Catherine, Empress of all the Russias

by the same author

THE GOLDEN HONEYCOMB
THE WISE MAN FROM THE WEST
THE LAST MIGRATION
A PEARL TO INDIA
THE LETTER AFTER Z
A CALENDAR OF SAINTS
THE COMPANION GUIDE TO PARIS
LOUIS XIV
FOUR WOMEN IN PURSUIT OF AN IDEAL
THE FLORENTINE RENAISSANCE
THE FLOWERING OF THE RENAISSANCE
NAPOLEON
LOUIS AND ANTOINETTE

CATHERINE

EMPRESS OF ALL THE RUSSIAS

Vincent Cronin

COLLINS
St James's Place, London
1978

William Collins Sons & Co Ltd
London · Glasgow · Sydney · Auckland
Toronto · Johannesburg

First published 1978

ISBN 0 00 216119 2

Set in Monotype Garamond
Made and Printed in Great Britain by
William Collins Sons & Co Ltd Glasgow

For
CHANTAL

Contents

Illustrations

THE HOUSE O

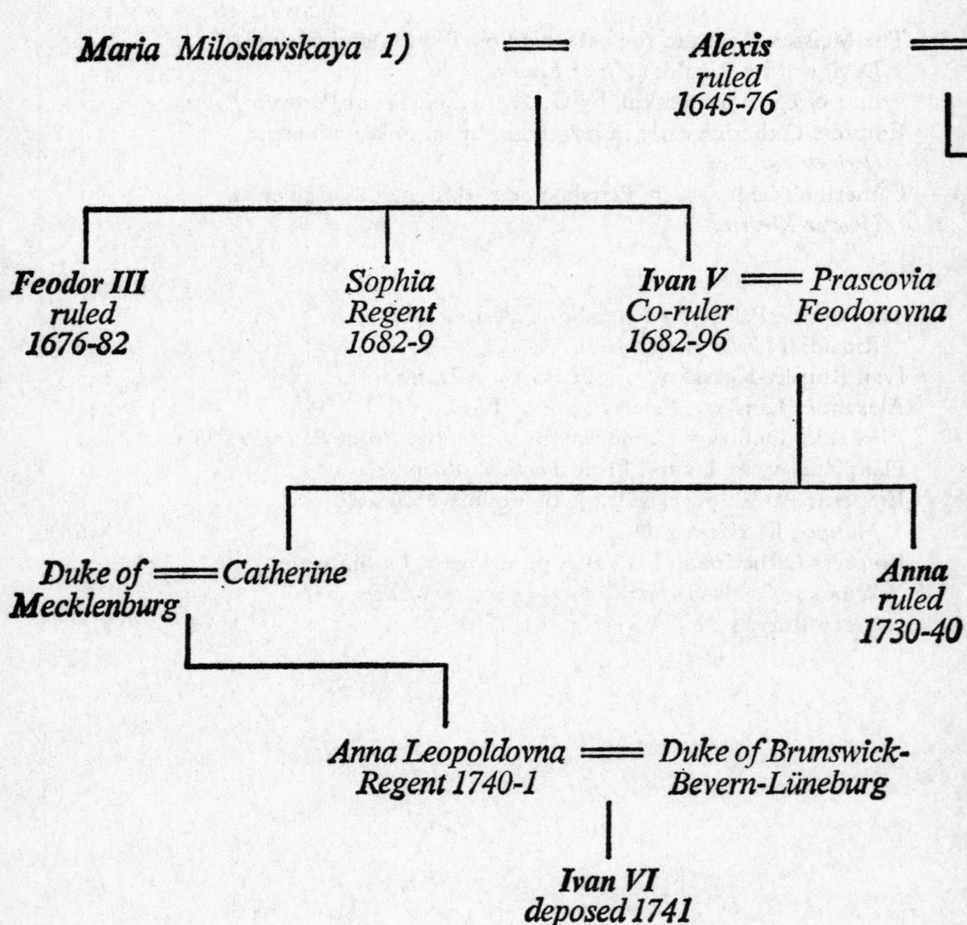
Maria Miloslavskaya 1)
Alexis
ruled
1645-76
Feodor III
ruled
1676-82
Sophia
Regent
1682-9
Ivan V
Co-ruler
1682-96
Prascovia
Feodorovna
Duke of
Mecklenburg
Catherine
Anna
ruled
1730-40
Anna Leopoldovna
Regent 1740-1
Duke of Brunswick-
Bevern-Lüneburg
Ivan VI
deposed 1741

OMANOV

2) Natalia Naruishkina

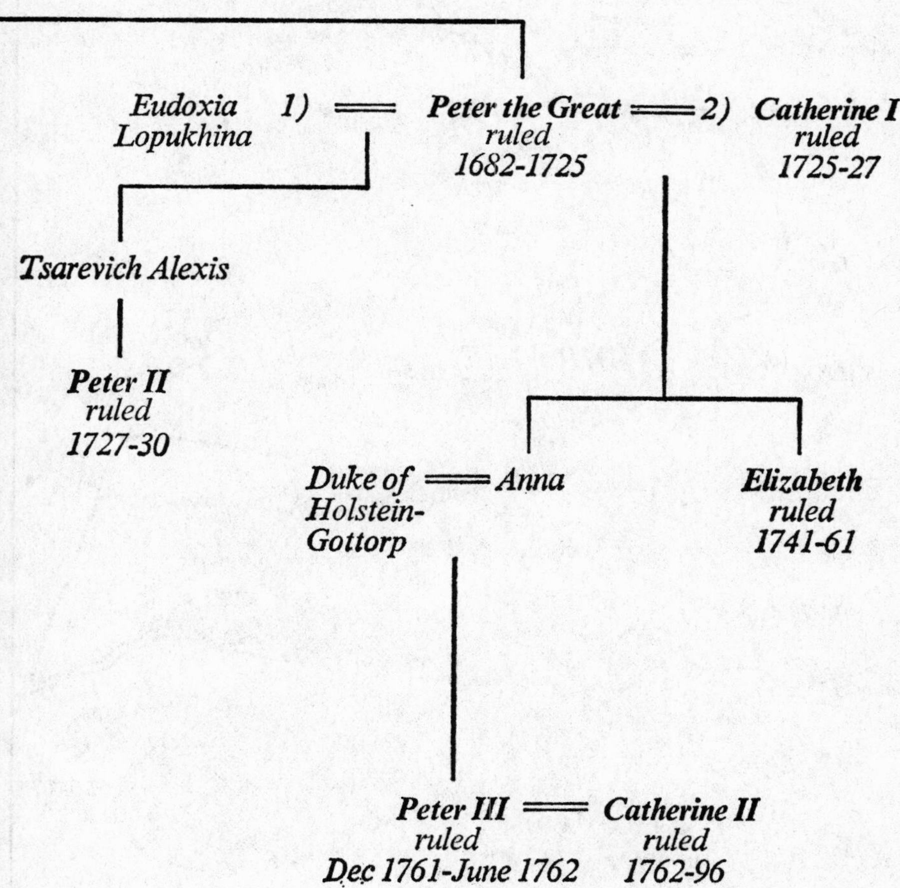

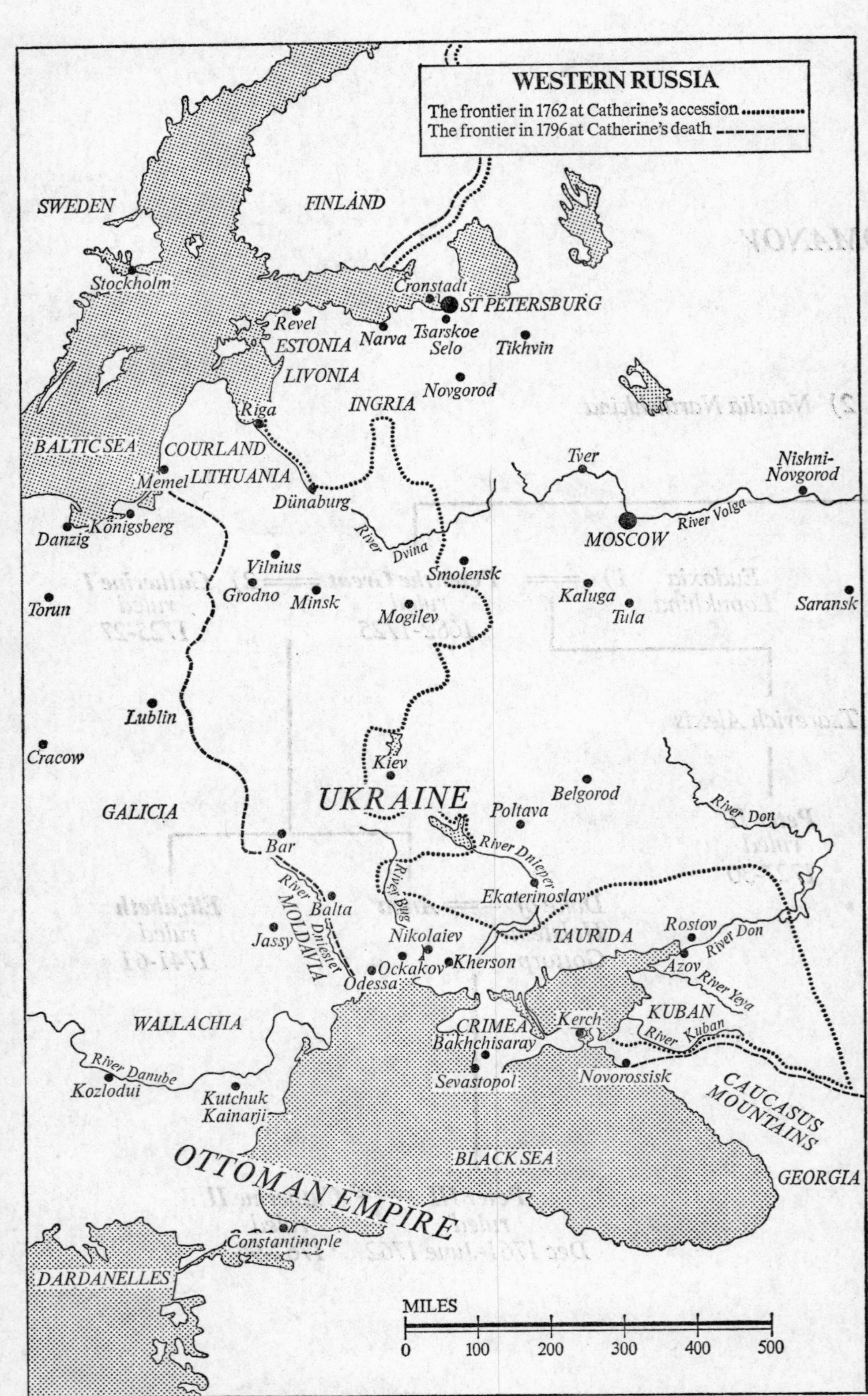
WESTERN RUSSIA
The frontier in 1762 at Catherine's accession
The frontier in 1796 at Catherine's death
SWEDEN
FINLAND
Stockholm
Cronstadt
ST PETERSBURG
Revel
ESTONIA
Narva
Tsarskoe Selo
Tikhvin
LIVONIA
Novgorod
Riga
INGRIA
BALTIC SEA
COURLAND
LITHUANIA
Memel
Tver
Nishni-Novgorod
Dünaburg
Königsberg
Danzig
River Dvina
MOSCOW
River Volga
Vilnius
Smolensk
Grodno
Minsk
Kaluga
Tula
Saransk
Torun
Mogilev
Lublin
Cracow
Kiev
UKRAINE
Belgorod
GALICIA
Poltava
River Don
Bar
River Dnieper
River Bug
Ekaterinoslav
River Dniester
MOLDAVIA
Balta
Jassy
Nikolaiev
TAURIDA
Rostov
River Don
Azov
River Yeya
Ockakov
Kherson
Odessa
KUBAN
WALLACHIA
CRIMEA
Kerch
River Kuban
Bakhchisaray
Novorossisk
River Danube
Kozlodui
Kutchuk Kainarji
Sevastopol
CAUCASUS MOUNTAINS
OTTOMAN EMPIRE
BLACK SEA
GEORGIA
Constantinople
DARDANELLES
MILES
0
100
200
300
400
500

Preface

The daughter of a minor German prince who received a French education and at thirty-three won for herself the crown of the Tsars was known during her reign as Catherine, Empress of all the Russias, That is the title I have chosen for my biography, preferring it to Catherine the Great, which came into use only after her death. Whether in fact Catherine was a great person or a great ruler, or both, or neither – these are questions which I hope the reader will be able to decide for himself after following the events of her life.

Catherine has several claims on the modern reader's attention. She is one of the most interesting and influential figures of the second half of the eighteenth century, so like our own age in its lack of religious faith, and the fact that she lived outside Europe gave her unusual insight into what in European thought was permanently valuable, what ephemeral.

Secondly, Catherine was one of the first career women, and as such she had to find a place in her life not only for her very exacting work but for the man, or men, she loved, for her home and for her family. Catherine's arrangements are perhaps unlikely to become standard practice in the West, but at least they represent a brave and sincere attempt to solve the problem.

As a woman politician Catherine is also of great interest to us today, when there are already several women heads of government, and likely to be more before the century is out. Plato saw man's soul writ large in the State; Catherine's reign shows us a woman's soul writ large in Russia. Many of the problems she faced face heads of government today, particularly in developing countries, and it becomes helpful, even important, to see what a woman not born to power made of her demanding role. Was she more successful than a man would have been and did she use her power differently from a man?

Catherine is one of those rare persons who had both an eventful private life and an extremely full public life. Faced with so much material, most of her biographers have chosen to deal with either one or the other. But Catherine the woman and Catherine the ruler were one and the same person, and in order to achieve a full and balanced portrait I believe that both aspects of her life must be viewed as parts of a single whole. That is the intention of the present biography.

It is one of the paradoxes of Catherine that a life which is very well documented should be the subject of so many legends. Catherine's love affairs in particular have been romanced and vulgarized *ad nauseam*, and even today some people picture the Empress as a cross between Lady Macbeth and a nymphomaniac, roaming dimly lit palace corridors by night in search of new victims or lovers.

The stories on which such a picture is based can all be traced back to a handful of French writers in the years immediately after Catherine's death when republican France was fighting for its life against a coalition that included Russia. One of the writers, Jean Laveaux, had twice been imprisoned for libel during the French Revolution, when libel had to be unusually venomous to warrant imprisonment.

An evaluative assessment of sources, then, was the first prerequisite in preparing a new biography, and it is published as Appendix A. The Russians of Catherine's day were not prone to put pen to paper; very few of them kept diaries and few wrote in other than general terms about their Empress. Hence the importance of reports by foreign residents and foreign travellers. One of the travellers was John Parkinson, a middle-aged clergyman and Fellow of Magdalen College, Oxford, who accompanied a young Lancashire gentleman, Edward Wilbraham-Bootle, on a tour of Russia, Siberia and the Crimea from 1792 to 1794. Despite a tendency to see behind every sudden death a cup of poisoned coffee, Parkinson observed keenly and usually accurately. His journal was published as recently as 1971, and adds many hitherto unknown details to our knowledge of Catherine's reign.

Among manuscript sources I have drawn chiefly on the despatches of foreign ambassadors, notably those of the Danish ambassador, a particularly well-informed observer during Peter III's reign, the letters of certain British ambassadors to Lord Holderness, head of the northern department, which give more personal details than do their despatches, and Robert Keith's special report on the Grand Duchess Catherine prepared for King George III, now among the Egerton Manuscripts in the British Library, which clears up one of the puzzles of Grand Duchess Catherine's relations with the Empress Elizabeth. Other useful manuscript material came to light in the National Library of Scotland and in the Library of Congress.

Finally, a wealth of material has appeared, especially since 1945, in specialized academic journals of limited circulation on the domestic politics, economics and foreign policy of Catherine's reign. Where these have illuminated my subject I have drawn on them. To their authors, named in the notes, I am indebted, and also to Professor K. A. Papmehl, for advice and for allowing me to use material from his forthcoming book about Dr Matthew Guthrie, the Scot who was for twenty-five years physician to the diplomatic corps in St Petersburg and knew personally many of the leading protagonists in Catherine's life.

During the eighteenth century Russians used the Julian, or old-style, calendar, which lagged eleven days behind the Gregorian, or new-style, calendar used in Europe. Events before Catherine went to Russia in 1744 I have dated new style; thereafter they are dated old style.

In transliterating Russian names I have adopted with a few exceptions the system used by the British Library; as regards Christian names I have used sometimes Russian, sometimes English versions, depending on which falls more naturally on the English ear. As for the value of the rouble, at the middle of Catherine's reign the exchange rate was 4.6 roubles to the pound sterling, and 4 roubles to the French *livre*. Living costs were higher in St Petersburg than in Moscow, partly because few market gardens could be laid out in the marshy terrain around the northern capital; for this and other reasons no exact comparison with present-day prices and currencies is possible. As a rough working equivalent and limiting ourselves to food, clothing and fuel for heating, we could say that one rouble would have bought in Catherine's Russia what £2 sterling buys today in Britain and $3.40 in the United States.

CHAPTER I

A GENERAL'S DAUGHTER

Berlin in the early eighteenth century was a small town of cobbled streets, canals, gabled houses and one magnificent building, the Königliches Schloss, lately enlarged to resemble Versailles and filled with showy French furniture, including Savonnerie carpets and silver armchairs. Here, on the 25th February 1713, a stocky young man with a round head on a bull neck and stern blue-grey eyes succeeded his father as King of Prussia. A few hours later, shutting himself in the study, the new King called for Herr von Printzen, the Lord Chamberlain, and desired him to bring the list of Court officials. He ran his eye down the chefs and footmen, the ushers and pages, the coachmen and kennelmen, the painters and sculptors, the actors and musicians, the one hundred chamberlains, the twenty-six drummers and trumpeters who used to announce the late King's every movement: the whole Versailles-like Court which Frederick the Ostentatious had assembled in order to disguise the fact that the Prussian crown was only twelve years old. Taking a quill pen, the young King drew a heavy black line from top to bottom of the page, and it was one of the symbolic lines of history, dividing two epochs: behind lay the pretentiousness of a petty German Court; ahead the powerful efficiency of Prussia. 'After my father's funeral,' said the new King, 'I intend to suppress them all.'

Two months later the able-bodied had been drafted into the army, the others retired on half-pay. The ground floor of the Schloss was converted into offices, and the treasury installed in the cellars, emptied of their vintage wines. These, the silver furniture, the gold plate, the State carriages had been auctioned to pay the late King's debts. Whole wings of the Schloss were closed, and twenty-four-year-old Frederick William reserved for himself just five rooms, in which he placed plain wooden furniture, but no carpets or draperies, for he hated dust.

Frederick William was a spoiled, self-willed only son, but in his soul Calvinism ran deep. The world was full of dust and dirt, muck and sin, and his job in life was to clean it up. Work moreover kept a man out of the devil's reach, so the young King arrived in his study each morning at seven. He wore a green overall to protect his uniform from inkstains and after touching anything even faintly dirty he washed his hands. All day he worked hard ruling and improving his kingdom; he personally did all the jobs his easy-going father had deputed to ministers, and he paid special attention to verifying accounts down to the last thaler. 'Things do not go as they should,' he explained, 'if one does not stick one's nose into every dirty mess.'

Against the dirt, the disorder, the ultimate terror of life, work was one bastion. The other was soldiers. With the clean-limbed men in blue uniforms, clean white gaiters and polished buttons the King felt safe. His 'dear blue boys' he called them and they became the passion of his life. He introduced conscription and doubled his army to 83,000 out of a population of 2.3 million, which made it proportionately by far the largest in the world. He turned the Schloss garden into a parade ground, and himself drilled the troops. Any soldier whose movements were slow he struck with the cane he always carried. But he listened personally to any grievances and when justified put them right.

Frederick William was not a bellicose man and of his foreign policy Tsar Peter I said, 'He likes to go fishing but not to get his feet wet.' War brought danger and disorder, whereas his beautifully drilled regiments represented order, and safety in every sense of that word. As the years passed Frederick William made his army almost the *raison d'être* of the State, and an extension of his own Calvinism. 'When one takes the oath to the flag,' he wrote in his new regulations, 'one renounces oneself and surrenders entirely, even one's life and all, to the monarch, in order to fulfil the Lord's will, and through this blind obedience one receives the grace and the confirmation of the title of soldier.'

Beautiful, smartly dressed, gracious ladies were rare in the courts of North Germany. Frederick William's wife, Sophia Dorothea, was sad-eyed, plump and gossipy. But Frederick William showed himself wearisomely faithful to her, giving her fourteen children, for, as he used to say, 'Harlotry, that is the most terrible sin.' To encourage his new manufactories he made her wear dowdy woollen dresses and once, when he asked her the price of eggs and she did not know, he said, 'After I am gone you will end on the dunghill.'

His evenings Frederick William spent not with his wife but with senior officers in the 'Tobacco Parliament', a panelled room where they smoked pipes, drank beer, scoffed at books and at philosophy –

which the King called 'breaking wind' – and contrived that the Court fool, an unfrocked Tyrolean friar, should sit on a stool whose legs had been sawn through. One evening the teaching of a rising professor at Halle was mentioned. 'What does Christian Wolff mean by his "pre-established harmony"?' asked the King. 'It means,' was the reply, 'that if one of your grenadiers runs away, he can, properly speaking, not be justly punished, because his running away is merely a piece of the pre-established harmony.' The King gave Wolff twenty-four hours to quit Halle.

Under such a king generals naturally had great importance: indeed they now ranked second in the State, while civilian ministers were downgraded to fifth place. The King's most trusted general was Leopold of Anhalt-Dessau, an impressive-looking long-jawed nobleman with prominent black eyebrows an inch wide and moustache to match. Known as 'Old Snoutnose', he was reckoned, since the death of Charles XII of Sweden, to be Europe's bravest soldier. It was he who set the psalms to march tunes and devised the fifty-four movements of Prussian drill, including the ceremonial march past with unbent leg that came to be known as the goose-step.

Another general much prized by Frederick William was Leopold's cousin, Prince Christian August of Anhalt-Zerbst. Born in 1690, Christian August served with distinction against the French in the Netherlands and at Malplaquet, 'the very murdering battle' as Marlborough called it. He was a handsome, open-faced man, cautious on the battlefield but absolutely trustworthy, and in contrast to Leopold, who married an apothecary's daughter, he made a very grand match to Johanna of Holstein-Gottorp, daughter of the Protestant Prince Bishop of Lübeck and a great-granddaughter of King Frederick III of Denmark.

Johanna was a very attractive girl of fifteen, less than half the age of her husband, with aquiline nose, arched eyebrows and curly fair hair. Immediately after their marriage in 1727 Christian August was appointed by the King to command the garrison at Stettin, a town recently acquired from Sweden which he was developing into a port for Berlin.

The King paid notoriously low salaries and was known to reply to requests for a rise in atrocious Latin or with rude verses: '*Non habeo Pekonia*,' or '*Gold kann ich nicht scheissen, Friedrich Wilhelm, König in Preussen*.' Even a general received very little, and since Christian August and his bride had only a small private income, they rented a modest grey stone house from a certain Herr von Aschersleben, in the district of the Marien Kirchen. Its address was no. 791, Stettin.

Here, at two-thirty in the morning of Monday, 2nd May 1729, Johanna gave birth to her first child, a girl, who was christened in the nearby Lutheran church with the names Sophie Auguste Friederike. They chose Sophie, the French version of Sophia, because although Christian August had fought France he and Johanna admired French civilization. Friederike may have been chosen as a tribute to the King. The baby was provided with a wet nurse, a soldier's wife, but her life looked like being very short, for someone – probably Johanna, who was inclined to be slapdash and still very young – knocked over a warming-pan in the nursery and set fire to the floor, happily without causing bodily harm.

Sophie was a lively child with very fair skin, blonde hair and blue eyes. When she was eighteen months old a brother, Wilhelm, was born, but he developed rickets and had to be sent for treatment to Karlsbad. In 1734 a second brother, Friedrich August, enlarged the family, but until then, during the first five years of her life, Sophie had no playmates in her own family. She learned how to amuse herself and she preferred making a toy out of a handkerchief or a game with her hands to playing with dolls.

Sophie spent all her childhood in the chilly grey town of Stettin, on the edge of a sandy plain at the mouth of the River Oder, swept by mist and winds from the Baltic. But the port offered some excitement: sailing ships unloading cloth and coffee, and sometimes very tall soldiers for the King's regiment of giants. Her father was promoted Governor of the town and moved into the ducal castle, a solid sixteenth-century building of Hartz granite in the main square. He was now the King's personal representative, and very impressive he looked to Sophie, taking the salute in his blue general's uniform, straw-coloured waistcoat and breeches, sword at his side.

When Sophie was four, the King visited Stettin. A ruddy-faced stout man, he wore a blue jacket cut tight and short, with lapels and cuffs of scarlet, chamois-leather breeches and white boots. Summoned into his presence, Sophie walked up to the great man in order to kiss the hem of his jacket, as told by her mother. But every time she reached up to try to catch his jacket, he pulled it away. So Sophie turned to her mother and said loudly, 'His jacket is so short I cannot reach it. Isn't he rich enough to have a longer one?' The King wanted to know what she had said. It was repeated to him, though with some embarrassment, because the short cut of his jacket was in fact an economy measure. The King said, 'The little girl is very saucy.' But he laughed and whenever her father went to Berlin or the King came to Stettin he inquired for Sophie.

Sophie was given a French governess, Elisabeth Cardel, the stout sensible daughter of a Huguenot refugee, and from 'Babet', as she called her, Sophie learned French almost as soon as she could speak German. Sophie was given La Fontaine fables to learn by heart, and reciting these was probably the origin of Sophie's fondness for mimicking animals. Other subjects Sophie learned were handwriting and drawing, which she did well, and music, at which she was not good at all. If she did her lessons without mistake, Babet would read her a play, Sophie's favourites being the Molière comedies, *Le Médecin malgré lui* and *Le Malade Imaginaire*, that poke fun at doctors.

Babet, who had had a refugee's hard life, set high store by courage and on not moaning without reason. She told her pupil the following story, which Sophie was to remember always. Once upon a time a peasant lived contentedly with his wife. One fine summer's day the wife began to cry. Her husband asked her what was wrong. For a long time she refused to say, but at last she confided the reason. 'Alas, Thomas! You have just hung your axe on that nail on the wall. Suppose I were to have a baby, and to put the baby to sleep in a cradle under the nail. Then your axe might fall, and the baby would certainly be killed.' With that the woman began to cry more loudly than ever.

Sophie's father was a devout Lutheran and, wishing his daughter to have a sound religious education, he chose an army chaplain to give her lessons in history, geography and Scripture. Pastor Wagner was a disciplinarian who underlined long passages in the Bible in red ink and required Sophie to learn them by heart. If she missed a word he beat her. 'The joys of the world are not worth its pains,' was one of his maxims, another was, 'The world is not good for much because of original sin.'

Sophie's nursery was on the top floor of the castle, next to a church, and when the church organ was played, she could hear it. In the evenings she would reflect on Pastor Wagner's grim warnings about the Last Judgment and the arduous task of working out one's salvation; with the organ thundering next door it proved too much for a little girl, and Sophie would sit by her window in tears.

Babet found out, spoke to the Pastor and got him to moderate his tone. The light and sun of the Mediterranean dispersed the mists of the north, and what might have been a cripplingly one-sided Prussian education was relaxed in favour of Gallic common sense.

Courage, truthfulness and obedience – these were the virtues instilled in Sophie. As for book learning, she was not specially good at it, for she possessed what Babet called an *esprit gauche*, meaning that she approached facts unconventionally. This showed itself quite early in a determination to question things and to think for herself. Sophie considered it a great injustice that Titus, Marcus Aurelius and all the heroes of antiquity should be damned because they did not know about Christ – a doctrine that was later to jar also on young Napoleon Bonaparte. A second difficulty was the nature of the universe before the Creation. Pastor Wagner said there had been chaos, Sophie wanted to know what chaos had been like, and when the Pastor could not give her a satisfactory answer remained sceptical of so elusive a thing.

A third battle centred on circumcision. Sophie wanted to know what the word meant, and the Pastor refused to say – understandably, since Sophie until her marriage day did not even know what differentiated the sexes. Sophie secretly considered the Pastor a blockhead and refused to accept his doctrinaire rulings, whereupon he would threaten to beat her. Babet, whom Sophie by now adored, would intervene, soothing the chaplain and once again pleading for common sense. Sophie would yield to Babet, but never to the Prussian who threatened her: 'all my life,' she was later to write, 'I had this inclination to yield only to gentleness and reason – and to resist all pressure.'

Sophie possessed what the doctors called a sanguine temperament. She had colour in her cheeks, saw the bright side of things and was so boisterous that one day she pulled over her heavy toy cupboard; it fell on top of her, but with its doors open, so that she was penned in instead of being crushed. Then at the age of seven, this healthy, happy child was suddenly stricken down.

One evening as she knelt to say her prayers, Sophie began to cough so violently that the strain caused her to fall on her left side, and she had such sharp pains in her chest that they almost took her breath away. She was carried to bed where she lay coughing, turned always on her left side, with a high fever and sharp chest pains.

The local doctor and the apothecaries prescribed various medicines, and three weeks later Sophie was allowed to get up. As she was being dressed, a frightening discovery was made. Her spine was no longer straight. The right shoulder and right hip were now two fingers higher than the left shoulder and hip, while her trunk curved to correct the balance. Seen from behind, her young body had the shape of a Z.

The discovery came as a great shock to Sophie's parents. Wilhelm was lame and walked with a crutch, now lively little Sophie looked like being a cripple. They immediately swore everyone in the house to secrecy and began to consider what they should do.

It might have seemed desirable to call in a specialist from Berlin or Switzerland or to send Sophie to the waters at Teplitz or Karlsbad. But Christian August rejected these courses, probably because he could not afford them – Wilhelm's treatment was already straining the family finances – and perhaps also because, should her illness become known, it would lessen Sophie's chance of marrying.

Christian August and his wife began instead to search for some local person with experience of curvature of the spine. The only one they could find was the Stettin hangman. They were naturally reluctant to call in so sinister a figure and for a long time they hesitated. Finally, under a pledge of secrecy, they asked him to visit the castle, the only persons to be told being Babet and a housemaid.

The hangman examined poor twisted Sophie and told her parents what must be done. Every morning at six an unmarried girl must come to the castle on an empty stomach and rub Sophie's shoulder and spine with her saliva. Next, Sophie must wear a wide black ribbon going round the neck, crossing the right shoulder and the upper part of the right arm, to be fastened at the back. Finally, he made a stiff, tightly fitting bodice, probably fashioned round a wooden frame, which she must wear day and night. It went over her vest and under her dress, and the only time she might remove it was when washing and changing her linen.

With this insect-like carapace on her body Sophie dragged herself round the castle month after month with no noticeable improvement. It was a lesson in humiliation and in patience. Then, after a year and a half, to everyone's relief and most of all Sophie's, the spine began to straighten, the right shoulder and hip to resume their normal positions.

Probably Sophie had a tendency to rickets, which lack of sunshine and a diet low in fat had aggravated, inducing scoliosis. Though she continued for some time wearing the cage-like bodice as a precaution, at nine and a half she was cured, and quickly regained her former energy. After being put to bed she would seat herself astride her pillow and pretend to gallop until she felt tired enough to sleep. When staying in her uncle's medieval castle, she shared a bedroom with Babet, and her game there was to wait until Babet went down a little corridor to the lavatory, whereupon Sophie would dash four flights up a large stone staircase, then down again and so into bed, to lie motionless and apparently asleep when Babet returned.

Sophie's parents were happily married but had very different characters. Off the parade ground her father was a quiet, thrifty man who preferred books to parties, real worth to show, whereas Johanna loved company, excitement and flitting from Court to Court; 'I'm a will-o'-the-wisp,' she used to say. With one eye on her daughter's future and another on her own pleasure Johanna took Sophie to spend a winter in Berlin. The King was absent; the Queen, with a double chin and eyes sadder than ever, grumbled that her husband was brutalizing Crown Prince Friedrich, whom he considered a milksop. She hated Berlin and compared it unfavourably with her native Hanover. Sophie played with another of the Queen's sons, Heinrich, and made a friend of him.

From Berlin Johanna and Sophie continued to Brunswick, where Johanna, one of a numerous family with little money, had been brought up by her godmother, the rich, childless Duchess of Brunswick-Wolfenbüttel. After Spartan Berlin the ducal castle of Brunswick seemed wonderfully splendid, with yellow-liveried footmen in attendance and pictures by Rembrandt and Van Dyck.

Sophie and her mother arrived in a plain carriage with very little baggage and no footmen. The poor relation, if a girl, has to be kind and tactful, not tell tales and be willing at all times to lend a helping hand. Sophie evidently complied with these conditions for she and her mother were invited to Brunswick seven successive summers. Balls, operas, banquets, concerts, hunting parties, carriage drives followed one after the other, day after day.

Sophie was also taken to visit two eccentric maiden aunts. Aunt Hedwig, her mother's sister, lived in the fashionable Protestant convent of Quedlinburg, where she held the rank of prioress; she was very short and fat, and kept sixteen pugs in her room; their smell made a strong impression on Sophie. The other aunt, Sophie Christiana, her father's sister, was very tall and thin, her face badly disfigured by a burn in childhood. A Canoness in the convent of Gandersheim, she filled her room with birds, particularly injured ones. There was a thrush with only one foot, a lark with a broken wing, a one-eyed goldfinch and many others. One day Sophie was left alone in the room; feeling suddenly sorry for the cooped-up birds, she opened a window and watched half the aviary fly to freedom. Her aunt was very angry and never let Sophie enter the room again.

While Johanna and her daughter travelled the rough roads of North Germany keeping family links in good repair, the man on whom they ultimately depended, King Frederick William, travelled the same roads keeping the State in good repair. He occupied himself with forests, mines, ports, customs, transit duties and the tax on salt. Giving negligent officials a cut with his cane, he was now 'making a plus' in every department. He colonized East Prussia, building there eleven towns and over three hundred villages, and he introduced compulsory education – one of the first rulers to do so. A drill-sergeant he might be, but he worked tirelessly for his people.

As he grew older King Frederick William became an increasingly heavy eater. Using an old-fashioned two-pronged fork, he would stuff himself – especially when someone else was paying – with pork, goose, truffles in oil and eight dozen oysters. His face became blotchy, his legs 'like two barrels', and part of his dining-room table had to be cut away to accommodate his Majesty's stomach.

Every autumn he hunted the stag and wild boar, standing on the scales in the evening to see how much flesh he had sweated off. Christian August would receive 'gifts' of haunches of venison – with a note saying how much he must pay for them: three to six thalers, according to size.

The King began to suffer from gout, then from dropsy. He had fits of remorse and self-doubt. He painted unflattering portraits of himself signed '*F.W. in tormentis pinxit*.' 'God knows what a low opinion I have of myself,' he wrote to Old Snoutnose. But then he would lash out at a careless servant with his cane.

In 1740 he fell seriously ill. Lying in his bedroom, its walls hung with portraits of all the captains in his regiment of giants, he summoned his chaplain for anguished talks about his chances of salvation. At night his sleep was troubled by dreadful nightmares.

On the last day of May 1740 he wheeled himself into the Queen's bedroom. 'Get up, I am going to die.' When his chaplain began to sing the hymn 'Naked shall I, too, appear before Thy stern countenance', the King shouted, 'No, no. I shall be buried in my uniform.' There was to be no funeral oration, just twenty-five fieldpieces each firing twelve rounds, and a fortnight later the chaplain was to preach on the text 'I have fought the good fight.'

The King ordered his horses to be led out of the stables and, from the window, chose one for Old Snoutnose. As the grooms were putting a blue saddle on a yellow horsecloth, when the colours should have matched, he sent a general to beat them with his stick. Then he tottered back to bed and at three that afternoon he died.

Christian August received the news in Stettin. He had fought for Prussia and all his adult life served the King, loyally. He felt a sense of deep personal loss, as he ordered the flag with its black eagle to be lowered to half mast and prayers to be said in all Stettin's churches for the repose of the King's soul. Johanna too shared her husband's sorrow. She had liked the Berlin Court, with its meticulous military etiquette, preferring it even to Brunswick. She at once put herself and Sophie into black mourning, and suggested to the ladies of Stettin that they should do the same. However they, having lived longer under Swedish than Prussian rule, felt no such deep loyalty to the Hohenzollerns, and declined to wear black. On Sunday at church Johanna felt herself conspicuous in black and after the second Sunday she decided to conform to local opinion and laid her mourning aside.

Johanna went to Berlin shortly afterwards, taking Sophie. There the behaviour of the Stettin ladies came up in conversation. Was it true that they had declined to wear mourning for their late lord and master, and that the Governor's wife had followed suit? Johanna denied the whole story, and this caused Sophie astonishment. 'Is it possible,' she asked herself, 'that my mother should have forgotten something that happened so recently?' She was on the point of reminding her, but something made her stop, and later she realized she had been well advised. Truthfulness was so much taken for granted in her family that until now, aged eleven, Sophie had never heard a lie.

King Frederick William was an important figure in Sophie's girlhood and because he became the model for some other rulers during her adult life he was to continue important. She parted company with both her mother and her father in her assessment of his reign. Frederick William had made his country prosperous and strong, put Prussia on the map, but in Sophie's eyes that was not enough. 'Never, I believe, did a people show more joy when learning of his death. On the streets passers-by embraced and congratulated each other, calling him by suitable epithets . . . He was severe, rough, close-fisted and hot-tempered; although he undoubtedly had great qualities as a king, there was nothing lovable either in his public or his private life.' Sophie noticed, by contrast, the people's joy over the accession of the Crown Prince, 'who was respected and loved'. Already Sophie had decided that what she admired in a ruler was not just getting things done, but winning the people's affection.

CHAPTER 2

INVITATION FOR TWO

In November 1742 Prince Christian August succeeded his first cousin, Johann August, who died without a son, as sovereign ruler of Anhalt-Zerbst. Resigning from the Prussian army with the rank of Field Marshal, Christian August left Stettin and moved with his family 150 miles south-east, into the heart of Germany. Anhalt-Zerbst was not part of Brandenburg-Prussia, though close to its western border; it was a small sovereign principality, with only 20,000 inhabitants, but with five hundred years of independence behind it. Its rich soil produced wheat, hops, potatoes, flax and tobacco; its forests were well stocked with deer and boar, its rivers with salmon and lampreys. The town of Zerbst, surrounded by medieval walls, towers and a moat, possessed handsome gabled houses, a brewery where the famous Zerbst beer was made, and a bronze female figure on a column of uncertain meaning, known as 'the butter girl'. The small baroque palace where Christian August and his family now settled was sixty years old, and in it were treasured letters from Luther to one of Christian August's forebears, who had protected the reformer in his early struggles, and a Luther Bible with woodcuts coloured by Lucas Cranach the Younger.

Earlier in the year Christian August had had a stroke, which paralysed his left side, but he recovered from it quickly and began to develop his little domain with energy and a kindly paternalism far removed from Frederick William's bullying style. He continued his frugal way of life, and devoted most of his revenues to providing for his people's welfare. To Sophie he appeared a model ruler. 'The strictest rectitude guided his footsteps. I can only say I never in my life heard him speak a word inconsistent with his character.' Evidently the people of Anhalt-Zerbst thought well of him too, for a foreign traveller in North Germany had this to write of them: 'They live in the land of milk and honey; indeed these were the only people, considered as a State, which before or since that time I ever heard talk without complaining.'

Sophie's social position now improved. She was in the full sense of the word a princess, and heir in her own right to the domain of Jever, in Lower Saxony, which passed to princesses of the house of Anhalt-Zerbst. There were liveried servants in the palace, a painted carriage in the mews, and to her mother, who liked such things, the leading ladies of Zerbst dropped a curtsy.

Sophie was growing up tall. She had dark chestnut hair and her eyes were now greyish blue. She was not a pretty girl, or so everyone told her. Her mouth curled up at the sides, her chin was pointed and prominent – Babet kept telling her to pull it in, or she'd be hitting people with it. She was taught to have a horror of coquetry, and indeed did not know exactly what the word meant. She took no trouble with her clothes, and had to be scolded even to curl her hair. She was repeatedly told to make up in kindness and intelligence for what she lacked in beauty.

Many Germans at this time believed in the occult, in ghosts, and in the 'white lady' whose dread form was said to have walked through the palace before Frederick William breathed his last. Sophie's mother believed in such things and consulted clairvoyants, while her lady companion, Fräulein von Kayn, was forever seeing ghosts and apparitions. Between them the ladies built up a chilling, even at times unhealthy atmosphere.

During a stay in Brunswick Sophie slept in a very small 'poor relations' room with Fräulein von Kayn. Their beds stood close together near the windows, between which on a table stood a water pitcher, a silver basin, and a night light. The one door, near the foot of the beds, they locked when they retired.

Towards midnight Sophie was suddenly awakened by someone getting into her bed beside her; opening her eyes, she saw that it was Fräulein von Kayn. Sophie asked her why she wanted to come into her bed, and the other, trembling and almost speechless with fright, stammered, 'For God's sake, let me be and go to sleep quietly.' But Sophie wanted to know what the matter was, and at last the lady said, 'Don't you see what's going on in the room and what there is on the table?' With that she drew the bedclothes over her face.

Though just a girl not yet in her teens, Sophie sat up in bed on her knees, coolly opened the curtains and looked around. She saw nothing unusual: the door was closed; candle, basin and silver pitcher were on the table. She told her room-mate this, and Fräulein von Kayn calmed down a little, though a few minutes later she got up to bolt the already locked door.

Next morning, seeing her room-mate looking pale and distraught, Sophie asked what she thought she had seen, but the other would not say. She was a Sunday child, she added darkly, and perceived unspeakable things hidden from other people. Sophie related the incident to her mother, who believed that Fräulein von Kayn had indeed seen something chilling. Sophie's dominant impression of the night's events was surprise that she hadn't felt any fear.

Another summer Sophie accompanied her parents to the family estate at Jever, near the North Sea coast of Lower Saxony, and from there went to stay in Varel with the dowager Countess von Altenburg. This lady had a twenty-eight-year-old daughter, the Countess von Bentinck, said to be of very independent character, separated from her husband and living, probably in a lesbian relationship, with a Fräulein Donep.

As they approached Varel, this lady rode out to meet her guests. She was rather plain and masculine-looking, but high-spirited and good-humoured. Sophie, who had never seen a woman on horseback, was fascinated by the young Countess and thought she rode 'like a riding-master'. When they arrived at the house Sophie followed the Countess into her room, where she changed from her riding-habit, then into Johanna's apartment, where the Countess suddenly took it into her head to sing and begin to dance round the room. Sophie entered into the spirit of the thing and soon the two of them were dancing a Styrian dance. This drew everyone to the door to look, and afterwards Sophie was scolded by her parents.

In spite of the scolding Sophie went next day to the Countess's apartment. On the wall was the portrait of a handsome man. The Countess looked at it and said, 'If he had not been my husband, I should have loved him madly.' In the room was a beautiful three-year-old boy and when Sophie asked about him the Countess said he was the brother of Fräulein Donep. Then she put her bonnet on the boy: 'Isn't he like me?' she said. Sophie thought he looked sweet and urged her to take the child, with the bonnet on, to show the Countess von Altenburg. The other objected that her mother did not like the child, but Sophie pleaded, and finally they led the boy upstairs. However, when she saw him from a distance, the old lady signalled to take him away. Sophie was puzzled until she learned from someone else in the house that the beautiful boy was the Countess von Bentinck's natural son by a page. Sophie's fascination with the lady grew still further.

The Countess promised to let Sophie ride in the afternoon and even undertook the difficult task of obtaining Christian August's permission.

Sophie was helped on to the horse by the Countess and made several rounds of the courtyard; from that moment she conceived a passion for horses. But her parents worried about the influence of this 'bad lot' on their darling daughter and, making their visit as short as they politely could, returned to the safety of the family castle at Jever.

Johanna was looking for a possible husband for Sophie. Her brother the Bishop of Lübeck had recently taken into his palace at Eutin an orphan: Peter Ulrich, Duke of Holstein-Gottorp. This boy, a year older than Sophie, was heir to the throne of Sweden. So Johanna arranged to pay a visit to Eutin, taking Sophie. Peter turned out to be a pleasant boy with regular features, very strictly brought up by his Swedish tutor, Otto von Brümmer. Sophie found him handsome, amiable and well-mannered, but Peter was more interested in beautiful Johanna than in Sophie, then at the awkward age. She consoled herself by going to the kitchen between meals to make herself a favourite milk-soup.

Later Sophie heard her uncles and aunts drop a word here and there which made her believe that she and Peter were intended for each other. 'I felt no kind of resistance to it,' she later recalled. 'I knew that he would be King of Sweden sooner or later, and although I was still a child the title of Queen flattered my ear.'

It was Johanna who had imparted to Sophie her own fondness for crowns. She liked to dwell on her royal connections and while staying in Brunswick she had taken Sophie to a fortune-telling monk, who surprised the Court and delighted Johanna by claiming to see not just one but three crowns on Sophie's brow. Despite this and the fact that she had arranged the meeting with Peter, on reflection Johanna came to have doubts about this particular match. Whenever Sophie's prospects were discussed and the young Duke was mentioned, Johanna said, 'Not to him: he needs a wife who can support his rights and claims by the prestige of a family more powerful than ours.'

When Sophie was twelve, Peter left Germany for St Petersburg, where he had been summoned by his maternal aunt Elizabeth, who had recently seized the throne of Russia. Peter disappeared from Sophie's horizon, apparently for good. Less than a year later he renounced the Swedish crown, was adopted by Elizabeth and designated heir to the Russian throne. About the same time, by the terms of a peace concluded between Russia and Sweden, Empress Elizabeth designated as heir to the Swedish throne Adolf Friedrich, Bishop of Lübeck, Johanna's brother.

There was much rejoicing in Johanna's family at this unexpected news. Thrilled at the prospect of becoming sister to a king, Johanna joined her mother in Hamburg to see her brother off by ship to Stockholm. Sophie shared in the rejoicing and took special pleasure in seeing a lot of her mother's youngest brother, Georg Ludwig, twenty-four years old, good-looking, and a lieutenant in the Prussian Cuirassiers. Uncle Georg had a cheerful disposition and Sophie found it fun to be with him.

When mother and daughter travelled from Hamburg to Brunswick, Uncle Georg came too. 'I shall be in a difficult position there,' he confided to Sophie. 'I shan't be able to talk to you so freely.' 'Why?' she inquired. 'It would lead to gossip,' he said.

In Brunswick Uncle Georg did indeed see less of his niece. One evening, however, they happened to meet and the remark escaped him that he had one great sorrow in life, namely that he was her uncle. Sophie did not know what to think. Had she perhaps made him angry with her? 'Not in the least,' said Uncle Georg. 'The trouble is that I'm too fond of you.' Sophie thanked him for having given her his friendship, but this made him exclaim sharply: 'You're a child. There's no talking seriously with you.' Sophie wished to excuse herself and begged him to tell her what was wrong. 'Very well,' he said. 'Are you friend enough to give me the comfort I want?' Sophie said yes. 'Then promise to marry me.'

'It struck me,' Sophie later recalled, 'like a bolt of lightning out of a clear sky. I had not imagined anything like that. My friendship was pure and I loved him as my mother's brother, who had shown me many kindnesses. Love I did not in the least understand and had never suspected it in him. He saw that I was taken aback and fell silent. But I said, "You are joking; you are my uncle, my parents would not wish it." "Nor would you," he answered. My mother called me and there, for that evening, the matter rested.'

A union between uncle and niece could take place with the Church's dispensation, and Georg happened to be a special favourite with Johanna. Sophie noticed that though her mother did not speak of Georg she began to show her more affection and deduced from this that she favoured his suit. Sophie's Brunswick relations, however, would have much preferred her to marry the new King of Prussia's second brother, Heinrich. He had played with Sophie as a child in the palace of Berlin and had grown into a vivacious young man, lean, with a wedge-shaped nose and a slight squint, but intelligent and charming. He played the violin but was also a promising colonel in the Thirty-fifth Regiment. At a Court wedding he had danced a minuet with

Sophie and afterwards his sister had told Johanna that Heinrich was interested in Sophie.

At the mention of Prince Heinrich, whose praises were beginning to be on everyone's lips, Georg began to sigh and to show the weak side of a petted youngest brother. Instead of going manfully to Christian August and asking for Sophie's hand, he sat about in complete silence. 'He was a timid lover,' Sophie recalled, 'quite shut up in himself; he ate and drank nothing, lost his sleep and above all his cheerfulness. I did not know what to do with him.' In the autumn she returned with her mother to Zerbst. Neither Georg nor Heinrich had made a definite proposal, and Duke Peter of Holstein seemed to have been swallowed up in Russia.

Johanna, meanwhile, had entered into relations with the new Empress of Russia, for it so happened that another of Johanna's brothers, Karl August, had been engaged to the Empress before her rise to power. Karl August had gone to Russia in 1726 and died there of smallpox before the marriage. Johanna wrote to the Empress, congratulating her on her accession and recalling the tenuous sentimental link, whereupon the Empress graciously deigned to accord Johanna's mother a large pension of 10,000 roubles. Encouraged by this, Johanna wrote again, in December 1742, when she gave birth to a second daughter, a sister for Sophie, asking the Empress if she would stand godmother to the child. The Empress agreed, the baby was named after her, and Johanna received a portrait of the Empress set in large diamonds.

The next present to arrive from this country of wonderful presents was the designation of Johanna's brother to the Swedish throne. For so signal a favour Johanna wrote the Empress a warm letter of thanks and in the hope of diverting to her elder daughter some of the largesse, in the summer of 1743 she had a portrait of Sophie painted by Balthasar Donner, and through a friend in the Russian service sent it to the Empress. Sophie was still not pretty, but Donner, a Court painter, knew how to embellish, and in due course Johanna received a letter saying, 'The Empress is charmed by the expressive features of the young Princess.'

The portrait had been sent before Georg Ludwig had fallen in love with Sophie, and any vague unspoken hope Johanna may have entertained of catching Grand Duke Peter's eye was now superseded by her desire that Georg Ludwig should marry her daughter. Sophie, on the other hand, had renewed her interest in Peter as soon as he was adopted and designated heir to the throne, for in his new position Grand Duke

Peter would no longer require a wife from a powerful family. 'In my secret thoughts,' Sophie was later to recall, 'I decided upon him, because of all the matches that had been proposed this was the most brilliant.'

On New Year's Day 1744, after service in the palace chapel, Christian August, Johanna and Sophie were sitting at dinner when a servant brought in a packet of letters. Christian August tore the outside cover off the packet and handed his wife several letters addressed to her, on one of which Sophie thought she recognized the handwriting of Otto von Brümmer, Peter's Swedish tutor, now in Moscow, with whom over the past five years her mother had exchanged occasional letters. As Johanna opened the letter Sophie caught sight of the words 'with the Princess, your elder daughter'.

The letter was long but Johanna said nothing about its contents and after dinner shut herself up in a drawing-room with her husband, from time to time summoning a friend or an adviser. Sophie gathered that her mother had been invited to go to Russia to thank Empress Elizabeth for having chosen her brother as King-designate of Sweden. But would that alone have been cause for the mysterious consultations?

The secret talks continued off and on for three days. Sophie thought it odd that her mother, usually pretty open with her, still said not a word to her about the matter. On the evening of the third day she went to her mother's room. 'You seem to be very much excited,' Johanna said. 'You are dying of curiosity.'

'Yes, indeed,' Sophie replied. Then jokingly, 'I know through my powers of divination what is written in your letters.'

'Aha, what is it then?'

Sophie was ashamed to confess that she thought it was concerned with her marriage and, mimicking one of Johanna's fortune-teller friends who claimed the power of predicting the name of a sweetheart, answered, 'I will question my oracle.'

'Very good, young lady,' said Johanna. 'We shall see what you make of a twelve-page political letter.'

Next day Sophie brought her mother a slip of paper on which she had written:

'The omens agree –
Peter the Third your husband will be.'

Johanna looked sharply at her daughter. 'You're a little rogue, but you will learn nothing more about it.' She got up and went to Christian August. Soon she returned and told Sophie that it was true propositions of that kind were being made. The relevant part of Brümmer's letter ran as follows:

'At the explicit command of her Imperial Majesty, I have to inform you, Madame, that the sublime Empress desires your Highness, with the Princess, your elder daughter, to come to our country as soon as possible, and repair without loss of time to the place where our Imperial Court may then be found.' The ostensible purpose of the journey would be to thank her Imperial Majesty for the benefits she and her family had received. But, continued the letter, 'Your Highness is too intelligent not to understand the true meaning of Her Majesty's great impatience to see you here, as well as the Princess your daughter, of whom report has said much that is lovely. There are times when the voice of the world is no other than the voice of God. At the same time our incomparable Monarch has expressly charged me to inform Your Highness that His Highness the Prince, your husband, shall under no circumstances take part in the journey. Her Majesty has very important reasons for wishing it so.'

This was an extraordinary invitation to arrive in a small German town from a lady living more than a thousand miles away whom neither Christian August nor Johanna had ever set eyes on. It was almost a fairy-tale invitation, especially as Brümmer, knowing Christian August was not well off, enclosed a money order to defray the cost of the journey, should they decide to make it. But for all that the invitation did not please the Prince of Anhalt-Zerbst, and his pointed exclusion from it played only a small part in his displeasure. For Sophie to accept, he declared, 'would be too much of a risk, too dangerous'. Christian August had in mind less the long journey, hazardous in winter, than the nature of the destination, Russia itself, its style of government, its dark recent history, and the manner in which the lady who issued the invitation had come to power.

CHAPTER 3

ALL THE RUSSIAS

To anyone living in Europe in the 1740s the prime fact about Russia would have been its immense size. From Poland in the west to the Pacific in the east it stretched at least five thousand five hundred miles, and even on the latest map the unexplored eastern limits were left a blur. It was so vast that almost any statement about it could be immediately contradicted. It was very flat but had some high mountains; for months it lay ice-bound, but produced grapes and melons. Only its vastness could not be contradicted.

Russia's population, estimated at 19 million, though large in relation to Prussia's 2.3 million, was smaller than France's and made for extremely low density. In the ninth century Russia had been a homogeneous community on the Dnieper, but as it expanded it absorbed many neighbouring states and peoples, and its name grew too, to become 'All the Russias', embracing by 1740 no less than eighty peoples of four races – Slavs, Finns, Mongols, Tartars. They included Cossacks on swift wiry ponies, turbaned Turkic-speaking Kirgiz falconers, Circassians in black lambskin caps, reindeer-herding Evenks, and the Yakuts of Siberia, living on the milk of cattle and horses.

So vast and variegated a country, with a babel of tongues and extremely slow communications, plainly had a strong inherent centrifugal tendency; indeed it could cohere at all only under a very strong centralized government. Though political influences played their part, it was chiefly in the facts of geography and demography that Russia's distinctive form of rule was rooted.

That rule was an autocracy in the exact sense. The Tsar possessed legislative and executive power, could imprison or put to death without trial, was more absolute than the King of Prussia. He might or might not take advice from elder statesmen, and he ignored at his peril influential groups such as the army and leading families, but except in Church matters where the Patriarch spoke with an equal voice, he ruled as he willed.

The Tsar expressed his will in the form of an *immenoy ukaz*, or named decree. This was a document which he caused to be drawn up and which he signed simply with his Christian name, not requiring approval by any other body and, having been published, it became one of the laws of the land. With the Tsar's authority government bodies also issued ukases, without the qualification 'named', to bodies under them.

As well as by its size and the nature of its government, Russia differed from European states by virtue of its history. If the constituent elements of Europe are taken to be the Western Roman Empire, the Roman Catholic Church, the Renaissance and the Reformation, Russia lacked all four. Russia also lacked feudalism: there had never been a strong nobility to contest the Tsar's claim to treat all Russia as his patrimony, and to rule it as an autocrat.

Russia, it is true, shared a common religion with Europe, but the Orthodox Church differed so much from its western counterparts that it was precisely in the spheres bordering on religion that Russia diverged most from Europe. For example, education in the West had been pioneered by Benedictine monks, but in Russia monks were forbidden to teach, their role being limited to prayer and worship. So Russia had never known the monastic tradition of learning, episcopal and cathedral schools, or even universities. At the time when France produced La Rochefoucauld and Molière, England Milton and Dryden, apart from the small Court, some nobles and the clergy, Russia was virtually illiterate.

The Church's ideal was unchangingness. Just as the best icon of Our Lady was the one most like that which St Luke had painted from life, so the best men and women were those who most resembled their forebears. Since music, traditionally, was an element in the Church's liturgy, non-sacred music was forbidden. So were shaving the beard and smoking tobacco. As a result all modern techniques, from clock-making to canal-building, had to be performed by foreigners, mainly Dutch, German and English. But the more backward Russia became, the better pleased were the clergy. Holy Russia, they claimed, by its unworldliness set an example to the world.

Such was the position in 1682, when young Peter I inherited the crown. Peter stood six foot eight, could bend a horseshoe in his hands, drank brandy by the keg and once, embracing a friend in an affectionate bear-hug, absent-mindedly broke the man's ribs. With this exceptional strength went courage and a keen practical intelligence. Basically, Peter was a soldier-patriot. He found the Swedes in possession of Russia's Baltic provinces, determined to throw them out and, in order to do so, had to change the face of Russia.

Seeing that the great obstacle to change was the Church, Peter decided to break its power. He cocked a snook at it by smoking a pipe, by his famous edict against beards, and by enrolling courtiers in a ribald Church of Bacchus; he seized monastic estates, he drew away ecclesiastical wealth to equip his army. Finally he abolished the office of Patriarch and instituted the Holy Synod, ten clerics and a lay *Ober Kurator*, to run the Church, so ending the situation whereby the word of the Patriarch was equal to the word of the Tsar.

Peter developed forests, mines, the fur trade; he slapped on new taxes. Like Frederick William, he geared the State to the army. But even when Westernizing most, Peter retained a measure of cruelty unthinkable in any European monarch. During one of his absences abroad the Moscow Guard revolted; hurrying back, Peter roasted 1700 of the Guard over slow fires until they 'confessed', and cut off the heads of four with his own axe.

Two changes introduced by Peter deserve mention because they were to be of great importance later. First is the institution of an elite Guards regiment, the Preobrazhensky, named from a village where Peter spent his childhood and meaning Transfiguration. This regiment was devoted to Peter and after his death to Peter's family, as well as to his ideal of a strong independent Russia.

The other change was to oblige Russia's 50,000 gentry to enter State service either as soldiers or civilians for twenty-five years. A gentleman's status henceforth no longer depended on birth but on merit: to be precise, on his position in a Table of Ranks – fourteen altogether – based on Prussian and Danish models.

Peter fought the Swedes for twenty-one years. He beat them decisively and recovered the mouth of the Neva. He built St Petersburg, first as a naval port, then as a second 'European' capital. As a reward for his victory he arranged for the Senate to call him 'the Great' and styled himself for the first time 'Emperor'.

In the Germany of Sophie's childhood Peter was remembered with awe. On his first visit to Brandenburg the Tsar had been so anxious to see a man broken on the wheel he had offered one of his own servants for demonstration purposes when no suitable Prussian candidate had been available. He had become very bad-tempered when this offer had been declined, and no less put out when his host refused to put to death a footman who had startled the company by dropping a silver platter on to the marble floor.

On a more recent visit Peter had brought his second wife Catherine – his first he had shut up in a convent. A Lithuanian servant girl who had formerly been the mistress of Peter's best friend, Catherine was thickset and suntanned. She wore a greasy dress, according to Frederick William's daughter Wilhelmine, worked with the double eagle; attached to it were a dozen orders and as many portraits of saints and relics, so that when she walked 'she jangled like a harnessed mule'. During dinner Peter had one of his fits, his face became convulsed and he seized Queen Sophia Dorothea's hand, squeezing it so violently that she cried with pain. This brought a roar of laughter from the Tsar, who remarked, 'My Catherine's bones are not so soft.'

Peter's son Alexis married Princess Charlotte of Brunswick, but Peter wrecked the marriage. Wishing to make a soldier of his frail dreamy son, for long periods he kept Alexis and Charlotte apart. Charlotte was miserable and soon died in childbirth, while Alexis died young too, of an inhuman flogging ordered by his own father.

Despite his obvious personal failings Peter amply deserved to be called 'the Great' if only because, almost single-handed, he heaved Russia out of the past into the present. But in order to do this, he had to increase still further the power of the autocracy by, as has been said, making the Church subservient to the throne – for which in his lifetime he was deemed by many Russians to be Antichrist – and by changing the law so that the Tsar could choose his own successor.

When Peter died, his wife Catherine reigned two and a half years and was succeeded by her step-grandson, Peter II, who ruled for almost three years and in turn was succeeded by Peter the Great's niece, Anna Ivanovna. The widow of a Baltic German duke, Anna Ivanovna entrusted State affairs to her lover and former secretary, Ernest Biron. He was a Courlander of German origin. His name was really Bühren but he so admired France that he gallicized it to Biron, and adopted the arms of the extinct Birons of France.

Biron was a pretentious upstart who used his wide powers to enrich himself and to crush all opposition. Once, on a journey, finding the bridges in such a poor state of repair that his carriage was damaged, he summoned the Senators and informed them that in order to repair the bridges he would have *them* laid down instead of planks. It was no empty threat. During Anna's ten-year reign the number of persons Biron killed, mutilated or exiled is said to have reached five figures. He never even deigned to learn Russian.

Before she died Anna Ivanovna appointed Biron Regent for the new Tsar, Anna's two-months-old great-nephew, Ivan VI. This proved too much for self-respecting Russians, in particular for the Preobrazhensky Guards, who helped Ivan VI's mother, Anna Leopoldovna, to seize the Regency and to exile Biron to Siberia.

Anna Leopoldovna was half-German, her father being a Duke of Mecklenburg; she had been educated in Germany and married a German, Anton Ulrich of Brunswick. A shy lady who kept to her apartments, she failed to learn the lesson of recent events and placed State affairs in the hands of two Germans, Ostermann and Münnich.

These men were very efficient, more so than most Russian senior officials. They spoke Russian, they were not high-handed like Biron. Nevertheless, there grew up strong opposition to this 'Germanization'. At his death Peter the Great had been hated for his cruelty and tradition-smashing; now, fifteen years later, he came to be hero-worshipped as the founder of a strong independent Russia who, though he fostered ties with German dukes, had always given top jobs to Russians. Xenophobia spread and was made more virulent by the Church. In confession priests told penitents that just as the people of God might not mix with the Moabites, so the people of Holy Russia must not mix with foreigners. Both clergy and sections of the Guards wanted Peter's only surviving daughter, Elizabeth, to seize the throne.

Elizabeth had been born in 1709, two years before her father married her mother. She saw little of her parents, who were often away, her education was neglected, and she was never taught the habit of work. She did, however, learn to speak French and German. Peter, who called her his 'little chicken', would send for her to entertain his guests by her graceful performance of the quadrille. She had inherited his fine physique, and grew up tall and very pretty. Peter tried to marry her to a French prince, but Louis XV objected to her tarnished birth. Negotiations to marry her to the great soldier Maurice de Saxe also fell through, whereupon Elizabeth declared that she was very pleased, because she wished to marry for love.

After the death of her parents, of her fiancé Karl August, and of her beloved sister Anna, Elizabeth led an independent life centred on the outdoor sports for which her strong body suited her. She rode to hounds, hunted bear and lynx, shot partridge, danced with Guards officers. She turned down two more grand political marriages and took at least two lovers, an army officer and a sergeant. She was affable, devout like her mother, quick-tempered like her father. She did not specially want to rule, and when Peter II had died she had not raised a hand to press her claims to the throne.

Ostermann became worried about Elizabeth's popularity with the Guards. In December 1741 he decided on a plan. He would order the Guards to march against Sweden, which had recently declared war, and during their absence arrest Anna Leopoldovna's potential rival.

Elizabeth was a lady who found it difficult to act. 'We may say of her,' wrote the British Minister, 'as Shakespeare makes Julius Caesar say . . . that her Highness is too fat to be in a plot.' Then, one day, her physician, Lestocq, learned of Ostermann's plan, hurried to Elizabeth and handed her a card, on one side of which he had sketched a crown, on the other the figure of a nun surrounded by hanged men. 'Your Highness,' he said, 'must choose between these two alternatives – *now*.'

Urged on by Lestocq and other friends, including a budding politician named Michael Vorontsov and two gentlemen of her household, Alexander and Peter Shuvalov, Elizabeth agreed to send for two brave Guards officers, whom Lestocq had already sweetened with money lent by the French Minister, La Chétardie. She asked the officers whether she could rely on them. 'Yes, little mother,' they answered. 'We are ready to die for you.'

Elizabeth entered her chapel and fell on her knees before an icon. Only after a long time in prayer could she bring herself to overcome her hesitation; then, doubtless recalling the cruelties still held against her father, she vowed that if she became Empress she would never sign a death warrant. Coming out of the chapel, she nodded to her friends and sent the officers back to barracks, promising to join them.

The revolution took place that night. The Preobrazhensky Guards forced an entrance to the palace but shed no blood. So slow were communications, so few the educated families and so centralized the government, that a handful of determined people in one city, having won the support of a Guards regiment, were able to change the ruler of one seventh of the earth's surface. By dawn Peter the Great's daughter was Empress of all the Russias, Ivan VI and his parents were prisoners, Ostermann and Münnich about to take the road to Siberia. In her first manifesto Elizabeth promised to deliver Russia from the control of foreigners.

Elizabeth saw herself as the continuer of Peter the Great's policies. Whether she might one day make a political marriage and bear children was anyone's guess; for the moment she summoned to St Petersburg the young Duke of Holstein, because he was Peter the Great's only surviving grandchild and, as has been said, she designated him her successor. So far Elizabeth had treated Peter well, but it was a truism that those who usurped power tended sooner or later to become suspicious of their successor. And now, at the end of her second year on the throne, the Empress of all the Russias had sent to a remote German town an invitation which had already plunged the Anhalt-Zerbst family into three days of excitement, doubt, fear and speculation.

CHAPTER 4

JOURNEY TO MOSCOW

'Neither your father nor I wish to hear anything more about it,' Johanna said to Sophie of Brümmer's letter. They disliked the idea of their fourteen-year-old daughter going to Russia on approval and were already agreed that Sophie should decline the invitation. But Johanna did ask her daughter, 'What do you think of it then?'

'If it doesn't please you,' Sophie replied, 'it would ill become me to desire it.'

'It seems that you have nothing against it.'

Sophie replied that not only did she have nothing against it, but as for the dangers God would take care of them if such was His will.

'But what will my brother Georg say?' This was the first time Johanna had mentioned Georg Ludwig.

Sophie blushed. 'He can only wish my happiness and good fortune.'

Aware that she was losing ground, Johanna went to fetch Christian August. The Prince shared his wife's view of the uncertainties of Russia and of Russian politics; he recalled the disastrous match between Tsarevich Alexis and Charlotte of Brunswick, but he had a more particular worry. If Sophie were asked to marry Peter, she might also be urged to join the Orthodox Church. The prospect of anyone trying to override his daughter's Lutheran conscience deeply disturbed the Prince. Really he should be beside Sophie, acting as her spiritual adviser. But the invitation said, 'The Prince, your husband, shall under no circumstances take part in the journey.' All things considered, Christian August opposed his daughter's going to Russia.

Sophie had been strictly brought up. She ended letters to Christian August with words that were more than a mere formula: 'To the end of my life, my Lord, I shall hold you in inviolable respect, and remain Your Highness's very humble, very obedient and faithful daughter and servant.' But Sophie also had a will of her own. When, the year before, Babet had fallen seriously ill, Sophie had defied her mother's order not to enter the sickroom for fear of infection: she had run to Babet as often as she could, preparing her tea one day when her maid was out, another day giving her her medicine.

Perhaps too Sophie had inherited from the Zerbst princes that spirit of daring which for five centuries had kept their small territory independent. At any rate, rather than acquiesce in a safe marriage to her timid uncle she preferred, if she could, to take her chances.

Sophie pleaded with Christian August. The journey, she said, would not commit her to anything. Once they arrived her mother and she would see whether it was advisable to return home or not. Above all, nothing would be lost by going. So would he give his approval?

Christian August was very fond of his daughter. As a soldier he admired the courage with which she had surmounted her childhood illness; in fact according to Sophie he considered her an angel. He again enumerated the drawbacks. But finally he said, 'I don't want to expose myself to self-reproaches later because I have made you unhappy.' Her mother must certainly make the journey as an act of gratitude. If Sophie truly wanted to go also, he would not stand in her way.

Sophie burst into tears of relief. 'Seldom in my life have I been so touched: a thousand different feelings moved me: gratitude for my father's kindness, distress lest I should displease him, the habit of obeying him blindly, the tender love I had always had for him, and most of all respect for him.'

Mother and daughter began to pack. Sophie had few possessions, and since she was only going on approval, Johanna decided she would not take a trousseau. A week later carriages were waiting, trunks ready. Christian August was to come part of the way, so Sophie did not say goodbye to him now. But she kissed her nine-year-old brother Friedrich – poor rickety Wilhelm had died – and her baby sister Elizabeth, who was to live only to the age of two; and she kissed Babet, unable to tell her where she was going, because her parents had demanded secrecy. Sophie was always to keep a fond memory of Babet, a gentle lady in a foreign land who had accepted a position of inferiority and still contrived to keep her self-respect.

First stop was Berlin, where Frederick William, dead these three and a half years, still lived on in his army and in the son he had bullied, half-strangled, court-martialled, imprisoned and generally brutalized. Frederick II had certainly had the effeminacy knocked out of him, but at the cost of his religious faith and any possibility of a tender relationship with women. He was left only with the huge army his father had been too cautious to use and an overwhelming passion for Prussia that filled the void in his soul. For Frederick the old restraints of European society – chivalry, law, treaties, the New Testament – simply did not exist. Seven months after coming to the throne he had marched 32,000 troops into Silesia, a large rich province belonging to Austria to which Frederick had no legal right, and had swiftly conquered it. He had, in his own words, made 'a total reversal of the old political system'.

Frederick received Johanna in audience and to her surprise said he knew all about her secret destination. In fact he claimed to have arranged the invitation to Moscow. Johanna may have been corresponding with Brümmer, but had Frederick and his ambassador been idle? By no means, and the young King tapped a file of letters. Johanna had sent a portrait of her daughter to Elizabeth in 1743; but Frederick had sent off Sophie's portrait, by the esteemed painter Anton Pesne, a full twelvemonth earlier. It was not Brümmer, said Frederick, or Johanna or the Empress who had engineered the coming *entrevue* between Peter and Sophie; it was part of his own new political system of aligning, under Prussia's hegemony, all the northern powers. Why else had he affianced his beautiful sister Ulrike to Johanna's brother, King-designate of Sweden?

Frederick then got down to the hard bargaining he liked. Johanna had hopes that her sister, the prioress who kept sixteen pugs in her room, might one day become Abbess of Quedlinburg. The abbey happened to be under Brandenburg's patronage, and Frederick hinted that this delicate matter might be arranged. Meanwhile, Johanna could help him. There were one or two people in Moscow he wished her to talk to. They would give her further instructions. But the whole matter must be kept secret.

At dinner in the palace that evening, Sophie sat next to Frederick and had a chance of observing a man who was to play an important part in her life. Thirty-one years old, he had a high brow, the same wedge-shaped nose as his brother Heinrich, and penetrating blue-grey eyes. A soldier by force of upbringing, he also loved learning and the arts. He broke through Sophie's shyness and, gesticulating with his very white hands, talked wittily of the opera they had seen before supper. At the end of the meal Frederick invited Sophie to hand a dish of jam to a distinguished courtier. As she did so, he said, 'Accept this gift from the hand of the Loves and Graces.' At the awkward but well-meant compliment Sophie blushed with pleasure.

Fifty miles from Berlin, at the cross-roads town of Schwedt, Christian August said goodbye to Johanna and Sophie. If his daughter stayed in Russia, she was, he told her, to hang on firmly to her Lutheran creed, as Princess Charlotte had been allowed to do when she married Alexis.

Christian August gave Sophie a book by a professor at Halle on the differences between the Lutheran and Orthodox Churches, and four pages of practical advice, including 'Save up your pocket money.' Sophie knew that she might never see her father again, and before he turned off to Stettin clung to him for a long time, crying.

Mother and daughter headed east in a heavy carriage through Danzig and Königsberg, accompanied in a second coach by a lady companion, a chamberlain, a cook and two maids. At their overnight stops Johanna, following Brümmer's directions, gave their names as 'Countess Reinbeck and daughter'. Countess Reinbeck, secret agent – it was a role that appealed to Johanna's liking for mystery and she sent a message to Empress Elizabeth saying that 'she only lacked wings, otherwise she would fly to Moscow.' To add to their excitement, as they passed through Courland – roughly present-day Latvia – they saw a comet, large and very near the earth. Sophie thought it terrifying.

They left the post road and took their chance on hiring fresh horses from peasants. One night, Johanna wrote to her husband, they had to spend in the innkeeper's own room: 'he, his wife, their dog, hens and children – children especially, in cradles, in beds, on the stove, on mattresses – strewn any old how like cabbages and turnips. But it couldn't be helped – I had a bench carried in and stretched out on that in the middle of the room.' It was so cold – well below freezing – that Sophie's feet swelled and on one occasion at least she was unable to walk and had to be carried from her carriage to the inn. The food was so bad that one day Sophie drank beer to wash it down and suffered an upset stomach, after which, she wrote to her father, 'Dear Mamma has forbidden me beer and I am well again.'

After three weeks of this mother and daughter arrived in Riga, a Baltic town of narrow streets and houses with steep-pitched roofs which marked the frontier between Polish Lithuania and westernmost Russia. As their carriage crossed the frozen River Dvina they arrived officially in Russia, and two things happened. They turned the calendar back eleven days, for Russia used the Julian calendar; and Countess Reinbeck became the Princess of Zerbst, guest of her Majesty the Empress, greeted by Court officials with a gift of sables, a regiment of light horse and a brass band. Johanna wrote home that it was 'like a dream': 'I can hardly believe that all this is for my poor self, who in her whole life has never had more than a drum beaten in her honour.' As for young Sophie, less concerned with appearances than her mother, she questioned one of the welcoming generals about the key figures at Court and asked him to write her notes on their characters, promising not to tell anyone.

The snow now lay so deep that they had to transfer to a Russian sleigh. A wooden hut on runners, with small windows on either side, it had shelves for provisions and a wax candle lantern suspended from the roof. The floor was covered with cushions and bedding. Chamberlain Simon Naruishkin explained to Sophie how to insert herself feet first into the bedding. '*Il faut enjamber; enjambez donc*' – a new word to Sophie that struck her as funny and made her laugh.

Lying in the comfortable bedding, heated stones at their feet, mother and daughter set off in their sleigh, drawn by six horses and preceded by a squadron of cavalry. They were a little cheered by their welcome but this feeling lasted only a short time. Leaving Riga, they passed a line of black coaches with blinds drawn, under heavy armed guard. Ivan VI, the boy Tsar whom Elizabeth had deposed, was being transferred with his mother and German father from the fortress of Dünaburg to an even safer prison nearer Moscow. The black carriages moving across the white snow were like a counterpart of the ominous comet that had frightened Sophie.

For five days they journeyed like this, into Estonia, a very poor province where flaxen-haired peasants speaking a language akin to Finnish eked out a living by growing turnips and white cabbages. At last, at noon on 3rd February according to Russian reckoning, they entered the city Tsar Peter had created in a waste marsh beside the River Neva. Mostly composed of log cabins, it had a few fine stone buildings, notably the Admiralty, and a population twice that of Berlin. Johanna and Sophie were welcomed at a big painted baroque building, the Winter Palace, by a handful of officials, most of the Court being in Moscow.

After dinner in the palace the visitors were shown the wooden barracks of the Preobrazhensky regiment: 'Here,' they were told, 'our Empress Elizabeth rallied the troops before beginning her Revolution.' They were shown an artificial toboggan run and then, probably for Sophie's benefit, fourteen performing elephants. These had been sent as a gift by Shah Nadir of Persia, who despite his name was a very great king and wished to marry his son to the Empress. By now Johanna was feeling the strain of the long journey but Sophie, she wrote to King Frederick, 'like the young soldiers who scorn danger because they do not know about it, delights in the splendours by which she is surrounded.'

After three days in St Petersburg Johanna and Sophie again set off in their sleigh, speeding day and night over the packed snow, stopping only to change horses. The long-haired peasants could not afford candles; they lighted their rooms with long slivers of pinewood, and they slept – the whole family – either on top of their stove or on shelves above it.

Racing through one of the villages their driver took a corner too sharply and hit a house. The crash caused the iron bar supporting the roof of the sleigh to fall heavily on Johanna's neck and arm. But for her furs she would have been badly hurt; as it was, after having brandy rubbed on the bruises and resting for a little, she was able to continue.

Fifty-two hours after leaving St Petersburg Johanna and Sophie arrived on the northern outskirts of Moscow. Here they received a message from the Empress directing them to wait until nightfall before entering the city. This secretiveness was not exactly encouraging but Sophie profited from the delay to change into her best dress, of rose-coloured moire and silver. At six o'clock they began to drive through Moscow, seeing almost nothing of its buildings in the darkness, to the city's southern outskirts. Their sleigh drew up outside a big, brightly lit building like a European baroque palace but in wood. This was the Annenhof Palace, and they had arrived.

Johanna and Sophie entered a splendid hall, leading to a wide staircase, decorated in white and gold, lit by crystal chandeliers, where the whole Court stood awaiting them, headed by the Adjutant General. Bowing, this official gave his hand to Johanna and led her, followed by Sophie, up the grand staircase to their apartments, where they removed their furs and hats.

Presently a plump little man in his fifties with sharp dark eyes in a small head and a cheerful manner came in. This was Count Lestocq, physician and close adviser to the Empress who, he said, was now ready to receive her guests in the ante-chamber of her bedroom.

Sophie, who had seen the Empress's portrait on a snuffbox, was prepared for a beautiful woman and was not disappointed. Her first impression was of tallness and stateliness. Then aged thirty-four, Elizabeth was very fair, with large sprightly blue eyes, fine teeth and a well-shaped mouth. Her face could be criticized as too round, her nose as being slightly turned up, her figure as too plump, but so majestic was her presence few noticed these imperfections. She was wearing a shiny silver taffeta gown, with a hoop skirt to offset her embonpoint; in her light brown hair were diamonds and a single upright black feather.

Johanna kissed the Empress's hand and said in French, 'I have come to lay at your Majesty's feet feelings of the deepest gratitude for the benefactions which your bounty has heaped upon my family.'

The Empress replied, also in French, 'What I have done is little compared with what I should like to do. Your blood is as dear to me as my own.'

The Empress embraced Sophie, then led her and Johanna into her bedroom. As Johanna seated herself on a stool the Empress surprised them by leaving the room abruptly. Later they were to learn why. It was seventeen years since Johanna's brother Karl August had come to Russia and died of smallpox, but Elizabeth still treasured her fiancé's memory and kept his portrait always by her. Struck by Johanna's resemblance to Karl August, she had left the room to be alone and shed a few silent tears.

At suppertime Peter appeared. He had a long pale face, fair hair, a straight nose and a firm chin. His shoulders were narrow and he seemed small for his age: he was about to be sixteen. He had a great deal of nervous energy and was never still a moment. Sophie found him good-looking but was surprised by the childishness of his conversation, though this could be a misconception on her part, for Sophie was older than her fourteen years and everyone agreed that Peter was a youth of great promise. Certainly he treated her with friendliness, and to her mother he said, 'I found the last hour of waiting so unbearable I should have liked to harness myself to your sleigh to hurry it on.'

The Empress looked in during supper to make sure things were going smoothly. When the meal was finished, Sophie said goodnight and went to her bedroom. On the double window were two thermometers, one outside showing the mercury below freezing, the other inside, registering the warmth generated by a big tiled stove. It was one reminder among many of the fact that she was now eleven hundred miles in a straight line from her little bedroom in Zerbst, from her father and from dear Babet. The forty days' journey from a new to an old world, from a familiar scene to an unfamiliar, was over, and she was about to spend her first night in Moscow. Sophie decided she liked what she had seen of the Empress and of Peter. But would the Empress and Peter like her, and would they ask her to stay?

CHAPTER 5

BECOMING CATHERINE

The next day Peter celebrated his sixteenth birthday and Sophie attended a dinner he gave for most of the Court. The following days she spent paying and receiving visits with her mother; in the evenings Peter came to their apartments to play cards. Because Lent had begun there were no dances, but Johanna was more than satisfied. 'We are living like queens,' she wrote to her husband. 'Everything is adorned or inlaid with gold – wonderful!' Sophie too liked what she saw of Russian life and, as at the Court of Brunswick, tried hard to make herself popular. She had the satisfaction of learning that Peter had said he would marry no one but her.

Sophie knew that the Empress's view of her would count for more than Peter's, but it would be tinged by politics as much as by personal feeling. As Princess of Anhalt-Zerbst Sophie had almost no political weight, but having been taken up by Frederick II she could be said to stand with Prussia and, through her uncle, with Sweden. Now Vice-Chancellor Bestuzhev, a man of commanding presence and one of the most experienced of Elizabeth's advisers, opposed a northern alliance, favouring a southern alliance with Prussia's enemy, Austria, and with Saxony; in fact Bestuzhev wanted Peter to marry Princess Marianne, daughter of the late Elector of Saxony and King of Poland, who was said to be very beautiful. In pursuance of this, Bestuzhev was trying to get the Archbishop of Novgorod to oppose any marriage between Peter and Sophie, on the grounds that they were cousins. Frederick II on the other hand had offered the Archbishop 3000 roubles not to oppose a marriage.

The Empress was as secretive about her opinion on this as she had been about Sophie's journey. Her main interest, as soon as Lent started, seemed to be prayers in her chapel, for she had inherited the piety of her relic-jingling mother, Catherine. She soon disappeared on pilgrimage to the Troitsa-Sergievskaya Monastery, but before leaving asked Archimandrite Simon Todorsky to give Sophie a course in the Orthodox faith. Peter had had to renounce Lutheranism and embrace the Orthodox faith as a condition of being adopted by Elizabeth.

Archimandrite Todorsky had spent four years at Halle University, quite near Zerbst, where there were two schools of theological thought: the historico-critical, which emphasized differences between creeds, and the Pietist, which put the inner thought of Christianity above outward forms. Todorsky followed the Pietist school and returned to Russia convinced that Germans and Russians at heart believed alike; indeed to Johanna he seemed virtually a Lutheran. So it was an astute move on Elizabeth's part to get him to instruct Sophie.

In his first lesson Todorsky explained Orthodox beliefs in Pietist terms. Sophie found nothing objectionable in what he said and added a postscript to Johanna's letter to Christian August: 'The Church here is forced to be different in externals because of the coarseness of the people.'

Nevertheless, when she attended Mass in the imperial chapel, Sophie like any observant person would have seen that such essential matters as transubstantiation, the veneration accorded the Mother of God and the saints, not to mention the belief that the Holy Spirit proceeds from the Father only, were in evident contradiction with Lutheranism.

Sophie found herself in a dilemma. On the one hand lay the family's long attachment to Luther, and her father's evident preference that she should retain the faith in which he had brought her up. On the other hand stood this bearded Russian, so much more learned than she, who claimed that any differences were merely apparent. Was he a tempter or a sage? 'The change of religion gives this Princess infinite pain,' the Prussian ambassador wrote to Frederick. 'Her tears flow abundantly when she is alone with persons of whom she is not suspicious.'

This was a moment when Sophie would have benefited from advice from a strong mother. But as in the matter of wearing mourning for King Frederick William, Johanna took the easy way out. Although she told Christian August that she found the formal ceremonies 'very different from ours', she did not question Todorsky's interpretation, and told her husband that she 'left the choice to Sophie's own free will'.

After receiving further instruction from Todorsky Sophie wrote to tell her father that she was convinced by his arguments. To this she received the following reply: 'Search yourself with care whether you are really in your heart inspired by religious inclination or whether, perhaps, without being aware of it, the marks of favour shown you by the Empress and other high-placed persons have influenced you in that direction. We human beings often see what is before our eyes.

But God in His infinite justice searches the heart and our secret motives.'

If this was hard, it was also shrewd. Sophie evidently did search her heart and what she saw there proved too much for her. Alone, trapped, her loyalties divided, exhausted by tears, she broke down physically and took to her bed with severe pains in her right side and a high fever.

Johanna at once panicked. It so happened that she hated the sight of blood and she refused to let her daughter be bled. The Dutch Court physician, Boerhave, wrote to Lestocq, who had accompanied the Empress on pilgrimage, telling him that unless she were bled Sophie would die.

The Empress, informed of this, hurried back to Moscow, removed Johanna from the sick-room, seated herself at the head of the bed and held the now unconscious Sophie in her arms while the Court surgeon opened a vein in her foot and let two ounces of blood. Sophie came to, saw the Empress bending over her and again lost consciousness.

At first smallpox was suspected, but when no pustules appeared Bestuzhev triumphantly declared it to be tuberculosis, and that this ruled out Sophie as a wife for Peter. The palace servants held a different opinion – that Sophie had been poisoned by the Saxon Minister, and in her delirium Sophie began to believe that too. In fact she was suffering from severe pleurisy, brought on partly by the change of climate, partly by the mental anguish of her religious crisis.

Sophie hovered between life and death. It was a grim experience for her to be so ill in a strange country, treated by doctors she had never seen, speaking a language she could not understand. The only good thing about it was the Empress's kindness. She came every day to be with Sophie and she, certainly, had no fear of blood for she had Sophie bled no less than sixteen times.

On the fourteenth day of the illness Johanna felt sure Sophie was dying. Still not allowed in the sick-room but wishing in some way to be effective, she sent a message to Sophie asking whether she would like to see a Lutheran pastor.

Sophie was now cut off from both her parents. She felt entirely dependent on the Empress, in whose palace she lay and who was nursing her so lovingly, and despite Christian August's warning, it was her that she wanted to please. To the offer of a Lutheran pastor Sophie said, 'Why? Please send for Archimandrite Todorsky. I should like to speak to him.' This answer, she noticed, raised her in the eyes of the Empress and the whole Court.

Slowly the fever lessened. Sophie became strong enough to sit up in bed, then to get up, and in April to resume her lessons from the Archimandrite. By asking him to come to her sick-bed she had not committed herself to changing her religion, but she had put herself in a position where that course seemed to follow as a next step.

It was now explained to Sophie that renouncing Lutheranism was not just a course that would please the Empress; it was, in the Empress's staunchly Orthodox eyes, an absolute condition of her marrying the future Tsar of Russia. This put the matter in a new light for Sophie. Unless she changed her faith, her long journey, her mental torments, her dangerous illness would all have been for nothing.

On 3rd May Sophie made her choice. 'As I find almost no difference,' she wrote to her father, 'between the Orthodox and the Lutheran faiths, I have decided to change my religion.' 'Almost' is the key word, its implications becoming plain in the light of a letter that followed, written after Sophie had received a gift of money from the Empress: 'I know that your Highness has sent my brother to the waters at Homburg, and that this has entailed heavy expenses. I beg your Highness to leave my brother there as long as is necessary to restore him to health; I will undertake to pay all the expenses.'

Without actually feeling guilt, Sophie evidently did not feel at ease about what she had done. If she had leapt the chasm signified by the word 'almost', she had done so because she wanted to wear a crown. In short she had not been absolutely truthful with herself. Now she was hoping that charity would make amends to truth, but, as Christian August would have told her, this is not a permissible bargain.

As she convalesced Sophie began to learn Russian, first the Greek-derived alphabet, then basic words, and verbs with more metamorphoses than the gods of Olympus. Russian is richer in hard, concrete words than French or German, and therefore a better instrument for speaking about the visible world; Sophie liked it from the start because it is 'so rich, so energetic, and you can manipulate it as you wish'. She quickly learned to speak Russian well, with only a very slight German accent, but her writing of it was always to be marred by bad spelling.

In making her confession of faith Sophie would have to read some fifty large-print quarto pages of Russian. Simon Todorsky taught her to use the accent of his native Ukraine, pronouncing unstressed O's more distinctly than Moscovites do, and G rather like an H, while Sophie's Russian teacher, Basil Adodurov, urged her to use a Moscow pronunciation. In order to please Peter, Sophie referred the problem to him, and was advised to use the Moscow pronunciation.

Things went smoothly until three weeks before Sophie was due to make her confession of faith; then an event occurred which looked like dashing all hopes of the marriage.

Sophie's mother had been kindly treated by the Empress, and at Easter had received from her a valuable diamond ring. But she had not forgotten that she was Frederick's secret agent and on her arrival in Moscow had begun working with the Prussian ambassador, Mardefeld, and the French envoy, the Marquis de La Chétardie. Johanna's task was to influence the Empress against Austria, and to topple Bestuzhev. Unfortunately for Johanna the British envoy, Lord Tyrawley, noticed her game and informed his friend Bestuzhev, while La Chétardie, a rash vain Southerner who had lost his former influence with the Empress and resented the fact, wrote a number of indiscreet letters which Bestuzhev intercepted.

At the beginning of June, to fulfil a vow made during Sophie's illness, the Empress, accompanied by Peter, Johanna and Sophie, again went on pilgrimage to the Troitsa-Sergievskaya Monastery near Moscow, a vast high-walled complex of buildings founded in 1342 and important in national history. There the Empress was handed seven of La Chétardie's letters, duly deciphered, in which the Frenchman described her as 'lazy' and 'extravagant', said that her chief pleasure in life was changing her dress four or five times a day – this was true – and referred to Johanna's secret plotting on behalf of King Frederick.

The Empress arrived unannounced in the cell-like bedroom Johanna shared with Sophie, and asked Johanna to follow her out. Sophie remained with Peter, who began to tell her amusing stories. Both were seated on a high window-seat, laughing, when Count Lestocq came in. 'You will soon be laughing on the other side of your faces,' he told them, adding to Sophie, 'What you have to do is to pack.'

'What does this mean?' Peter asked.

'You'll find out later,' said Lestocq, leaving the room.

Peter turned to Sophie. 'If your mother has done something wrong, that does not mean that you have,' he said, to which Sophie replied, 'My duty is to follow my mother and obey her commands.'

A long time passed before the Empress and Sophie's mother returned, both red in the face, and Johanna's eyes swollen with crying. The Empress considered, with reason, that Johanna had repaid her kindness very badly but once the other had apologized she softened and decided after all not to pack her home. She contented herself with ordering La Chétardie to leave Russia, and with refusing an alliance to Frederick.

The Empress and her guests returned to the Annenhof Palace and there, in the chapel, on 28th June, less than five months after arriving in Russia, Sophie went through the ceremony for which she had long been preparing. Wearing a crimson and silver dress like the Empress's, she read the long confession of faith unfalteringly, recited the Nicene Creed in its Orthodox form, declaring the Holy Spirit to proceed from the Father only, not, as in the Lutheran creed, from the Father and the Son, and formally became a member of the Orthodox Church. This was a turning-point in Sophie's life, marking, as it did, a break with her childhood and with the categorical imperatives learned in Stettin and Zerbst; her adopted religion was never to have the same force for her as Lutheranism had had.

Sophie then received the sacrament of confirmation and with it a new name. Sophie had bad overtones in Russia, being the name of Peter I's treacherous half-sister, and the Empress chose Catherine, the name of her mother and of the saint of Alexandria who combined looks and learning, who had been wedded spiritually to the Christ Child, and who was put to death on four wheels bristling with nails and saws. So Sophie said goodbye to part of herself, the appellation she had borne for fifteen years, and became Ekaterina, which is the Russian form of Catherine.

That evening, still feeling awkward in her strange-sounding name, Catherine entered for the first time the walled complex of medieval palaces and churches known as the Kremlin. After spending the night in these gloomy surroundings Catherine, accompanied by Peter, followed the Empress, who wore her crown and was attended by Court dignitaries, across the square to the Cathedral of the Assumption. There amid the glittering jewelled icons the young couple were blessed by the Archbishop of Novgorod and plighted their troth by exchanging plain gold rings, which each placed on the third finger of the right hand. Peter was already known as 'Grand Duke', and Catherine, in a special ukase read after her betrothal, was declared 'Grand Duchess', with the title 'Imperial Highness'.

One result of the betrothal was to change Catherine's relations with her mother. Catherine now took precedence over Johanna and had the right to have her hand kissed, like the Empress. To spare her mother's feelings, when she returned to the palace Catherine tarried in the doorway so that they passed through together, and avoided occasions when her mother might feel slighted. Some officials – but not Bestuzhev – helped by kissing Johanna's hand as a token honour, and she wrote delightedly to Christian August that during the betrothal reception her hand had been kissed so often it had a red mark the size of a florin.

In late July the Empress set off on a two-month tour of the Ukraine. She wished to consolidate her power by showing herself to the people, and especially to the clergy of the holy town of Kiev, but on the way she did some hunting. Catherine, with her mother and Peter, went also and during the tour she had an opportunity of observing Elizabeth more closely.

It was noticeable, first, that the Empress as a ruler felt no embarrassment on account of her womanhood. Lacking Aristotle and the Western Fathers, the Russians had no belief that woman is 'inferior' and that it is 'unnatural' for her to rule over men.

Catherine noticed also Elizabeth's religious exactitude. She went to church three times daily, for matins, Mass and vespers. She observed – and saw that Catherine observed – the four Lents and other fast days: altogether, during thirty weeks of the year, no meat, eggs, milk, butter or cheese were served, only fish and vegetable oil, while during the first and last weeks of the four Lents only mushrooms and pickled cucumbers might be eaten. The Empress also made frequent pilgrimages on foot; these, like her fasting, were good for her figure as well as her soul.

As the daughter of a Lithuanian mother who in early life had been a Roman Catholic, that is a heretic, Elizabeth evidently felt the need to stress her Russianness. She even on occasion dyed her fair hair black. This helped Catherine to explain several puzzles. Why had Elizabeth been so insistent that Catherine give up Lutheranism? Because Lutheranism was the religion of Germans. Why had her father been asked not to come to Russia? Because he was a German prince, whose presence would emphasize Catherine's German origins. Why indeed had Elizabeth chosen Catherine to marry Peter? Not, as Catherine had originally supposed, because of her Prussian links, but because, through her mother, she belonged to the Holstein-Gottorp family, whom Peter the Great had cultivated because of their connections along the Baltic useful to Russia.

Catherine also learned something of Elizabeth's private life. As a princess Elizabeth had tried to make her chapel services as beautiful as possible and recruited the best voices for the choir. One such recruit was Alexis Razumovsky, son of a small farmer in the Ukraine. A solo he sang so moved her that Elizabeth had him presented to her after the service. She found a tall, dark, very good-looking man, his arched black eyebrows especially fine, the same age as herself and with the sunny disposition more usual in Ukrainians than in Russians of the north. Elizabeth felt strongly attracted to Alexis and arranged for him to be attached to her household. His duties were to sing to her and to play the *bandura*, and his perquisites included a jug of vodka a day and several jugs of beer.

The ex-chorister became Elizabeth's lover and very probably, in autumn 1742, after she became Empress, her husband. Publicly to marry a lowly farmer's son would have weakened her authority and affronted the influential gentry, so Elizabeth kept the marriage secret. Alexis's official position was Grand Huntsman, but his quarry was not the deer; unofficially he was called 'the night-time Emperor'.

Catherine came to know Alexis on the journey because they all stayed with him at his estate in Kozelets. She thought him one of the handsomest men she had ever seen and liked his unassumingness. When the Empress loaded him with honours he said, 'Do what you like, you will never make people find me imposing.' He did not want power and kept out of politics. What he liked was music, opera bouffe and, something he shared with the Empress, missions to convert the infidel.

Catherine enjoyed her journey through the rich wheat-growing plains and nothing before or later made such an impression on her as the gorgeous splendour of the eleventh-century Church of the Assumption in Kiev, in which all the holy pictures were covered with gold, silver and jewels.

Catherine was meeting ordinary Russians and trying to understand the national character. Two early incidents impressed her. The people of Kiev put on a firework display for their distinguished visitors. The first rockets zoomed into the night sky, only to fall on the imperial tent, narrowly missing the Empress and causing the carriage horses to shy dangerously. Evidently the Russians were not very practical.

The other incident occurred at one of the Tuesday masquerade balls, when the Empress made men dress as ladies and ladies as men. Catherine in tight hose was dancing a polonaise with Chamberlain Sievers, a very tall man wearing a wide hoop skirt lent by the Empress. 'Countess Hendrikova,' Catherine recalled, 'who was dancing behind me, was knocked over by Sievers' hoop skirt as he gave me his hand in turning. As she fell she struck me in such a way that I tumbled beneath Sievers' uptilted hoop skirt, causing him to trip over too. All three of us lay on the floor with me entirely covered by his skirt. I was dying of laughter and trying to get up but we were so entangled that none of us could rise without making the other two fall and eventually we had to be lifted to our feet.'

This free-and-easy, almost knockabout atmosphere pleased Catherine.

She liked spontaneity, hence her interest in her eccentric aunts in their convents, and she saw that the Russians liked it too. For example, when someone was portrayed on a coin or medal, he was depicted warts and all, not as in Europe given conventional good looks.

Naturalness of course had its less pleasing side. Catherine saw that many Russians were moody and intemperate; one contemporary observer put this down to the fact that as children they had been looked after exclusively by peasant nurses who indulged and fawned on them. Also, as their recent history showed, they were intolerant, especially of Europeans.

This brought Catherine's considerations back to herself. She liked Russians and liked what she had seen of their country. But would they like her, a European? To be liked, she must become in some ways Russian. Yet it was already part of her philosophy – despite her concession over Lutheranism – that she must be true to herself, and that self was European. The tensions inherent in Russia's geography and history could well become tensions within her personally.

Having looked around her and weighed up her experiences since her arrival Catherine decided on a three-point plan of action. It was disarmingly simple, she did not yet realize that one point might turn out to be incompatible with another, but she decided on it none the less:

(1) To please the Grand Duke
(2) To please the Empress
(3) To please the Russian people.

On the tour of the Ukraine and afterwards in Moscow Catherine saw quite a lot of Peter. Not only his conversation but his behaviour struck her as being unusually young for his age. He could not get enough of playing with toy soldiers, practical jokes, romping, games and entertainments. He seemed to have no serious interests and liked turning every occasion into a joke. Partly, she supposed, this arose from his early background. His mother Anna, daughter of Tsar Peter and sister of Empress Elizabeth, had died a few weeks after his birth, leaving Peter to grow up in Kiel, a solitary only child, until the age of thirteen when he had been whisked from familiar surroundings to the even greater loneliness of a Russian Court.

Catherine decided to adapt herself. She played blind man's buff with Peter; out of mattresses, a sofa and the big wooden case of a harpsichord she constructed an indoor slide, on which she, her maids-in-waiting, Peter and his attendants used to play like ten-year-olds. She also took

ophie's parents.
rince Christian August of
ınhalt-Zerbst rose to be a
ield Marshal in the
russian army. His wife
ɔhanna had royal blood
ıd a taste for splendour.

Sophie of Anhalt-Zerbst, aged about fifteen.

Grand Duke Peter, Catherine's husband.

John Atkinson, a British artist patronized by Catherine, made some of the earliest etchings of daily life in Russia. *Above:* Village scene. *Below:* A peasant's house. For warmth in the Russian winter the inmates slept above the stove. On the left a lamp burns before icons.

dancing lessons in order to learn the minuet and polonaise, for balls, especially in fancy dress, were a feature of Court life, and offered an occasion for being with Peter on a slightly less childish basis.

What disturbed Catherine more than anything was that Peter never sought occasions for being alone with her, never spoke tenderly or told her that he was happy to be with her. Did he even care for her? During the angry scene at the Troitsa-Sergievskaya Monastery when she had said, 'My duty is to follow my mother home,' Peter had not seemed upset at the prospect of her leaving and had made no protest.

Catherine had outgrown her awkward age and was now a fresh, pretty young girl, a constant smile on her lips, as one courtier noticed, and eager for a few compliments from her fiancé. She decided to see what a little jealousy could do. Among Peter's attendants was a certain Lieutenant Andrey Chernuishev, very good-looking and pleasant. Catherine began to flirt mildly with this young officer in the Life Guards, hoping that it would encourage Peter to make a show of his feelings for her. Peter did indeed notice Catherine's interest in the officer, but instead of becoming jealous, he turned the affair into a joke. 'Andrey Chernuishev is your new fiancé,' he quipped, and he kept referring to the Lieutenant as 'your future bridegroom'.

Puzzled, Catherine returned to the old round of games and entertainments. Then, one day, a Swedish envoy arrived in Moscow. Count Charles Gyllenborg had first met Catherine two years before in Hamburg, been struck by her conversation, and told Johanna that she had a very intelligent daughter. When the Swede saw Catherine's new way of life, he was surprised. 'You think only of clothes,' he told her. 'I bet you haven't opened a book since you came to Russia.' Catherine admitted it. Gyllenborg then said he felt sure Catherine had the mind of a budding philosopher, and she ought to train it. As a start he recommended Montesquieu's *Cause of the Romans' Greatness and Decadence*. Perceiving the motive for her frivolous life, he told Catherine, 'I can't help feeling this marriage of yours is a mistake.'

Catherine esteemed the serious-minded Swede. She got hold of Montesquieu's book and tried to read it. But after two days she gave it up and returned to her romping and easy amusements.

In December the Court moved to St Petersburg. On the way Peter caught smallpox and for six weeks lay seriously ill in a farmhouse, the Empress nursing him day and night as devotedly as she had nursed Catherine. For almost two months Catherine was not allowed to see her fiancé. Then, one February evening, in the Winter Palace, St Petersburg, Peter came to see her, but he was so changed Catherine would not have recognized him. His cheeks were pitted and still swollen, and on his head, which had had to be shaved of all its hair, he wore an ungainly wig.

Some girls, especially those who are beautiful, attach small importance to masculine good looks. Catherine was not that sort. Perhaps because she was herself no more than pretty, she felt the need of good looks in her future husband. Peter's two attractions for Catherine had been his good humour and his good looks. Now his looks were marred.

Nor was his good humour by any means constant. If thwarted, he would stick out his tongue at his tutor, and criticism made him cross. One day Catherine's mother was sitting in her room writing a letter, when Peter came in. Beside her on a chair lay a leather case in which she kept valuables, including correspondence, and she asked him to be careful of it. Peter began romping round the room in his usual style and eventually sent the leather case flying on to the floor. Johanna thought he had done it on purpose and flared up. Peter said it was an accident and instead of accepting her rebuke grew angry, leaving Catherine to smooth things over.

Catherine's heart was not at ease and when a date in the summer was set for her marriage she heard it without enthusiasm. She began to have unaccountable moods of sadness and as at the time of her dilemma about religion, often found herself crying.

In May 1745 the Empress and Peter went to live in the Summer Palace, while Johanna and Catherine were allotted a stone building on the Fontanka river. Peter sent Catherine a servant to tell her that he now lived too far away to visit her often, and he did in fact very seldom come. Catherine had too high an opinion of herself to believe that Peter disliked her or was shying off the marriage; she told herself merely that as yet he did not love her. Nevertheless, she recalled, 'This lack of attention and coldness did not exactly prepossess me in his favour, and the closer the wedding day came the less I hid from myself that I was perhaps going to make a very bad marriage.'

Catherine had fought to leave Zerbst. She had made the long icy journey to Moscow. She had fought pleurisy, she had overcome her scruples in order to accept the Orthodox faith, she had learned Russian, she had made herself popular at Court – was she now going to draw back, scuttle home and settle down with timid Lieutenant Uncle Georg of the Cuirassiers?

She would have liked to turn to her mother for advice. But her mother, Catherine knew, had set her heart on this second royal marriage in her family and besides she was not very perceptive about character:

like so many others, she simply saw Peter as a promising, if sometimes tiresome, young prince.

Catherine glimpsed the Empress only on Sundays and was not close enough to confide in her. Yet she loomed large on the young girl's horizon. When Catherine left by sleigh for St Petersburg with her own hands she had tucked an extra fur round her. She used to say she loved Catherine almost more than Peter. Hardly a week passed but she gave Catherine some valuable piece of jewellery. As a result Catherine transferred much of her filial affection to the Empress, finding her, she confessed, 'like a divinity in whom there could be no fault'.

The Empress wanted the marriage, and Catherine increasingly wanted to please the Empress. She also, subconsciously, desired one day to be like this lady who was so strong, so kind, and able to do so much good. By marrying the heir to the throne she could realize that desire. And so, just as she had fought down her religious hesitations, Catherine fought down her fears that she might be making an unhappy marriage, and allowed no one to see her tears.

On the morning of her wedding day, 21st August 1745, Catherine got up at six o'clock. She had recently had her hair cut and was having it arranged as she liked, curled with a fringe, when the Empress came in and, after kissing her, began to scold her hairdresser Timothy for curling Catherine's hair. 'She must wear it smooth,' said the Empress, 'otherwise her jewels will not stay in place.' Then she left the room.

Catherine decided that she wanted her hair arranged in her own way; after all it was her wedding. So she got Timothy to enlist the help of the Empress's bosom friend, Countess Rumyantsova, who happened to like curls and to hate smooth hair. The Countess went back and forth between the Empress and Timothy three times, and finally the Empress relented.

When her hair was arranged as she wished, in curls and a fringe, Catherine put on her wedding dress, of heavy silver glacé with silver embroidery only seventeen inches round the waist, and the Empress again came in, to arrange the grand ducal crown on her head.

At three o'clock Catherine and Peter drove in the Empress's State coach to the Church of the Holy Virgin of Kazan, in St Petersburg's main street, the Nevsky Prospect. Its square nave, crowded with courtiers and dignitaries, was separated from the sanctuary by an altar-screen on which hung a jewelled copy of the miraculous icon of the Virgin of Kazan.

The benign-looking Archbishop of Novgorod was waiting in cope and mitre. He blessed gold filigree crowns, which were then held over the heads of Catherine and Peter during the marriage ceremony – hence its other name of coronation. The Archbishop addressed Catherine first. 'Do you, Ekaterina Alekseievna, of your own free will and firm purpose, take this man, Peter Feodorovich, whom you see here, to be your husband?'

Catherine replied, 'Yes, Reverend Father, I do.'

'Are you engaged to anyone else?'

'No, Reverend Father, I am engaged to no one else.'

In the Orthodox Church the bride gives no promise to love, honour and obey. The same questions having been put to Peter and answered in the same way, the Archbishop raised his eyes: 'Lord most holy, bless this marriage and grant to these thy servants peaceful life, length of days, sobriety, mutual love in the bond of peace, long-lived posterity, grace in their children, and the unfading crown of glory.' Peter and Catherine then exchanged plain gold rings, placing them on the same finger as their engagement rings. This was a solemn moment. Since the Orthodox Church did not permit divorce except on the grounds of the wife's adultery, Catherine had committed herself to Peter for life.

The young couple returned with the Empress to the palace for a grand dinner, followed by the dancing of polonaises. For the same reason she had excluded him from the original invitation, Elizabeth had not invited Catherine's father to the wedding, but Christian August swallowed his pride and sent along a homely gift, probably all he could afford. It appeared at the dinner, when guests, along with the champagne and golden Tokay, also drank glasses of best Zerbst-brewed beer.

CHAPTER 6

THE MARRIED PRISONERS

Saying goodbye to her mother, who after the wedding returned to Zerbst, Catherine settled down to married life. In autumn and winter she lived in a suite of rooms on the first floor of the Winter Palace, separated by a landing from Peter's rooms and the Empress's apartment. They were heated by Dutch wood-burning stoves, and from the windows Catherine had a fine view of the port of St Petersburg, closed by ice in winter, but at other times busy with ships sailing to and from Europe. Catherine had eight maids to look after her rooms, her clothes, her lace and ribbons, jewels, powder and combs, rouge and mouches. As companions she had three young maids-in-waiting of good family, under the supervision of Madame Maria Kruse, an officious lady, mother-in-law of Count Sievers, with whose hoop-skirt Catherine had become entangled at the fancy-dress ball.

Peter, though slim, was tough – even in freezing weather he insisted on driving in an open sleigh – and during the winter months he kept fit by taking fencing lessons. He played the violin well and Catherine took harpsichord lessons so as to be able to join him in little concerts. He constructed a puppet theatre and gave performances for Catherine, her maids-in-waiting and his own attendants, Andrey Chernuishev and Andrey's equally amiable cousins, Ivan and Zachary Chernuishev, who were also Guards officers. Catherine and Peter had to attend Court performances of plays and Court balls, which they found dull; what they liked much more was to give small supper-dances for friends of their own age. Both Catherine and Peter loved dancing, Peter being specially fond of English country dances, which he learned in houses of the English colony.

In March or April the ice on the Neva would thaw and after a short delicious spring they moved at the beginning of summer to the country, usually to Oranienbaum. The name means Orange Tree, a few such trees being grown under glass, and the house, built by Peter the Great's favourite, Menshikov, before his exile to Siberia, consisted of a dome-roofed central structure and two long pavilions joined to it by long galleries, the whole commanding a fine view of the Gulf of Finland.

'I would rise at three in the morning,' said Catherine, 'and dress in man's clothes. An old huntsman of mine would be waiting for me with guns. He had a fisherman's skiff all ready on the seashore, nearby: we crossed the garden on foot, shouldering our guns, got into the skiff, he, a pointer, a fisherman and I, and went out shooting duck in the reeds which fringe the sea on both sides of the Oranienbaum Canal, stretching about a mile into the sea. We often rounded the canal and so sometimes found ourselves in stormy weather out at sea in the skiff. The Grand Duke used to join us an hour or two later, after he had had his breakfast.'

Catherine and Peter continued duck-shooting until ten o'clock, then returned to the house for dinner. After a siesta they went long rides on horseback through woods of larch and birch. Catherine had begun to take riding lessons soon after her arrival in Moscow; riding had become her favourite sport and according to one British Minister, 'it really is not flattering to say that few men ride better.' The more violent the exercise the more Catherine enjoyed it, so that if a horse ever broke away it was she who galloped after it and brought it back.

Sometimes the Empress took Catherine and Peter on little trips, her favourite destinations being Tikhvin, where there was a miracle-working icon of Our Lady, and Alexis Razumovsky's country estate, Gostilitsy. Then, in September, they would all return to St Petersburg for the long dark winter.

Peter was a cheerful companion, who liked nothing better than a practical joke. One day while preparing a puppet show he heard animated voices in the next room. Curious about them, he got hold of a carpenter's brace and bored holes in a blocked-up door. Looking through, he saw the Empress at the dinner table with about a dozen guests: mostly below-stairs staff whose company she enjoyed – lackeys, choristers and serving women – but also her favourite Alexis who, having taken a purge, was wearing a brocade dressing-gown. This was better than a puppet show. Peter called his suite to look through the peep-holes, and even carried in benches, chairs and footstools, for the comfort of the audience, he said. He called Catherine too but she was frightened that the Empress would find out and be upset, and she refused to look.

Nothing happened until two days later. It was a Sunday, and Catherine arrived in church a little later than usual. Back in her room she was going to change from her Court dress when she saw the Empress come in, looking very irritated and rather flushed. As she had not attended the church service but had been at Mass in her private chapel, Catherine had not seen her before on that day and went up to her as usual, the moment she saw her, to kiss her hand. The Empress kissed Catherine, ordered that Peter should be called and, while waiting for him, scolded Catherine for coming late to church and giving preference to matters of vanity over those of God. She added that in the time of the Empress Anna, though she did not live at Court, but in her own house some distance away, she had never missed church and very often got up in the middle of the night with a candle to attend the service. Then she called Catherine's coiffeur and told him that if in future he dressed her hair as slowly as he had done that day she would have him dismissed.

Peter, who had undressed in Catherine's room, now walked in wearing a dressing-gown, carrying his nightcap in his hand. He looked gay and spruce, and rushed to kiss the Empress's hand. She first kissed him and then asked how he had dared to behave as he had; she went on to say that she had walked into her dining-room and found the door riddled with holes, all immediately facing the place where she usually sat. She could only suppose that in doing what he did he forgot all that he owed her; he was the epitome of ingratitude. Her father, Peter the First, she went on, also had an ungrateful son whom he had punished by disinheriting him; in earlier days she herself had always shown the Empress Anna the respect due to a crowned head, anointed by God – and there, furthermore, was an Empress who had allowed no nonsense and imprisoned all those lacking in courtesy towards her; as for Peter, she concluded, he was nothing but a boy and she would soon find a way of teaching him how to behave.

Here Peter began to lose his temper and wanted to retort, hotly. He even stammered a few words in rebuttal, but she ordered him to be silent. The corners of her eyes twitched and her anger reached such a peak that it seemed to Catherine she completely lost control. She showered furious condemnations and gross words upon Peter, betraying as much contempt for him as anger.

Catherine was as much dumbfounded and perplexed as Peter, and though the scene had nothing to do with her, it brought tears to her eyes. The Empress noticed and said to Catherine: 'What I am saying is not directed at you. I know that you took no part in all this and neither looked nor wanted to look through that door.'

This remark, thought Catherine, at least proved the Empress's sense of justice, and seemed to calm her. After this she bade the two of them goodbye and left, very red in the face, her blue eyes flashing.

Peter went back to his rooms and Catherine undressed in silence, thinking over what she had just heard. When she was fully undressed Peter joined her and said, half contrite, half sneering, 'She was like a Fury and did not know what she was saying.' Catherine said, 'She was extremely angry.' They repeated to each other what they had just heard, after which they dined together alone.

When Peter had retired to his room, Catherine's senior lady-in-waiting, Madame Kruse, walked in, saying, 'One must admit that the Empress behaved today like a real mother.' Catherine could see that she wanted to draw her out and therefore remained silent. Madame Kruse continued: 'A mother gets angry and scolds her children and then it all blows over; you ought, both of you, to have said to her: "*Vinovaty, Matushka* – We beg your pardon, Maman" – and she would have been disarmed.'

Catherine replied that she was so perplexed and shaken by her Majesty's anger that all she could do was to listen and remain silent. Madame Kruse then left, but the phrase *Vinovaty, Matushka*, remained in Catherine's memory.

Mostly these early days of Catherine's marriage passed in light-hearted occupations and amusements, so that the young couple's apartments rang with laughter. The nights, however, were less happy for Catherine. On their wedding night, after the polonaises, when Peter got into the poppy-coloured bed beside her, he had confided with a giggle that his manservant would think it very funny if he could see them in bed together; then he had turned over and gone to sleep. On the nights following he had shown equally little interest in his bride.

Catherine tried to be understanding. Peter was young for his seventeen years; everyone said he was a late developer. Then again, he and she were second cousins, and it was well known that between cousins the spark of physical love could be weak and slow to come. Louis VII of France had long been cold towards Eleanor of Aquitaine, Louis XIII towards Anne of Austria. But as weeks passed and then months, Catherine decided to do something to make Peter notice her as a woman. Peter's handsome attendant, Lieutenant Andrey Chernuishev of the Life Guards, was the best-liked member of their set: invariably gay, he could get round Madame Kruse, Catherine's spoil-sport lady-in-waiting, by playing on her weakness for the bottle, thus allowing the rest of the group to dance and play without hindrance. Catherine started again to flirt with Andrey, throwing him warm glances and singling him out for attention. But Peter either did not notice or chose not to show it. In bed he still treated her like a sister.

Catherine suffered from headaches at the time of her periods. On one of these occasions she remained in her bedroom, waiting to be bled. It was May 1746, nine months after the wedding. Suddenly the door of her bedroom opened but instead of the expected surgeon in walked the Empress. She was looking very angry indeed and, as on the occasion when she had lost her temper with Peter, the corners of her eyes twitched.

'You are trying to wreck your marriage,' she said severely to Catherine. 'And you're doing it to please the King of Prussia. I know your tricks and deceitfulness, I know everything. It is your fault if the marriage hasn't been consummated.' The Empress paused for breath. 'If you don't love the Grand Duke, I'm not to blame. I certainly didn't force you into the marriage. The explanation is, of course, that you're in love with another man.'

Catherine was so astonished and so frightened she burst into tears. The Empress continued to lash her and when Catherine, through her sobs, tried to defend herself, 'Be silent,' the Empress cried, 'I'm sure you have no possible answer.' For a solid half-hour she berated Catherine for not producing a child, while the younger woman, her head pounding, listened miserable and helpless.

At last it occurred to Catherine to use the phrase which Madame Kruse had recommended. '*Vinovata, Matushka*,' she managed to stammer out, making the first word singular. The effect was remarkable. The Empress began to calm down and without making any further attacks left the room.

Catherine felt shattered. She had failed to please the adored divinity, who had behaved towards her like an angry Juno. She had done this at the very time Catherine was trying her best to arouse Peter. It was, thought Catherine, totally unjust.

Catherine lay on her sofa sobbing, feeling dreadfully alone. Ever since her arrival two and a half years before she had tried to please Peter and to please the Empress. Plainly she had failed, and having failed she did not want to go on living. Noticing a knife on a nearby table she picked it up and in an agony of despair decided she would stab herself. Probably this incident with the knife was more a symbolic expression of Catherine's wish to be dead than a purposeful attempt at suicide; at any rate while she was cutting open her stays to bare her breast, Catherine's maid entered the room, saw what was happening and grabbed the knife. Catherine came to her senses and swore the maid to secrecy.

It was customary at Court to receive Holy Communion once a year, at Easter, so Catherine was surprised when shortly after this interview she and Peter were instructed by the Empress to receive Communion for the second time that year and, as always, to go to confession first.

Catherine's confessor was the archimandrite who had instructed her, Simon Todorsky. When she stood before him in the chapel he asked her whether she had kissed one of the Chernuishevs. Much surprised, Catherine said, 'No, Father.' 'How is that? The Empress has been told that you gave a kiss to Andrey Chernuishev.' 'It's not true, Father. It's a slander.' Evidently the archimandrite caught the note of sincerity in her voice, for Catherine heard him say to himself, 'What wicked people!' He admonished her to be on her guard and never in future to give grounds for such a suspicion. Then, when she had confessed her sins and expressed sorrow for them, he gave her absolution in the customary manner, placing the two ends of his stole on her head. Afterwards he went to the Empress, apparently to report to her.

The sequel turned out to be anything but amusing. Lieutenant Andrey Chernuishev suddenly disappeared. It was supposed that he had been posted to a distant garrison, but after numerous inquiries Catherine learned that he had been arrested by the secret police and was being held in one of their prisons.

The Empress decided that the best means of getting Peter and Catherine to consummate their marriage was to prevent either of them having special friends, male or female, and to place an exemplary married couple in charge of their household, with orders at all costs to forward the wished-for consummation. The Empress's choice fell on Nicholas and Maria Choglokov, a good-looking pair in their twenties who produced children at the rate of one a year. Maria was the Empress's first cousin, being the daughter of Catherine I's sister and Simon Heinrich, a Lithuanian peasant later ennobled as Count Hendrikov. Nicholas, a chamberlain, occasionally performed minor diplomatic missions.

Catherine was able to feel little esteem for the Exemplary Couple. They had no conversation and were happiest playing faro for money. Nicholas she thought a pompous ass; Maria peevish, uneducated and almost as stupid as her sister who, after the birth of a son, boasted of her midwife's powers of prediction: 'She told me I would have either a boy or a girl.'

Catherine's life before the Choglokovs' arrival had already been subject to strict control. Her first spring in the Winter Palace, when after the long trying winter she had opened her window wide to let in the fragrant air, Madame Kruse had made her close it again because, she said, the Empress had not yet opened hers. Now, however, the strictness became ten times worse. The Choglokovs kept a sharp eye on Catherine's and Peter's activities, whom they spoke to and for how long. They rummaged through their papers, they would not let them out of the palace without special permission and every evening locked them in their bedroom, like cattle to be coupled. At the slightest infringement of rules Maria Choglokova would say, 'I will make a report to the Empress.'

When the bedroom door had been locked for the night, Peter would turn to his toy soldiers. He had a big collection of them, made of wood, lead, starch and wax, and would line them up on a table beside the bed. He nailed narrow strips of wire across the table with strings attached to them, and would pull the strings, causing the strips of wire to make a noise which, he said, was just like the rolling of guns.

Peter invited Catherine to take part in the parades and war games he invented for his toy soldiers, and reluctantly she did so. They lasted until the small hours of the morning, and they were the only games played in the conjugal bed. Gradually Catherine began to see that Peter's interest in his toy soldiers and his lack of interest in her were linked.

All the soldiers wore the blue uniform of Holstein, and their regiments were Holstein regiments. Because, Peter explained, Holstein was the most splendid country in the world. It was his native land, and that of his fathers, the background to a boyhood of exceptional intensity, and he would describe it to Catherine by the hour.

Peter's Holstein was a dukedom sixty miles wide straddling the peninsula between the North and Baltic Seas, Denmark to the north, Hamburg to the south. Peter had been born in the capital, Kiel, a fine-looking town with proud traditions. After his birth his mother Anna had stood beside his cradle at her open bedroom window, watching the celebratory fireworks. When her ladies warned her against the icy February air, Peter the Great's daughter replied with hauteur, 'I am Russian, remember.' Three days later she died of pneumonia.

Peter was reared by his father in the new strict military tradition whose presiding genius was Frederick William of Prussia. Uniforms, belts, shoulder straps, drill, deployment, rank, promotion, duty, punishment, the fatherland – these were the key words. One day nine-year-old Peter stood guard in his blue uniform at the door of the *Tafelsaal* when he was summoned by his father the Duke and promoted to the rank of Lieutenant, with the immediate right to take his place at table with his brother officers. It was, said Peter, the happiest day of his life.

This world of boots snapping to attention, of kettledrums and bugles, excluded what was soft and gentle. Women were partly feared, partly resented. Its effect on King Frederick II and his brother Heinrich, with whom Catherine had danced in Berlin, was to render them incapable of normal married life. The Duke of Holstein treated his son less severely than Frederick William treated his; on the other hand Peter had no mother to turn to for soft words and kisses. So the leather shoulder belt of army life cut deep into his young spirit.

As she came to understand Peter's boyhood, Catherine decided that the best means of weaning him from it was to go along with his war games and to be sympathetic to all his odd activities. The way to his heart would be via Holstein.

So Catherine, who anyway had never cared much for dolls, learned the names of the regiments of toy soldiers and joined with zest in the bedroom battles between them. When Peter took to dressing up his servants in blue uniforms, and giving them military rank, Catherine too called them Corporal, Sergeant or whatever. To please Peter she even sometimes shouldered a musket herself, allowed Peter to drill her and stood guard at his door.

Peter bought a big military whip and would stand in the centre of his room cracking the long lash. One day he caught his cheek with the lash, making it bleed. He was terrified that the Empress would notice the gash, but Catherine came to the rescue, applying a thin layer of zinc ointment to the cut. When they went to chapel Nicholas Choglokov said to Peter, 'Wipe your cheek, there is some ointment on it.' Catherine quickly intervened, saying to Peter jokingly, 'And I your wife forbid you to wipe it.' Peter turned to Choglokov. 'You see how these women treat us. We mayn't wipe our faces without their permission.' The unsuspecting Choglokov was taken in and said, laughing, 'A real woman's caprice.' Afterwards Catherine had the satisfaction of being thanked by Peter.

Another incident occurred one Holy Saturday. 'As I had to keep vigil that night,' Catherine recalled, 'I went to bed about five in the afternoon to sleep until the hour when I had to dress. I had scarcely got into bed when the Grand Duke came rushing in and told me to get up and come quickly to see some oysters he had been sent from Holstein. For him it was a wonderful, a double treat when these oysters arrived. He loved them and they came from Holstein . . . It would have meant disappointing him not to get up, so although I was exhausted by the devotions of Holy Week I went to his room.' There she sat down and started on the oysters, being careful however to eat only a dozen, for Peter would have been displeased if she had eaten more. After that he allowed her to return to bed, while he remained with his oysters.

One winter Peter took it into his head to build a pavilion in the park of Oranienbaum. Exotic or quaint pavilions were all the fashion: thatched cottage, pagoda and so on. Peter wanted a Franciscan friary and at his bidding Catherine drew a sketch of such a building. Then it turned out that he wanted Catherine, himself and their suite to live in the friary when it was built, dressed as friars and nuns, wearing brown habits, cowls and sandals, and fetching water and provisions on donkeys. Though he almost certainly did not realize it, Peter's plan was just another pretext for avoiding sexual relations; nevertheless, all that winter Catherine helped him to work out designs for the celibate establishment.

Knowing that the eye of the Empress was upon her and that her own future happiness was at stake, Catherine kept trying, week after week, in the short hot summers and the long snowbound winters, gently to wean Peter from his military boyhood to an adult attitude to women. One year passed, two years, three years; Catherine reached what seemed to her the incredibly old age of twenty, and still night after night she slept in the same bed with a man who showed much interest in shoulder straps and gorgets but none in her fresh young body, increasingly attractive though it was to other men. She was deeply unhappy and felt a failure. Then, one day in 1749 – they were spending that year in Moscow – she saw something which revealed to her that Peter was just as unhappy as she, and doubled therefore her sense of gloom and failure.

Peter by then had taken to training hunting dogs, which he exercised and kennelled in their apartments, rushing about indoors with them amid much cracking of whips and beaters' cries. 'One day,' said Catherine, 'I heard a dog whine piteously for a long time. I opened the door of my bedroom where I was sitting and I saw that the Grand Duke was holding one of the dogs in the air by its collar, while a young boy of Kalmuik origin who was in his service held its tail; it was a poor little English King Charles, and the Grand Duke was flogging the dog as hard as he could with the handle of a whip. I tried to intercede for the poor animal but this only increased the blows. Unable to stand a spectacle that seemed quite horrible to me, I retired to my room in tears.'

CHAPTER 7

HUMILIATION

Catherine and Peter had been married four and a half years, and at the beginning of Lent 1750 were living in the Winter Palace, still subject to the Exemplary Couple, and to increasingly strict rules, whereby they might not go for even a short drive without obtaining the Empress's permission. It was customary during Lent to take a steam bath before receiving Easter Communion and Catherine, doubtless wishing to escape from her palace-prison for an afternoon, sent Madame Choglokova to ask the Empress's permission to take her bath in the Choglokovs' house.

On Tuesday evening in the second week of Lent Madame Choglokova came to the grand ducal apartments and told Catherine that her Majesty gave the desired permission. She then turned to Peter and said that he would do well to bath also. Peter like everyone else had been living for a week on a few mushrooms and pickled cucumbers and was not in the best of moods. 'I have no intention of taking a bath,' he replied. 'I have never taken one and I never will.' The Lenten bath, he added, was a ridiculous and unimportant ceremony.

'It would please her Majesty if you went to the bath,' pursued Madame Choglokova.

'Not at all,' said Peter. 'And I'm not going.'

'I'm surprised,' said Madame Choglokova, 'that you show so little respect for her Majesty's wishes.'

'Whether I go to the bath or not has nothing to do with the respect I owe her Majesty. I'm astonished that you dare suggest it has. Were you a man I'd teach you a lesson or two.'

This threat caused Madame Choglokova to lose her temper and raise her voice. 'Don't you know that for such talk and disobedience towards her Majesty you could be shut up in the Fortress?' The Fortress of Saints Peter and Paul, on an island in the Neva, was a State prison administered by the secret police.

'Are you saying that on your own responsibility or does it come from her Majesty?'

'I'm just pointing out the consequences your thoughtless behaviour could have. If you wish, her Majesty will repeat what I've just said.' Then she added darkly, 'Remember what happened to Peter the Great's son on account of his disobedience.'

At this allusion to Alexis's death by flogging the Grand Duke moderated his tone. 'I would never have believed that I, the Duke of Holstein and a sovereign prince, would be treated so shamefully. If her Majesty isn't satisfied with me, she has only to let me return to my own country.' He then sank into thought, strode up and down the room, and at last began to cry. At this Madame Choglokova left, with her usual exit-line, 'I will make a report to the Empress.'

Next day she returned and told Peter that, having been informed of his behaviour, the Empress had said, 'Very well then, if he is so disobedient, I will kiss his damned hand no more.'

'That's up to her,' Peter replied. 'But I shan't go to the bath. I can't stand the heat there.'

This incident gave Catherine further insight into her husband's character. The strict Lutheranism of Holstein, in which he had been educated, put a cloak of secrecy and even shame about a man's private parts. Catherine recalled that Peter never undressed or dressed in their bedroom, he always retired to one of his own rooms and shut the door. Bathing in Russia was mixed, and probably Peter did not wish to appear nude in front of Catherine.

But Peter had another motive in refusing the steam bath, a complex one having its roots in the recent history of Holstein. In 1713 Denmark had invaded the duchy of Holstein and seized the important province of Schleswig. Peter's father had gone to St Petersburg and secured a solemn promise from Peter the Great, his future father-in-law, that Russia would force Denmark to restore Schleswig to Holstein. But in the peace negotiations following Russia's long war with Sweden Peter the Great, bowing on this to European opposition, broke his promise and allowed Denmark to retain Schleswig. Young Peter, brought up originally for the Swedish not the Russian throne, had been taught to see Russia as the great betrayer of Holstein. So that interwoven with Peter's love for his native land, and its emblem, a silver nettle-leaf on a red background, was a deep hatred of Russia and its black double-headed, not to say two-faced, eagle. Elizabeth might be his aunt, but more importantly she was a daughter of the Tsar who had left little Holstein in the lurch.

Peter, therefore, in standing up to the Empress was standing up for Holstein, but the significance of the steam bath did not end there.

It was a quasi-religious ablution, a purificatory rite linked to Easter Communion, which was the high point of the Orthodox year. Now Peter, as Catherine learned, had shown a great deal of fight when his aunt ordered him to be instructed in the Orthodox faith. Aged only thirteen, he had contested every single point with Simon Todorsky and would not have yielded at all had not the Empress intervened. In refusing to take a steam bath Peter therefore was expressing his resentment not only against the Empress but against the Russian religion which at her bidding he had been forced to take into his soul.

Now that she possessed this new clue to Peter's character, Catherine was in a better position to understand his behaviour towards her. In these early years she practised her adopted religion with much fervour; heaven knew, she had need of God's help; but she was also copying the Empress she so admired, partly wishing to win her approval. She fasted not only for the first and last weeks of Lent, but for all six weeks. Every evening she said her prayers in a small chapel near her dressing-room. On one of these occasions the Empress's favourite lady-in-waiting, Madame Izmailova, found her in the chapel, spoke to her, looked at her prayer book and said she would be spoiling her eyesight if she read such small type by candlelight. Next day Catherine received with an approving word from the Empress a prayer book printed in large type.

Peter on the other hand scoffed at Orthodox ritual. At Mass he mooned about, declined to make the customary signs of the cross and sometimes stuck his tongue out at the celebrant. Merely to see one of Catherine's maids light a candle in front of an icon filled him with rage. Sometimes during Lent he got his servants to smuggle him slices of meat.

Catherine noticed that Peter resented her fervent practice of the Orthodox religion and scolded her severely for fasting all through Lent. The conclusion was plain. Peter thought that by behaving in this way Catherine was siding with the Empress against him. So, in their bedroom at least, Catherine was now doubly the enemy, both a woman dangerous to a virile soldier and an ally of that darkest of all dark women, perfidious Russia incarnate in the Empress.

Yet the more strictly he was treated by the Empress, the angrier her threats, the more Peter felt the need to confide in someone. 'I realized his position,' said Catherine, 'and was sorry for him, and therefore tried to offer all the consolation that was in my power. Often I would be annoyed by the visits he paid me, lasting several hours, even exhausted by them, because he never sat down and one had to walk up and down the room with him all the time. He walked fast and took long strides, so that it was difficult to follow him and at the same time continue a conversation about very specialized military details, of which he spoke with relish and, it sometimes seemed, interminably.'

Out of the military details, the religious objections and the stories of Holstein Catherine was at last able to detect a theme and draw a conclusion. Peter was waiting for her to align herself with him against the Empress. He had hung on to a Lutheran prayer book and sometimes read it; he wanted her to do the same. He liked talking German, and though it was forbidden by the Empress he wanted Catherine to speak German too. He wanted his wife to enter into his fantasy world, at the centre of which lay Holstein, to wax lyrical over Kiel University, the splendid Holstein cows and the even more splendid Holstein soldiers. He wanted her in short to hate, as he hated, the Empress and Russia; then perhaps, when she was subject to him, the Duke of Holstein, he would accept her physically as his wife.

When she had made her three-point programme, Catherine had given priority to pleasing the Grand Duke, but she had not realized then that this would mean displeasing the Empress and the Russian people. She was extremely anxious to make her marriage a success, she had a hunger now for tenderness and affection. Yet how could she bring herself to do as Peter seemed to require? It would be folly, this pitting of tiny Holstein against Russia, of a Lutheran past against the Orthodox present. It would be dangerous lunacy to be definitely European in a land where Europe was suspect.

So Catherine continued to tread the more difficult path, trying to get Peter to accept the reality of his position in Russia. If the Empress had treated her nephew with more consideration, Catherine might have succeeded. But she kept Peter on an ever-tightening lead, she no longer kissed his hand, and this increased his resentment towards Catherine too. It became gradually evident to Catherine that she and Peter were drifting apart.

In summer Catherine and Peter continued to travel with the Empress, now to review warships, now to kneel before a rare icon. On these occasions Catherine found she needed more sleep than Peter, especially at the time of her periods. She would then go to bed early, be wakened when Peter joined her and be unable to sleep again. During one of their summer journeys, probably when staying in lodgings at the miracle-working shrine of Tikhvin, Catherine, suffering from a headache, decided to sleep in a separate bed; this was possible because the

Exemplary Couple's vigilance relaxed on journeys. Not to hurt Peter's feelings, Catherine explained to him that she found the bed in their lodgings uncomfortably narrow.

When she was feeling well again Catherine suggested to Peter that they should resume their usual sleeping arrangements. To her surprise Peter replied with a written message: 'Please don't bother to come and sleep with me tonight. I've had enough of your pretending the bed is too narrow. Today marks two weeks of separation from you. Your very unfortunate husband – whom you never deign to treat as such – Peter.'

When they returned to St Petersburg, they were again locked every night in their bedroom and slept together, but Peter continued with this new, odious claim that, if they were not fully man and wife, Catherine, not he, was to blame.

At the age of twenty-one Peter began to take an interest in other women. The winter they lived in Moscow he paid attention to a certain Princess Dolgorukova, whose husband had been Grand Chancellor to Tsar Peter II. He called this middle-aged lady 'the beautiful widow' and addressed her with soft looks and words. She, however, treated him like a child. In fact, she had children of her own about the same age as Peter.

When he left Moscow Peter forgot about 'the beautiful widow' and began to pay attention to Catherine Biron, daughter of Ernest Biron, Empress Anna's cruel Minister, then living in exile on the Volga. Catherine Biron had run away from home, where she was unhappy, and had become lady-in-waiting to the Empress. She was small, pretty, with chestnut hair, and clever, but stoop-shouldered almost to the point of being hunchbacked.

Peter liked the Biron girl for three reasons: her deformity made him feel superior; she was not a Russian; and she spoke German with him. He began to send her little presents: wine and her favourite dishes from his table, shoulder straps and Grenadier caps.

One evening in March 1750 after a game of cards Peter and Catherine were supping with their guests in the Choglokovs' apartment, Peter ogling Catherine Biron and flirting with her in German. Catherine happened to have a headache; leaving the table before supper was finished, she went to her bedroom. While undressing she was joined by her chief lady-in-waiting, Madame Vladislavova, an elderly woman who had succeeded Madame Kruse – dismissed for drinking – and whom Catherine called a 'living archive' because she knew so many stories about the leading families.

Madame Vladislavova had watched the supper through a keyhole; she attributed Catherine's indisposition to jealousy, and began to speak against the German cripple, blaming Peter and adding a full measure of sympathy for Catherine. Catherine realized that Madame Vladislavova meant well, but she could not bear being pitied by anyone. She burst into tears, Madame Vladislavova withdrew and Catherine eventually fell asleep.

She was woken by Peter coming into the bedroom. He had drunk quite a lot of wine and although he knew Catherine had a headache began to talk about the Biron girl, her personal charm, her talents and her gift for conversation. Catherine gave a cross reply and pretended to go to sleep again. Peter got into bed and began talking more and more loudly to wake her up. Then, seeing that his wife showed no sign of waking, he turned over and went to sleep, first giving her a couple of hard punches in the side.

Sobbing from the pain of the punches, from her headache and from Peter's humiliating treatment of her at supper, Catherine lay awake beside her heavily sleeping husband. Her instinct told her that Peter was not seriously in love, any more than he had been with the maternal widow, but this was poor consolation. Rather it served to emphasize his incapacity for ever forming an adult sexual relationship.

Catherine felt utterly miserable, and all through that long winter night tears ran down her cheeks. The ice was thawing, spring with its flowers was near, but for her, in the fifth year of a hollow marriage, plainly there would be no spring.

The further Peter drew away from her, the more Catherine felt the need of friends. She liked company and attracted people to her by her gaiety, warmth and informality: 'no one,' she claimed, 'ever spent a quarter of an hour in my company without feeling at ease.' The first friend she had was one of her maids, Maria Zhukova, a sweet cheerful girl, whom Catherine made a fuss of and entrusted with the key to her jewels.

After a brief journey to Krasnoe Selo Catherine returned to the Summer Palace and found that Maria Zhukova had left. When she asked why, she was told that she had gone to visit her sick mother. She never returned.

Catherine next became fond of a Finnish girl, Catherine Voinova, who besides sweeping her room and doing her bed would make her laugh by mimicking Madame Choglokova. Putting a cushion under the front of her skirt, the buxom Finn would waddle through the room, exactly like the Exemplary Wife when, as so often, she happened to be in the family way. This girl too was removed, married off by the Empress's express command. Soon afterwards Catherine's valet and coiffeur Timothy Evreinov, a devoted servant for five years, was deported to Kazan.

Catherine's friends of her own class were viewed by the Empress with just as much suspicion. Because Catherine enjoyed their company, Ivan and Zachary Chernuishev, cousins of the imprisoned Andrey, were posted to their regiment. Prince Basil Repnin was another friend sent back to the army, and Count De Vier, Chamberlain to the grand ducal Court, paid for his popularity with Catherine and Peter by also being dismissed. Catherine reached the point where she hesitated to be specially nice to anyone, for fear it would mean his or her dismissal.

Among the influential, Catherine's one friend was Count Lestocq, physician and adviser to the Empress. He had a curious way of encouraging Catherine to stand up to misfortune. There seems to have been some private joke between them, in allusion to which he called her Charlotte, and whenever she passed him at Court Lestocq would glance up at her with his witty eyes and say, 'Charlotte, hold yourself straight.' But this friend in high places also disappeared: accused of taking bribes from Frederick of Prussia, he was tortured and sent to Siberia.

These sudden dismissals and disappearances, so unlike anything in Europe, shocked Catherine deeply. She wanted to tell her mother about them, for she, knowing the characters in Catherine's drama, would have been able to give much-needed sympathy. But to her astonishment Catherine was told that the Empress did not consider it suitable for a Russian Grand Duchess to write to a foreigner. The College of Foreign Affairs would draft an occasional letter to the Princess of Zerbst; Catherine must not make suggestions about its contents or add even the shortest postscript. All she might do was append her signature.

Catherine therefore found herself virtually cut off from her own home. She could not even receive letters from her mother, and it was by way of a cold diplomatic despatch that she came to hear of a particularly sad piece of family news. Her father Christian August had died of apoplexy at the early age of fifty-seven.

Catherine was deeply saddened. She had had a close relationship with her father and had admired him as a model of chivalry. She spent long hours alone in her room, weeping for her father, saddened still more that she had not been at his bedside and could not stand at his grave.

For a week Catherine was allowed to cry as much as she wished: after that Madame Choglokova came to tell her that there had been enough tears and that the Empress ordered her to stop crying as her father had not been a king and the loss was not so great as all that. Catherine was outraged and gamely retorted: 'It is true that my father was not a king, but he was after all my father; I presume it is no crime to mourn for him.'

The Empress, Catherine knew, was displeased that the marriage she had arranged was turning out badly, but could that alone explain such harsh behaviour? Was she jealous of Catherine's affection for her father? Suspicious of her devotion to a German? Was it a symptom of frustrated motherhood? Or sadism inherited from Peter the Great? As yet Catherine could not tell, indeed she preferred to believe that Madame Choglokova had somehow got the message wrong. Nevertheless she was obliged to emerge from her room and allowed to wear mourning for only six weeks, half the customary period, again on the grounds that her father had not been a king.

Catherine found herself trapped between the Empress for whom she was too European and a husband for whom she was not European enough. Frustrated, isolated from family and friends, blamed – unjustly, she thought – by the majestic lady she sought to please, 'I led a life,' said Catherine, 'which would have driven ten other women mad and twenty others in my place would have died of a broken heart.'

If Catherine's heart did not break, it was because she drew on strong heredity – an Anhalt-Zerbst did not whimper – a strong will and a sound education. Catherine thought often of dear Babet, the lonely refugee who had never complained. 'I concealed my tears,' she said, 'because I had always thought it base to arouse the sympathy of others.'

Though she mastered them at the conscious level, deeper down the tensions spread. Something had to snap, and it turned out to be Catherine's health. Just as her religious dilemma had brought on pleurisy, so this longer running battle entrained a succession of illnesses, only partly attributable to winters when the mercury dropped to minus 20 degrees centigrade.

Catherine's first ailment was headaches at night, causing insomnia. Madame Kruse, sympathetic, would bring her a glass of golden Tokay wine in her bed; this Catherine invariably declined and Madame Kruse invariably quaffed – drinking to Catherine's health, she explained. Dr Boerhave examined Catherine; he found that her cranium, at the top, was still not fully formed, and there was a gap in the middle sensitive to changes in temperature which produced headaches. His prognosis was not exactly encouraging: the headaches, he said, would continue at least another eight years.

So they did. But headaches were only part of the trouble. Catherine caught German measles, she caught measles proper; every winter she had severe, what she called 'twelve handkerchiefs a day' colds. Then she began to spit blood, and was warned that she must take care or she would become tubercular.

During the first winter of her marriage on the eve of an important reception Catherine developed toothache. She confided in an amusing naval officer, Captain Korsakov, who fetched a big iron nail and told her to pierce the gum where it hurt. Catherine did so and the toothache vanished. Probably the toothache had been a subconscious appeal by Catherine's neglected body for attention, and when the attention was given, the pain went.

Toothache became the most frequent expression of Catherine's mental anguish. Captain Korsakov sailed away, taking his wonderful nail with him, and Catherine subsequently had to undergo less gentle treatment. The worst occurred when Catherine had been suffering for five months from a painful wisdom tooth and against the advice of Dr Boerhave, whom she esteemed, insisted on having it extracted. She sat on the floor, Boerhave on one side and Nicholas Choglokov on the other to hold her down, while with one hand the Court surgeon, Gyon, grasped her jaw and with the other tightened his pincers round the tooth. At first he could not draw the tooth, then clumsily he began to twist it, and finally he pulled it out with part of Catherine's jawbone adhering to the root. The pain was almost unendurable: blood gushed from her mouth and for two to three minutes she says tears streamed from her eyes 'as though poured from a teapot'.

The Empress had a habit of appearing whenever Catherine was ill or in pain. She did so now. She had a strong stomach for other people's suffering but on this occasion, said Catherine, 'she could not keep back her tears upon seeing me suffer so terribly'. For weeks after the extraction the mark of Gyon's fingers remained in the shape of five dark bruises on Catherine's very white skin.

CHAPTER 8

MOTHERHOOD BY COMMAND

If the first six years of her marriage were in many ways miserable, Catherine managed to come through them by looking for, and finding, new interests and new friends, and by being able to laugh at the various odd happenings that were part of life in Russia.

There was, for instance, the incident of the house that slid down the hill. The Court had gone to stay in a new house on Alexis Razumovsky's estate when early one morning Catherine and Peter were abruptly awakened by Nicholas Choglokov shouting, 'Get out of the house at once.' The bedroom was rocking, as though an earthquake had struck it. Peter fled; Catherine went to wake Madame Kruse. By the time Madame Kruse had dressed, the floor had begun to heave violently and both women were knocked flat. A Guards sergeant clambered up the remains of the staircase, which had collapsed, took Catherine in his arms and carried her away to safety, then rescued Madame Kruse. It turned out that some unsightly supporting timbers in the hall had been removed against the builders' instructions, causing the house, which stood on a slope, to slide downhill and partly disintegrate. The Empress was furious, Alexis Razumovsky fell into a despair of shame and threatened to shoot himself. Catherine, though frightened at the time and badly bruised, in retrospect found the whole event hilarious.

Even more so was the discomfiture of the Choglokovs. Week in, week out the Exemplary Couple were held up to Catherine and Peter as paragons. Forever billing and cooing, they had now produced six bonny infants, one for each year of their idyllic marriage. So beautiful, everyone gurgled, including the Empress, and there would be other infants presently. Indeed there would, but not quite in the way the Empress expected. Lo and behold, Nicholas Choglokov fell in love with one of Catherine's maids-in-waiting, Maria Kosheleva, a stupid clumsy girl endowed with a beautiful white skin, and made her pregnant. When she found out the Empress was furious and announced her intention of sacking Choglokov, a course from which she was dissuaded only when he and his wife fell on their knees at her feet and begged her to forgive him. After that, much to her relief, Catherine heard considerably less about the fruitful married life of the Exemplary Couple.

In 1751 a new gentleman-in-waiting to Peter was appointed. Leo Naruishkin came of one of Russia's best families – Peter the Great's mother had been a Naruishkin. Leo was a big, heavy-jowled bachelor four years younger than Catherine, ungainly, dishevelled, and usually with little cuts on his face, because he liked to shave himself and did it badly. Though very fat, he loved dancing; though very rich, he never had a penny in his pocket. Above all, he was wonderfully funny, a born clown. He possessed a superficial knowledge of every subject and was capable, said Catherine, of giving a dissertation on art or science, would use technical terms and talk for a quarter of an hour; at the end neither he nor anyone else could make head or tail of the flow of words streaming from his mouth, and all would end in a general burst of laughter. He went in for paradoxes, such as 'Comedies shouldn't be well-written, otherwise they're boring', but it was less what he said than the way that he said it, and his whole manner of being – the witty, deceptively helpless courtier – that endeared Leo Naruishkin to Catherine and made him a godsent distraction.

Catherine was very fond of clothes and took pleasure in dressing well. Her riding habit was of best silk camlet and as camlet shrinks in the rain and fades in the sun she was constantly having a new one made. At a grand ball she would change her dress three times. Once she appeared in a plain white dress with no ornaments other than a rose in her hair and a second rose in her corsage. The Empress, a connoisseur of clothes, admired it. 'Good God,' she said, 'what simplicity! Not even a mouche.' Catherine jokingly answered that she did not wish to add even that much weight to her attire, whereupon the Empress produced a box of mouches, chose a small one and placed it on Catherine's face: a mark of approval that quickly went round the ballroom.

Some time later, on the feast of St Alexander, Catherine thought she would try white again. She chose a satin flounced dress, with a zigzag border in gold, in the latest French fashion. She curled her hair and wore emeralds. But on this occasion the Empress eyed her dress crossly and paid her no compliment. On the contrary, after the ball, she sent Madame Choglokova to tell Catherine that she thought the dress quite unsuitable, giving as a reason that it resembled the dress of the Knights of St Alexander. But Catherine saw that this was just a pretended reason, for the Knights wore a flame-coloured jacket over their white uniform.

Catherine wondered why the Empress chopped and changed towards her. It began to look as though she was driven from time to time by some secret fear relating to Catherine, but what that fear might be for the moment remained hidden.

Foiled in her attempt to shine sartorially, Catherine decided to direct her aesthetic interests to furniture. The same beds, chairs, tables and looking-glasses were carted round with the Court on its migration from palace to palace and city to city. Often what suited one room looked awkward in another, and the furniture inevitably got knocked about, chipped and dilapidated. Little by little, out of her annual allowance of 30,000 roubles, Catherine bought tables, chairs, chests of drawers and other items, until she had prettily furnished her rooms in the Winter and Summer Palaces and at Oranienbaum. Furniture that was hers and familiar gave her a little reassurance.

Still strong in Catherine was the vein of secret defiance that had impelled her as a child to run up and down stairs at Dornburg after lights out. It so happened that she was very fond of writing and receiving letters, and it annoyed her intensely not to be able to correspond with her mother. After much searching she found a reliable person willing to pass letters, an Italian named d'Ologlio. Catherine wrote her letter very small, rolled it up and hid it in her glove. Then during a palace concert she would cross the hall and stand behind d'Ologlio's chair – he played 'cello in the orchestra. Pretending to take his handkerchief from his coat, d'Ologlio opened his pocket wide, while Catherine slipped the note from her glove into the pocket and walked to the other side of the room, nobody being any the wiser. Soon she had the satisfaction of being in regular correspondence with her mother.

Andrey Chernuishev was very much on Catherine's mind, for by flirting with the handsome officer she felt partly responsible for his imprisonment by the secret police. She tried in vain for two years to discover his whereabouts; then learned from her valet that he had been transferred from the Fortress of Saints Peter and Paul to a little wooden house in St Petersburg belonging to the Empress. Catherine decided she would try to get in touch with him, observing as much secrecy as when writing to Zerbst.

At this time Catherine still had her Finnish maid, Catherine Voinova, and one evening she spoke to her at the only moment she could be sure of not being overheard: when using her night-commode. She asked the maid to get in touch with her fiancé, also a Court servant, and to arrange a secret meeting between them and Andrey Chernuishev in the fiancé's house.

On his name-day Andrey drank his guards under the table and slipped away to the rendezvous, where he handed the Finnish maid a letter. When this letter was slipped to Catherine on her night-commode, she put it in her garter; then, when her ladies undressed her, slipped it into her nightdress sleeve. She read Andrey's letter that night in bed, answered it and afterwards burned it. She wrote a number of letters to her imprisoned friend and, since he was short of money, even smuggled him several hundred roubles. Such triumphs as these, small though they were, helped Catherine to keep her spirits up.

Another of Catherine's distractions that soon became a major interest was books. One of the first she enjoyed was the *Letters* of Madame de Sévigné, who had the gift of saying wise things lightly and who was to influence Catherine's own letter-writing. Then she read *Cause of the Romans' Greatness and Decadence*, in which Montesquieu attributes the greatness to a division of political power, just laws and a citizen army, the decadence to monarchy and to mercenaries. This was a new point of view for Catherine and she stored it away for possible future use. Later she was to go on to the same author's *Spirit of the Laws*, and find further arguments in favour of a division of power within the State. She read Barre's *History of Germany* in nine quarto volumes, and Péréfixe's *Henry IV*, whose early life was quite as oppressed as her own but who went on to become France's most popular king. She read the works of Plato, meeting in his *Republic* the philosopher king, who alternates between contemplating the Ideal and putting it into practice in a rigid class society of which Montesquieu would have disapproved.

She read above all Voltaire, loving him for his sound common sense, his humour and his attacks on prejudice, particularly religious intolerance. In contrast to Montesquieu Voltaire thought sensible monarchy the best kind of government. Catherine read every work by the sage of Ferney that she could lay hands on, virtually did an extra-mural university course in Voltaire's ideas: 'his works formed my mind and spirit,' she was later to say. Catherine learned from Voltaire to apply to everything, even to sacred cows, the criterion of usefulness, and the need to respect other people's consciences.

Catherine chanced also on a few novels. The one that impressed her most, doubtless because of its hero, was *Tiran le Blanc*, Caylus's French version of a Spanish, or more probably Portuguese, romance. Tiran is the son of Blanche, Duchess of Brittany, hence his sobriquet. A knight as brave as he is handsome, he sails to England, where he makes a name in tournaments and battles, is awarded the Garter, and pleases the King's daughter, described in a striking phrase: 'her skin was so white and finely textured that when she drank red wine you could see it pass down her throat.' Catherine remembered the description – her own skin being so white.

From England Tiran sails to the East, saves Rhodes from the Turk, in Alexandria frees four hundred slaves, and continues to Byzantium. Here he falls in love with the Emperor's daughter; chivalrous rather than domineering, he kneels before this honey-complexioned girl and swears 'she will always be mistress of his fate, and he will always regard her as his Sovereign.' The Emperor gives his consent to their marriage, but – and this was unusual in an eighteenth-century French novel – so deeply are they in love that before the wedding day arrives they sleep together. Soon afterwards Tiran falls in battle. The Emperor's daughter cannot live without him, she dons her wedding dress, clasps a crucifix to her breast and falls lifeless on Tiran's body. 'A great light filled the palace room, it was the angels carrying her soul and Tiran's to Paradise.'

This novel and others like it were not mere distractions for Catherine. She began to think in terms of a tender, chivalrous hero for whom love is the mainspring of action. Was there any Tiran le Blanc on her horizon? As it happened, there was.

The summer of 1749 Peter and Catherine spent at Rayovo, Choglokov's estate half-way between Moscow and the Troitsa-Sergievskaya Monastery. A dreary place, it stood on marshy ground surrounded by thick woods, and looked on to an ornamental pond full of muddy water, but Choglokov believed that everything belonging to him – wife, children, hunting dogs – were the world's best, and he considered Rayovo a garden of Eden. Catherine spent her days on horseback, either galloping alone or hunting hares.

One day Cyril Razumovsky rode over. The much younger brother of Alexis, the Empress's favourite, Cyril had been given the advantage of a university education in Königsberg and Strasbourg, so that whereas Alexis remained limited intellectually, Cyril was President of the Academy of Sciences, could recite long sections of the *Aeneid* and beat anyone at chess. He was four years older than Catherine, dark and very good-looking. Wealthy, thanks to his brother, he kept open house for rich and poor alike. He was married quite happily and much run after by society girls.

Catherine liked Cyril. She enjoyed his conversation, which was more intelligent than the usual courtier's, and found him good fun. He evidently liked her too, because he used to ride over regularly from his estate twenty miles away to spend the day with her and Peter, then return home at dusk. Nicholas Choglokov thought he came to enjoy the beauties of Rayovo, while Maria, seeing him joking and laughing, did not suspect Cyril's true feelings. Riding and hunting with him much of the summer, Catherine became very fond of Cyril Razumovsky, and when she returned to St Petersburg she began to exchange friendly notes with him.

Cyril's attentions to Catherine evidently displeased the Empress. She did not say so, for she and Catherine now rarely spoke in private, but Catherine concluded as much from what she did. Although he was not a soldier or even a natural leader, the Empress appointed Catherine's admirer Hetman of the Ukraine, a post equivalent to military governor; Cyril went to live in Cossack country and, for the moment, vanished from Catherine's horizon.

Back in St Petersburg, Catherine met Count Zachary Chernuishev again. She remembered this dashing Guards officer, a cousin of Andrey Chernuishev, as Groom of her Bedchamber during her betrothal and early days of her marriage. But five years ago his mother had said to the Empress, 'He's constantly watching the Grand Duchess, and when I see that I tremble with fear at the follies he might commit.' So Zachary had been sent on a diplomatic mission to Bavaria, then to his regiment, from which he had now been granted several months' leave.

Zachary said to Catherine, 'You've grown beautiful.' Catherine, who had never been paid such a compliment before, was young enough to believe him. They met at dances, where Zachary continued the compliments. Then he sent Catherine a motto enclosed in a three-dimensional emblem such as was then the fashion; the verses expressed tender esteem. Catherine chose a friendly but non-committal motto in reply and sent it to Zachary in an emblem like an orange. Zachary then wrote her a note, and again Catherine replied.

At the first masked ball of the season Zachary partnered Catherine. Handsome, well educated, a good talker, and an outstanding young colonel, he had many of the attributes of a Tiran le Blanc, though inclined to be pleased with himself. He whispered to Catherine that he had a thousand things to tell her that could not be entrusted to paper. Couldn't she find a suitable occasion of allowing him to come for a few minutes to her apartment? Catherine replied that that was quite impossible. No one had access to her apartment, nor was she free to leave it at will. Zachary proposed to disguise himself as a servant, and again Catherine rebuffed him.

But Zachary proved importunate, and Catherine was becoming attracted to him. Eventually she softened, and twenty-one little notes which she wrote to Zachary and which he carefully preserved chart their relationship. 'If you are not too tired,' Catherine wrote in an early note, 'and can leave the Grand Duke's apartment between eleven and midnight, take a coat from your carriage and come to my apartment by the little staircase, I shall see that the door is open.' In another: 'I thought that if you were to pass my windows between five and six, perhaps you could come in and spend the evening in my apartment, though my maid-in-waiting will probably be there too.'

In the course of such stolen meetings Zachary fell in love with Catherine, and she with him. She wrote that she loved him as no other woman had loved him, that she could not imagine Paradise without him. 'I am very glad you left your snuff-box in my room, for it gives me an occasion to write this note and say that I love you very dearly, that I wish only for your happiness, that I shall certainly lend myself to it, but I need a little time to preserve appearances at least, and to make it easier for you to come here again. Trust me, I shall do what is useful to us and necessary. You show me such passion that I should truly be very ungrateful if I didn't give you proof that I respond. Only don't torment me, I beg you. I shall make more headway if you leave me to myself than if you straight off try to browbeat me, for my head is made of iron and very resistant. You might succeed against other wills but not against mine. Yet that will, left to itself, becomes wax when it is a question of pleasing someone I love. Now tell me, am I not in love with you? Can you doubt it?'

Whereas her friendship with Cyril had unfolded in the open air, to the scent of leaves and saddle-leather, Catherine's loving glances and whispered words to Zachary took place in a wintry city, sometimes in crowded ballrooms, sometimes at the opera. In keeping up appearances Catherine sometimes caused Zachary to feel jealous and to sulk, but on the whole things ran smoothly between them. They were watched, however, and meetings proved hard to come by. Catherine seems not to have reached the stage where her will became 'wax'.

When Zachary had to be absent a week, Catherine wrote: 'The first day was still as though I was waiting for you, because you have so accustomed me to seeing you. The second day I was in a reverie and remained alone; the third I was bored to death; the fourth I lost my appetite and sleep, everything became unbearable, I didn't care what dress I put on. The fifth day tears flowed, and relieved me a little, for all the earlier days my heart had been heavy. They say I've grown thin and am in a black mood. Shall I call things by their right name? Well then, I love you.'

But time was running out. Their love was a winter love, fated to end immediately after Carnival, when Zachary had to rejoin his regiment, with no prospect of another such long leave. Carnival came. The young Grand Duchess and the colonel said goodbye, and parted with all the sorrow parting lovers feel. Catherine had no means of corresponding secretly with Zachary, and so the affair stopped there. Nine years were to elapse before Catherine saw Zachary again. He would then try to resume their sentimental relationship, only to find that Catherine had by then given her heart to someone else.

A very different possible candidate for the role of Tiran le Blanc entered Catherine's life about the same time as Zachary. Serge Saltuikov belonged to one of Russia's most ancient and noble families, allied to the Romanovs through the mother of the Empress Anna, who was a Saltuikov, but of a different branch from Serge's. Serge had *fin de race* good looks – a long face, languid dark eyes, small mouth with fleshy lips – and was a born courtier, gay with a winning manner and a feel for the ins and outs of palace life. He occupied the post of gentleman-in-waiting to the Grand Duke. He was twenty-six and had been married for two years to Matryona Balk, a frivolous young lady whose joy in life was teaching Catherine's pet poodle to walk on its hind legs, curling its coat and knitting it sweaters.

Catherine employed Serge to carry notes to Cyril, and when Cyril went to the Ukraine and Zachary rejoined his regiment, Serge aspired to take their place in Catherine's affections. He discovered in the heavy-minded and unimaginative Nicholas Choglokov a secret passion for writing lyric poetry. Serge asked to see some of the poetry, praised it and encouraged the older man to write more. In the evening he would invite the would-be poet to write new verses, saying his boon companion, Leo Naruishkin, would set them to music, whereupon Nicholas Choglokov would retire with pen and paper to a corner near the stove, leaving Serge free to flirt with Catherine.

At first Catherine welcomed Serge's attentions. She was pleased to find another admirer, and listened with surprise, then with a satisfaction she was careful to hide, to well-turned compliments her husband would never dream of paying her. It soon became apparent that Serge was smitten. 'What about your wife?' asked Catherine, reminding Serge of how he had seen her one afternoon on a swing, fallen passionately in love and proposed next day. Serge answered with a courtier's platitude: 'All is not gold that glitters, and I'm paying a high price for a moment of folly.' His feelings for Catherine, he assured her, were much deeper and more solid.

One summer's day Peter, Catherine and their suite were invited by Nicholas Choglokov to a hunt on an island in the Baltic. They crossed by boat, their horses having been sent ahead. 'As soon as I arrived,' Catherine was later to recall, 'I mounted a horse and went to join the hounds. Serge Saltuikov only waited for the moment when the others were pursuing the hares to come up to me and start upon his favourite subject; I listened to him more patiently than usual. He drew me a picture of the plan he had evolved in order, as he said, to envelop with great mystery the happiness two people might experience in circumstances such as ours. I remained silent. He profited by my silence to persuade me that he loved me passionately and begged me to permit him to believe and hope that I was at least not wholly indifferent to him. I told him that he could hope what he pleased as I could not prevent his thoughts. Then he started comparing himself with other men at Court and made me admit that he was preferable to them; from this he concluded that he was preferred. I laughed, but had to admit that he was agreeable to me.

'After about an hour and a half I told him to go because our conversation might give rise to suspicion. He told me he would not go unless I said I tolerated him. I replied: "Yes, yes, but go away!" He said: "I will remember that," put spurs to his horse, and while I was shouting: "No, no!" he kept repeating: "Yes, yes!" '

After the hunt a storm blew up, sending waves so high they reached the steps of the hunting lodge. The storm and flooding delayed their departure until two in the morning and allowed Serge to linger with Catherine. 'You see,' he whispered, 'Providence is on my side.' But two days later he told Catherine that Peter had complained to his valet that they talked too often together. Catherine advised Serge to be more circumspect, but they continued to see a lot of each other, Serge declaring his love, while Catherine, though doubtful of his character, could not help listening to him because she found him handsome as the dawn.

Catherine's relations with the Empress meanwhile continued to puzzle her. Sometimes the Empress was kind: when she got sunburned at Rayovo the Empress had given her an excellent lotion of lemon, white of egg and French brandy. But another time, on a shooting trip when they were all camping in tents and Catherine appeared in an expensive jacket, the Empress became very angry and said that at Catherine's age she had dressed plainly in a black grisette skirt and a white taffeta jacket. *She* hadn't overspent her allowance, and why? Because she knew that if she died in debt her soul would go to Hell. Catherine was saved from further scolding by the Court jester who, announcing that he had caught a strange animal, held out his hat in which lay a baby hedgehog. As it raised its head the Empress thought it was a mouse, an animal of which she was very much afraid, and with a piercing scream ran to her tent.

The summer when Catherine and Serge were seeing so much of each other, the Empress gave a party at Peterhof. Catherine rode over wearing riding breeches and a smart blue and grey jacket with black velvet collar. When the Empress had last seen Serge Saltuikov and Leo Naruishkin they had been wearing her livery – silver and black – but now they, and everyone from Oranienbaum including Peter, were wearing blue and grey. This had been Catherine's idea, because it allowed her and Serge to meet without attracting notice.

This time the Empress did not scold Catherine directly, but she did give Madame Choglokova a furious dressing-down. In a stormy interview that lasted most of the afternoon she made much of the fact that Catherine's riding breeches were wholly unsuitable and furthermore, when she herself rode in breeches, she always changed into a skirt immediately afterwards.

By now Catherine was beginning to understand the Empress better. She knew she was terrified of the dark, went to bed very late – always in a different room – and lay awake for hours with her women to keep her company and soothe her by stroking her beautiful legs and small feet. This fear of the dark reflected a fear of twelve-year-old Tsar Ivan, locked in Schlüsselburg, where he was known as Prisoner Number One, but still in the eyes of many the rightful occupant of the throne. One day a strange man with a knife had been found concealed in the imperial palace; on another occasion an army officer had been caught plotting to dethrone Elizabeth. With each new alarm the Empress felt more insecure, and became more impatient to secure the succession. Frustrated motherhood added to her frenzy. At one moment she felt she needed Catherine, at other moments she was jealous of her, suspicious of her, furious with her for not providing Peter with an heir. And because she saw the world in terms of clothes, the Empress often vented her feelings against Catherine's dress. Underlying her anger about the riding breeches was the belief, held by many doctors, that riding a horse made it more difficult for a lady to become pregnant.

Madame Choglokova appeared extremely shaken by her stormy interview with the Empress. Soon afterwards, in an unusually serious mood, she took Catherine aside. 'I must really talk to you frankly,' she said. She started in her usual way with a long dissertation on her affection for her husband, on her wisdom, on what had or had not to be done to secure love and facilitate conjugal relations, then she suddenly declared, 'There are certain situations of major importance that form exceptions to the rule.'

While Catherine wondered what she could mean, Madame Choglokova continued, 'You will soon see how much I love my country and how frank I can be. I have no doubt of one thing: your heart is set on a certain man, either Serge Saltuikov or Leo Naruishkin, and I rather think it's Leo.'

'No, no; not at all,' exclaimed Catherine.

'Well, if it's not Leo, it can only be Serge.' Catherine said nothing; then Madame Choglokova added significantly, 'You will see that I shall not be the one to create any obstacles for you.'

At first Catherine made a show of not understanding, but Madame Choglokova continually reverted to the subject, until there could be no doubting what was meant. Catherine believed that so unorthodox a proposal had not originated with the Exemplary Wife, and that probably it came from the Empress, with whose secret fear it would well accord.

Catherine at once found herself facing a dilemma. She was very much attracted to Serge, he evidently loved her, and she longed for the kisses and caresses so long denied her. On the other hand, if she gave herself to Serge, and even more if she bore his child, she would be wronging Peter. He, it could be argued, was wronging her. But was he? Could he be blamed for being an orphan or for his damaging education? Should she not continue a little longer to try to win his love?

But when she turned to Peter as he now was Catherine found nothing to suggest that he would ever improve; rather the contrary. A Danish envoy had recently arrived to ask Peter to cede his beloved Holstein to Denmark in exchange for the nearby territory of Oldenburg, and the Empress was putting pressure on him to yield. This made Peter even more resentful of the Empress and the wife she had chosen for him, so that his behaviour was becoming very odd indeed. Catherine entered his room one day to find a huge rat hanging from a small gibbet, with all the paraphernalia of torture. When she asked the meaning of it, Peter replied that the rat had been convicted of a crime and deserved the severest punishment according to military law. What was the rat's crime? It had climbed over the walls of a cardboard fortress and eaten two sentries, made of starch, one on each of the bastions. Peter had put his setter to catch the rat, which he had then court-martialled and hanged, and it would be exposed to the public as a warning for three days.

All things considered, Catherine found the personal ties binding her to Peter very loose indeed. Sexual ties there were none. As for the ties imposed by society, these too were loose, for Russians treated extra-marital affairs with indulgence, partly because divorce was difficult to obtain, partly because the Church itself treated them leniently. Indeed the pious Empress in her youthful days had had more than one lover.

What might well have checked Catherine were the moral imperatives of Lutheranism. In Zerbst a wife did not lightly set aside her marriage vows. But in becoming Orthodox Catherine had to a large extent put those girlhood imperatives behind her. So now the question really narrowed to this: was it to her own advantage to do as Madame Choglokova had suggested, indeed kept on suggesting? The proposal itself might of course be a trap – Madame Choglokova, feeling the pressure on her from above, trying to take an easy way out. But if it was not a trap, and she were to bear a child reputedly Peter's, Catherine would be pleasing the Empress and pleasing the Russian people. Unable to fulfil the first point in her original programme, she would at least be fulfilling points two and three.

Also to be considered was what might happen to her if she declined to co-operate. The Empress's tone was hardening daily. At a dinner party she had noticed Peter paying a lot of attention to a lady named Martha Shafirova, whereupon the Empress remarked that Martha had a neck like a crane's. 'That sort of neck,' she added darkly, 'is convenient for hanging.'

So Catherine made her choice. She would yield to Serge if he wished it. As it happened, he left Oranienbaum for part of the summer because his mother died, but he returned more dashing, more charming, more pressing than ever. In his blue and grey jacket, he seemed to Catherine as handsome as Tiran le Blanc, and hadn't the Emperor's daughter yielded to Tiran without marriage or any other formal tie, simply from love? That autumn, when the birch leaves were turning gold, aged twenty-three and after seven years of white marriage, Catherine gave herself to Serge Saltuikov.

In the weeks that followed Catherine was undoubtedly very happy. At last she knew fulfilment as a woman and at last was able to make a man happy. Serge might come of a family that had passed its peak but Catherine found him an attentive, high-spirited lover. She realized, however, that she had begun to play a dangerous game and there must surely have been times that autumn when she feared to meet the Empress's eye.

While these important events were taking place in Catherine's life, Nicholas Choglokov had begun to take a more active role in the grand ducal household. About the same time as the Empress had given Maria Choglokova a severe talking-to, she had informed Nicholas that she was gravely displeased by his failure to turn Peter into a satisfactory husband. Since his unfortunate love affair with Catherine's maid-in-waiting Nicholas Choglokov was most anxious to redeem himself before the Empress and began to consider rather more drastic measures than those hitherto taken. He did not tell his wife about them, partly because relations between them were cooler than before, partly because he wished to astonish everyone by suddenly producing an ace from the pack.

In confidential conversation with the Court doctors Nicholas Choglokov arrived at the conclusion that Peter's fear of women could be overcome only if, in the right circumstances and at the right time, Peter could be, so to speak, 'seduced' by a young woman who was sexually experienced and also his social inferior. After much searching such a woman was discovered, the young widow of a Stuttgart painter, L. F. Grooth, who had been employed at the imperial Court.

The unknown quantity was Peter himself. For almost two years he had been particularly bearish, as he held out against the Empress and her Chancellor, both trying to make him cede his beloved Holstein to the arch-enemy Denmark, predator of Schleswig. With the moral support of Catherine, who considered her husband had every right to hold on to his ancestral domains, Peter persevered bravely in his refusal and in autumn 1752, to everyone's surprise, including probably his own, he won a victory. The Empress dropped her pressure and the Danish envoy returned home empty-handed.

Peter's success gave him the self-confidence he had formerly lacked. He no longer felt himself to be a pawn in his aunt's hands. When this second 'beautiful widow' showed herself attentive and admiring, in a warm atmosphere of music, good humour and wine, Peter felt able to respond. He overcame his fear, took Madame Grooth to bed and proved himself a man. Once the initiation was over, Madame Grooth was withdrawn behind the scenes by an exultant Choglokov.

The Empress and her Court spent the following year, 1753, in Moscow. Medieval and Asiatic, its streets laid or lined with wood, a city Catherine sensed was full of dark passions, Moscow could always be relied on to produce strange scenes, and that year at Court an almost fantastic situation came to pass. Much assured, much more interested in women, Peter still did not feel himself ready for so considerable a person as Catherine, and he divided his time between making passes at her ladies-in-waiting and giving violin recitals. Catherine continued her love affair with Serge in obedience to the mysterious message which might or might not emanate from the unapproachable sleepless Empress who, every Tuesday, indulging a taste for man's clothes, would appear at the Court ball now as a Cossack, now as a Guards officer. In the evenings when the Grand Duke and Catherine stayed in, Nicholas Choglokov was gulled by Serge into writing poetry, which Leo Naruishkin set to music, while in the wings Madame Choglokova, who everyone understood was trying to bring Peter and Catherine together, was in fact exercising all the experience of a wife who had just produced her eighth child to get Serge into bed with Catherine the most number of times.

To add to the impression of phantasmagoria several inmates of the palace really did go mad, among them a monk from the Voskressensky Monastery who, perhaps influenced by the sect of Castrators, slashed his private parts with a razor, and a major of the Semeonovsky regiment who professed a firm belief that Tahmasp Kuli Khan, the dethroned Shah of Persia, was God. The Empress had them placed near Dr Boerhave's apartments, so that a small Court lunatic asylum gradually built up. There were doubtless moments when Catherine felt that she too would soon be there.

As if this were not enough, on the afternoon of 1st November 1753, when Catherine was sitting quietly in Madame Choglokova's rooms in the palace, Peter, Serge and Leo suddenly burst in with shouts of 'Fire! Fire!'

Catherine rushed out to the first-floor landing and saw that flames from the fire, which had started in one of the hall stoves, were already licking at the staircase. Her first thought was of her books, hard to come by in Russia, and she hurried to her room to save in particular Bayle's *Dictionary*, which she was half-way through. Soldiers and volunteers arrived to help her and to drag out the furniture. The palace fire-fighting equipment, stored in the hall, had become inaccessible and despite the recognized alarm – whirling of wooden rattles – equipment from elsewhere was slow to arrive. The occupants of the palace, including the lunatics, were helped to safety, and the wooden building left to burn. The Empress was furious at the loss of her wardrobe of 4000 dresses. As for Catherine, the image that stayed with her, watching the glare and smoke from a muddy street, was a prodigious number of rats and mice pit-patting down the palace entrance stairs in a file, and despite the flames showing very little hurry.

After the fire Catherine moved to a private house and Serge to unobtrusive lodgings. This facilitated their meetings. Before the next important Court ball Catherine pretended to be indisposed; what ensued she later revealed to a friend, referring to herself in the third person: 'As soon as she heard that everybody was gone to Court and the ball was begun, she got up, dressed herself, and went in a hired coach to Saltuikov's lodging. The lover thanked her three times for the honour she had done him, and she got safely back to her own apartments before the ball was finished.'

In the New Year Catherine found herself pregnant. The previous summer she had had a miscarriage at two months, but she was feeling stronger now than then, and took special care with her health. The Empress, informed by Madame Choglokova, showed intense relief and satisfaction. Without asking Madame Choglokova about how or who, she ordered Catherine to travel to St Petersburg in a carriage drawn at a walk, appointed a midwife to be with her day and night, and in the summer invited Catherine to her seaside estate at Peterhof, where Rastrelli had improved Peter the Great's barracks-like building with a long baroque façade. Peterhof had beautiful gardens, fountains and a cascade with chimes; here Catherine spent a quiet summer, not once mounting a horse, and going for long walks, enjoying the Empress's solicitude for her, hoping with all her heart that she would bear a healthy child, and that it would be a boy.

Peter knew of course that he was not the father of the child his wife was carrying. Probably by this time he had a shrewd suspicion who the father was. Neither of the courses open to him appeared very enticing. He could kick up a fuss, but only by revealing his prolonged incapacity as a husband. Or he could accept the situation, allow everyone at Court to believe that the child was his, and reap the rewards in terms of greater freedom and consideration by the Empress. This is the course he chose.

In August Catherine returned to her rooms in the Summer Palace, looking north and east over the river, and made attractive with her own tastefully chosen furniture. On 19th September 1754, when Catherine felt her first pains begin, the Empress had her moved into a room furnished with red damask adjoining her own apartments. Wearing a blue satin cloak, for the room was cold, she spent that night at Catherine's bedside. In the morning Catherine was lifted from the four-poster to a plain hard labour-bed. Peter came in, the midwife bustled and issued crisp orders, doctors waited in an ante-room. At noon, after a difficult labour, Catherine gave birth to a healthy child, a boy.

Catherine found the baby beautiful, and experienced all the pent-up joy of maternal fulfilment. The child was swaddled and immediately christened Paul, a name chosen by the Empress to emphasize its supposed descent from Peter the Great, who had called the eldest son of his second marriage Paul. As she listened to the church bells ring, as people sang and danced in the streets, and later as she saw celebration fireworks bang and flash and dazzle outside her window, Catherine knew that at last she had succeeded in pleasing the Empress and in pleasing the Russian people.

CHAPTER 9

INDISCRETIONS

After the birth of Catherine's son, the Empress had the midwife carry the child to her own apartments and Catherine found herself left alone, still on the hard bare labour-bed, in an unfamiliar room. Behind her were two windows and to the left of the bed two doors, none of which closed properly. Catherine, susceptible to draughts, felt herself catching a chill and asked to be moved, but no one dared take that responsibility without permission from the Empress, who was fully occupied with the baby. It was late afternoon before Catherine could be moved to her own bedroom, with its comfortingly familiar furniture, but by then she had caught a rheumatic chill down her left hip.

The pain in her hip prevented her sleeping and made her days miserable as well as lonely. The Empress inquired about her blue satin cloak, which she had mislaid, but not about Catherine's health. Peter spent only one evening with her; Serge, as Peter's gentleman-in-waiting, was able to pay her frequent but necessarily hurried visits. As for little Paul, he was still with the Empress.

On the sixth day after the birth, when Paul was baptized by immersion, the Empress gave Catherine a case of jewellery, but when she opened it Catherine was hurt to find that the two rings, the ear-rings and necklace contained not one stone worth more than a hundred roubles. The Empress also brought her the customary present of 100,000 roubles. This meant much to Catherine, for she would be able to pay off the 70,000 roubles of debts her mother had left behind and which Catherine had shouldered. But Peter said he ought to receive 100,000 roubles too. He made such a fuss that the Court treasurer came to see Catherine, explained that the treasury was empty and asked her to lend the Empress the money she had just received – temporarily of course. Catherine did so and the 100,000 roubles were paid to Peter.

Catherine was worried that she still saw nothing of her son. She heard that the Empress, childless herself, positively doted on the boy, fussing over him from morning to night. Fearful lest he should catch cold, she kept him in a very warm room, wrapped in flannel, in a crib lined with black fox-fur, under wadded satin and a red velvet coverlet lined with black fox-fur. The baby, Catherine heard, was almost continually bathed in perspiration.

When she was well enough to get up Catherine began to inquire discreetly when she would be allowed to look after little Paul. At first the answers that trickled back from the Empress's apartments were vague and stalling. Catherine persisted and at last learned the full truth. Now that she had produced a child, her job was over. This boy born to be Emperor belonged to Russia and would be brought up by the Empress. Catherine might expect to see him a couple of times a year, no more.

Simultaneously with this shock, Catherine received a second. Serge's visits were making all the difference to her during these dark days of convalescence; he in some measure compensated for little Paul. Then an order issued from the Empress: Serge Saltuikov is given the honour of taking the glad news of the birth of the Grand Duke's heir to the King of Sweden and will depart forthwith for Stockholm.

Catherine felt she was being very unfairly treated. All that winter she exerted herself to get Serge recalled for Carnival, and through influential friends finally succeeded. On the eve of Shrove Tuesday Catherine waited in her room, where Serge had promised to meet her. Midnight struck and still there was no sign of her lover. Catherine waited till three in the morning before going sadly to bed, alone.

Serge appeared at Court next day. He explained that he had been invited to a Freemasons' meeting and had he declined would have brought suspicion on them both. Catherine allowed herself to be convinced. She picked up the threads of their affair, but she soon realized that Serge was very far from being the hero she had hoped. Wearing a silver-embroidered jacket he had once described himself as 'a fly drowned in milk': Catherine saw now that the passive metaphor correctly reflected the man. Serge had flirted in Stockholm, and on his return preferred the light intrigues of Court society to his now dangerous liaison with Catherine. Not to put too fine a point on it, he feared the Empress. Catherine and he saw less and less of each other, and his departure as Resident Minister to Hamburg marked the close of a dwindling affair.

Catherine suffered from these difficult months. It pained her that Serge should prove inadequate, it pained her even more to see him leave.

Her baby had been virtually kidnapped, and now she had lost her lover. She felt desperately alone and began to revive only with the hot summer and her move to seaside Oranienbaum.

There Peter was for the first time allowed to play with flesh and blood Holstein soldiers. A battalion had arrived from Kiel, and Peter was in the seventh military heaven, drilling his blue-uniformed Germans, reviewing them, taking them on manoeuvres. In the evening he sat up late with the officers drinking English-brewed stout.

One morning Peter walked unsteadily into Catherine's rooms, followed by Herr Zeitz, his secretary for Holstein affairs, who was brandishing a document. 'Look at this devil of a man,' Peter said thickly. 'I had too much to drink last night, I'm still in a haze, and here he comes running after me with papers and accounts. He even follows me into your room!'

'Everything I have here,' Zeitz explained to Catherine, tapping a sheaf of papers, 'needs just a yes or a no. The whole lot wouldn't take more than half an hour.'

Catherine glanced through the papers, then asked Zeitz to read aloud the pertinent questions. He did so, and according as she judged best Catherine answered yes or no. Zeitz turned to Peter, who had been listening, plainly impressed. 'You see, sir, if you agreed to do this twice a week, everything would go smoothly. They are only small matters, but they have to be dealt with, and the Grand Duchess disposed of the lot with six yeses and about the same number of noes.'

Peter did agree, and henceforth Catherine dealt regularly with Holstein affairs. She enjoyed turning chaos into order and showed a real gift for quick sensible decisions. Peter was delighted, for he could now devote all his time to the parade ground, and he called Catherine admiringly 'Madame la Ressource'.

The distant duchy of Holstein, which had kept the young couple apart for nine years, now brought them together. Peter, proudly commanding his very own Holstein troops, saw his wife ably running Holstein's civil affairs; he was grateful to her, he felt that at last she was actively on his side, and that summer for the first time he sought to have sexual relations with his wife.

Catherine granted them. After Serge's sophisticated courting Peter's approach to her doubtless struck her as disconcertingly blunt. Inhibitions still dragged on him, he was no ardent lover, and Catherine took little pleasure in his infrequent embraces. Though she felt a certain satisfaction in having at last become a wife in the full sense, the real revelation of that summer to Catherine was the pleasure she found in Holstein politics and administration.

She had started with a mere yes or no, but very soon took the initiative, particularly in righting cases of injustice. She found for instance that a senior administrator named Homer had been held in a Holstein prison without trial for six years; examining the documents and discovering that there was no case against him, Catherine obtained his release.

Holstein was so small that its affairs occupied only a part of Catherine's day. With no lover and no child, she had time on her hands but, having matured with motherhood, she no longer found satisfaction in party games and balls. She needed something meatier. From Holstein, she found herself moving on to the far greater problems of Russia and began to study Russian history. As the available books were inadequate, she went to the State archives and there read many original documents, such as Ivan the Terrible's treaty with Elizabeth of England. The more she read, the more interested she became, and the more she looked forward to the day when she would be helping Peter to rule Russia. That summer, when Catherine was twenty-six, the old dream of a crown simply for the sake of a crown was replaced by a more mature and a much more positive ambition: to bring the fruits of her reading – she was never now without a book of history or political theory in her pocket – to benefit Russia and the Russian people.

This important change in Catherine's life coincided with an equally important change in the Empress's. Since about the time his house had slid downhill Alexis Razumovsky also had been sliding downhill. In frequent vodka sessions the gentle chorister changed into an aggressive fist-fighter, the charming young lover into a touchy middle-aged unofficial husband. He began to bore the Empress. He remained Grand Huntsman but the role of night-time Emperor was transferred to a young gentleman of poor but distinguished family.

Ivan Shuvalov was a cousin of Peter and Alexander Shuvalov, who since helping the Empress to the throne had gained much power, Peter holding the monopoly for salt, tobacco and tunny-fish, Alexander that for champagne, as well as being head of the Secret Chancellery, which controlled the secret political police. Ivan was twenty-two when he became the Empress's favourite. He did not have the striking good looks of Alexis Razumovsky – his portraits show him to have had narrow slanting eyes and a drawn, difficult mouth – but he was more intelligent and by reading widely in French had given himself a good education. The Empress was in many respects ignorant: when ordering statues for the Summer Gardens, for instance, she was imposed on, an old bearded man being passed off as Sappho and an old woman with shrunken breasts as Avicenna. But she very much liked the French theatre and French finery, and it was here that she and Ivan Shuvalov found a common interest to counterpoint their physical attachment.

Peter and Alexander Shuvalov were both pushing men. They intended to use their cousin's position as favourite to get more political power. Peter had a hand in everything – he even invented and manufactured an efficient howitzer, and when Nicholas Choglokov died Alexander got his job as head of the grand ducal household. The brothers already had commercial links with France and as a means to marketing Russian tobacco in that country wished to conclude a Russo-French alliance. After her experience of La Chétardie the Empress was cool, so they were particularly anxious to gain control of the Grand Duke and to convert him to the idea of a French alliance.

The obstacle was Catherine. All across Europe her father had fought France, traditional enemy of Prussia and the German principalities; but it was above all her own observation of France's declining power and of the feebleness of Louis XV's diplomats that convinced Catherine that an alliance with France would be the worst possible thing for Russia.

When they saw that Catherine stood unshakable in this view and through her new-won influence was holding Peter to it also, the Shuvalovs decided to try to break Catherine. The English ambassador described one of their early moves. 'Madame [Peter] Shuvalov, who is the Czarina's favourite, and who is in the secret of all her amours, held the young prince [Paul] in her arms and said (out of malice to the Grand Duchess), Who is he like? Like the father, said the Empress; that can't be, said [Madame] Shuvalov, for he is very brown, and the father is fair. Well then, said the Czarina, he is like his grandfather. Not at all, replied [Madame] Shuvalov, which answer put the Empress in a passion, and made her say, Hold your tongue, you b[itch], I know what you mean, you want to insinuate he is a bastard, but if he is, he is not the first that has been in my family' – the Empress herself having been born before her parents married.

The Shuvalovs were not deterred by this initial setback. They kept the rumour going that the Grand Duke was not the father of little Paul, and capped it with a second, even more damaging. Who, they asked, had any proof that Paul was the son of Catherine, who after all had been nine years sterile? Night and day Paul was dandled by the Empress, he lived in her apartments; much more likely that Paul was the Empress's own son. In either case, they hinted, Catherine might well be expendable.

At the very moment when she had formed a clear ambition of helping Peter one day to rule Russia, Catherine found that ambition menaced by the Shuvalovs. She could not help noticing that with the rise of Ivan Shuvalov the Empress had withdrawn her favour, and on the anniversary of her coronation, seated on her throne in the Kremlin, had dined in solitary state, without associating Peter or herself in the ceremonial, an action that some observers had interpreted as public rejection of the Grand Duke and Duchess.

Catherine had been reading Tacitus's *Annals*, the masterly account of intrigue in the early Roman Empire, and under the influence of that book 'I began,' she said, 'to see everything in black and searched to find deeper and more interested motives for the happenings around me.' In her insecurity Catherine built up a dark fantasy of the Shuvalovs. Alexander Shuvalov happened to have a twitch affecting the right side of his swarthy face from eye to chin; this Catherine attributed to long hours in the torture chamber of the Secret Chancellery. Alexander's wife, who had succeeded Madame Choglokova as thwarter-in-chief of Catherine's freedom, was a stiff woman who never smiled. Catherine named her 'the pillar of salt' and came to believe that she, her husband, and her brother-in-law were bent on destroying her.

Catherine had hitherto behaved well at Court, seeking to please and to make friends. But now, driven by fear of being displaced from the succession and by this dark fantasy, she began to behave very indiscreetly indeed. Her first indiscretion was to go round dropping sarcastic remarks about the Shuvalovs. She pointed out that Madame Shuvalova, though very rich, skimped on her skirts, which were always too narrow and an inch shorter than the fashion; at the card table she made everyone laugh with a clever imitation of Alexander Shuvalov's facial twitch. Even Peter, who did not particularly like the Shuvalovs, thought she was going too far and urged her, in both their interests, to stop. But Catherine would not listen to him. She had cast the Shuvalovs in the role of deadly enemies and felt she must either break them or be broken.

Catherine looked around for an ally. Count Alexis Bestuzhev had started his career as Russia's envoy to Copenhagen and there, working with the chemist Landike, had discovered and patented a sedative – ethereal tincture of ferric chloride – which had become well known as Bestuzhev's drops. A big strong-faced man with a livid complexion, now aged sixty-three, he had been Grand Chancellor for eleven years.

Plagued by an eccentric wife and an errant son, Bestuzhev drank heavily but still got through a great deal of work. He had treated Catherine's mother harshly and had drawn up the strict rules for the grand ducal household enforced by the Choglokovs. But over the years Catherine came to esteem his intelligence and his policy of friendship with Austria – France's enemy. Bestuzhev, on his side, was beginning to feel threatened by the young Shuvalovs and their friend, Vice-Chancellor Michael Vorontsov, also a Francophile, so that when Catherine suggested that in future they should forward each other's interests he guardedly agreed.

Shortly after Catherine had moved closer to Bestuzhev, a new British ambassador arrived. This in itself was of interest to Catherine. She knew that Russia had a long trading relation with England, interrupted only in 1649 when Tsar Alexis objected to the Englishmen's 'most evil deed: their sovereign King Charles they have done to death', and through Montesquieu she had come to admire England's constitutional monarchy.

Charles Hanbury-Williams was born in Monmouthshire in 1708 to a family grown rich on iron. After schooling at Eton he married Lady Frances Coningsby, by whom he had two daughters. The marriage was not a success and after ten years they separated. Hanbury-Williams entered Parliament as a Whig, was well-liked and made a name in fashionable London by his witty poems, notably an 'Ode to an Oyster'. In appearance he rather resembled an oyster, with a droll moon face and, in portrait, upturned eyes. Among his baggage was Lord Chesterfield's gift of goldfish, which Horace Walpole said could not live in Russia. He took up residence in a house rented from Count Skavronsky: 'It costs me £10 a year for being guarded against nobody by a sergeant and 16 men who live in my house and like my mansion better than I do their company.' He did, however, have a view over the Neva, in winter 'the finest street in Europe'.

Catherine liked Sir Charles at once, finding him frank, original and amusing. When she learned that he was trying to negotiate an alliance between Russia and England, France's enemy, she liked him even more. She listened with interest as he talked about his last post, Berlin, and the shocking way King Frederick persecuted his sweet young wife. Discerning in Sir Charles an eighteenth-century Galahad, Catherine let him learn, discreetly of course, that she too had her difficulties.

Hanbury-Williams already knew Catherine to be a friend of Bestuzhev and therefore a valuable potential ally. When he heard about her ill-treatment, a new light came into his eye and he treated Catherine with fond attention. At a ball he admired her dress, modelled on that of a Georgian princess, whereupon Catherine sent him a copy of the dress for his daughter, Lady Essex. Their friendship ripened. Catherine found in the Englishman an attractive spontaneity and warmth lacking in Bestuzhev. Feeling very lonely and still deeply alarmed by the Shuvalovs, Catherine began writing letters to Hanbury-Williams, telling him her fears almost as though he were a father confessor. She was seeking comfort from an independent man she genuinely liked, but it amounted to a second indiscretion. For a Grand Duchess of Russia to carry on a secret political correspondence with a foreign ambassador was an act punishable by excision of the tongue or exile to Siberia.

Catherine wondered why the Empress appeared less and less. She had enjoyed good health in her youth; despite her weight she seldom had any ailment worse than constipation or indigestion. But the twitch at the corner of her eyes had been a warning sign that Peter the Great's blood ran in her veins and now, in her forty-seventh year, the Empress began to suffer, as Peter had done, from convulsions. Some spoke of hysteria, others of apoplexy or even epilepsy. But the convulsions, whatever their cause, left her cold and unconscious for hours. In summer 1756 her condition became alarming, and her doctors believed the Empress would not live long.

Unlike Louis XV on his sick-bed, the Empress suffered no remorse about her favourite. Ivan Shuvalov had access to her bedroom day and night, and through him Peter and Alexander Shuvalov got hour-by-hour news. Catherine and Peter, however, were denied admittance.

Catherine's worry about the succession now grew into alarm. By a law of Peter the Great the monarch alone designated his or her heir, who need not be the nearest blood relative. The Empress had declared her nephew her heir at the time of his adoption. But that had been fifteen years ago, and she had done nothing since to confirm the original declaration. Catherine's position was even shakier than her husband's. Peter the Great had had his wife crowned at the time of his own coronation; otherwise there was no good precedent for Catherine to share in her husband's rule – if, that is, he ever came to rule. At the time of her betrothal her mother had suggested that Catherine be designated *naslednitsa*, meaning that she would succeed to the throne should her husband die, but the Empress had refused.

Catherine knew to be bogus her chief claim on Russian affections, namely that she was the mother of Peter's son. She knew too that the

Shuvalovs suspected as much, and probably the Empress too. What more likely than that the Shuvalovs would choose the Empress's illness formally to exclude her, their enemy, and perhaps Peter also, from the throne? Catherine heard rumours that the deposed boy Tsar Ivan VI had been brought to the palace and that the Empress had had a secret interview with him. Ivan might be designated heir, with the Shuvalovs as Regents. Or, even more probable, little Paul, now almost two, again with the Shuvalovs as Regents.

In this crisis Catherine acted with great energy. She approached Bestuzhev and persuaded him to draw up a secret contingency document, associating her with Peter in the government. Then she went to Sir Charles. She desperately needed money, she told him, to bribe the Empress's maids for news of her condition, and to win the influential friends she would need in case the Empress died. 'In Russia,' she explained, 'nothing is done without money.' If King George II would make her a loan, she would give him her note-of-hand and repay it when she could, and she promised to use it solely for their common service. 'How much do you need?' asked Sir Charles. Without batting an eyelash Catherine replied, 'Ten thousand pounds.'

The sum was very large. But Sir Charles convinced Whitehall it was not too high a price to pay to prevent the Anglophile Grand Duchess being excluded from power and, as she promised, to help him block the Shuvalovs' plan for a Franco-Russian alliance.

Catherine got her ten thousand pounds. Taking money from a foreign power to meddle in Russian politics – this was her third indiscretion. At once she laid out part of it in bribes. 'Provided,' she wrote to Sir Charles, 'my arrangements for being informed in time do not fail, and that even one among eight people gives me warning, it will be my fault if they [the Shuvalovs] gain the upper hand. Be assured that I shall never play the King of Sweden's easy-going and feeble part, and that I shall either perish or reign.' To which Sir Charles replied, 'You are born to command and reign, and old age alone will kill you.'

Catherine then worked out a detailed plan of action in case the Empress died. She would grab little Paul and carry him to her room, send for Bestuzhev and another friend, General Apraxin, then go to the bedroom of the dead Empress, summon the captain of the guard, and make him take the oath not only to Peter as Tsar but to herself as Tsarina.

Catherine was strong enough to perfect this daring plan, but she was not strong enough to keep it to herself. She absolutely felt the need of confiding in her chosen friend. So she wrote it all in a letter to Sir Charles, and he wrote back, suggesting wise improvements: 'If a will is found, and it is not altogether favourable to you, it would be best to suppress it. Lay claim to no title but the lineage of Peter the Great.'

Meanwhile Catherine had to fulfil her side of the bargain. One of the things Sir Charles had asked her to do was to prevent an exchange of ambassadors between Russia and France – there had been none since La Chétardie's gaffe. When a Cabinet paper approving such an exchange was passed to Peter for his signature, Catherine in her role as Madame la Ressource advised him not to sign it. Peter agreed with her. 'They will never,' he said, 'force me to play the part of a dishonest man by signing something of which I do not approve.'

Catherine reported this to Sir Charles. But the Empress became furious with Peter, and three days later Catherine wrote to Sir Charles: 'The Grand Duke appended his signature this morning, saying to Alexander Shuvalov that it was from a desire to please the Empress, and not in any way because he approved.' Uppermost in Peter's mind of course was the succession.

The French were flooding St Petersburg with agents. Mackenzie Douglas, a Jacobite posing as a mining engineer, and the Chevalier d'Eon, a transvestite who found ladies' clothes an agreeable disguise, were the two most active, and Catherine had been asked by Sir Charles to foil them. One day a brilliant French miniaturist, Sampsoy, came to show Peter some of his work. He struck up a conversation, got in some digs at Douglas and continued on a questioning note: 'It is said that your Imperial Highness is very annoyed about a French ambassador, and that you are afraid the man who comes will intrigue against the succession.' 'Mind your own business,' replied Peter, but limply, and Catherine, who had overheard, decided it was not good enough. She felt sure Sampsoy was working with Douglas and, calling him into her room, closed the door.

'Do you know the laws of the country in which you are meddling with matters of this kind?'

'No,' said the Frenchman, beginning to tremble.

'Well,' Catherine retorted, 'you *should* know them. Whoever speaks of things like these, or even mentions them, is sent to the Fortress. Tell those who approve of what you are doing or who send you to make such remarks that their messengers will be thrown out of this window.' Then she dismissed him and from that time on had no further trouble with French spies.

All through summer and autumn 1756 the crisis continued. The invisible Empress seemed to be sinking: on 14th October, for instance, 'her feet and arms were cold as ice, her eyes sightless'. Ivan Shuvalov remained at her bedside, while Catherine, with Sir Charles's money, perfected her plans for foiling the Shuvalovs, both in regard to the throne and the alliance with France. The tension on Catherine began to build up: 'I have a sick headache nearly every day,' she confided to Sir Charles, himself ill with diarrhoea, then with liver trouble.

Sir Charles was well pleased with Catherine's vigorous work on his behalf. This extremely pretty young lady was also, unlike her mother, an extremely efficient secret agent. Catherine, for her part, felt deeply grateful to Sir Charles for his loan and his encouragement. As danger drew them even closer, she felt the need of confiding in him the whole story of her life. She poured out to Sir Charles, in a 40-page written memoir, her long-pent-up string of misfortunes and the nine-year frustration of her marriage.

Sir Charles was flattered, touched and deeply moved. His comments about Catherine in his official despatches became markedly warm and began to evoke speculation in London. Lord Holderness commented, 'I think I see a Signum Salutis in some of your letters; you have more weapons for the service of the King than your tongue and your pen.' 'A man at my age,' replied Sir Charles, who was forty-eight, 'may be a very good friend, but would make a poor lover, my sceptre governs no more.'

Sir Charles was underestimating Catherine's attractions and his own susceptibility to them. Alone in his guarded house by the Neva, amid his goldfish and Dresden china, suffering from the cold and discouraged by what seemed the Shuvalovs' growing power, Sir Charles lived more and more for Catherine's letters and his rare secret meetings with her. At last he too poured out his feelings. 'My heart,' he wrote to Catherine, 'my life, my soul are yours. I regard you as a creature wholly superior to myself. I adore you and my adoration goes so far that I am persuaded that I can have no merit apart from you.'

It was extraordinary for a Grand Duchess of Russia to receive a declaration of love from an English ambassador, but in those tense months of devious plotting and counter-plotting, when the norms of life seemed to be suspended, this extraordinary happening was capped by one even more extraordinary.

Sir Charles had brought to Russia his secretary, a young Polish gentleman, Stanislaus Poniatowski. The fifth child of Count Poniatowski, a poor nobleman of Italian descent, and Princess Constance

Czartoryska, a member of one of Poland's powerful families, Stanislaus had served as aide-de-camp to Marshal de Saxe and completed his education in Paris under the tutelage of Madame Geoffrin, where he shone by his conversation and was much liked. Now aged twenty-two, he had come to Russia to make contacts useful to the Czartoryskis, who were pro-Russian.

Stanislaus had a handsome, heart-shaped face, with prominent eyebrows and a tapering chin. His short-sighted hazel eyes gave him an idealistic expression, and this fitted his character, for Stanislaus was a high-principled young man who had promised his mother not to gamble, not to drink wine or spirits and not to marry before the age of thirty. Yet Stanislaus was by no means dull. He spoke six languages and could discuss books and pictures with amusing good sense; he was in short a model cultivated European.

Soon after arriving in St Petersburg Stanislaus met Catherine. He described her thus: 'A dazzlingly white complexion, large blue eyes, long dark eyelashes, a straight nose, a mouth that seemed to ask for kisses, perfectly shaped arms and hands, a slim figure; she was above middle height and very light on her feet, yet dignified; her voice was pleasant, her laugh gay; she was equally at home playing the most childish and maddest games as she was adding up a difficult column of figures.'

Catherine began to find herself the object of Stanislaus's attentions. At Court balls he danced with her as often as he could; at the opera his eye was more often on her box than on the stage, and he paid her discreet little compliments. Catherine knew that Sir Charles thought the world of Stanislaus, and she herself found him not only handsome – she particularly admired his eyes – but most interesting: well-educated young men with Parisian manners were a rarity in Russia. She enjoyed his company and when he had to make a brief visit to Poland found that she missed him. On his return, promoted now to the post of Saxon Minister to Russia, she went for midnight sleigh rides with her new admirer. Then, in a most remarkable coincidence, just about the time when she received Sir Charles's declaration, Stanislaus told Catherine that he had fallen in love with her.

Between the older man, very dear to her but dear chiefly as a father confessor, and handsome young Stanislaus, with a Polish touch of poetry to all he said and did, Catherine did not hesitate long. She was already under the charm of this stranger of whom she was later to say, 'I esteem and love him above all the rest of the human race.'

Once they knew each other's feelings, and Stanislaus pressed her to become his mistress, Catherine was faced with the question, What to do next? She recognized the danger. To have an affair with a Russian courtier at the Empress's command was one thing; quite another to have an affair with a foreign diplomat who, in addition, was disliked by the Empress, no one quite knew why; presumably because his grandfather had been an enemy of Peter the Great. To enter such an affair at a time when the Empress looked like dying and Catherine had to strain every nerve if she wanted to secure the succession – this would be dangerous almost to the point of madness.

If she had held calculatingly to the three-point programme devised at the time of her marriage, Catherine would have held back from Stanislaus as he sought to kiss the mouth that seemed to him to ask for kisses. But Catherine was not just a calculating woman. She felt lonely, insecure and in need of love. Either from choice or inner necessity she decided that there are times when a woman should follow her feelings. 'One cannot,' she wrote, 'hold one's heart in one's hands, now forcing, now releasing it, tightening or relaxing one's grasp at will.'

Catherine's chances of succeeding to the throne depended above all on her being 'Russian'. Yet now, at the crucial moment, during the winter of 1756, Catherine chose to follow her heart and in the person of Stanislaus to take a non-Russian lover. It was her fourth and most dangerous indiscretion.

CHAPTER 10

DISGRACE

Every day of her childhood Catherine had been aware of the Prussian army, squads of blue-uniformed, meticulously-drilled soldiers whom her father commanded and who were inspected regularly by stern, cane-wielding Frederick William. Parade-ground troops in those calm days, they had been turned by Frederick II into the terror of Europe. This new-style king who lived seven days a week for Prussia's aggrandizement had already wrested Silesia from Austria; in August 1756 he embarked on a second war of conquest, marching his steely grenadiers into Saxony.

Prussia was the ally of England, Austria of France. Russia had a ten-year-old defensive treaty with Austria, and was not bound to join in when Austria, and later France, went to Saxony's aid. Catherine for one thought it would be a mistake to do so. But the Empress hated Frederick – 'He turns everything sacred into ridicule, and never goes to church'; encouraged by the Shuvalovs, ill though she was, in January 1757 she joined Austria and France against Prussia in the conflict which was to become known as the Seven Years' War.

As soon as war threatened talk in St Petersburg turned to troops, guns, ammunition, supplies; and Peter Shuvalov, Grand Master of Artillery, became more prominent than ever. He received permission to raise 30,000 recruits under his sole direction and command, to be called the Reserve Corps. This was the worst possible news for Catherine, who in an emergency could count on only five Guards officers commanding 250 men, and she wrote to Sir Charles about Peter Shuvalov: 'People argue and differ about it, but all call him a second Godunov.' The first Godunov was Boris, an ambitious boyar who became Tsar in 1598.

What to do? Among the friends Catherine had been cultivating for several years was General Stephen Apraxin. He belonged to the ancient nobility and had served in the Turkish war of 1737–9, distinguishing himself at the siege of Ochakov. Then he became ambassador to Persia, softening considerably during his stay in that land. He had a lot of money, entertained lavishly, set great store by status, refusing a gold-hilted sword from George II because it was not bejewelled, and he owned a unique collection of snuff-boxes, one for each day of the year. Now aged fifty-four, Apraxin was described by Sir Charles as 'a very corpulent man, lazy, luxurious and certainly not brave'. He was however influential, being a close friend of Grand Chancellor Bestuzhev, and he very much liked Catherine.

Catherine and Bestuzhev now approached Apraxin and asked him whether he would be prepared to take on Peter Shuvalov, should the latter use his Reserve Corps to seize power. Apraxin, after reflection, said he would, and Catherine was able to breathe freely again. But her peace of mind did not last. A ukase suddenly came from the Empress appointing Apraxin commander-in-chief against Prussia with the rank of Field Marshal and ordering him to leave without delay for the front.

Catherine and Bestuzhev saw the Shuvalovs' hand in this. They both believed that Russia had nothing to gain from fighting Austria's battles, and they themselves everything to lose by Apraxin's departure. They found that Apraxin himself was none too eager to shoot it out with Frederick's veteran grenadiers. Catherine then took a bold step. With Bestuzhev's approval she urged Apraxin to delay his departure, and once again the snuff-box General obliged her. To mask these intrigues Catherine wrote Bestuzhev the following note, for his files: 'I have heard with pleasure that our army is about to put our Declaration into action – we should be covered with shame if it is not fulfilled. I beg you to urge our mutual friend [Apraxin], when he has beaten the King of Prussia, to force him back to his old frontier, so that we may not have to be perpetually on the *qui vive*.'

Apraxin lingered in St Petersburg through the spring of 1757 on the pretext that his travel allowance amounted to only 6000 roubles, four times smaller than his rank demanded. But when that and other matters were adjusted, he had to obey his Empress; she, though still not fully recovered from her illness, was now out of danger. With 500 horses to draw his personal luggage the portly, red-faced Marshal left St Petersburg by carriage in mid-May. Once he smelled gunpowder he regained his youthful form; he drove the Prussians out of the fortress of Memel and on 10th August 1757 won a thundering victory at Gross Jägerndorf. All East Prussia lay open to him, and the Russian Court expected him to overrun the whole of that province. Instead, he hesitated for two whole weeks; then, burning his ammunition and abandoning his guns, he returned by forced marches to the safety of Memel.

When she heard the news of Apraxin's retreat the Empress staggered out of the country church where she was hearing Mass and collapsed unconscious on the grass. After being bled she was carried home on a sofa, speechless. When she was able to receive visitors, the newly appointed French ambassador and the Austrian ambassador complained bitterly to her, comparing Apraxin's 'flight' unfavourably with her father's glorious victories in the same region.

Catherine was secretly pleased by Apraxin's withdrawal, for from Memel the Field Marshal could help her in a crisis. When she came to write her Memoirs Catherine denied that she had played any part in persuading Apraxin to withdraw, and this is probably true, since the actual withdrawal seems to have been occasioned by a breakdown in food supplies. But probably, in conjunction with Bestuzhev, Catherine did persuade Apraxin that the issue of the succession mattered more than defeating Frederick. At all events, as she told Sir Charles Hanbury-Williams, Apraxin said to Catherine before leaving St Petersburg: 'If the King of Prussia attacks me, I'll fight; if not, I'll lie low.' And Catherine did write more than one letter to the Field Marshal. When she heard of his withdrawal to Memel, she deemed it prudent to write him another letter, this time intended less for his eyes than to cover herself with the government. She warned Apraxin of the virulent rumours, explained that his friends found it difficult to justify the speed of his withdrawal and begged him to resume his advance.

The Empress, pressed by the French ambassador and the Shuvalovs, ordered Field Marshal Apraxin to be relieved of his command, placed under arrest and court-martialled. The shock proved too much for the corpulent Marshal; on the very day he was due to be cross-examined he suffered an apoplectic stroke, collapsed and died. But not before he had handed over his personal papers and letters, including those in Catherine's beautiful flowing hand, to Peter Shuvalov.

This was a very bad blow for Catherine. She would have liked to confide in dear Sir Charles but her English friend, having failed to block a Franco-Russian rapprochement, had had to return home – Catherine wrote to him, 'I love you as my father, I account myself happy to have been enabled to acquire your affection,' and wept all through the day of his departure. The alarming thing was that the Empress called Sir Charles 'a deceiver, a traitor, an intrigue-maker' – words that suggested she knew more than Catherine wished her to know. Meddling in military affairs, taking money from Prussia's ally – in the context of a full-scale war these activities amounted to high treason punishable by death.

Meanwhile Catherine was in the exciting first stages of her new love affair. Disguised as a man she would slip past 'the pillar of salt' and hurry to a secret rendezvous, often in the apartment of Leo Naruishkin, who acted as go-between. At other times, wearing a blond wig over his dark hair and telling the sentries he was one of the Grand Duke's musicians, Stanislaus would arrive in her bedroom by the servants' staircase. He was readier than Serge to take the risks that Catherine herself enjoyed. He was much straighter too: when he told her he would love her always Catherine knew she could believe him. Then again, he had so many interesting things to tell her. He knew London and had stories of the King whose money she had borrowed; he was a connoisseur of painting; the French authors she had read he had met; and if he rather overdid his filial affection for Madame Geoffrin, whom he called 'Maman', at least Madame Geoffrin was someone Catherine held in respect.

Catherine handled her love affair discreetly, for she did not want to complicate further her position, and she continued to have conjugal relations with Peter on the infrequent occasions when he invited her. Then, in spring 1757, she found herself pregnant. She was fairly sure the child was her lover's, but she hoped that Peter would believe it to be his.

Peter, however, had noticed not only Catherine's swelling figure but her frequent evening absences, and he made an angry scene to Leo Naruishkin. 'I have no idea,' he cried, 'whether this child is mine and whether I ought to recognize it as such.'

When Leo repeated this to her, Catherine realized that she was once again in deep trouble. After due reflection she decided that the best form of defence was attack. 'Ask the Grand Duke,' she told Leo, 'to swear on his honour that he has not slept with his wife. Tell him that if he is ready so to swear, you will immediately inform Alexander Shuvalov, head of the secret police, so that appropriate action may be taken.' Leo did as Catherine said and Peter, ruffled, took the easy way out. 'Go to hell,' he told Leo. 'Don't mention the matter again.'

Catherine's child was born on 9th December 1757. This time it was a daughter. Catherine suggested it should be called Elizabeth, but the Empress pointedly declined the compliment, named it Anna and removed it to her apartments, where flannel and fur were waiting, so that Catherine had no time to fondle her baby, no time to get to know it. Happily, Peter chose to consider himself the father, and ordered a public holiday in Holstein, while Stanislaus came to see her in her bedroom. When Peter Shuvalov unexpectedly entered to present plans for the celebration fireworks, Stanislaus hid behind a curtain – a situation which caused him and Catherine much amusement.

With the birth of Anna and the lulling of any suspicions about Stanislaus, Catherine could congratulate herself on having safely sailed through this particular squall. But, while still convalescing from the birth, one Sunday in February Catherine was handed a note by Leo. Opening it, she recognized Stanislaus's handwriting and read as follows: 'Last night Count Bestuzhev was arrested and relieved of all his charges and decorations.' The Grand Chancellor of Russia, twelve years pillar of state – arrested! Her one sure friend in high places – stripped of office! At first Catherine could not believe it. Yet it was quite true. A whole company of grenadiers had been called out to check any popular protest, for Bestuzhev was esteemed by many beside Catherine.

That evening Catherine was due to attend a wedding, that of her friend Leo Naruishkin. Though alarmed about the implications of Bestuzhev's arrest, she went to the wedding and to the ball afterwards. A three-man commission had been appointed to question Bestuzhev and during the ball Catherine went up to Prince Nikita Trubetskoy, an elder statesman who was on the commission.

'What are all these wonderful goings-on?' Catherine whispered. 'Have you found more crimes than criminals, or more criminals than crimes?'

'We did what we were ordered to do, but as for the crimes, we are still searching for them.'

The search led painfully close to Catherine. An Italian jeweller named Bernardi, who had passed messages for her and knew of her correspondence with Sir Charles, was arrested; so was her close friend Adodurov, who since teaching her Russian had made a name as a writer of mathematical treatises. What they would confess under torture Catherine dared not think. What she did soon know for certain was that among Bestuzhev's papers was found the document for associating Catherine in the government.

It looked as though Catherine was as good as lost. She found herself shunned at Court. No one wanted to know the friend of the fallen Grand Chancellor. No one dared be seen with the foreign lady who had been mixed up with treacherous Apraxin. Burning certain papers and accounts, Catherine shut herself in her room, her only company, in default of her children, her dog and a parrot.

The war was having its effect on Peter also. Seeing himself as the great military expert, he had expected a place in the War Council or

Empress Elizabeth, daughter of Peter the Great.

Above: Catherine's first lovers, Serge Saltuikov
and Stanislaus Poniatowski, later King of Poland.
Below: Gregory Orlov and Catherine's
son by Orlov, Alexis Bobrinsky.

at least a command in the field. Instead, he was ignored until the Shuvalovs, hoping to win his gratitude, offered him command of the St Petersburg Cadet Corps. Peter accepted, but drilling cadets was baby stuff, and at heart he felt humiliated.

Peter as a boy had stayed for a time in Berlin and been deeply impressed by the parades there: rank upon rank of impeccably turned-out soldiers moving like clockwork. He admired Frederick of Prussia and thought wistfully that had he not come to Russia he would have held the rank of colonel in Frederick's crack army. As his own life became more frustrated, Peter began to hero-worship Frederick. He even came to hope that the soldier-King would win victories and so humiliate the aunt who was humiliating him: the bitch of the North, as Frederick pithily called her.

Peter felt a secret despair at Gross Jägerndorf and the further Prussian reverses that followed that defeat. He lapsed into a deep moroseness. He penned notes in bad French to Ivan Shuvalov, describing himself as 'ill and melancholic to the utmost degree' and begging the favourite to persuade the Empress to let him travel abroad for a couple of years.

Peter would have needed his wife at this period. But as part of her punishment Catherine had been forbidden by the Empress to have anything further to do with Holstein, and the man who had helped her administer the duchy – von Stambke – was sent home. So her role as Madame la Ressource had lapsed, and in the evenings she always seemed to have a headache – or so she claimed – but Peter was beginning to have his suspicions, and these did nothing to cure his moroseness.

Peter thought he would console himself by courting one of Catherine's ladies-in-waiting. Elizabeth Vorontsova was the niece of Michael Vorontsov, a friend of the Shuvalovs, lover of France – the furniture in his house had been given to him by Louis XV, some said it was Madame de Pompadour's throw-outs – and Bestuzhev's successor as Grand Chancellor. Elizabeth was very plain but because of her uncle something of a power at Court. Catherine felt threatened by Elizabeth in a way that she had not felt by Peter's other flirts. It particularly annoyed her that when she passed Peter and Elizabeth *tête-à-tête*, instead of rising, as politeness demanded, Peter remained seated.

Though shunned at Court, Catherine continued to see Stanislaus, in fact she was as much in love with him as ever, so she had no just grounds of complaint against Peter for consoling himself with Elizabeth. Yet such was the state of her nerves that Catherine did in fact complain – at least to herself. Merging the pain she felt at her fall, which after all was partly merited, with the pain she felt at Peter's affair with Elizabeth – induced by her own affair with Stanislaus – Catherine drew herself up to the heights of an emotion she rarely indulged in: persecuted self-righteousness. She thundered to her soul, and to her parrot, that she was being treated with barbaric, with intolerable cruelty. No self-respecting woman would endure longer such torture as was being inflicted on her. The Empress, the Shuvalovs, Peter, Elizabeth Vorontsova – in the solitude of her room Catherine furiously denounced them and all their works.

Meanwhile, the three-man commission continued its inquiry into Bestuzhev's affairs. The short, fiercely cold days of winter, which precluded walking or riding, made Catherine feel doubly a prisoner. Soon Lent would be upon her, with its meagre fare and absence of all amusement. Though her very dangerous political position called for prudence, Catherine was now almost completely at the mercy of her nerves. Instead of lying low, she felt an overpowering need to assert herself before her enemies.

Now Catherine's one friend was the handsome Pole. Whatever the feelings of anyone else, Stanislaus adored her. So Catherine, in those harrowing first weeks of 1758, conceived a plan. She would emerge unexpectedly from her self-imposed exile on Carnival Eve. She would wear her most sensational dress, she would drive with her ladies to the theatre, where a Russian play was being performed – Peter, who did not care for Russian plays, would stay in the palace – she would watch the play from the grand ducal box with Stanislaus beside her; later at the Court ball she would dance in Stanislaus's arms the whole night through.

Shrove Tuesday arrived. Hardly had Catherine begun to dress when Peter entered her room in a terrible rage. 'You enjoy upsetting me,' he shouted. 'You're only going to the theatre because you know I hate Russian plays. I shall countermand your carriage.'

'In that case,' Catherine replied, 'I shall walk.'

They argued for some time at the top of their voices; Peter was evidently so furious because Elizabeth would be in attendance on Catherine and he would have to spend the evening alone.

Peter finally stalked off. When it was almost time for her to leave, Catherine sent to ask whether her carriages were ready, whereupon Alexander Shuvalov appeared. 'The Grand Duke,' he told her, 'has said the carriages are not to fetch you.' At this Catherine lost her temper. 'I shall complain to the Empress,' she cried.

'What exactly will you say?' asked the other coolly.

'I will tell her how I am being treated, and how, so that the Grand Duke can enjoy the company of my ladies-in-waiting, you encourage him to prevent me from going to the theatre where I may have the happiness of seeing the Empress . . . I'm going to write to her Majesty this moment – and you will deliver my letter!'

There and then Catherine took up pen and paper; in the most pathetic tones she could summon she thanked her Majesty for all the kindness and graciousness she had shown her since her arrival in Russia, but said that, alas, the present situation proved she had not deserved it, as she had only provoked the hatred of the Grand Duke and the marked disfavour of her Majesty. Deprived of the most innocent entertainments, she was reduced to sitting in her room in distress, solitude and steadily declining health.

Having penned this one-sided little dirge, Catherine called Alexander Shuvalov back and gave it to him. She was now told that her carriages were waiting and, pleased at having got her way, she dispensed Elizabeth from accompanying her. As she left the palace, she noticed Elizabeth settling down to a game of cards with Peter, and both rose as she passed. Satisfied with this sign that they acknowledged her victory, Catherine responded with a studied low curtsy.

Catherine drove to the theatre and there was Stanislaus. After combating the trickery of her husband and Alexander Shuvalov, Catherine welcomed all the more her lover's straightforwardness and inner strength. Before the deluge of Lenten devotions began on the morrow she spent one perfect evening with him, first watching the play, then at the ball, whispering, laughing, dancing minuets and polonaises, flaunting their joy before the cold Court.

Catherine was rather proud of her letter to the Empress. She believed its pathetic tones might soften her Majesty. She certainly was not prepared for yet another attack on her beleaguered position. Yet that is precisely what happened. In the second week of Lent Madame Vladislavova, Catherine's trustworthy maid for nine years, was relieved of her duties. When Alexander Shuvalov brought her the news Catherine broke down and, something she hated doing in front of such a man, burst into tears.

They were tears for her own plight, and for her own indiscretions. She had begun to be indiscreet in order not to be excluded from the succession; now the Empress had recovered Catherine feared that she had excluded herself – by meddling in the war and by her affair with Stanislaus. The next blow, she felt sure, could fall on her personally, and indeed rumours began to circulate that Peter planned to divorce her and marry Elizabeth.

Catherine decided that she must see the Empress. It might do harm. It might precipitate any action the Empress was contemplating against her, such as trial for high treason. On the other hand, it might conceivably do good. At any rate, it was in Catherine's character not to wait passively but to act.

Through Alexander Shuvalov Catherine began asking for an interview. Nothing happened. She stepped up her pleas, and received only vague assurances. Lent ended, Easter came, then the month of April. Her sense of doom growing, still avoided by all at Court, Catherine decided finally on drastic measures. She went to bed, announcing that she was ill, feigned a high temperature and weak pulse, told her doctors that it was spiritual help she needed, and sent for her confessor, Theodore Dubyansky. Knowing all she said to him would be repeated, for Theodore was also the Empress's confessor, Catherine spoke to the bearded figure in black for an hour and a half, pouring out her troubles, inveighing against the Shuvalovs, and begging for an interview with the Empress as the only means of restoring her to health.

Next day Alexander Shuvalov informed Catherine that the Empress would see her that evening, provided she was well enough to get up. Catherine replied that she was feeling much better and pondered a plan of action. She held no strong cards, so must play the Empress's weak suit. Hard-pressed by the war, argued Catherine, the Empress would be particularly anxious not to give any purchase to her enemies abroad. The tension between Europe and Russia – the old story in a new setting – this was the weakness Catherine decided she would play.

At ten o'clock in the evening Catherine was dressed, waiting to be ushered into the imperial apartments. But the Empress and delay were synonymous and Catherine had to wait with thudding heart until half past one in the morning; only then was she escorted through the long corridors of the silent palace to a long room, the sumptuous furniture of which included a sofa, several high screens, a table and a dressing-table, where lay a beautiful toilet set of gold.

Dominating the room, as she dominated any place she happened to be, stood the Empress. She had taken to dyeing her hair black, her face was lined by her recent illness and she was overweight, but she still possessed beauty and majesty. To Catherine's consternation she was not alone. Flanking her were the two men Catherine now regarded as her enemies-in-chief: her husband and Alexander Shuvalov of the facial twist, Head of the Secret Chancellery. It was not after all going to be a woman-to-woman talk.

Long ago, when she had been taught and first used the phrase '*Vinovata, Matushka*', Catherine had understood that the Empress liked to exercise the power of forgiveness, and she had been ill often enough to know how softened the Empress could be by the sight of pain and tears. So the first thing Catherine did was to fall on her knees at a suitable distance before the Empress and burst into tears.

'I am utterly miserable,' she sobbed, 'at having lost your Majesty's favour and incurred the Grand Duke's hatred.' She explained what she had touched on in her letter; that she sat all day in her room, alone and deprived of even innocent amusements. Such was her anxiety that her health had collapsed, and now the point had come when she must do all in her power just to preserve her life. That is why she approached her Majesty, begging to be allowed to go to a spa in Europe and take the waters that yet might halt her decline.

Catherine then took her courage in both hands. Though it was the last thing she desired, with urgent voice she cried, 'I beg your Majesty, after I have taken the waters, to send me back to my mother. I will spend the rest of my days at home with my mother praying to God for your Majesty' – Catherine took care to stress the praying – 'praying for the Grand Duke, praying for my children and for all those who have been kind – and unkind – to me.'

The Empress crossed the room and touched the kneeling figure, indicating that she should rise, but Catherine remained in her suppliant posture. 'How can you speak of being sent away? Remember that you have children.'

'My children are in your hands and could not be in better ones.'

'How would I explain such a thing to the people?'

'Your Majesty will, if she finds it opportune, enumerate all the reasons for any disfavour, as well as for the Grand Duke's hatred.'

'How will you provide for yourself, living with your family?'

'I will do as I did before you honoured me by taking me away.'

'Your mother is in hiding: she had to leave her home and has gone to Paris.'

'I know,' replied Catherine, adding something she hoped would help. 'She was suspected of having the interests of Russia too much at heart and the King of Prussia persecuted her.'

'Stand up,' said the Empress, and Catherine obeyed. She now noticed a big screen not far from where the Empress stood. She guessed that Ivan and Peter Shuvalov were hidden behind it, listening to every word she said. Later she was to learn that she had been half right: Ivan was behind the screen.

The Empress came close to Catherine. 'God is my witness to how I wept when you were so desperately ill on your arrival; had I not loved you I would not have kept you here.' Catherine thanked her for her past kindnesses, but insisted on her disastrous present position. The Empress's tone hardened. 'You are excessively proud. Don't you remember how I came up to you one day at the Summer Palace and asked if your neck were painful, because I had noticed that you had hardly bowed to me; and that it was because of your pride that you merely gave me a nod?'

'Good heavens, Ma'am, how could you imagine that I should show pride in your regard? I swear to you it never crossed my mind that the question you put to me four years ago could have meant anything of the sort.'

'You fancy that no one is as intelligent as you are.'

'If I ever had such a fancy, nothing would be more likely to destroy it than my present situation, and this very conversation, particularly as I realize that my stupidity was to blame for misunderstanding you four years ago.'

Peter now spoke for the first time. 'She is terribly cruel,' he interposed to his aunt, 'and incredibly stubborn.'

'I have become stubborn,' Catherine retorted, 'since I realized that my meekness has only brought me your hatred.'

The Empress moved about the room, then returned to Catherine. 'How could you venture to send orders to Marshal Apraxin?'

'I, send orders? It never entered my head.'

'Your letters are over there,' and the Empress pointed to a tied-up packet in her gold wash-basin.

'I did write three letters,' Catherine admitted. 'But I never sent him orders. In one I told him what was being said about his behaviour.'

'Bestuzhev says there were many other letters.'

'If Bestuzhev says so, he is a liar.'

'Well, if he spreads lies about you, I will put him on the rack.'

'As Empress, you are free to do so. But I have written only three letters to Apraxin.'

As the Empress considered this in silence, Peter, who had been muttering to Alexander Shuvalov, spoke up. He was very angry indeed. He accused Catherine of working against his interests, and of marital infidelity. She asks to be sent home, he said. An excellent idea. Let her go at once. A separation could be arranged; then he would be free to marry Elizabeth Vorontsova.

As Peter so outspokenly took her bluff at face value, Catherine felt afraid. She could defend herself only by going into details about Peter's conjugal behaviour. But to do so to his face in front of Alexander Shuvalov and whoever stood behind the screen would be so humiliating to Peter that their marriage would be irretrievably ruined.

Peter continued with his charges – and he had plenty of incidents to cite. Fortunately for Catherine the Empress seemed to sense the motives for Catherine's silence. Just when the interview seemed at its blackest, she came up to her and whispered, 'I have many more things to say to you, but I find it difficult at the moment – I don't want to make things worse between you than they are already.'

Catherine noticed a friendlier tone and whispered back, 'I too find it difficult to speak now, in spite of the great desire I have to tell you all there is in my heart.' She thought she saw tears in the Empress's eyes; then, quite suddenly, Peter and she were dismissed.

So ended the interview. On balance Catherine considered it had gone fairly well: no proof of her involvement in Apraxin's withdrawal, and her threat to return to Europe had had the desired effect. However, Peter's accusations about her infidelity – these remained to be answered.

A second interview followed in May, this one between the Empress and Catherine alone. When she came to write her Memoirs, Catherine broke off at the beginning of this interview with the sentence: 'The Empress asked me for details about the life of the Grand Duke . . .' It was a critical moment in their relationship, evidently one that Catherine wished to reflect on long before committing to paper, for until this interview the Empress had been unaware of why the marriage had broken down, and naturally attributed it to Catherine's philandering.

What happened at the second interview has been the subject of conflicting speculation, but now we know for sure what took place, thanks to a hitherto unpublished paper addressed by Sir Charles's successor, Robert Keith, to Lord Holderness for young George III, who liked such 'anecdotes' as they were then called.

'The Grand Duchess,' wrote Keith, 'had certainly a very hard game to play; for . . . the Empress [is] prejudiced against her upon account of her youth, beauty and other accomplishments, of which her Majesty is extremely jealous.' This element in the Empress's character is one of which Catherine incidentally seems to have been unaware, probably because she herself hardly ever suffered from jealousy.

The Empress then went straight to the central issue: Stanislaus

Poniatowski. Catherine, said Keith, 'had the courage in answer to some reproaches made by her Majesty on the subject of her lover, not only to avow the thing, but even to justify herself, by representing what sort of husband the Grand Duke was; how little comfort she could have with him; and what she had to suffer from him. This she did in such a manner that the Empress, tender-hearted herself, pitied her, entered into her reasons, excused her weakness.'

This was the moment Catherine had been hoping for. The Empress at last understood the misery of her marriage, and having understood would surely allow the kind of love affair she herself enjoyed with Ivan Shuvalov. But in this she had miscalculated. The Empress, sympathetic on the score of Catherine's marriage, proved adamant about Stanislaus. Not because he was a Pole, not because he was a foreign Minister, not because he was the son of her father's enemy, but because he professed the Roman Catholic faith, and this was abhorrent to all devout members of the Orthodox Church. 'The Empress,' continued Keith, 'excepted to her having a heretic for her lover. This may seem pretty extraordinary and even improbable to your Lordship, but I can assure you, every circumstance of it comes from the Great Duchess herself.'

Catherine emerged from this second interview stronger than from the first. Rather than see the Grand Duchess leave Russia, the Empress was prepared to overlook her political meddling, and even to give instructions that Catherine should be respectfully treated. Now that she knew the whole truth about the marriage, she was prepared also to overlook Catherine's occasional love affair. But on one point – the one where it hurt Catherine most – the pious Empress refused to yield. The Grand Duchess must cease to see Stanislaus. Orders were given to ensure his immediate recall to Poland.

CHAPTER 11

PREPARING TO RULE

Catherine's three-month disgrace had ended. But its shock still sent tremors along her nerves. When she said goodbye to Stanislaus, Catherine decided she had better make a fresh start, and follow to the letter her original three-point plan. Her motto in future must be: good behaviour.

She would begin by trying to patch things up with Peter. But Peter was now under the spell of Elizabeth Vorontsova, who had become his mistress. Pock-marked and not too bright, Elizabeth rarely washed, and spat when she spoke. Compared by one ambassador to the lowest run of barmaid, she evidently pleased Peter by a sort of military roughness – she swore like a trooper – and by a pair of very large breasts. How was Catherine to win over such a woman? Evidently not by discussing Voltaire.

Catherine was fond of dogs and parrots, and had a happy gift of being able to mimic various birds and animals, their cries as well as their postures and walk: in particular she could give a funny 'cats' concert', when she would growl, spit and box her own ears for all the world like two gesticulating cats. This imitation sent simple people like the Choglokovs into stitches of laughter and Catherine probably used it to break down Elizabeth Vorontsova's hostility – Elizabeth's sister at any rate mentions the cats' concert admiringly.

The other side of Catherine's relationship with those at Court, and *a fortiori* with Elizabeth Vorontsova, was a refusal to brook disrespect. An illustration of this may be seen in Catherine's handling of Leo Naruishkin. Usually so gay and easy-going, Leo had recently entered a bad patch – he may have been secretly jealous of Stanislaus. He began to treat Catherine with rudeness and impudence, and to talk against her friends. One day, entering her room, Catherine found Leo sprawled on her sofa. He did not acknowledge her presence and went on humming a nonsensical song. Catherine decided to teach him a lesson. With two lady friends she picked large bunches of stinging nettles; slipping quietly into the room they gleefully struck the reclining

Leo with the nettles on hands, legs and face. The resultant red swellings kept him from Court next day; they also shook him out of his rudeness. From then on he behaved impeccably to Catherine.

The exact methods Catherine used for winning Elizabeth Vorontsova over are not known, but almost certainly they were based on her twin gifts for making people laugh and keeping them up to the mark, aided by the strength of mind she had shown on the night when she got Peter to reverse his order about the carriages.

During the summer of 1758 Catherine reached a position with Elizabeth where she could set forth her terms. She would, she said, allow the younger woman to continue as Peter's mistress, provided Elizabeth helped to reinstate her as wife.

It is a measure of Catherine's skilful handling of her rival that Elizabeth agreed to these terms, and it was actually by means of Elizabeth, Keith reports, that Catherine was reconciled to the Great Duke. By September all was smooth and the ambassador could write: 'The Great Duchess and His Imperial Highness continue to live in the greatest harmony.'

Catherine had made a promising start in her policy of good behaviour. The next thing was to prepare Peter for the throne. Catherine was not alone in seeing that her husband had a number of faults, and that these must be corrected if he were to rule well. Whenever he had the chance Peter would snub the Guards, whom he considered chocolate soldiers; aware of the future importance to Peter of the Guards' allegiance, Catherine persuaded him to show a more friendly attitude at least to the officers. In church Peter continued to worship in undemonstrative Lutheran style; Catherine explained that he was alienating influential dignitaries and persuaded him at Mass to 'make ten or twelve more signs of the cross'. She showed Peter that his habit of praising Frederick was, at the very least, poor taste at a time when thousands of Russians were being killed by Frederick's troops, and she persuaded him to play a more patriotic role by attending meetings of the War Council.

To compensate for his frustrated military ambition, Peter took to recounting stories about his military boyhood. Catherine disapproved of this habit, which only served to foster Peter's unhealthy day-dreams about Holstein. One day she heard him tell a friend how he had been placed at the head of a company of Guards and sent by his father to capture a gang of gypsies who had been committing horrible highway robberies near Kiel. Peter described his prowess in detail, the ruses he had employed – how he encircled them and challenged them to combats in which he gave proof of prodigious valour – and how he finally led them all captive into Kiel.

'How long was this before your father's death?' asked Catherine quietly.

'Three or four years.'

'Well, you must have started your exploits very young. You would then have been only six or seven. Do you want us to believe that the Duke sent his only son, aged six or seven, to fight dangerous robbers?'

Peter flew into a rage and accused Catherine of wishing to discredit him. 'It's not I, it's the calendar,' she replied, and after this heard less of Holstein.

Catherine was pleased at her new relationship with Peter. It was not perfect having Elizabeth in the picture, but at least it was a big improvement on having Peter work against her. The Empress too was pleased with the reconciliation and the improvement in her nephew, and as a reward for her good behaviour she allowed Catherine to see her children once a week. So at last Catherine enjoyed to a limited degree the joys of motherhood. She watched little Paul, aged four, as he played in the palace garden, and pretty Anna, aged nearly one, begin to crawl.

The following year, 1759, when Catherine reached the age of thirty, was in many ways an unhappy one. In March Catherine had a great sadness. Little Anna fell suddenly ill and within a few days died. Catherine, Peter and the Empress laid the little body to rest in the monastery of St Alexander Nevsky, in St Petersburg. It was a painful loss to Catherine, but at least it was less bad than losing Paul, her chief claim to the succession.

Also that year Catherine had news of Sir Charles Hanbury-Williams. She had told him that on coming to power 'I shall raise statues to you, and the whole world shall see how highly I prize merit.' On returning to England poor Sir Charles became alarmingly eccentric, then quite mad and very soon died. Having served his country with zeal, he was buried in Westminster Abbey. He had been a loyal friend to Catherine and she mourned him.

During Catherine's first interview with the Empress, Catherine's mother had been mentioned as living in Paris. It was Catherine's former suitor, Prince Heinrich of Prussia, who had invaded Anhalt-Zerbst, driving out her brother, who had joined the Austrian army, and Johanna, who had fled to Paris, dabbled foolishly in alchemy, then fallen ill of dropsy. Catherine, distressed, sent her mother parcels of China tea and of rhubarb, the new Russian cure-all medicine which, unfortunately, did not cure Johanna. She died in Paris aged forty-seven. It was a painful blow for Catherine who, despite differences of temperament, had loved her sometimes scatterbrained mother. Johanna left debts of half a million francs, which the Empress reluctantly agreed to pay, not from friendship but to save a debtor's soul from Hell.

Shaken by these three deaths and the devastation of her homeland, Catherine at this period evolved a kind of Stoic philosophy. She no longer thought in terms of political intrigue – which anyway now lay beyond her, for Bestuzhev had been found guilty of *lèse-majesté* and rusticated to his country house. She thought, rather, in terms of enduring what had to be endured and, however adverse the circumstances, of behaving dutifully; then, at a moment fixed by no earthly power, she would attain what was decreed for her by Providence.

Catherine was now reading a great deal and looking critically at the way Russia was being ruled. In her almost twenty years of power the Empress had done practically nothing to improve the country. Her policy, like the Church's, was unchangingness. She had rashly let herself be drawn into the Seven Years' War yet practically never attended the weekly War Council. She could decide what dresses to order but about matters of State she showed pitiful indecision. When the Anglo-Russian treaty was submitted for her signature, Sir Charles was told by Bestuzhev first that the Empress had tumbled downstairs and bruised her right shoulder; then that 'she catched a violent rheumatism which is very unluckily fallen into her right arm'; a few days later, while she was in the nursery, a pole by which the cradle was suspended fell and would have hit her on the head had she not, with great presence of mind, parried the blow with her right arm – bruising it and making it impossible for her to hold a pen! Such were the stories put out by her Minister to cover the Empress's indecisiveness, under which Russia stagnated.

Catherine wanted to see Russia ruled energetically. Deeply shocked by the cruelty with which families in Moscow treated their servants, she wanted to see new laws enacted to prevent brutality and, generally, to ameliorate the lot of the serfs. She wanted to end Elizabeth's mercantile policy and reduce tariffs. She wanted new schools, universities, a hundred improvements suggested to her by reading Montesquieu and contributors to the *Encyclopédie*.

Catherine came to these authors as a German, and the fact calls for emphasis. The modern French theorists, and even more the English on whom they were based, believed man had rights that had to be protected against unbridled political power, whereas the German tradition stressed man's duty to the community and State. So Catherine, when reading Bayle and Montesquieu, necessarily did so with a German bias: what interested her was not the division of the legislature and the executive, but humane laws and practical steps to general prosperity.

As she evolved her own idea of the good State, Catherine saw that in many respects it differed from Peter's. Peter held that Russia had been ruled too long by petticoats. What was needed was Frederick William's cane, Old Snoutnose's goose-step, and the iron will of Frederick, whose portrait Peter wore on a ring. Catherine disagreed; she shared Sir Charles's view of the Prussian people, 'all equally miserable, all equally trembling before [the King], and all equally detesting his iron government'. When Peter said he would reintroduce the death penalty, Catherine argued strongly against it but was unable to shake her husband.

As regards the future, then, there arose a kind of impasse between them. 'I therefore decided,' said Catherine in grandiloquent vein, 'to continue, as far as I could, giving him the advice which I believed to be for his good, but never to insist, at the risk of angering him . . . to open his eyes to his true interests whenever occasion offered and to withdraw the rest of the time into total silence; but to pursue, on the other hand, my own interests as far as the Russian people were concerned in order that the latter, in case of need, would see in me the saviour of the nation.'

Catherine in short was determined to dissociate herself from Peter's Prussian-style State, the unpopularity of which she had experienced first-hand as a girl, and she made this clear to her increasingly wide acquaintanceship at Court.

One of those who listened to the Grand Duchess was Catherine Dashkova. Married to a Guards officer, Prince Dashkov, she was a younger sister of Elizabeth Vorontsova, but no two girls could be more different. Dark, with a high, broad forehead, deep-set intelligent eyes and high cheek-bones, Catherine Dashkova was one of the first in the long line of Russia's 'eternal students', seeking after Truth with a capital T. She did not care about dresses and would not wear the white paint and rouge almost statutory at Court; what interested her was books. Though only sixteen, she had a library of 900 volumes, and had read them all. The authors she preferred were Bayle, Montesquieu and Voltaire. From them she had imbibed a great respect for tolerance, human rights and the Republic of Holland. As Peter's godchild she sometimes talked politics with him; once, when Peter defended the death penalty, Catherine Dashkova took issue with him, and Peter's only reply was to stick out his tongue at her. This shocked the reasonable seeker after Truth, and caused her to listen even more attentively to Peter's wife. Catherine, said Princess Dashkova, 'forthwith captured my heart and mind and inspired me with enthusiastic devotion'.

In the summer, when she drove from Oranienbaum to see little Paul at Peterhof, Catherine formed the habit of stopping at the Dashkovs' house. There the woman who had practical experience of politics and the sixteen-year-old bluestocking discussed what might be done in the next reign. During these discussions Princess Dashkova became convinced that Catherine, not Peter, would be the 'saviour of the nation', and that she alone must succeed to the throne. Catherine was flattered by the suggestion, and by a laudatory poem her friend wrote her, but she did not encourage so rash a plan. She wished to come to power as Peter's wife, and to influence Peter to govern well.

Catherine continued her good behaviour throughout 1759 and into the new year. She was still deeply in love with Stanislaus, and the only indiscretion she allowed herself concerned him. Once again Keith is our source. 'She wants of all things in the world to have her friend back from Poland, which she will certainly not succeed in, and this engages her in a thousand little intrigues which give jealousy to a greater lady than herself, and this often brings little mortifications upon her, which cannot fail to give her great uneasiness. When her young daughter died lately, all the ladies of the Court were allowed to wait on and comfort her; but within these few days an order from above has been given, forbidding those visits, and desiring her to confine herself to the ladies properly of her own court.'

Catherine had by now learned to live with the Empress's nettling. She practised her Stoic philosophy and continued to behave. She corresponded with Stanislaus, recalled their good times together, and promised herself they would one day meet again. No one in Russia, she thought, came within measurable distance of Stanislaus.

Early in 1760 Catherine happened to be standing at her window in the Winter Palace on the side facing the Moika Canal when she noticed on the path beneath an officer in Guards uniform. He was good-looking, tall – over six foot – and carried himself straight, but with his head bent forward. He happened to look up at her window and their eyes met. Catherine learned that the officer was one of the five Orlov brothers, all over six foot tall and well known as tough, devil-may-care fighters. The toughest was Alexis, who in middle age was to tip the scales at 23 stone, a huge man disfigured by a sabre cut down the left side of his face, received in a pothouse brawl.

The Orlovs were a boisterous clan. They hunted bear, went cock-fighting and organized boxing matches – two teams, each of fifty boxers, in a long line. Their jokes were rough and hearty – Alexis once toasted a friend: 'May you never die – except at my hands.'

Gregory, the second brother, was the one Catherine had seen from her window. He had fought at the terrible battle of Zorndorf, where 20,000 Russians fell. He was wounded three times but refused to leave his platoon. In recognition of his bravery he had been given the honour of escorting a distinguished Prussian prisoner to St Petersburg and appointed aide-de-camp to Peter Shuvalov, Grand Master of Artillery. He had then proved himself as successful in the lists of Venus as in those of Mars by winning and making his mistress beautiful Princess Kurakina.

Gregory was a new type of man for Catherine. He possessed a dimension lacking in Serge and Stanislaus, for he had looked death in the eyes. With his smell of leather and gunpowder and tavern beer, he struck Catherine as splendidly virile, 'a hero similar to the Romans of the golden age of the Republic, possessed of courage and generosity'. When he began to show interest in her, then to court her, Catherine immediately felt attracted.

Catherine was determined to keep to her line of good behaviour. To fall in love with a war-hero could hardly displease the Empress or the Russian people; but Peter it would displease, and so Catherine took the utmost care to keep her meetings with Gregory secret – and she had by now considerable experience in the technique of secrecy. Their affair developed quickly; Gregory was soon calling her, the Grand Duchess, his senior by five years, Katinka or Katyusha. In late 1760 or early 1761 Catherine became the mistress of Captain Gregory Orlov.

Gregory was not of sufficiently distinguished birth to cut a figure at Court, but as a war-hero he was *persona grata* to her Majesty. The Empress had become much absorbed by her personal crusade against atheistic Frederick. 'I intend to continue the war,' she told the Austrian ambassador when Austria showed signs of wilting, 'even if I have to sell half my diamonds and my dresses.' The reference to dresses was not flippant: the Empress had replaced those lost in the Moscow fire and now possessed 15,000, many adorned with pearls or diamonds.

The most dazzling ball dresses she wore less and less. She had never fully recovered from her illness of 1756–7. She suffered from frequent nosebleeds, and, lately, from dropsy, made worse by overindulgence in pâtés, sent express from Périgord by her ambassador to France. The majestic presence swelled and swelled, like something in a fairy-tale. In the middle of December 1761 the Empress suffered convulsions followed by a haemorrhage, and was declared by her doctors to have only a few days to live. This time there could be no hope of a rally.

In the Winter Palace talk shifted from munitions to medicines, and the generals ceded to physicians-in-ordinary. As before, Ivan Shuvalov remained at his mistress's sick-bed, joined now by Alexis Razumovsky, and his brother Cyril, who had hurried back from the Ukraine. There was, however, one big difference between this illness and that of 1756: Peter Shuvalov no longer hovered at the head of his private army. He had suffered a heart attack and lay in bed, seriously ill.

On 20th December, past midnight, Catherine was lying in bed but not asleep when a slim figure, huddled in furs, slipped up the servants' stairs and entered her bedroom. It was Princess Dashkova. Catherine felt astonishment, for the previous day her young friend had been unwell and confined to her bed, and the temperature that night had dropped well below freezing. 'Come into bed and warm your feet,' said Catherine solicitously. The other did so, and explained why she had come. She had been unable to bear the uncertainty of the dark clouds gathering over Catherine's head. 'You must look to your safety,' she told Catherine gravely. 'Have you worked out a plan?'

Catherine said she had not. Then, taking the girl's hand in her own: 'I shall meet bravely whatever may befall me.'

'Then, Ma'am,' said her *exaltée* admirer, 'your friends must act for you.'

'For heaven's sake, Princess,' said Catherine pleadingly, 'don't expose yourself to danger on my account. Besides, what can anyone do?' Prince Dashkov could muster fifty Guardsmen, Gregory Orlov perhaps double that number, but to what purpose, since no plans had been made? Half-cock action, especially if premature, could ruin everything, even provoke the Empress into specifically excluding her from any part in future government. So with firmness Catherine restrained her impetuous friend.

To the sick-room the Empress's confessor, Theodore, was now admitted, and with the smell of medicines mingled the tart scent of incense as Theodore prepared his holy oils and administered Extreme Unction to the prostrate monarch. 'Holy Father,' he prayed, 'Physician of souls and bodies . . . heal your servant Elizabeth of the bodily and spiritual sickness of which she is afflicted.'

The hours ticked away. Catherine, shivering in the draughty palace, waited anxiously, trying to show the bravery of which she had boasted. At last the longed-for summons came. Peter and she were for the first

The Coronation of Catherine in the Assumption Cathedral
in the Kremlin, September 1762.
Catherine placed the crown on her own head.

Four of Catherine's friends. *Above:* Zachary Chernuishev and Nikita Panin.
Below: Alexis Orlov and Sir Charles Hanbury-Williams.

time admitted to the imperial bedchamber and could look at the pale face on the pillow, drawn by pain, the nose already bearing the pinched look of death.

The Empress spoke to them, and already her voice seemed to come from a distance. She made Peter promise to care tenderly for little Paul. She also charged him to harbour no grudge for old wrongs, and to treat as friends all her servants and dependants. She had no specific message for Catherine, but allowed her to remain at her bedside with Peter.

Catherine stayed there for two nights. To see a beautiful woman of absolute power reduced to a dropsical contorted figure gasping for breath was doubtless a chastening experience. Catherine forgot the wrongs done to her and remembered that this was the woman who had called her to Russia and, in the past two years, treated her with understanding.

The Empress gave no sign of new wishes regarding the succession, so the designation of Peter made twenty years ago still stood. It seemed unlikely that the Shuvalovs would try to contest it. The Empress, whatever her shortcomings as a stateswoman, had been loved by the Church and the Guards; Peter had been behaving himself; and her wishes would doubtless be complied with.

Christmas Day dawned. The Empress asked Theodore to read her the solemn prayers for the dying and herself, faintly but fervently, made some of the prescribed responses. When he ended, she made him begin again.

Catherine still sat by the sick-bed. Peter had left the room to talk to an official. A maid entered and whispered in Catherine's ear a message from Prince Dashkov: 'You have only to give the order and we will enthrone you.' Catherine reflected a moment and whispered a reply: 'For God's sake don't plunge us into chaos.'

A few minutes later Prince Trubetskoy, senior Senator, opened the double doors of the ante-chamber and faced the waiting courtiers and palace servants. 'Her Imperial Majesty Elizaveta Petrovna has fallen asleep in the Lord. God preserve our gracious sovereign, the Emperor Peter the Third.'

Catherine left the bedroom to accompany her husband to the palace chapel. There in front of the Archbishop of Novgorod a senior civil servant read the manifesto drawn up by the late Empress in 1742 declaring her nephew to be the true and lawful heir to the throne, and exhorting him to follow in the footsteps of his grandfather. The Archbishop then hailed Peter as Autocrat; he made no mention of

Catherine or little Paul. The Senate and senior dignitaries, hand on Bible and cross, then took the solemn oath of allegiance to their new Emperor. Peter Shuvalov kept to his bed.

As her husband strode to the great drawing-room to receive the allegiance of three Foot Guards regiments, Catherine went to her bedroom. Everything had unfolded smoothly, one might almost say providentially. She had attained her ambition, was wife to the Emperor of Russia. But as she began the long mourning rites she reflected on the complications awaiting her in the new reign. She was carrying – had been carrying for five months – Gregory Orlov's child.

CHAPTER 12

PETER'S REIGN

The late Empress's body was washed, disembowelled, embalmed and arrayed in a beautiful silver tunic with finest lace sleeves – even in death Elizabeth was the best-dressed woman in the palace. On her head was placed a golden crown inscribed with her name and the words 'Most Pious Autocrat'. Beside her body was laid the traditional plate of boiled rice with raisins, and in her right hand Theodore placed the customary scroll, wherein a confessor commended a departed soul to St Peter.

The body lay in the imperial bedroom under a baldaquin, while priests recited the Gospels and soldiers stood guard, heads bowed, arms reversed. After three weeks one of many Requiem Masses was said; the body was placed in an open coffin, carried to one of the large State rooms and laid on a dais under a canopy hung with ermine and crowned with a golden two-headed eagle. Here, for a week, the people of St Petersburg filed past to pay their last respects to an Empress more visible now than during her lifetime.

Catherine knew that the Church and Russians generally set great store by exact observation of mourning rites. She questioned three experienced Court ladies and, wishing to create a favourable impression, put their advice into practice. She knelt for long hours before the Empress's body, recited the prescribed prayers, succeeded in finding black material with which to hang her rooms – because the Empress had disliked mourning, it was scarce and cost five roubles a yard – and she wore only dresses of deep black, a colour which conveniently disguised her condition.

One month after death the Empress made her last journey across the Neva to the cathedral of St Peter and St Paul, there to be buried beside her mother Catherine the First, and her sister Anna. Walking behind the coffin, Peter grew impatient at the slow pace of the cortège: he unexpectedly quickened his step, causing the train of his black robes to slip from his trainbearer's hands and flap loudly in the wind. Catherine covered this little indiscretion by continuing to walk with leaden step and by letting her tears be seen.

Immediately after the funeral Peter moved into the late Empress's apartments and began to exercise fully the functions of his new office. Until she had had her child, Catherine did not wish to take part in public ceremonies, so she stayed in her old rooms, watching how Peter shaped, but not going out. She explained that she had a bad cough, then a swollen cheek, then toothache.

The new Emperor got up at seven and even while dressing listened to reports. At eight he received in his study Michael Vorontsov, whom he retained as Grand Chancellor, the chief of the St Petersburg police, the head of the War College – equivalent to War Minister – and other senior executives. The Shuvalovs were no longer a force: Peter died two weeks after the Empress, and Alexander was moved to a colonelcy in the Guards. In taking decisions Peter consulted only one man: Dmitri Volkov, a capable middle-of-the-road civil servant, who had been Elizabeth's Cabinet secretary.

Peter next went the rounds of the Colleges, ensuring that everyone from presidents to copyists was hard at work. Then came two hours on the parade ground, after which he dined, inviting to the meal anyone whose views he wished to hear. Afternoons were spent visiting State manufactories or civic services such as the fire brigade, for since Peter the Great's time a Tsar was expected to fight fires. Peter asked questions, nosed out grievances, devised improvements. This heavy day continued till nine, when he ate supper, his table guests being chosen not by birth but by lot; after which he smoked a clay pipe and drank stout with a few close men friends.

Peter started off excellently by reducing the tax on salt and fixing a maximum price for it, thus removing an oppressive burden from the poor. He recalled all political exiles save Bestuzhev; among those who reappeared after more than twenty years were Field Marshal Münnich and Ernest Biron: white-haired, in old-fashioned suits, like figures in the last scene of a masque. Peter permitted the return of religious dissenters banished by his aunt and allowed them to practise their rites 'since bitterness or violence is not the proper way to convert them'.

Peter at once began negotiations to end the unpopular war, which had cost Russia 100,000 men and most of its small navy. At one point Russian forces, with their Austrian allies, had occupied Berlin and sacked Charlottenburg, but England had made plain she would never allow Russia to make territorial gains in East Prussia, so Peter negotiated on the basis of pre-war frontiers.

Though the Russian infantry had proved itself the equal of any, senior officers had made a poor showing. Apraxin of the snuff-boxes had been succeeded later in the war by Serge's brother Peter Saltuikov, who incidentally had married hunchbacked Catherine Biron. Peter Saltuikov handled his armies so clumsily he was called by Frederick 'the stupidest of all Russia's fools' and had to be relieved of his command.

Pondering on these and many similar failures, the new Emperor decided to go to the root of the matter. Peter the Great had obliged all gentry – owners of land and serfs – to serve in the army or civil service. At the age of ten sons had to be inscribed; later they passed very elementary exams before entering the lowest of fourteen grades, so beginning twenty-five years' service. As the army offered more posts than the still embryonic civil government, most of the gentry, however unsuitable by physique or character, rose to command troops.

The new Emperor decided that the best means of getting an efficient officer class was to confine entry to well-chosen professionals. He therefore issued a ukase ending obligatory service for the gentry. In fact most gentry still continued to serve the State, because of the pay and possibilities of family advancement, but Peter's ukase, motivated by military concerns, was welcomed by the gentry because it removed the element of compulsion, and hearing the news Prince Dashkov, who had so opposed Peter's accession, exclaimed to Catherine: 'The Emperor deserves a statue in gold.'

The part of his day to which Peter attached most importance was between eleven and one. Wearing full uniform, top boots and a tricorne, he would march smartly out to the parade ground beside the Winter Palace and inspect the regiment drawn up there, ensuring that buttons were well polished and leather gleamed. Then he would drill the regiment, snapping out the commands himself: 'Shoulder arms!' 'Order arms!' 'Present arms!' Next he exercised the regiment: quick march, slow march, counter-march, wheeling, and the many other precise regular movements which, for those who subscribed to the military cult, had all the fascination of a Bach fugue. The regiment Peter took most pains with was the Preobrazhensky: after putting it through its paces he would order an issue of vodka to every man. At the conclusion of the morning's drill he would take the salute, or, on days of special importance, proudly march at the head of the regiment, leading the unswerving ranks across the parade ground, swinging in his right hand a kind of halberd called a spontoon, and at the moment of climax giving a signal for all the cannon in the Citadel and Admiralty to fire – so many at once that the whole city shook.

By attaching such importance to a well-drilled army Peter was following Frederick II and, through him, Frederick William. Like them, Peter saw the army as the symbol of, and model for, a new strong virile State.

The man who as Grand Duke had put Catherine into uniform and made her shoulder a musket naturally profited from his new position to urge all senior officials, even civilians, to don army uniform and join in the parade-ground drilling. Even Prince Trubetskoy, in his sixties, putting on an officer's uniform, marched, counter-marched and wheeled on gouty legs. Only Paul's tutor, Nikita Panin, an ex-ambassador who hated barrack-room ways, declined the honorary rank of general and its accompanying gold-braided uniform. This puzzled Peter, who said sadly, 'I understood Panin to be intelligent,' but he comforted himself with a plan for making seven-year-old Paul a Guards warrant officer.

Catherine was well pleased with Peter's promising beginning. She felt the satisfaction of a producer who has spent long hours, month after month, training an unlikely actor for the exacting leading role in a drama that would last as long as his life and where the supporting cast numbered, literally, millions. Each day Peter seemed to accomplish more, now inspecting an ordnance factory, now the Mint, then speeding to put out one of the big fires that so often swept the wooden houses of St Petersburg, and all the time making numerous administrative improvements – admittedly mainly on points of detail.

If a friendly adviser had drawn up a three-point long-term programme for the new Emperor, it would have read as follows: Try to please the Church, the Guards and the Russian people. Catherine had doubtless outlined some such programme. But the new Emperor for all his keenness was the same man who had rebuffed her invitations to tenderness and her pleas that he should stop beating his King Charles spaniel. Peter would follow Catherine's advice – anybody's advice – so far and no further. The rest of the way he would decide and act for himself.

Soon after seizing power Elizabeth had gone to Moscow to be anointed and crowned. It was expected that Peter would do the same. Instead, he announced that he would defer his coronation indefinitely. His pretext was lack of money; his real reason probably that Frederick II, on succeeding, refused to go through with such 'mummery'. Whatever his motive, Peter offended the Church.

The Russian Church honoured the New Testament's First Commandment but paid scant attention to the Second. As a result serfs on monastery lands were overworked and knouted cruelly. Pious Elizabeth had done nothing to help this oppressed group. Peter, however, acted at once. He issued a ukase nationalizing all monastery lands. This was a good reform, but Peter carried it out precipitately and with the same lack of tact he showed when, needing horses to remount his cavalry, he commandeered the bishops' horses, with the result that bishops could no longer come to Court. Taken with his known Lutheranism and his postponement of the coronation, the seizure of their lands roused the Church against Peter.

To the Guards Peter adopted an ambivalent attitude. While cultivating and improving the senior regiment, certain others he considered over-privileged chocolate soldiers. He therefore disbanded the Life Guards. He gave officers and men a choice of serving in the regular army or retiring on half-pay; only six chose the first option. At the same time, in the interests of better parade-ground appearance, he made certain changes in the grass-green and red uniforms which Peter the Great had bestowed on the Preobrazhensky regiment. This angered its members and caused them to believe that they too might be downgraded to the level of a regular regiment.

For six agonizing years Russians had shed their blood against Frederick's armies. They were relieved when Peter made peace, and they could even accept that the alliance Peter concluded with Frederick was to Russia's political advantage. What displeased the Russian people was the extraordinary tone adopted by their new Emperor. Peter wrote the Prussian King effusive letters, calling him 'one of the greatest heroes the world has ever seen'. He named a Russian ship of the line *Fredericus Rex*. He asked for, obtained and wore the orange ribbon of the Prussian Black Eagle in preference to all others. He adopted the disconcerting habit of referring to Frederick as 'our master'. At the banquet celebrating peace he toasted Frederick to the roar of 50 cannon fired at once, and was heard to say to the Prussian ambassador, 'You can inform our master the King that he has only to give the order and I shall make war, with all my empire, on Hell itself.' Even Frederick was amazed, saying, 'I am his Dulcinea. He has never seen me and has fallen in love with me, like Don Quixote.'

This behaviour might have been excused as youthful eccentricity. But, as Catherine knew to her cost, Peter possessed a more dangerous eccentricity than hero-worshipping Frederick. For twenty years he had obstinately maintained that he was Duke of Holstein first, and Grand Duke of Russia second. The question arose whether, on mounting the throne, he would alter that priority.

In January 1762 Peter took a step little noticed at the time but of great subsequent importance. He summoned to St Petersburg two of his Holstein cousins. One, the Prince of Holstein-Beck, he made Governor-General of Estonia and Ingria; the other, Prince Georg of Holstein-Gottorp, who was Catherine's uncle and as a Lieutenant in the Cuirassiers had wanted to marry her, he appointed Senior Field Marshal in the Russian army. To both Peter accorded public honours, and to Prince Georg he made a present of Bestuzhev's luxurious town house. Finally he appointed both these Holsteiners to his War Cabinet; this meant that two foreigners would sit in Russia's nine-member top military committee.

Peter could argue that his cousins, one a first-rate ex-Prussian army colonel, would prove very valuable in making Russia's army more efficient. That may have been true. But Peter overlooked, or chose to ignore, Russia's hostility towards Westerners, particularly Germans. It hurt the Russian to call in help from outside, it wounded his pride, it made him fear to lose his identity in imitating the foreigner. It made the gentry jealous to see Prince Georg getting 4000 roubles a month and being treated, in the words of the Danish ambassador, as 'an oracle and judge without appeal'.

Had he stopped there, it is just possible that Peter might have continued to carry with him the goodwill of his people. But, like his more famous namesake, he lacked restraint. Continually before his mind was an event that had happened fifteen years before he was born: Denmark's seizure of Schleswig, part of the Duchy of Holstein. Peter the Great had promised his father to recover that small mist-bound territory, and had failed to do so. What was to stop him, son and grandson of the two men involved, from fulfilling the promise now?

On the day before Easter Peter moved from the old draughty, partly-demolished Winter Palace to the new stone building commissioned from Rastrelli eight years before by his aunt and only now complete. The new Winter Palace, much larger and more lavish than its predecessor, rather went to Peter's head. In his brand-new study, furnished with deep carpets and gold fittings, he took up his pen and gave to his words a new touch of majesty. 'My glory,' he wrote to Frederick, 'obliges me to secure satisfaction from the Danes for the outrages committed on my person, above all on my forebears.' He asked for the loan of a base and by a strange irony Frederick offered him Catherine's birth-place, Stettin.

It became known that the new Emperor was planning war on Denmark, an ally of Peter the Great which had never harmed Russia, and that he was doing so with Holstein advisers in the interests of

Holstein. In effect he was waving the silver stinging nettle of his homeland in the faces of the Russian people.

'He is mad,' said Stanislaus Poniatowski, recalling that Peter, in uniform and tricorne, resembled at times a swaggering bully, at other times a fop in Italian comedy. If he had been only mad, the Russians might have borne with him, for they had borne with more than one very peculiar Tsar. But Peter was, from their point of view, something worse than mad. He was a European in the sense that he seemed determined to put European interests before those of Russia.

Catherine meanwhile remained in her rooms in the old palace: on plea of indisposition she had not yet moved to the new. Her news of Peter came only indirectly. Gregory Orlov told her of anger in his regiment, of the guardsmen's wounded patriotism, of resentment at a Tsar who preferred speaking German to Russian. Princess Dashkova spoke of the need for schools and books, not more cannon and bloodshed, while the Princess's kinsman, Nikita Panin, complained of Russia's empty treasury, of troops stationed in Prussia unpaid for two months. All of them said to Catherine: 'Do something to stop your husband.'

In principle Catherine was more a free agent than she had been while the Empress lived. In fact, however, she was subservient to the child she was carrying. Until its birth she was powerless to act. Besides, at the moment she rarely saw Peter. So she said to her friends: 'Wait. Let us see how things develop.'

On 11th April 1762, in the old Winter Palace, alone except for the midwife and maids, Catherine gave birth to her third child, a boy. The first two had been taken from her at birth, and it might have been thought that she would cling to this one. Imperative reasons of State made that impossible. This was not just Catherine's child, it was a bastard of the Tsar's consort, and were its true identity ever known could be a dangerous weapon in the hands of enemies. So Catherine, after naming the boy Alexei Grigorovich, sent him away to foster-parents. Because she wrapped him in the fur of a beaver, the Russian for which is *bobyor*, the boy came to be known as Alexei Grigorovich Bobrinsky.

After she had sent her son to the country, Catherine moved to apartments in the new Winter Palace. Elizabeth Vorontsova was already installed there, but she and the Tsar had frequent fights, and Catherine still retained an ascendancy over her rival. In fact, a few days after the Empress's death, when Elizabeth in a bout of jealous rage announced her intention of going to live in the country, Catherine had persuaded her to stay. She knew she had little to fear from this plain, unintelligent girl who was coming to be a victim for Peter's bullying.

Catherine had not forgotten her friends' pleas. Now that she could assess Peter's political position for herself, she saw that he had indeed aroused deep resentment. She knew that, despite the birth of Gregory's child, Peter still respected her, still regarded her as Madame la Ressource; in fact he had recently paid all her debts, 600,000 roubles. She decided therefore to take the first opportunity of showing her disapproval of his recent behaviour.

Catherine reappeared in public on her thirty-third birthday. She received with marks of pleasure a letter of congratulation from the new young King of England, George III, who as the son of Princess Augusta of Saxe-Gotha was Catherine's cousin in the third degree; but she reserved her warmest attention for Count Mercy, Austrian ambassador. Knowing that he feared the Russo-Prussian alliance was directed against Austria, Catherine said pointedly to Mercy, in the presence of all the Court and diplomatic corps, 'I assure you that my goodwill towards your country remains unchanged.' Translated into plain language Catherine's message read, 'I think the Emperor would do well to continue Russia's long-standing friendship for Austria, instead of rushing into this new alliance with a hated aggressor.'

Catherine made her second protest by inviting senior clergy to consecrate a small chapel in the new palace, which would be in effect for her use only, since Peter now rarely went to Mass. The ceremony took place with due pomp in the second half of May. The clergy were pleased but Peter flew into a rage. He sent a letter of reprimand to all his aides who had attended the ceremony, and told one of his helpers, Melgunov, an ugly scoundrel who drilled the cadets, to tell Catherine that if she ever again acted independently like that he would shut her up in a convent for the rest of her life. Catherine cried, made excuses and begged Melgunov to appease the Emperor. When Melgunov returned to his master and tried to do so, Peter believed that his order had not been executed exactly, and sent Prince Georg to repeat the scolding vigorously, and he made three of his aides stand outside the door to listen and report back to him.

Catherine made her third protest direct to Peter, and again in public. On 11th June the Emperor celebrated the signing of his Prussian alliance with a military review followed by a banquet in the splendid hall of the new palace. At Peter's wish, lots were drawn for places, and Catherine found herself at the opposite end of the hall from her husband, with an amusing courtier, Count Stroganov, in attendance behind her chair. Everyone who mattered was present: gentlemen in uniform, ladies in long dresses wearing their diamonds, the diplomatic corps, and Peter's favoured cousins: the Prince of Holstein-Beck and Prince Georg of Holstein-Gottorp.

Before the banquet began Peter stood up and proposed the toasts. 'To the health of the imperial family!' he said, lifting his goblet, while the cannon he loved to hear fired a salvo. Everyone rose to drink the toast, save Catherine, who drank it seated. Peter noticed and at once sent his aide-de-camp, General Godovich, to ask Catherine why she had not risen. 'The imperial family,' Catherine replied, 'consists of you, myself and my son, who is not present. So naturally I remained seated.' 'What about my cousins?' asked Peter, indicating the Holstein princes. Catherine did not answer, nor did she need to, for by remaining seated she had already signified to the assembled guests that she, wholly a Russian, no longer acknowledged blood ties with Germany, and expected the Emperor to renounce those ties also. But Peter, flushed by his military parade, resented the implied criticism. Angrily he shouted one word across the hall at Catherine: '*Dura*!' meaning 'Fool!'

Shocked silence followed, then a buzzing as guests discussed this extraordinary behaviour. Catherine must have known that her protest, if it failed to bring Peter to his senses, would incur his anger, so it was to hide not wounded pride but disappointment that she turned in tears to Count Stroganov and begged him to tell her a funny story, any story, to give her a countenance. Then the dinner was served, and somehow Catherine struggled through it.

After the banquet it became clear that Peter was unmoved by his wife's protest, for he actually spoke about having her arrested, and was only dissuaded from doing this by Prince Georg, who, though now married, retained a warm affection for his niece. At the same time he made active preparations for leading a Russian army against Denmark and, to the general dismay, announced that during his absence – 'those stupid Danes are not likely to keep me busy more than two months' – all troops remaining in Russia would be under the command of Prince Georg.

On the day after the dinner Catherine received visits from those who had previously urged her to check Peter. They were now much more pressing. Gregory Orlov told her that he, his brothers and several close friends detested Peter's pro-Holstein policy, Princess Dashkova that Cyril Razumovsky and Russia's best cavalry officer, Michael Volkonsky, had been won over to the opposition. A growing body of influential people believed that Peter must go, and go quickly. To replace him they wanted Catherine. Indeed, without Catherine as an alternative ruler, they hardly dared to act.

Catherine now found herself in a situation of great complexity. On the one hand it was possible that Peter would moderate his behaviour – Frederick was advising caution and trying to mediate between Peter and Denmark; in that event there would be no need to remove him. On the other hand, Russian xenophobia could not be underestimated – it had cost Anna Leopoldovna the Regency. Should it even now be on the point of erupting against Peter, and Catherine had failed to take a positive stand against him, she could be engulfed with him. After all, she even more than Peter was a foreigner, the hated Prince Georg was her uncle, and the base against Denmark her birthplace.

When her friends invited her to head a coup Catherine faced three possible courses. First, she could stand by her husband, invest him with the respect she had acquired in high quarters, and perhaps strengthen him to a point where no plot could succeed. Secondly, she could remain neutral, retire to her rooms and occupy herself with needlework and the study of history. Thirdly, she could accept her friends' invitation and head the conspiracy.

'My disposition is such,' Catherine once wrote, 'that my heart would have belonged entirely and unreservedly to a husband who gave me his love.' Had Peter loved her and she him, Catherine would probably have followed the first course. But Peter had withheld his love, and Catherine far from loving Peter, now actually bore him positive hatred, for, having subjected her to years of misery and ruined her marriage, he now looked like ruining her whole life: certainly he had put it – and his own – at grave risk.

So Catherine rejected the first course, and because she was energetic and a born leader, the second. There remained the third, and this is the one that carried immense risks. For her, a foreign-born petty princess, with only a handful of friends, to lead a rising against her own husband, Peter the Great's grandson – even in Russia no such daring a coup had ever before been heard of. Yet this is the course that appeared necessary. Catherine had a double motive for favouring it: she wanted to rule, believed she could rule well; and she wanted to avert the downfall facing her if she did not act. So on 12th June, when Peter left suddenly for Oranienbaum, telling his wife to follow him six days later to Peterhof, Catherine took one of the great decisions of her life. She told her friends she would lead a *coup d'état*.

Lead was the word, for the conspirators made a mixed bunch. Gregory Orlov was a tough army officer, more at home in the barrack-room than in a palace, yet he loved Catherine deeply and was acting from love. His even tougher brother, Alexis of the scarred face, despised the would-be soldier Tsar and was acting partly from fraternal feeling, partly because he thought Catherine would make a good commander-in-chief. Princess Dashkova bookishly saw Catherine as a peace-loving philosopher-queen, and would have been disappointed to learn she was the mistress of a man like Gregory. Nikita Panin, who wore a full wig and thought in terms of protocol and precedents, was a budding statesman, who distrusted soldiers, even brave ones, and smiled at Princess Dashkova's naivety. He, and the man he had recruited to the plot, Cyril Razumovsky, wanted little Paul to become Tsar, and his mother to be merely Regent. Catherine for the moment allowed Panin and Razumovsky to believe that this would happen.

The conspirators met probably in any room save Catherine's, and always in a different one. After discussion they agreed on a plan: they would lock Peter in his apartment and declare him incompetent to rule, while the Guards, acted on by the Orlovs and their friends, rallied to proclaim a successor. To be sure of victory it would be useful to turn public opinion even further against Peter, and to get hold of money to sweeten uncommitted Guardsmen.

As regards public opinion, the conspirators began spreading highly coloured stories, some true, some false, against Peter. He was planning, they said, to bring in Holsteiners to replace the Guards, to dower selected Russian girls and marry them in a Lutheran church to his German aides. His private life was as reprehensible as his public. He drank to excess, regularly fell under the table and had to be carried to bed. He ordered sixty marriages to be performed at Court – an English agent picked up this story and passed it to George Grenville, head of the northern department – 'and four beds of gauze in the same chamber for those who should give the greatest proofs of their *capacity*'.

Catherine made contact with the English, hoping again to get money; what happened illustrates one aspect of her many difficulties. The ambassador, Keith, was a devotee of Peter, who dined *tête-à-tête* with him and Elizabeth Vorontsova and said openly that Catherine was finished politically. Lord Bute in London did not believe Keith, and sent out Thomas Wroughton, who knew and liked Catherine, as British Resident, with £100,000 for Keith to lend Catherine. Keith was hurt at Bute's action, declined to use the money and offered to resign.

Bute calmed down Keith, while Catherine, disappointed at getting no money, gave Wroughton a secret letter in which, recalling her long friendship for England, she asked Bute to make Keith stop speaking against her.

This did not end the matter. Peter, who was no fool, noticed the appointment of a man he knew to be sympathetic to Catherine; he immediately protested through Keith and got Wroughton transferred to Warsaw. The upshot was that Peter's suspicions were aroused, while Catherine had no money to bribe the Guards.

Hence the importance to Catherine of Gregory and his brothers. They worked tirelessly on her behalf, going round their fellow officers and converting several more, including the much-respected Captain Passek. In the very short space of five days Catherine had gathered into her hands all the threads of the plot and specified a date for seizing the Emperor: as soon as he returned to St Petersburg.

On 18th June Catherine said goodbye to Gregory and Princess Dashkova, whose husband – it looked suspicious – Peter had appointed ambassador to Turkey. Then, following Peter's instructions, she drove to Peterhof, the huge imperial residence overlooking the Baltic. She slept there and next day drove a further nine miles to Oranienbaum to join her husband.

Peter was marking time, waiting for what looked like a satisfactory outcome to the conference on Schleswig convened by Frederick in Berlin, but continuing war preparations in typically idiosyncratic style. Admiral Taluizin having reported that great numbers of ratings were on the sick list, Peter published an angry ukase ordering the men to get well at once because illness was not one of their duties. When Frederick suggested that he should take with him 'all those who might in your absence prove dangerous', Peter laughed the warning off; he had nothing to fear, he said, the Russians loved him.

Her head still full of the plot, Catherine was now obliged to join in light summer entertainments, and try to amuse Elizabeth Vorontsova, who was quite unaware of her sister Princess Dashkova's activities. The day she arrived at Oranienbaum Catherine attended an opera, at which the husband she planned to dethrone sat in the orchestra, happily playing the violin. Later there would be garden parties and a fancy-dress ball, leading up to a gala dinner at Peterhof on 29th June, Peter's name-day. After that he would return to St Petersburg – and his fall.

On 24th June news arrived that 12,000 Danish troops had invaded the free city of Hamburg and extracted by force a loan of one million écus, desperately needed to put Denmark's defences in order. It was an extraordinary, wholly unexpected happening. 'The Emperor,' wrote Keith, 'considers it a direct aggression on the part of Denmark.' He cancelled plans for returning to St Petersburg; instead he 'has publicly declared his resolution of setting out from here . . . to put himself at the head of his army, now in Pomerania.' He would leave after his name-day, and he gave orders for the Preobrazhensky regiment to prepare to march with him.

As soon as she heard that Peter would not be returning to the capital, Catherine realized that the coup would have to be postponed. She sent a secret message to her fellow-conspirators to damp down the plot.

CHAPTER 13

OAK LEAVES AND POISON

The night had been very short and so light that it would have been possible to read without a candle. At six o'clock in the morning of Friday 28th June, when the sun was already shining warm from a cloudless sky, a hired carriage drew up outside Peterhof park and a tall man with a scarred face got out. He was wearing the grass-green and red uniform of a captain in the Preobrazhensky guards. Entering the park, he walked fast through a wood of larches into the garden, skirted the cascade, the fountains and the immense palace, its rooftop statues recently re-gilded, and arrived at a brick pavilion close to the sea known as Monplaisir. Here he knocked, gave his name to the maid and was shown to a heavily curtained bedroom.

Catherine, who had been wakened by her maid, recognized the officer as Alexis Orlov. 'Everything is ready for the proclamation,' he told her. 'You must get up.'

Alexis explained to Catherine how, on the previous day, a guardsman in his regiment had picked up a rumour to the effect that the Emperor had arrested his wife and was holding her in custody. Very upset, the guardsman went to his officer, who happened to be Captain Passek, and said grievingly, 'I suppose this is the end for our Little Mother.' 'Not at all,' replied the captain, and tried to cheer up the guardsman. But he, still alarmed, went to another officer, told him the rumour and repeated his conversation with Captain Passek. This officer was not one of the conspirators; horrified that Captain Passek had listened to the guardsman's implied disloyalty to the Emperor without arresting him, he informed his superior, Major Voeikov. After questioning the guardsman, the Major placed Passek under arrest. As soon as he heard this Alexis had consulted Nikita Panin. Panin recognized the danger that Passek would reveal the plot under torture, and though normally cautious, approved Alexis's wish to hurry to Peterhof.

Catherine listened closely, noticing with satisfaction how calm Alexis was. She thought it probable that Peter, who was spending the night at Oranienbaum, had been told of Passek's arrest. If so, there was not a minute to lose. To mount the coup without first arresting Peter would vastly increase her difficulties, but Catherine decided all the same that this was her only course.

While Alexis returned to the carriage to wait for her, Catherine hurriedly put on a black dress, for in order to associate herself in people's minds with the late Empress she still wore mourning. Accompanied by her maid, a lackey and a groom, she slipped out of the pavilion and across the park in the direction Alexis had indicated. But she lost her way and it took her a whole hour to find the carriage. She got in, while Alexis climbed into the driving seat and whipped up the horses.

During the thirty-mile drive to St Petersburg Catherine made plans. First thing, she would go to the Guards, a cross-section of educated men and the nearest thing to an assembly Russia possessed. If the Guards wanted her, they would acclaim her, as the legions used to acclaim a new emperor. In St Petersburg as in Rome it was popularity that counted, not primogeniture. She would explain to the Guards that her life was in danger – not strictly true, but it would, she hoped, arouse their chivalrous feelings.

The carriage raced along the bumpy road and presently met another going in the opposite direction. In it was Catherine's hairdresser, whom she had asked to come to Peterhof to dress her hair for the morrow's festivities. Catherine told the hairdresser that she wouldn't be needing him, then continued on her way.

Five miles short of St Petersburg Gregory Orlov was waiting for Catherine. He too was wearing Preobrazhensky uniform. He took her and Alexis from the hired carriage into his own, and the three of them drove to the barracks of the Izmailovsky regiment, on the outskirts of the city. Finding a drummer and a few guardsmen in front of the wooden barracks, Gregory ordered the drummer to beat the call to muster. Drumsticks rattled on stretched sheepskin, at once creating an atmosphere of excitement. Guardsmen hurried out of the barracks. Their colonel, Cyril Razumovsky, had made clear his dissatisfaction with the Emperor but on Catherine's instructions had held his hand regarding any protest action, so that the guardsmen were unprepared for Catherine's early morning visit. After their first surprise they pressed forward to kiss her hands and feet, and the hem of her black dress.

Catherine spoke to the guardsmen in the simple concrete language she habitually used. The Emperor, she said, is planning to kill me and my little son, but I have come to you less on my own account than for the sake of Russia and the Orthodox faith.

In this kind of situation what matters is self-confidence, and self-confidence Catherine plainly possessed. The soldiers responded with eager promises of help. Two of them fetched their chaplain, and there in the open the Izmailovsky guardsmen kissed the chaplain's crucifix and swore an oath of allegiance to Catherine.

Catherine resumed her seat in the carriage, where she was joined by Cyril Razumovsky, so that she now had three popular Guards officers beside her as she drove, still in the city suburbs, to the barracks of the second of the four Guards regiments, the Semeonovsky. Some of the Izmailovsky hurried ahead to announce her coming, the rest escorted her carriage.

Ten officers on average in each of the Guards regiments had promised Catherine their support, and those in the Semeonovsky had done their job well. When Catherine arrived scores of guardsmen, wearing their distinctive red tunics and high black gaiters, were waiting to acclaim her. 'Long live our Empress,' they shouted.

Catherine now had the allegiance of two of the Guards regiments. They were the less important of the four, but she decided all the same to enter St Petersburg. Preceded by the regimental chaplains carrying crosses and followed by the cheering guardsmen, she drove to the Cathedral of Our Lady of Kazan.

Catherine knew that the guardsmen's acclamations, if they were not to be hollow, must be solemnly sealed by the Church. She had taken pains to dissociate herself from Peter's offensive actions to the clergy and to show her approval of the late pious Empress. She had thus won over a number of senior Churchmen, including Benjamin, Metropolitan of St Petersburg, who, having been alerted by the Orlovs, was waiting for her now. Catherine and her followers entered the church, less than thirty years old but venerable by virtue of the icon of Our Lady, gleaming with gold and jewels, on the altar screen. Here Catherine and Peter had been married; here now Metropolitan Benjamin read aloud the short proclamation drafted in the early days of the plot by Catherine herself. It proclaimed Ekaterina Alekseievna Sovereign Autocrat, and her son, the Grand Duke Paul, her successor.

Catherine walked from the cathedral into the summer sunshine. Bells were pealing, the soldiers exultant in their show of strength. All seemed well, as she drove the half-mile to the palace. But Catherine was far from satisfied. The most important regiment, the Preobrazhensky, was not to be seen. What had happened to it?

The answer is given by the poet Derzhavin, a musketeer in the

Preobrazhensky. As soon as they heard Catherine was in St Petersburg Derzhavin's company, without any orders from their officers, hurried to the regimental barrack-square, loading arms as they ran. Derzhavin saw another company – grenadiers – running along Lityeinaya Street and one of their majors – Voeikov, the same who had arrested Passek – was on horseback, cursing them and hacking at their muskets and caps with his sword.

'Suddenly the grenadiers gave a roar and threw themselves on Voeikov with fixed bayonets; he was obliged to gallop away from them with all his force. Afraid that they might catch him on the Semeonovsky bridge, he turned to the right and rode into the Fontanka canal up to his horse's chest. There the grenadiers left him alone.

'In that way the third company of the Preobrazhensky regiment, and all the other companies, ran one after another over different bridges to the Winter Palace. There they found the Semeonovsky and Izmailovsky regiments, which had already arrived and surrounded the palace, and put their guards on all the exits.' 'Forgive us for being late,' the Preobrazhensky said to Catherine. 'Our officers tried to arrest us, but here are four of them, whom we arrested to show you our zeal. We want what our brothers want.'

Catherine stationed the Preobrazhensky inside the palace, where all took the oath. The Horse Guards arrived last, led by their officers. Amid this the only man to suffer was Prince Georg of Holstein. An obvious target for xenophobia, he was roughly treated by the Horse Guards, and had his house plundered before Catherine sent a platoon to rescue him.

The senators, a small but respected judicial and law-framing body, probably at Panin's invitation, waited in the palace, with the exception of Prince Nikita Trubetskoy, who was in Oranienbaum. Conservatives, they disapproved of the Emperor's behaviour, and when Catherine appeared in their midst both they and the Holy Synod saluted her as their Empress.

Once she was sure of the capital, Catherine turned to Russia. She wrote a manifesto, stressing the danger threatening the fatherland and the Orthodox religion, and declaring that she had yielded to her subjects' wishes that she should mount the throne. Printed in the cellar of the Academy of Sciences, copies of the manifesto were rushed to Moscow and a score of towns, to the Ukraine, to Siberia. Catherine sent couriers to the army corps, including those in Pomerania, ordering commanders to administer the oath of allegiance, and Admiral Taluizin to do the same in the naval base of Cronstadt.

By early evening Catherine found herself in a commanding position. She was mistress of St Petersburg, acclaimed by the most important civil and military groups – and no blood had been shed. She doubtless felt a strong temptation to remain in the safety of her palace, trusting that Peter would crumble. Or, if she thought he would put up a fight, to send a trusted and daring officer like Gregory at the head of a thousand picked troops to seize the deposed Emperor.

Catherine decided on a more daring course, one that would keep her at the centre of events. First, she had herself declared colonel of the Preobrazhensky. Putting on their green and red uniform, and their black three-cornered hat, which she decorated with oak leaves, symbol of victory, she mounted a dappled grey stallion, placed herself at the head of the Guards regiments and certain regiments of the line, and at ten o'clock that evening led this large body of soldiers – fourteen thousand – out of St Petersburg on the road to Oranienbaum. It was a dramatic sight, later depicted by painters: the slim figure of Catherine, for eighteen years subdued and victimized, at last in command, perfectly assured on horseback, attractive in her Guards uniform, at the head of company after company of soldiers, their boots thudding the road in unison.

The man they were marching against had woken that morning with a hangover. Peter spent the early hours sweating it off on the parade ground and, pleased with his Holsteiners' performance, set off in a better mood for Peterhof where it had been arranged he would take his midday meal.

Peter arrived at Monplaisir with his suite in six carriages shortly after two o'clock. He was wearing blue Prussian uniform, for his friend King Frederick had recently given him the colonelcy of a regiment. He entered the brick pavilion, where, to his surprise, he saw neither Catherine nor her maid. He searched all the rooms, looking under the beds and even opening wardrobes. Nowhere in Peterhof was there any sign of Catherine.

Peter assumed his wife had gone to St Petersburg, perhaps on some innocent errand but perhaps – and he was thinking of Captain Passek – with sinister intentions. He therefore sent Prince Nikita Trubetskoy, Alexander Shuvalov and Grand Chancellor Vorontsov to St Petersburg to bring him definite information about Catherine.

At three o'clock, soon after the emissaries had left, a longboat was seen approaching over the calm waters of the Baltic. It tied up at the palace jetty and from it stepped a certain Lieutenant von Bernhorst, a bombardier specializing in fireworks who, like Catherine's hairdresser, had left the capital in order to prepare for the morrow's festivities. Peter questioned him anxiously but Bernhorst was either very discreet or very unobservant. All the fireworks-man would say was that there had been great comings and goings by the Guards that morning, and a rumour that Catherine had arrived in the city.

Peter began to pace the park in great agitation. Apart from a thousand Holsteiners at Oranienbaum, he had no troops. The nearest source of troops was the island of Cronstadt, five miles across the bay, and the first thing Peter did was to send a colonel by boat to fetch 3000 men from Cronstadt.

What would he do when they arrived? Field Marshal Münnich suggested he should go by sea to St Petersburg, show himself to the Guards, and exhort them to return to their allegiance. The Prussian ambassador, Goltz, urged him to make for Narva, seventy miles west, and join the army destined for Denmark. Others urged him to go himself to Cronstadt, or to flee to Holstein, to the Ukraine, even to Finland.

Peter paced up and down beside the canal that ran through the park, covering his doubts by dictating to four secretaries at once a string of unimportant orders and ukases; when they were written down he leaned the papers on a stone balustrade to sign. It took him almost an hour to reach a decision. He would stay and fight, not in Peterhof or Oranienbaum, which were difficult to defend, but in Cronstadt. At four o'clock, cancelling his previous order, Peter sent General De Vier and Prince Barayatinsky to Cronstadt, the former to take command, the latter to bring back news as soon as the port's loyalty was assured.

Three hours passed. Peter had heard nothing from Vorontsov and company: though he did not know it yet, they had defected. He had heard nothing either from a messenger sent to two regiments in St Petersburg who he believed would never desert him. Beginning to be alarmed, Peter summoned his Holsteiners and dug them in in that part of the park which served as a menagerie. He changed his Prussian uniform for that of the Preobrazhensky with the blue ribbon of St Andrew, worn by the sovereign. Then he ate supper on a wooden bench by the canal – a dish of meat and bread and butter, and several glasses of champagne and burgundy.

At ten o'clock Peter received his first piece of good news: Barayatinsky returned to say that Cronstadt lay at his Majesty's disposal. Gathering Elizabeth Vorontsova and those of his suite who remained, Peter led them down to the jetty. There they embarked on a galley and two small pleasure ships. Casting off, they struck out, under sail and oar, into the grey tideless waters of the Baltic. Helped by a favourable breeze, they made good headway and well before midnight drew close to Cronstadt's harbour walls, guarded by cannon.

In the milky light Peter could see that the harbour was closed by a boom. He ordered a small boat to be lowered and, getting into it with Field Marshal Münnich, was rowed towards the main fortress. As the boat neared the steep walls a midshipman hailed them: 'Keep back or I fire.'

Peter stood up in the boat and removing his cloak displayed, diagonally across his uniform, the blue ribbon of the Order of St Andrew. 'Don't you know me?' he shouted. 'I am your Emperor.'

Back from the grey walls came the midshipman's reply: 'We no longer have an Emperor. Long live Catherine the Second.'

Without disputing the man's claim, without even replying, Peter had himself rowed back to the galley, where he sank on to a bench, so shocked he could neither move nor speak. The would-be tough military commander, the man who had aspired to be a new Frederick, collapsed – and did so moreover in the face not of cannon on a corpse-strewn battlefield but of one midshipman on a distant wall.

Peter had not been betrayed by Prince Barayatinsky. It was perfectly true that General De Vier had taken command of the port. But after the prince had left Admiral Taluizin arrived. With news of the coup and an order signed by Catherine he had no difficulty in winning over the troops and ratings.

Peter's collapse was total. He abandoned all his plans, even plans to escape. Returning to Oranienbaum, he arranged for the safety of his suite and then wrote a letter to Catherine, telling the Vice-Chancellor, Prince Golitsuin, to deliver it into his wife's hands.

Catherine and her soldiers had marched fifteen miles and were resting at St Sergius's Hermitage. There Catherine received the letter. In it Peter apologized to his wife, and offered to share the throne with her. Catherine remarked to Golitsuin that the welfare of the State now demanded other measures. She did not reply to the letter and Golitsuin, instead of returning, swore allegiance to Catherine.

Peter waited in vain for the Vice-Chancellor's return. Then he wrote a second letter, this time in pencil, offering to give up the throne, and entrusted it to his adjutant, Izmailov. When Catherine read it, she said, 'Very well, I accept the offer, but I must have the abdication in writing.' She had Izmailov draft a form of abdication, and when it was worded to her satisfaction told Izmailov, with Alexis Orlov to keep an eye on him, to carry it to Peter.

Catherine decided to play out the next scene at the palace associated with Peter the Great and Elizabeth, and she did so with a sure sense of drama. She ordered her soldiers to Peterhof, and when they were rested and in position arrived there herself, still in her colonel's uniform, handling her grey stallion with ease, to be welcomed by enthusiastic cheers. She received the act of abdication – 'I, Peter, of my own free will solemnly renounce the throne of Russia to the end of my days.' Having verified her husband's signature, Catherine handed the document to an adviser for safe-keeping.

An hour later Peter arrived in a dusty, long-disused carriage. Feeling against him ran high and the soldiers would probably have done him harm, had not Panin picked and disposed 300 sure men in a protective square. Accompanied by Alexis Orlov, Peter was hurried to a wing of the palace. Catherine did not see him; their last meeting had been two days earlier at a friend's house, when he had told her to prepare for his name-day 'a dinner fit to eat'.

Now his name-day had arrived, but instead of fireworks and a banquet Peter saw hatred on the soldiers' faces, and muskets with fixed bayonets. He believed he had acted according to his deepest self during his reign, the little blue-uniformed boy of Kiel, and this was his reward, to be hustled under arrest to a menial's room in his own palace. There his captors removed from his body the uniform of the Preobrazhensky, the regiment to which he had taught German-style efficiency and issued free vodka. He was now totally stripped of Russia, and reverted to what he had always wanted to be, Duke of little Holstein.

But this metamorphosis happened not of his own will, but roughly, with indignity, at others' hands, as during a nightmare wishes are realized in horribly perverted form. It proved too much for Peter, and he collapsed unconscious on the floor.

When he came round, a more considerate person was in the room. Where would he like to stay, asked Nikita Panin, until arrangements had been made for his future? As Grand Duke, Peter had sometimes stayed at a medium-sized country house belonging to the Crown called Ropsha. It lay quite close and there was fishing to be had in its pond. Peter suggested Ropsha.

Catherine did not know yet what she would do with Peter. Tsar Ivan VI, deposed as a child, had been imprisoned for twenty-one years; it looked as though Peter would have to be imprisoned too. But Peter had made some popular reforms, his portrait was on the coinage, he could well become a focal point for trouble. When Panin returned from seeing Peter, Catherine agreed to Ropsha. But her husband must be very closely guarded. Catherine felt no tenderness for him, even in her triumph no indulgence. In other circumstances she might have said, Not a hair of this man's head must be harmed, but having led Russia to the brink of chaos Peter had forfeited her protection; indeed he was still a threat to Russia, and so she appointed as his gaoler the toughest of her friends, Alexis Orlov.

At six o'clock that evening a detachment of Horse Guards formed up in the courtyard, commanded by Alexis and including an efficient young warrant officer named Gregory Potemkin. A figure was hustled into a carriage with drawn blinds; then the carriage rumbled away, escorted by the Horse Guards.

Catherine was nearly exhausted. This day and its predecessor had taxed her nerves, her will and her body to the limit. Nevertheless, she again put herself at the head of her soldiers when she learned that that was what they wished and began the march back. At Prince Kurakin's estate she snatched a couple of hours' sleep, and on Sunday morning made a triumphant entry into the capital. This time there was nothing to mar the joy but her own tiredness. After attending Mass and a solemn *Te Deum* she ate a light meal and went to bed. She slept till midnight when a rumour that the Prussians were coming to carry her off ran rife among the tipsy soldiers, and she had to get up, dress, talk to the men and reassure them. Then she slept a further eight hours.

Next morning Gregory Orlov came to see her. He was delighted of course at the success of the coup. But in raising Catherine to the throne he felt that he had lost his mistress. He sensed that he was not cut out for Court life, that he would prove an embarrassment now to Catherine. So he came to ask her permission to retire to the country.

Catherine understood Gregory's feelings. He was a generous man, and this was a generous offer. In a way he was right. She knew that Panin and Princess Dashkova, to name only two, looked down on unpolished Gregory. But she was in love with him and he with her. So she asked Gregory – and it was almost an order – to stay. It would injure his work, she explained, if he allowed her to seem ungrateful to the very man who had helped her most. Then she placed over his uniform the red ribbon of the Order of St Alexander, one of Russia's highest, and handed him the gold key of Chamberlain, which carried with it the rank of Major General.

Peter meanwhile had arrived at Ropsha, where he was assigned a medium-sized ground-floor bedroom. The green blinds on its window were drawn so that soldiers patrolling the grounds day and night could not see in, and armed sentries stood guard outside the locked door.

Peter was accustomed to walking a lot, so he suffered from his cramped quarters. He still felt shame at showing his body, so he suffered too from having to use a close-stool with an officer watching. He lodged complaints on both scores, but no change was made. Then he wrote as follows to Catherine: 'If you do not want to kill a man already sufficiently miserable, have pity on me and give me my only consolation, which is Elizabeth Romanovna [Vorontsova].' This request Catherine refused.

Peter probably questioned Alexis Orlov about his future. He would have been told that most people expected him to be imprisoned in Schlüsselburg fortress. This must have come as a great shock to Peter, who had been hoping to go to Holstein. Only three months earlier, in an interview with Peter, Prisoner Number One had babbled a wild tale that Tsar Ivan had long since been taken up to heaven, and that he was a different Ivan who nevertheless supported his namesake's claims. It was obvious to Peter that a lifetime of solitary confinement had driven the deposed Tsar mad.

Fear of Schlüsselburg, fear of going mad himself in that prison – these began to weigh on Peter's depleted strength. On the third day of his captivity his health broke. He suffered from acute diarrhoea, probably caused by fear, and severe mental confusion.

Alexis Orlov informed Catherine by letter, referring to Peter not as 'the ex-Emperor' or 'the prisoner', but as 'the monster'. Plainly this was a term in use between Catherine and those who engineered the coup. It carried a considerable degree of hatred, and an alarming implication that Peter no longer possessed ordinary human rights.

'We and the whole detachment are all well, but our monster has fallen very sick and has had an unexpected attack of colic. I am afraid that he might die tonight, and fear still more that he might live. The first fear I have because he chatters pure nonsense, and that amuses us; and the second fear, because he is really dangerous for us all, often speaking as if he had his former position.'

Awkwardly expressed though they be, Alexis's feelings are clear. He believed Peter was going to die and on balance was pleased, not least because he disliked guarding a man who in some people's eyes was still Emperor.

On Wednesday evening Peter's physician, Dr Lüders, came to Ropsha, examined the prisoner and gave him medicine. On Thursday Lüders called in Staff Surgeon Paulsen for a second opinion. Later that same day both doctors declared Peter to have recovered. There was, they said, no longer any danger. And, as though to demonstrate their conviction, they left Ropsha.

Alexis had felt sure Peter would die. He had been counting on it, seeing all the advantages to him, such as being able to return to St Petersburg. He certainly felt a sense of being cheated at this news of recovery, and his hatred of the monster grew. Doubtless he fed it by thoughts of how dangerous Peter still was to Catherine; she was obliged to keep St Petersburg on a war footing: 'numerous pickets,' says Derzhavin, 'were posted on all bridges, squares and crossroads, with their cannon loaded and fuses ready to be lit.' It could be argued that it would be an act of patriotism not to let Peter live.

Among the officers at Ropsha was a certain Gregory Teplov, the son of a stoker of stoves, but intelligent and well educated, for many years Cyril Razumovsky's right-hand man. Orlov the soldier opened his mind to Teplov the hardened politician and the two formed a conspiracy within a conspiracy.

On Saturday morning, his seventh at Ropsha, Peter was sleeping in his four-poster bed, which at his request had been brought from Oranienbaum, when his valet, who had gone for a breath of fresh air in the grounds, was suddenly seized by command of the officer on duty, gagged, thrust into a closed carriage and sent away. At two o'clock Peter sat down to dinner. Perhaps he had again adopted his tone of rightful Emperor, which so provoked his gaolers. With the valet safely out of the way, it seems to have been at this meal that Alexis introduced poison – perhaps readily-available rat poison, containing arsenic – into the food or coffee. Having eaten and drunk, Peter was seized with severe stomach pains, and Alexis called a doctor.

Events so far are reported by a well-informed Danish envoy; the sequel is given by Keith's successor, Buckinghamshire.

The doctor 'found that wretched prisoner in a high fever and convulsed, but so far sensible as to know him. As he thought he discovered some symptoms of poison, he immediately desired some milk might be brought. Alexis Orlov and Teplov, who had the care of him, ordered with great seeming eagerness that some should be sent for immediately, but after having waited a considerable time the surgeon was told that no milk could be found in any of the villages; they then sent him away.'

Alexis dashed off a note to Catherine telling her that he did not expect Peter to live till nightfall, saying he feared her anger at having allowed his prisoner to die 'or that you should think that we were the cause of the death of the monster, monster to you and all Russia.'

Peter was still alive. Perhaps the poison would not kill him. If so, Alexis would be in deep trouble. It seems probable that alone or again with Teplov he decided to finish the job by other means. So thought Buckinghamshire. 'The Emperor was probably first poisoned and then strangled, as the appearance of his neck and countenance, when afterwards the body was exposed, seemed to indicate.' When the strangling was done and Peter lay dead, Alexis hurried to St Petersburg to inform the Empress.

What Catherine felt is unrecorded. It can only be conjectured. Probably her first reaction was shock, for Peter was only thirty-four and before the coup had enjoyed excellent health. Her second reaction was probably a form of gladness. It was good to be rid of a man hateful to her as a woman, dangerous to her as an Empress. But when she learned the manner of his death – and Alexis told her everything – Catherine was probably very angry. Many times she may have wished Peter's death in her heart, but wishing someone dead was a very different matter from murder.

Catherine immediately faced a dilemma. Was she going to make the truth known? If she did, she would be sending Alexis to prison, indirectly tarnishing her own name and perhaps dooming the golden age she hoped to give Russia. If she did not, she would be starting her reign with a lie. She faced in short the classic dilemma of a sovereign in every age: which comes first: conscience, duty to the truth, or the public good, duty to the State?

Catherine chose the second course, just as in an earlier dilemma she had chosen to become Orthodox, and so Peter's wife. She decided to make the murder look like natural death. She had the body dissected by a doctor she could trust, and a certificate signed explaining the death by natural causes. With the object of making Peter ridiculous in death as he had so often been in life, she issued a manifesto declaring that the late Emperor had died of a haemorrhoidal colic which had affected his brain and brought on apoplexy.

Describing the coup to Stanislaus Poniatowski, Catherine wrote, 'Everything was carried out on the principle of hatred of the foreigner, Peter the Third counted as such.' She therefore stated – and it may well be untrue – that when he knew he was dying Peter called not for an Orthodox but for a Lutheran priest. She had the body laid out in a blue Holstein uniform, complete with boots and gloves, his bruised and mottled neck partially hidden by a cravat. Because he had not been crowned, he could not lie with the Tsars, and Catherine had him buried in the St Alexander Nevsky Monastery. Catherine did not attend his funeral – 'for reasons of health'.

It was an unfortunate beginning. Catherine could hide the truth from the Russians, but not from Europe. 'When a heavy drinker dies of colic,' quipped Voltaire, 'it teaches us to be sober.' Newspapers in Paris and London, in Dresden and Leipzig, spoke of a return to the cruel days of Ivan the Terrible, while one German periodical compared Ropsha to Berkeley Castle, and Catherine to Isabella, Queen of England, who had instigated the murder of her husband King Edward II.

These were the speculations of distant observers. Catherine probably felt some guilt for having wished the death of her husband and she could not pretend that it would have happened if she had acted differently, but of her being involved in the murder directly or indirectly there is not a particle of evidence, while the evidence against it is plentiful. François Pictet, an honest Swiss who served as secretary to Gregory Orlov and later to Catherine, maintained that Catherine had never been an accomplice to her husband's death. One day, years later, when Leo Naruishkin had played an exasperating practical joke on her and the Prince de Ligne, Catherine said banteringly to Ligne, 'Come on, let's strangle him,' and Ligne took the use of such a word in such a context to be a sign of her innocence. There is also the verdict of Frederick, who had few illusions about human nature. Left to herself, he said, Catherine would have kept Peter alive, partly because she believed he could be made harmless, partly because she saw, or thought she saw, the effect that putting him out of the world would have on public opinion, both inside and outside Russia. He concluded that Catherine had taken no part, direct or indirect, in the murder. Finally, a piece of strong evidence was to emerge thirty-four years later. Shortly after Catherine's death her son Paul, we are told by Paul's friend Rostopchin, instituted a frantic search among her private papers for a document that would prove or disprove her involvement. He found a scribbled note, in Alexis Orlov's hand, that had been sent to her from Ropsha immediately after the event. He interpreted its contents as exonerating his mother from complicity in the murder, much to his relief. Later he burned the note.

On the very day she heard of Peter's death Catherine turned to the next part of her programme. The *coup d'état* had been only one half of a diptych; the other half was to be her coronation. Catherine knew that she was not yet fully Empress in the minds of her people, and would not become so until she had been anointed by the Church's representative and was seen to wear on her brow the crown of the Tsars.

On the first of September Catherine left St Petersburg with her advisers and all her Court, a mammoth migration requiring 19,000 horses. Nikita Trubetskoy, who had been sent ahead with 50,000 roubles, all she could afford, welcomed Catherine to Moscow with arches of greenery. Catherine as a rule disliked Moscow and its parochialism, but on this occasion she rejoiced in its age-old traditions, which alone could lend her authority. She lodged in the Great Palace of the Kremlin, and with her was her seven-year-old son. Assumed by all to be a Romanov, little Paul would be a useful figure in the ceremonies, since he linked Catherine with the first Romanov Tsar, Michael, crowned in Moscow in 1613.

Catherine approached the ceremonies with the utmost seriousness, reading up their history, taking the best advice and deciding to emphasize the quasi-priestly character of the monarch who in Russia was head of both State and Church. Knowing her own vulnerability as a foreigner, she wished in short to assume the full mantle of authority.

For two weeks Catherine fasted and remained secluded in the Great Palace. At five in the morning of Sunday, 23rd September 1762, twenty-one cannon fired a salute, and all taking part in the ceremony gathered in the Kremlin. At eight, soldiers surrounded the cathedral and the adjoining square, while all Moscow's church bells began to peal. At ten, to the sound of trumpets and kettle-drums, Catherine left her private apartments. Wearing a dress of ermine-trimmed silk brocade, its long train carried by six chamberlains, she walked with slow dignity to the audience chamber, where senior gentlemen and clerics greeted her; preceded by her confessor, who sprinkled her path with holy water, she went down the steps of the Beautiful Staircase, used only at coronations, and crossed to the almost adjoining Assumption Cathedral.

It was a small rectangular five-domed building, which in the West would have been called a chapel, but so crammed with gold and silver ornaments, jewelled icons, frescoes, crosses on chains and candlelit shrines that it gained in intensity what it lacked in size. From the central dome hung a silver chandelier weighing over a ton, while all the pillars were covered with frescoes on a gold ground.

Catherine seated herself on a diamond- and ruby-studded throne, set on a dais in the centre of the cathedral. After welcoming her, the Archbishop of Novgorod said, 'May Your Majesty deign, according to the custom of ancient Christian monarchs, to profess in the hearing of your faithful subjects the Holy Orthodox Faith.' Catherine then read aloud the Creed.

Had the ceremony taken place in Westminster or in Vienna, Catherine would have been a passive recipient; here in Moscow she took an active role. It was Catherine who placed on her own shoulders the imperial purple mantle, she who lifted the replica of a lost twelfth-century crown, known as the crown of Vladimir Monomachos, and placed it on her own head. She then picked up the orb in her left hand, the sceptre in her right, and stood very straight, arrayed with all the visible emblems of her imperial authority, while in the square outside cannon fired salvo after salvo.

Catherine knelt and prayed aloud. 'Thou, my Lord and God, instruct me in the work which Thou hast assigned to me, send me understanding and guidance in this great service. Let the wisdom which dwells at Thy throne be with me.' A Russian monarch took no oath to observe fundamental laws, made no promises to the gentry or to the people. The coronation was a pact between Catherine and God, and having been crowned her authority had no more limit than His.

The Archbishop began to celebrate Mass. During the Epistle and Gospel Catherine knelt; at other times she stood, wearing the crown. After the consecration she did something that even pious Elizabeth had not done. She passed through the doors of the iconostasis, which screened the sanctuary from the rest of the cathedral and which was reserved for priests. In this holy of holies she knelt, while the Archbishop anointed her as monarch on the brow, the breast and both hands. Rising, Catherine went to the altar and there she performed an action which was her right as monarch but which no woman ruler had exercised before. With her own hands she raised the chalice and partook of the consecrated wine in which was soaked the consecrated leavened bread.

The remaining prayers were intoned, the long ceremony drew to a close. Eighteen years before, Sophie of Anhalt-Zerbst had arrived in Russia dowerless and powerless. Now she found herself by the grace of God Catherine the Second, Empress Autocratrix of all the Russias, of Moscow, Kiev, Vladimir, Novgorod, Tsarina of Kazan, Tsarina of Astrakhan, Tsarina of Siberia, Lady of Pskov, Grand Duchess of Smolensk, Princess of Estonia, Livonia, Karelia, Tver, Perm, Vyatka . . . and of other places running to eight more lines of text; ruler – sole ruler, with no consort by her side – of an empire considerably larger than the Roman Empire at its height.

CHAPTER 14

REFORMING RUSSIA

In order to begin to rule the new Empress required to know certain basic facts. So she went to the Senate. 'How many towns are there in Russia?' Catherine asked this body of thirty distinguished men, which included the Heads of the Colleges or Ministries. No one knew. Catherine suggested looking at the map. There was no map. Catherine then took five roubles from her purse and sent a clerk across the Neva to the Academy of Sciences to buy a copy of the latest map of Russia. When the clerk returned, Catherine presented the map to the Senate and the towns were counted.

With that gesture and at that moment Catherine left the sheltered world of a civilized Court and stepped into Russia as it was: ignorant, superstitious, disorganized, unruly, sometimes hungry, often diseased, always to a European appallingly backward. She wanted to begin straight away bettering things, and for that she needed money. Again she turned to the Senate. What was the condition of the finances? This the Senate knew, roughly. As a result of the Seven Years' War, they said, Russia was heavily in debt and her credit so low that Holland had refused a two million rouble loan which Empress Elizabeth had tried to float. In the current year revenue of 28 million roubles would fall short of expenditure by the staggering sum of 7 million.

Catherine was shocked by the deficit and disturbed too when the senators, having imparted the figures, left everything for a complicated lawsuit about one meadow near the small town of Mosalsk, spending six whole weeks just listening to the records of the case.

Catherine decided that her first and overriding task would be to increase Russia's wealth. Everything else depended on that. And since Russia was primarily agricultural she began with the land. She sent experts to outlying regions to study soil and propose suitable crops; she made grants to landowners to learn the improved techniques being devised in England, whereby turnips, clover and rye grass were alternated with grain crops, and to buy the agricultural machines that were beginning to be invented there. She arranged for silkworms to be cultivated, and encouraged the rearing of honey-bees; she extended the Ukraine tobacco plantations and offered bounties for high yields; she commissioned a descriptive catalogue of Russian plants; she encouraged the introduction of modern methods of breeding sheep and cattle; she promoted scientific horse-breeding, and Alexis Orlov, one of the pioneers in this sphere, crossed Arabs and Friesians with notable success.

Catherine saw the need for creating a pool of practical knowledge. As a foreigner, she knew of societies and publications in other countries. With these in mind she founded the Free Economic Society where landowners could meet to exchange information and discuss problems. Technical essays were published in the Society's journal, which Catherine paid for, and in the Academy of Science's bulletins. According to a British visitor, Archdeacon Coxe, 'No country can boast, within the space of so many years, such a number of excellent publications on its internal state.'

To work the underpopulated land Catherine saw that more labour was needed. She set Gregory Orlov at the head of a board to encourage immigration. It placed advertisements in foreign, mainly German, newspapers, inviting settlers and offering attractive terms: six months' free lodging; seed, livestock and ploughs; exemption from taxes for five, ten or thirty years, according to a man's skills. The response was excellent; furniture piled into covered wagons, thousands took the road Catherine and her mother had taken twenty years before, to work the rich black soil of southern Russia. These settlers played an important part in feeding a population that was to grow steadily through the next three decades.

Catherine paid special attention to wealth under the earth. She sent geologists to collect and assess ores from Russia's seemingly desert lands, among them Samuel Bentham, the inventive engineer brother of impractical Jeremy, who collected in Siberia half a ton of assorted minerals, mainly copper and iron ore, including loadstones, and wrote a report for Catherine, suggesting that the ores be extracted not by gunpowder but by pulverizing machinery.

Once new deposits were found, Catherine allowed merchants to own and work the mines, not just the gentry, as in previous reigns. To provide technicians she founded in St Petersburg Russia's first School of Mines, including a simulated underground mine, with shafts and tunnels, where trainees could learn under realistic conditions.

Catherine took a special interest in silver, because by law that metal belonged to the crown and because when she came to the throne she found a grave shortage of silver roubles – only four per head of the population. Here she was fortunate to strike it rich. In 1768 her prospectors found important silver deposits on the frontier of Mongolia, and by 1773 supplies from these mines, 3000 miles away, were swelling her budget. From all varieties of metal Catherine was to increase mining revenue by 30 per cent during her reign to an annual 13 million roubles.

Furs had long been an important item in Russia's natural wealth. As early as 1245 the King of England's tailor went to Lynn in Norfolk and bought from Edmund of Gothland £174 17s 1d worth of 'greywork', the fur of the Arctic squirrels taken in winter by Russian trappers and marketed in Novgorod. Catherine encouraged the existing fur trade, mainly in Siberia, and promoted hunting expeditions to the recently-discovered Aleutian Islands: that of Dmitri Bragin, lasting five years, brought back 200,000 roubles' worth of furs, mainly sea-otter.

When she turned from Russia's natural wealth to manufacturing, Catherine found that under the dilatory Elizabeth, senators, notably Peter Shuvalov, had taken matters into their own hands and established a tight system of monopolies and controls. Catherine had an aversion to theories, particularly economic theories. She preferred to work from common sense and her observations of human nature, and these inclined her to what would be called free trade. One of her first actions on coming to the throne was to end these monopolies and controls. As early as October 1762 she decreed that except in Moscow, which was overcrowded, and in St Petersburg, which was a show city with its own needs, anyone could start a manufactory. Later she decreed that anyone could set up a loom and weave for profit. Soon enterprising State peasants were running quite large textile businesses, and there came into being a whole range of cottage industries: linen, pottery, leather goods and furniture.

For more sophisticated enterprises Catherine called on expert help from abroad, and partly because she wanted to play down her German connection she turned most often to England. She brought over Admiral Knowles to build warships and dockyards, paying him three times as much as a Russian admiral, and she sent workmen from the important Tula steelworks to England to study latest methods of making barometers, thermometers, mathematical instruments and spectacles. Sensitive to cold, Catherine made a point of placing a thermometer not only in certain rooms of her palaces, but in all the rooms, as well as outside all the windows. The incidence of breakage by servants was high, so Catherine arranged to buy up all the thermometers produced by the Tula works.

Catherine developed manufactories for textiles, especially in the Moscow region, for linen in the Yaroslav region, and for leather, tallow and candles along the central Volga. Altogether during her reign Catherine was to increase the number of manufactories from 984 to 3161.

Catherine brought in German, Austrian and French craftsmen to improve the imperial porcelain works; she also enlarged and improved the output of the imperial tapestry works. Tapestries were still an essential furnishing for well-to-do houses and handy as gifts to important friends. Catherine gave the second Earl of Buckinghamshire, the envoy who admired her horsemanship, a very fine tapestry depicting Peter the Great on horseback winning the battle of Poltava, which may be admired to this day in Blickling Hall, Norfolk.

In the sphere of foreign trade Catherine achieved remarkable results by the simple expedient of abolishing export duties. Russia's main exports were timber for masts, hemp, flax, their seeds and oils, fats, raw leather, furs, linen cloth and iron, 'Old Fox', the brand name of Urals iron, being particularly sought after.

Since Tudor times English merchants had enjoyed commercial privileges and gathered into their hands two-thirds of Russia's foreign trade. Friendly though she was to England, Catherine decided to end this special relationship. She signed a series of trade treaties with Spain, Portugal, Denmark, the two Sicilies, and, later in her reign, with France. Freer bargaining worked to Russia's advantage, and foreign trade was to rise sharply from an average 13.8 million roubles in the 1760s to 43.2 million in the early 1790s while Russia's favourable trade balance was to double, to 3.6 million roubles.

One aspect of Catherine's foreign trade is of great interest. When she came to the throne, China had just seized a district on the River Amur believed to contain silver which Russia claimed was hers. Catherine strengthened her army in Siberia to eleven regiments, then sent a special envoy to settle the dispute and to reopen trade. The Treaty of Kyakhta, signed in October 1768, soon had camel caravans passing to and from Manchuria. China exported cottons, silks, tobacco, porcelain, lacquerware, preserved and jellied fruits, silver and tea – superior, Russians claimed, to the tea drunk in Europe, which lost some of its flavour in the salt air of a long voyage. Russia sent China furs, leather, linens, foreign-made cloth, Bengal and Turkish opium. During the early part of her reign Catherine corresponded with Voltaire, then running his Ferney estate on sound business lines. Between fulsome compliments Voltaire asked Catherine if she would be kind enough to market some of the watches made at Ferney; Catherine agreed and the bales of one of her camel caravans carried Voltaire's Swiss watches to be sold to the mandarins of Peking. Russia's exports to China rose from nil at the beginning of the reign to 1,806,000 roubles in 1781, bringing Catherine customs and excise revenue of 600,000 roubles.

These measures, combined with tight cost control and an end to tax-farming, produced remarkably quick results. As early as 1765 Catherine had repaid three-quarters of the debt from Elizabeth's reign, and turned a budget deficit of seven million roubles into a surplus of 5.5 million, while State revenue was increasing by three per cent annually. She was now in a position to undertake major reforms.

Catherine found Russia divided into eleven *gubernii*, or governments, each administered by a governor-general, usually a soldier, who received no salary and had a tiny staff. The governor-general's task was to keep order with knout and bayonet; usually he also amassed enough in bribes to be able to retire at the end of three years in comfort.

Some of the *gubernii* were unmanageably large, and Catherine began by dividing the largest, making fifteen in all. She also sought to standardize, replacing the Hetman, or Military Commander, of the Ukraine by a governor-general acting for a Little Russian Board, and declaring that Livonia – the Baltic province, which retained many German ways – 'must be induced by the gentlest methods to consent to being Russified'. She brought to trial the Governor of Smolensk and his staff for taking bribes, and the Governor of Belgorod and his staff for running an illegal vodka distillery, replacing them with honest men, and paying all governors an adequate salary.

In April 1764 Catherine issued instructions to the governor-generals. They were to rule in an enlightened and rational manner; they were to take an accurate census, map their provinces, and report on the people, their customs, agriculture and trade. They were no longer just to keep order: they were to build and repair roads and bridges, fight fires, and ensure that orphanages and prisons were properly run. For this they would need staff. Catherine doubled the number of provincial civil servants and by 1767 was spending nearly one quarter of her budget on provincial government and services.

The second phase of modernization began in 1775, after a Cossack rising to be described later had shown that administration was still imperfect. Between January and May 1775 Catherine composed her Fundamental Law on the Administration of the Provinces. This reduced still further the size of administrative units, and increased their number from fifteen to forty-one (later forty-two). It established in each province a Board of Public Welfare, with an initial endowment from Catherine of 15,000 roubles, to which local gentry added according to their means. Local representatives sat on the board, whose task it was to run the schools and hospitals Catherine was beginning to build, and to ensure that local people – not only men on the governor's staff as in the past – administered justice. Henceforth the judge and members of the gentry's court, the members of the burghers' court, and the members of the peasants' court were all elected locally.

Catherine had good memories of her girlhood in Zerbst, the sturdy walled town with its craftsmen, its brewery, its strong community feeling. And near Zerbst were other thriving towns, such as Köthen, where the people made gold and silver lace, and where Bach had been Kappelmeister. She wanted to create such towns in Russia, where towns were so few that the Senate should certainly have known their number.

In 1763 the centre of Tver burned down. Instead of allowing it to be rebuilt in the old fire-trap style, pine or spruce houses set higgledy-piggledy in enclosures surrounded by animal pens and storage sheds, Catherine referred the matter to a Commission on Building, under Prince Ivan Betskoy, a former diplomat, fifty-nine years old, who had spent much of his life in Europe and had been a close friend of her mother.

On Catherine's instructions, Betskoy's Commission drew up a plan for Tver, which would also serve for all future towns. A main street joined two big squares, one for administrative buildings, the other for shops and stalls. From this radiated side streets, on the gridiron pattern of classical Roman times; in order to reduce the risk of fire they averaged 75 feet wide. The whole town was four versts (2.6 miles) in diameter.

With a gift of 100,000 roubles from Catherine and a 200,000-rouble Government loan, Tver was rebuilt on this plan. In the first eight years of the reign sixteen other towns burned down and were rebuilt on the same neat model.

In 1775, with the second stage of her modernization programme, Catherine began creating new towns as administrative centres for the new districts brought into being by her provincial reorganization. She gave merchants priority in buying lots in the centre of each town, where two-storey brick or stone houses were to be built, arranged interest-free loans to cover the cost and exempted owners from taxes for five years. The zone contiguous to the centre consisted of widely spaced one-storey stuccoed wooden houses on stone foundations; in the outer zone wooden houses were built in straight streets. Manufactories were restricted to the suburbs, those such as tanneries that polluted the water had to be sited downstream from the residential zones.

Not all Catherine's new towns were built from scratch. Sometimes a village got a few administrative buildings and a grand name: Black Muck for instance became Imperial City. On the other hand, a typical new town, Ostrakhov, possessed by the end of the reign 293 new houses, 73 of stone or brick, 132 shops, and a quota of those public welfare buildings which will be discussed presently. Catherine, who rarely boasted, took pride in the fact that between 1775 and 1785 in a land with no civic traditions outside the capitals, and little stone suitable for houses, she created 216 new towns.

Catherine had received a sensible education, and one way the good sense showed itself was her readiness to credit any sound habits she had to Babet. More than most people in the eighteenth century she believed in the power of education to improve a people, while in Russia she found a land almost without education. It lacked schools altogether other than a few Church schools – mainly seminaries – and Peter the Great's technical colleges for future army and navy officers. On all sides Catherine found that appalling ignorance coupled with complacency which Peter the Great's engineer, John Perry, had called 'the check and discouragement to ingenuity'.

At the beginning of her reign, in collaboration with Prince Betskoy, Catherine wrote 'A General Statute for the Education of the Youth of Both Sexes', publishing it in March 1764. It is just a short essay, but it states certain important principles on which Catherine intended to act: education is the responsibility of the State; it must begin early, at five or six; it must consist not only of book-learning but of character-training; and – this was a startling innovation – it must provide for girls as well as boys.

Catherine began with girls. She converted a St Petersburg convent built by Elizabeth into a boarding-school modelled mainly on Madame de Maintenon's Saint-Cyr. Girls entered the Smolny Institute, as it was called, at five or six and remained till eighteen. They were divided into two 'streams'. Daughters of gentry learned religion, Russian, foreign languages, arithmetic, geography, history, heraldry, the elements of law, drawing, music, knitting and sewing, dancing and society manners. The other stream, burghers' daughters, took many of the same subjects, but foreign languages were replaced by more domestic skills. Catherine laid down that from time to time a hundred poor women should dine in the school, so that girls could learn their responsibilities towards the unfortunate, and make them gifts of alms or linen. She often visited the school herself and watched performances of plays there; in 1773 she was seen by Diderot surrounded by all the girls – 440 of them – 'embracing her, jumping up to her arms, her head, her neck'. Diderot, who liked a good cry, gave the scene his accolade: 'It was a sight touching to the point of tears.'

The Smolny Institute was special to St Petersburg. In planning her State schools Catherine felt the need of advice and turned to a man who had been chaplain to the English factory in St Petersburg, and also to Sir Charles Hanbury-Williams. Daniel Dumaresq was a tall, ungainly, likeable scholar who had been born in Jersey and become a Fellow of Exeter College, Oxford, then rector of a Somerset village, Yeovilton. There, one day in 1764, a letter arrived not unlike the letter that had reached Zerbst one fateful New Year's Day. 'Mistaking my zeal and industry,' said Dumaresq, 'for marks of uncommon abilities, [the Empress] was pleased to call me from this quiet village, and . . . invited me to return to Russia to be consulted in matters that related to schools.'

The modest rector stipulated that he should have as colleague the learned Dr John Brown, vicar of St Nicholas's, Newcastle-upon-Tyne, author of a best-selling book criticizing luxury and effeminacy in English high society. Brown agreed to accompany Dumaresq and received £1000 from Catherine for his journey, but he was prevented by gout and rheumatism from starting. Finally, in a fit of melancholia, the unfortunate Brown cut his throat with a razor.

Dumaresq travelled alone to St Petersburg, where he was welcomed by Catherine and installed as an esteemed member of her five-man Educational Commission. Probably it was he who put forward the plan – recommended in the Commission's report – that Russia should have a secondary school in every provincial town. As his special field was philology – he had compiled 'A comprehensive vocabulary of the Eastern languages' – Dumaresq probably also advocated Latin and foreign languages.

If Dumaresq provided useful advice, it was from the Austrian educational system – then one of the best in Europe – that Catherine took most of her ideas. In 1782 she appointed a former Director of Schools in the Austrian province of Banat, Jankiewith de Mirievo, to be her adviser; in 1783 she founded a Teachers' Training School on Austrian lines and ordered Austrian textbooks to be translated, with suitable changes, for the use of trainees.

On 5th December 1786 Catherine issued her important Statute for Schools, the first educational act covering the whole of Russia. A 'minor school' with two teachers was to be established in every district town, and a 'major school' with six teachers in every provincial town. Major schools taught mathematics, physics, science, geography, history, and religion, which Catherine specified should be expounded by laymen; in the higher classes pupils going on to gymnasia and university would learn Latin and foreign languages.

The schools were free but attendance was not compulsory. As a newspaper advertisement explained, the new system was intended for all and 'the new schools are called "people's" schools because in them every one of Her Majesty's subjects can receive education suitable to his station.'

Catherine immediately opened 25 major schools in 25 provinces, and by 1792 every province save the Caucasus had a major school. Whereas in 1781, apart from the Smolny Institute, Russia had only six State schools with 27 teachers for 474 boys and 12 girls, by 1796 Russia had 316 schools, in which 744 teachers taught 16,220 boys and 1121 girls. Figures for a slightly later date show that 22 per cent of the pupils were middle class and 30 per cent State peasants.

Had she wished to dazzle Europe, Catherine would have opened more universities. But she knew that Russia lacked the teachers to staff such prestige institutions. She confined herself to drawing up projects for universities that she hoped would one day come into being and concentrated her resources on basic education, which was what Russia needed. She did, however, considerably increase the number of grants for study abroad. Law students she sent to Leipzig, budding prelates to Oxford and Cambridge, in order that they might there widen their learning 'for the use of the State'.

When, at the beginning of her reign, she looked at public health, Catherine found here the same dark void as in education. 'If you go to a village and ask a peasant how many children he has he will say ten, twelve, and sometimes even twenty. How many of them are alive? He will say one, two, three, rarely four. This mortality should be fought against.'

Catherine began by tackling one of the worst killers among children: smallpox. A Dr Thomas Dimsdale had just published *The Present Method of Inoculating for the Small-Pox*, describing his successes using a method invented by Robert and Daniel Sutton. It went through four editions in 1767, and Catherine, who kept abreast of new books, decided to invite the author to St Petersburg.

The Dimsdales were Quakers; Thomas's grandfather had accompanied William Penn to America in 1684 and for a time lived there. Thomas held the degree of M.D. from Aberdeen, and arrived in late summer 1768 with his son and assistant Nathaniel. They were given handsome lodgings on the Millyonaya Street and invited to dinner with the Empress.

Dimsdale found Catherine 'of all that ever I saw of her sex, the most engaging', while Catherine found the Englishman full of good sense, if somewhat cautious. All her life she had been afraid of smallpox, but now she wished to be inoculated as the best way of overcoming others' fears both of the disease and of inoculation. Dimsdale wished first to consult her doctors, but Catherine said this was unnecessary; Dimsdale then suggested that, as a trial measure, he should inoculate other ladies of her age and constitution, but again Catherine firmly said no. Finally they agreed on a date for the inoculation: Sunday, 12th October 1768.

On the 3rd Catherine stopped eating meat and drinking wine, and every third night at bedtime took a dose of eight grains of calomel, eight grains of powder of crabs' claws, and an eighth of a grain of tartar emetic, followed, on waking, by a dose of Glauber's salt. At nine in the evening of the 12th Dimsdale inoculated Catherine in both arms with matter taken from a boy with smallpox named Markov. Next day Catherine drove to Tsarskoe Selo, her country palace. She developed a moderate number of pustules and, twelve days later, a sore throat, for which she gargled with blackcurrant jelly. Dimsdale pronounced the inoculation a success, and three weeks later Catherine resumed her duties.

Many Russians believed that the donor of matter used to inoculate was doomed to die. To prove this belief mistaken Catherine permitted several persons to be inoculated with matter from her pustules, and also from those of her son Paul, whom Dimsdale inoculated in November.

Catherine's example was followed by one hundred and forty of the St Petersburg gentry, headed by Gregory Orlov; also – six years later – by young Louis XVI of France. In Moscow Dimsdale notched up another fifty successful inoculations. Both in St Petersburg and Moscow Catherine bought houses which Dimsdale fitted up as Inoculation Hospitals, and published in Russian a special booklet by Dimsdale: *A Description of the Methods proposed for extending the salutary Practice of Inoculation through the whole Russian Empire.* As a reward for his useful work Catherine made Dimsdale a Baron of the Empire, with the right to sport the double-headed eagle in his arms, and gave him £10,000 plus an annuity of £500.

Ever since Ralph Standish came out in 1557 to treat Ivan the Terrible, Russian sovereigns had shown a predilection for British doctors. Catherine chose as her physician a young Scotsman, John Rogerson, a graduate of Edinburgh and very able, who in time became a good friend. Like many who are strong and vivacious, Catherine thought that in the normal course of events she had absolutely no need of a doctor, and one of her amusements was to treat Rogerson as a kind of Molière charlatan: 'You couldn't cure a flea-bite,' she would say to him. Rogerson, good-natured, continued to urge her to take this or that pill, and on the rare occasions when he succeeded he would pat on the back the Empress of all the Russias, saying in a jolly tone, 'Well done, Ma'am, well done!'

In 1763 Catherine founded Russia's first College of Medicine, comprising a director, a president and eight members. It had an annual revenue of 470,000 roubles, plus one per cent of the salaries of military and civil service personnel, who in return received free medical treatment. The object of the College was to train sufficient Russian doctors, surgeons and apothecaries to serve all the provinces, and to further medical knowledge. In 1778 the College published the first *Pharmacopoeia Russica*; in 1789 rules for apothecaries and for midwives, and a scale of charges for medical treatment. In 1795 it was provided with its own printing press.

Peter the Great had founded good military hospitals; it was Catherine who founded hospitals for civilians. In 1763, when the document establishing the College of Medicine was presented for her signature, Catherine added in her own hand: 'The College must not forget to submit plans to me for hospitals in the provinces.' In 1775, when she reorganized the provinces, Catherine decreed that each provincial capital must have a hospital, each county – comprising between twenty and thirty thousand inhabitants – a doctor, a surgeon, an assistant surgeon and a student doctor. Salaries were higher in the remote provinces, and State doctors were allowed also to treat paying patients. Until there should be sufficient indigenous doctors, Catherine attracted many Germans with the offer of an 800-rouble retirement pension.

Catherine founded, in the name of her son Paul, a small model hospital in Moscow which the prison reformer John Howard, who visited Russia, said would do honour to any country. Another visitor, Francesco de Miranda, the future liberator of Venezuela, was struck by the Russian habit of transferring patients to summer hospitals, so that the winter ones could be cleaned and disinfected before the cold weather set in. He also noticed that the majority of patients had scurvy or V.D. In this connection Catherine founded, in 1783, a hospital in St Petersburg exclusively for venereal diseases. Of its sixty beds half were for men, half for women. It was not permitted to ask the name of any person who applied for admission: he or she was given a night-dress and a cap inscribed with the word Secrecy.

Catherine's example prompted efforts by her gentry. Baron von Keichen, for example, founded a 300-bed St Petersburg hospital overlooking the Fontanka canal, a brick building, to which in 1790 the College of Medicine added wooden annexes with 250 more beds.

Catherine gave special attention to orphans, foundlings and unwanted infants. She built a five-storey Foundling Home in Moscow, superior to anything in Europe, which included a lying-in hospital, a church and a dairy farm of eighty cows. Mothers wishing their children to be accepted had only to ring the doorbell; a basket was lowered, the mother placed her baby inside, stating its name and whether it had been baptized, and the basket was drawn up again. Each child had its own bed, the sheets of which were changed weekly, and the gifted children could continue their schooling, free, to gymnasium level. The Moscow Foundling Home took in 2000 infants annually and became the model for similar smaller homes in St Petersburg, Tula, Kaluga, Yaroslav and Kazan.

Storch in 1796 gives the following figures for infant mortality: London 32 per cent; Berlin 27.6 per cent; St Petersburg 18.4 per cent. St Petersburg of course enjoyed much better facilities than Russia as a whole, but Storch's figures speak well for Catherine's work in the field of child care.

So much for the visible results of Catherine's domestic reforms. There would be more reforms later in the reign, and achievements in many other fields. But the ones considered amount to civilizing in a fundamental sense: increasing the yield of the land, fostering trade, replacing military by civilian rule, founding towns and creating in each provincial centre, school, law courts and hospital.

CHAPTER 15

THE MOVE TO COMPASSION

These achievements, and the many others that were to follow, Catherine carried out by personal rule. When the idea of a permanent Council came up at the beginning of her reign, after consulting four trusted friends, Catherine rejected it, because she, and they, believed that in a country of slow communications only the speed and vigour of a decision by one person could get results. So throughout her reign Catherine, like her predecessors, ruled mainly by means of the *immenoy ukaz* or named decree, drafted by herself, revised and put into legal form by one of her three secretaries, and signed by Catherine with her distinctive signature, Ekaterina, the E looped and very large, the rest of the name, small, neat and straight. Once she had signed it, throughout the length and breadth of Russia the ukase had the force of law.

In formulating policy during the first part of her reign Catherine most often turned for advice to Nikita Panin. In 1762 he was forty-four years old, a plump little bachelor with small eyes and fish mouth, very plain but with a kind expression and perfect manners. He spoke through his short thick nose, had a habit of saying 'hem, hem' and fussed over his health and that of his friends: it amused Catherine to hear him repeat, when anyone ran a temperature, 'Take some quinine, sir, nothing but quinine.' He got up late, spent much of the morning looking at his collection of prints or newly-arrived books, and after a gourmet's dinner would take a siesta or play cards. Panin, in short, was lazy. But he was also completely truthful, a quality Catherine esteemed above all others, and Western in his political thinking: twelve years in Sweden had left him with a respect for constitutional monarchy. 'Kings are a necessary evil' was a phrase often on his lips, and when Catherine complained that this or that was going badly, Panin would say teasingly, 'Why are you complaining? If things were going well, we shouldn't need an Empress.'

In formulating policy Catherine also consulted her lover. Gregory Orlov was honest like Panin, but not guarded and slow; to any problem, said Catherine, 'solutions pour from his mouth like a torrent that almost suffocates him.' Russian through and through, with little education, Gregory believed that governments should be a warm personal affair between an all-wise mother and her adoring subjects. He often disagreed with Panin, but this very disagreement was useful to Catherine.

Catherine had started her reign with the urgent task of balancing the budget and beginning to civilize the provinces, but she harboured an ambition much larger than that. She confided the germ of it neither to Panin nor Orlov, but to the fly-leaf of a book she esteemed, Archbishop Fénelon's *Telemachus*:

'Be gentle,' she wrote, 'humane, accessible, compassionate, and open-handed: do not let your grandeur prevent you from mixing kindly with the humble and putting yourself in their shoes . . . I swear by Providence to stamp these words in my heart . . .'

This sympathy with the humble was more than a pious phrase because for eighteen years Catherine had been the underdog. She had suffered humiliation, insults and the dismissal, without explanation, of at least a dozen friends and servants. Under the twin persecution of Peter and the Empress she had wept for nights on end, lain ill and wished herself dead.

Catherine did not need to imagine – she had often seen them – the pillory, chains and thick leather knouts which were as much a feature of some Moscow houses as the Dutch-tile stove. In that city cruelty had become so ingrained, she said, that children grew up taking it for granted that servants should be whipped for the slightest offence. This is what Catherine decided she wanted to fight. She intended during her reign to create a new tone, to make Russia a less cruel, even a compassionate society.

She began by a small but symbolic act of personal example. People expected her to punish her vanquished enemies, but Catherine spared every one of them. She received old Field Marshal Münnich, who had urged Peter to oppose her with armed force, and told him that he had only done his duty. As for Elizabeth Vorontsova, who had repeatedly urged Peter to arrest her, Catherine allowed her to live in Moscow, and to keep Peter's gifts of jewellery worth 100,000 roubles, some of it purloined from Catherine's own jewel-case. When Elizabeth got married Catherine gave her a handsome wedding present and stood godmother to her first baby.

Catherine turned next to the case of a certain rich gentlelady who had become notorious for ill-treating her servants. Darya Nikolaievna

Saltuikova – no relation to Catherine's first lover – caused the knout to be used with such cruelty that more than one of her household died. Catherine decided to make an example of this woman. She had her arrested and brought to trial: a step almost unprecedented in Russian annals. The court found the woman guilty and gave her a stiff prison sentence. The case caused much comment and Catherine hoped that it would make plain her disgust with cruelty.

In 1763 Catherine issued the first of her humane edicts. She forbade an offender, once he had confessed, to be tortured in the hope of discovering his accomplices or other undetected crimes, and she forbade torture by officials in small towns, where too often local vendettas put on the mask of justice.

Catherine wished to go further, to the very structure of society. In simple terms, Russian society consisted of the Sovereign, the gentry, the Church, the State peasants, and the serfs. The gentry numbered 50,000; a handful were very rich, but three-quarters were small squires, owning land which required twenty or fewer male serfs. Male State peasants numbered about 2.8 million. They were bound to the land they worked, and paid the State an annual tax of around one and a half roubles per male. Male serfs numbered about 3.8 million. They belonged either to the Church or to the gentry and were kept by their masters. Some paid their masters *obrok*, dues in money or kind, others worked for their masters three days a week, sometimes more.

Serfdom had come into force between 1550 and 1650 as a solution to a specific problem: too few peasants to work the land. Because small proprietors were unable to compete with large proprietors for a limited labour force, nomadic in instinct, peasants were tied to the land they worked, and landlords became the Tsar's fiscal agents, responsible for paying his serfs' head tax.

Many serfs had just masters. According to Cook, a Scots doctor in Russian service: 'Though it may seem surprising, they are satisfied with their slavery. They commonly have good warm houses to live in. They have as much land as they can labour, and as much pasturage as they can store with cattle.' But if a serf had a cruel master, his life could be a hell. And though he did not legally belong to his master like a cotton-plantation slave in the United States, the State had few means of protecting him.

In assessing serfdom, Catherine had no clear-cut European attitude to guide her. The French Encyclopedists condemned it but Rousseau held that serfs should not be freed all of a sudden, while England, which Catherine greatly admired, was up to her elbows in the slave trade, shipping 20,000 Africans a year to the West Indies. Catherine however had no doubt at all where she stood on this particular issue. 'It is,' she wrote, 'contrary to the Christian religion and justice to make people, who are all born free, into slaves.'

Catherine's first measure to ameliorate oppression among the serfs came at the beginning of her reign. Peter had nationalized monastic land and serfs, and the Church, having helped Catherine to power, expected the new Empress to return them. Catherine did not want to do this, for she knew that the Church was the cruellest landlord of all. However, she was new on the throne and still unsure of herself. She handed the estates back to the Church but appointed a commission of three clerics and five laymen to study the question. The commission recommended nationalizing half the estates – those where oppression was worst – and in 1763 Catherine did this. In February 1764, by then sure of her authority, Catherine nationalized the remainder, thus upgrading all the Church's serfs to the improved status of State peasants. When Arseny, Metropolitan of Rostov, protested and compared her to the Emperor Julian, the Holy Synod unfrocked him, while Catherine soothed Arseny's see by walking in pilgrimage to consecrate a silver reliquary of St Dmitri. By the new arrangement the State gained one million roubles annually, while the Church lost that amount. Catherine could not resist saying to the disgruntled bishops: 'You are the successors of the Apostles, who were very poor men.'

Eighteenth-century political theorists stressed the power of good laws to change society. Catherine shared their belief. She wished to carry her policy a stage further by reforming the code of laws in such a way as to end oppression, be it of serf by master or poor citizen by government official. For eighteen months she steeped herself in the latest books, including Montesquieu's *Spirit of the Laws* and *The Punishment of Offences* in which a young Italian, Beccaria, for the first time argued against retributive punishments. At the end of it Catherine emerged with the notion not only of curbing oppression but of ending serfdom.

Catherine showed her proposal, in the form of maxims from her favourite authors, to Gregory Orlov. The generous war-hero who shared his money, when he had any, with his brothers, as they did with him, and who although three times wounded had stayed with his platoon in a post of danger, showed sympathetic interest in Catherine's proposal. By and large he favoured it. But Nikita Panin said to Catherine: 'These are maxims to cast down walls.'

What did Panin mean? First of all, that direct taxation and army recruitment were based on serfdom and would collapse without it. Not only that, once the serfs were freed, how would they live, since they had either insufficient land or no land at all? If you took land from the gentry – where did you find money to compensate them, since the Exchequer was still paying off debts incurred by Elizabeth? Panin, never one to hide the truth, may well have said to Catherine something like this: Go ahead and sign a ukase freeing the serfs. You will be hailed in Western Europe as a Liberator, your glory there will be unequalled. But it will be a glory similar to Peter's in Holstein. You will lose your throne and – something that means far more to you than that – you will be doing precisely what you refrained from doing when Prince Dashkov's message came to you at Empress Elizabeth's deathbed: you will be plunging the Russia you love so much into chaos – the kind of chaos that lasted from 1584 to 1613, when the central government broke down, causing anarchy, famine, invasion and much bloodshed.

Catherine had every reason to trust Panin. He was not one of the big landowners who had many serfs to lose, and generally he favoured her humane plans. Nor was Panin alone. Others to whom Catherine showed her maxims pronounced them unworkable or undesirable. Almost certainly Catherine read an essay written in 1761 by Lomonosov, the son of a poor fisherman who had risen to become a famous chemist, poet, historian and independent thinker. In his essay 'On Bettering the Russian People', Lomonosov advocated improved agriculture, education, medicine – the very things Catherine had already taken in hand – but it did not occur to him to mention an end to serfdom. For Lomonosov it was part of Russia's natural structure.

Weighing these views, Catherine decided that the ending of serfdom could not happen immediately, or even very soon. But she intended all the same that it should be ended some day. She continued to see it as a self-perpetuating injustice. When her secretary Sumarokov, reporting on her proposal, wrote that the serfs 'so far have no noble sentiments', Catherine tartly penned in her own hand, 'And cannot have under existing conditions.'

Catherine decided to press ahead with her plans to curb oppression by law. Both Panin and Orlov thought well of them, but Catherine wished to consult a cross-section of the Russian people, hear their complaints and invite them to formulate ways of righting them. She decided to summon a Commission of elected representatives. This in itself was an innovation – not since the seventeenth century had elected representatives met together – and Catherine meant it as a signal that she wished to legislate with the advice and in the interests of her people.

Catherine arranged that State peasants should elect representatives – this too was an innovation – and they chose eighty of a total of 672. The towns provided 208, the gentry 160, the Cossacks 60, other groups the remainder. On 31st July 1767 all the deputies who had by then arrived assembled in the Palace of Facets, Moscow, where Gregory Orlov began proceedings by reading key passages from a sixty-page document prepared by Catherine, entitled *Nakaz – Instruction*.

The opening words of the *Instruction* – the first phrase pronounced by Gregory – were like a clap of thunder: 'Russia is a European country.' Catherine took her stand on that unequivocally. The rest followed. As a European country, Russia must change its ways in accordance with the best European thinking. The government did not intend to force change, its role was to prepare and educate the people so that they themselves could introduce change. In a series of quotations, mainly from Montesquieu and Beccaria, Catherine set out the need for complete religious toleration, for freedom of the press within limits, above all for just and humane laws. Punishment should be for deeds only, never for thoughts or intentions: it should never outrage human dignity and generally speaking capital punishment should be avoided.

After listening to these views, which a majority would have found revolutionary in the extreme, the deputies were received by Catherine, who gave to each a chain and gold medal inscribed: 'The welfare of one and all'. Thereafter the deputies met sometimes in full session, sometimes in nineteen committees. They had brought with them lists of grievances, not unlike the *Carnets* of a French States-General, most relating to local issues: scarcity of timber, fences being knocked down, crops trampled by wandering cattle, the law's delay, the insolence of office. These they read and discussed. For the first time in the history of Russia representatives frankly, publicly and without fear of retribution spoke out about what troubled them and those they represented.

In February 1768 the Commission moved to St Petersburg and began debating Catherine's measures to mitigate serfdom. Catherine had enlisted the support of a few enlightened gentry. Koselsky and Korobin spoke in favour of legal checks on landlords' power over serfs, and of serfs being allowed some property, while Bibikov, whom the deputies had elected Marshal, urged that noblemen who tortured their serfs should be declared insane, which would allow the law to sequester their estates.

Catherine was hoping much from Count Alexander Stroganov, the courtier who had cheered her up after Peter had publicly called her a fool. She knew that he was a gentle and at heart a humane man. Moreover, he had received an excellent education in Geneva and Paris. But when he rose to speak Stroganov defended with passion and fury the institution of serfdom. Catherine was astonished and did not know whether to ascribe his behaviour to cowardice or the influence of his wealthy family.

More dangerous to Catherine was Prince Michael Shcherbatov, a stiff arrogant gentleman who considered the hereditary nobility God's special gift to Russia, hated Gregory Orlov as an upstart and believed that his country had been going to the dogs ever since Peter the Great began Westernizing. In a specious but forceful speech Shcherbatov argued that because Russia was a cold northern country, peasants would not work of themselves, they must be forced to work. The State could not force them – Russia was too large – only the gentry could do it – in the traditional way, without interference by government.

When she found that Shcherbatov was supported by a large majority of the representatives, including those who were not gentry, Catherine felt intense disappointment. Even her passing reference to the serfs as being 'just as good as we are' was deeply resented. Catherine described the majority of representatives as 'irrational and cruel' on this issue. 'I believe there were not twenty human beings who reflected on the subject at that time with humanity, really like human beings.'

Despite the low level of debate – thirteen per cent of the deputies were illiterate – and her disappointment that she had found no support for radical measures to mitigate serfdom, Catherine considered her Commission a qualified success. It met in all 203 times, established a precedent for free discussion, and its committees brought up a number of important grievances on which she was later to act, such as the need for smaller administrative units, for the gentry to participate in local government, and for a measure of self-government in towns. As regards the issue closest to her heart, in her own way and in her own time Catherine intended to work for more compassionate laws.

Turkey declared war on Russia in 1768, most of the representatives had to join the army, and Catherine adjourned the Commission *sine die* in 1769, though certain committees continued their work into 1772. The war drew Catherine's energy away from home reforms, until in 1773 an event occurred which raised the question of serfdom in a quite different and alarming way.

On 15th October of that year Catherine attended a routine meeting of her War Council, the members of which included Zachary Chernuishev, the handsome officer with whom Catherine had been in love twenty-two years before and whose military qualities were such that she had appointed him Head of the War College. Catherine listened closely as Chernuishev read reports from Orenburg, a garrison town south of the distant Urals, and from Kazan, 300 miles north-west of Orenburg, both telling of rebellious Cossacks. Ever since Russia began governments had had trouble with Cossacks, but this rebellion differed from its predecessors. According to the reports it was led by Tsar Peter III.

The rebellion had begun in this way. A certain Emelyan Pugachev was born on the lower Don about 1740. He was a Cossack, that is, he belonged to one of a dozen communities scattered over 5000 miles of south Russia: self-reliant frontiersmen who preferred banditry to taxation and the restraints of law. Pugachev owned a small farm, married a local girl and had three children. He was conscripted into the army, saw action and attained the rank of cornet. Then he went absent without leave, and after being flogged deserted altogether, entering on a vagabond career that took him to Poland, to the lower Volga, and finally to the Yaik Cossacks.

The Yaik Cossacks were fishermen and cattle-raisers. Many were descendants of Central Russians who had sought refuge in the south because they were Old Believers, members of a sect that clung to traditional rites and practices and refused the revisions made by Patriarch Nikon in the early seventeenth century. Old Believers, for example, gave the blessing with two fingers, representing Christ's dual nature, not with three, representing the Trinity, as Nikon laid down.

The Yaik Cossacks opposed Catherine's policy of settlement, taxation and service in the army. They also resented the efforts of hell-fire Orthodox missionaries sent to convert them, and in this connection revered the memory of Peter III, who had eased Elizabeth's stern measures against their sect. Pugachev was small and stocky. He wore his dark hair in a fringe over his low brow and had a short dark beard. His complexion was disfigured by white scrofula scars, and several of his teeth had been knocked out in fights. He did not resemble Peter III, but one day a Cossack who had seen Peter said he did. This remark, and the respect it brought him, were not lost on Pugachev.

He placed himself at the head of a band of outlaw Cossacks and began calling himself Tsar Peter III. He had a two-fold appeal to his followers: as a soldier who would protect their independence, and as a saintly, almost Christlike figure, who had meekly accepted dethronement by his evil wife, and who would, with God's help, end the harassing of Cossack Old Believers.

Peter Feodorovich, as Pugachev now styled himself, issued a manifesto exhorting Cossacks, Kalmuiks and Tartars to serve him, promising to grant them the river Volga, the land and the grass, as well as lead, powder and sufficient food. In short, he would protect the traditional Cossack way of life, threatened by Catherine's extension of government.

The Yaik Cossacks were superb if undisciplined cavalrymen. Led by Pugachev and lunging with their long lances, they defeated the first general Catherine sent against them, captured half a dozen forts, hanging the officers, raping and murdering the officers' wives. At the head of 10,000 Cossacks Pugachev then began to besiege Orenburg.

The town lay close to important privately-owned manufactories and foundries, where minerals from the Urals were processed by workers whose pay and conditions had deteriorated under Empress Elizabeth. Their grievances were being investigated by Catherine but had not yet been put right. The workers were led by a certain Afanasi Sokolov, better known as 'The Cracker', veteran of countless knoutings, his nose torn off to the bone, so that he kept his face covered with a net. 'The Cracker' passed Pugachev much-needed aid: food, money and muskets.

Pugachev failed to take Orenburg, which was defended by seventy cannon, and suffered a defeat by government troops under General Golitsuin. In summer 1774 he marched north and scored a great success by capturing Kazan, which he burned. He then headed towards Nizhni-Novgorod, calling on the serfs to join him. His appeal met with a widespread response. From estate after estate peasants, armed with knives and sickles, slipped away to follow the self-styled Tsar. By mid-July Pugachev had an army of 25,000, part Cossack, part serf. He then announced his intention of marching on Moscow.

On important occasions 'Tsar Peter III' now wore a red coat trimmed with lace, sceptre in one hand, silver axe in the other, while supplicants knelt and bowed their heads. He dictated orders, being unable to write or read, and stamped them with a counterfeit seal showing a double-headed eagle, explaining that he would write his name only when he mounted the throne. He conferred titles on his chief supporters, granted them estates in the Baltic region, and even made them gifts of serfs. Off-duty he drank with his men and sang Cossack songs. 'When I have captured Moscow,' he said, 'I shall order everyone to follow the Old Faith and to wear Russian clothes.'

The shade of poor murdered Peter pursuing his wife across the steppes – it has all the makings of an Aeschylean tragedy, and doubtless Catherine experienced an icy terror at the thought that her crown might be snatched from her by Peter-Pugachev in an act of cosmic justice. She knew that an earlier impostor, claiming to be Ivan the Terrible's son Dmitri, who died mysteriously while still a child, had seized the throne with Cossack support in 1605. She knew that foreign observers thought her days as Empress were numbered. She had heard that Pugachev intended to place her in a convent, an arrangement not at all to her taste.

Against this sudden eruption from Asia into her Europeanizing policy Catherine acted with speed and energy. She called back troops from the Turkish front, she recruited reliable Cossacks and Kalmuiks, she sent General Mikhelson to bar the way to Moscow. As a result Pugachev turned south. He won over the Volga serfs and began a march of terror. At Saransk he hanged 200 gentry; at Penza he burned down the governor's house with the governor and twenty gentry inside it; capturing Lowitz, an astronomer in Catherine's service, he had him hanged so that he might be 'nearer the stars'. Altogether Pugachev, his Cossacks and serfs murdered in cold blood more than 3000 men, women and children. 'Since Tamerlaine,' wrote Catherine, 'no one has destroyed so many human beings.'

Like a tracked animal, Pugachev headed for the Don and home. But no man is an impostor in his own country. 'Why does he call himself Tsar Peter?' asked the Don Cossacks. 'This is Emelyan Pugachev, the small farmer who deserted his wife Sophie and his children.' Pugachev saw his followers drift away, and on 15th September 1774 he was seized and tied up by three of his staff, handed over to the military governor of the nearest town, and sent to Moscow in a wheeled iron cage.

In her *Instruction* Catherine had urged humane punishment and where possible avoidance of the death penalty. But the note she had written in her copy of *Telemachus* goes on to say: 'See that this kindness, however, does not weaken your authority nor diminish their respect.' Wherever a threat arose to the authority of the crown, now and later Catherine was to show herself inflexible. Pugachev having confessed his guilt and expressed a hope for mercy, Catherine wrote to Voltaire: 'If it were only me he had harmed, his hopes could be justified, and I should pardon him; but this trial involves the Empire and its laws.'

Pugachev was tried by the Senate sitting in the Kremlin, found guilty and beheaded. Five of his henchmen were also found guilty and put to death. It was the army's task to deal with his followers in the south; they did this roughly and sometimes cruelly. Catherine herself ordered Pugachev's home village razed to the ground, and kept Pugachev's daughters in custody for the rest of her reign.

In his year-long rebellion Pugachev had fused two quite separate protests. The first was the Cossacks' protest at being settled and taxed. Catherine did not allow it. On the contrary, she speeded plans for strengthening administration in Cossack lands and for improved schooling. But she did restrain the Church in its campaign to convert Old Believers and singled out individual Cossacks for honour: she attended an important ceremony in 1774 with a personal bodyguard of 65 brave Cossacks. This was the beginning of what was to become a famous deep-seated loyalty of Cossacks to the crown.

The second protest was that of oppressed serfs, and this Catherine did allow. Although Pugachev's rebellion for a time still further hardened the attitude of the gentry, Catherine pressed on with measures to eliminate grievances. She took over the worst-run manufactories and manned them with State peasants, who received fixed wages. She arranged that the children of workers in private manufactories should receive schooling, and if they were of working age their parents were to receive compensation. She set out improved conditions in her Manufactory Manifesto of 21st May 1779, after which in this sphere there was no further trouble.

As regards oppression generally, Catherine acted in two ways. First, as a means of educating public opinion, she ordered her *Instruction* to be read three times a year in every law court and judicial institution. Here are some of the relevant passages:

> The law must ensure that no citizen fears another and that everyone fears only the law.
>
> A law may be productive of public benefit, which gives some private property to a serf.
>
> Equality consists in everyone being subject to the same laws.
>
> To ensure equality an institution must prevent the rich oppressing the poor and profiting from the rank, privilege and authority which are theirs only in their capacity as government officials.

In time these truths would come to seem self-evident to the point of platitude, but in the 1770s against a background of peculation and terrorizing they had a sharp cutting edge; indeed Catherine's *Instruction* was considered so advanced it was banned in France. In Russia it helped set a humane tone. 'At least people began to know the will of the law-maker,' said Catherine, 'and began to act in accordance with it.'

Catherine's second way of easing oppression was to make new laws

– piecemeal, so as not to affront the gentry. She made it legal for owners to free serfs and to bequeath them their freedom. She prohibited a freed serf from becoming a serf again. She rescinded a law whereby orphans, foundlings and illegitimate children became the serfs of those who took them in, and another law whereby if a free man married a serf he too became a serf. She opened her new State schools to serfs, who in the past had received no education, so that at the end of her reign serfs would provide about 11 per cent of the pupils, and in 1787 she specifically allowed serfs to enter university, declaring, 'The sciences are called free in order to give freedom to everybody to acquire them, and not in order to give this right only to free men.'

Catherine did not end serfdom; at that time probably not even a native Russian could have done so. What she did do was to educate public opinion against serfdom, where possible to curb and ease it, and, more generally, to set a compassionate tone. Ségur is specially trustworthy here, because as a Frenchman he had been brought up to see Russia in dark colours and as a future adherent of the Revolution he had his eyes open for injustice. Writing of the second part of Catherine's reign, Ségur says that serfs were treated mildly and, during his five years in Russia, he had never heard of a serf suffering cruelty.

CHAPTER 16

VICTORIES ABROAD

Arriving very young from a small country in which she had lived only a short while, Catherine had quickly fallen in love with Russia. When she gave up Lutheranism, much of the reverence that had gone into religion she transferred to the Russian land and people. In time Catherine conceived what can only be termed a cult of her adopted country, deeper than the patriotism of a native Russian, a cult as strong as Napoleon's was later to be for France or Alexander Hamilton's for the United States.

At the same time, coming from Europe, Catherine was also more aware than native Russians of Europe's disdain for the object of her cult. It pained Catherine that foreigners should consider Russia a second-class power, a source of troops for others' wars, to be pushed around by knowing European chancelleries. It was a driving desire to make her native Europe admire wonderful Russia that led Catherine to her first principle in foreign affairs: 'Make the State powerful, and respected by its neighbours.'

When she came to the throne Catherine found Russia anything but powerful. Her people were exhausted by five and a half years of war, two-thirds of her army unpaid and her navy, as she put it, was little better than a herring fleet. Within weeks of her coup Catherine was laying down keels of two ships of the line and driving in the first nails herself, but not with war in mind. Catherine's second principle was this: 'Peace is necessary to this vast empire; we need population, not devastation.'

Catherine's first actions as Empress were in fact actions of peace. She called off Peter's war against Denmark, and she began winding up the Seven Years' War, of which she had always disapproved. Since Russia had gone originally to the help of her ally Austria, it required considerable diplomatic skill by Catherine to persuade proud Maria Theresa to parley with the king who had twice made aggressive war on her. Catherine managed to bring both sides to the conference table and in February 1763, at Hubertusburg, Prussia and Austria made peace. Within months of that success Catherine faced her first big problem, that of Poland.

Poland, which included Lithuania, was then twice as large as it is today. It ran from the River Dvina in the north to the Turkish province of Moldavia in the south. Twelve million inhabitants and a 900-mile common frontier made it the most considerable of Russia's western neighbours. Once it had been very strong – in 1611 Polish troops burned Moscow – but now a peculiar government – a republic with an elective crown – made for weakness if not anarchy, and for long its Diet, under pressure usually from Austria or France, had been reduced to choosing a foreigner as king. When the throne had last fallen vacant the candidates had been the Elector of Saxony, supported by Austria and Russia, and Stanislaus Leszczynski, supported by Louis XV, who had married Stanislaus's daughter. The Empress of the day, Anna, sent in a Russian army which besieged Stanislaus in Danzig and drove him into exile in France, and the Elector of Saxony became King of Poland as Augustus III.

In September 1763 Augustus died. Many Poles wanted his son to succeed, and looked for support to their traditional friend, the King of France. But Louis XV was now a pitiful figure, stealing home from his private brothel to indulge diplomatic fantasies. Behind the back of his Foreign Minister Louis sent three different secret agents to Poland, each unknown to the other and with differing instructions. They ended by exasperating both the Saxon candidate and the Poles, who resolved to choose a native king.

Catherine decided to seize this opportunity of extending Russian influence by putting forward a candidate. The obvious choice was Prince-Chancellor Adam Czartoryski, a member of the leading Russophil family, possessed of a strong character and great riches. But Adam Czartoryski had a nephew who might suit Catherine's purpose even better. His name was Stanislaus Poniatowski.

For three years after Elizabeth had driven him away, Catherine had remained in love with Stanislaus. She had written very often to the father of little Anna and tried to secure his recall. Then she had met Gregory – less polished, less a gentleman, but with a strength and drive that deeply attracted her – and the new love superseded the old. Catherine knew, however, that Stanislaus still loved her, for as soon as she became Empress he had wished to rush to her arms, and she had had to write hastily to check him. It would be convenient to have a man who loved her on the Polish throne but, as Catherine was well aware, love could fade. If that were to happen, she would still have a hold on Stanislaus, because he was as poor as Adam Czartoryski was rich, and the peculiar elective crown of Poland would bring him only a pittance. It was chiefly because poverty would make him always dependent on her that Catherine decided to back Stanislaus.

Catherine easily secured the agreement of Frederick of Prussia, who wished to see the exclusion of his two enemies, France and Saxony, and in autumn 1763 she offered Stanislaus the throne of Poland.

'My dominant reflection,' said the faithful and gentle-hearted Stanislaus, 'was that if I became a king the Empress might sooner or later marry me, but that otherwise she would be unlikely to do so. Moreover, the despotic and implacable character of my uncle [Adam] made me fear that his reign would be hard for Poland.' So he accepted Catherine's offer.

A Polish king was elected by the assembled magnates and gentry. As soon as Stanislaus had agreed to be a candidate Catherine sent to Poland a comparatively small body of troops – 8000 compared with the 50,000 Empress Anna had sent in 1733 – to make her wishes clear. Delegates were more pleased at the prospect of a native king than angered by Russian interference; they unanimously elected Catherine's candidate, thereby fulfilling a prophecy. 'I flatter myself,' Sir Charles Hanbury-Williams had told Catherine eight years earlier, 'that one day you, and the King of Prussia as your lieutenant, will make him [Stanislaus] King of Poland.'

This lightning diplomacy was very different from that of Elizabeth, who had taken three months just to write her name on a treaty. The chancelleries of Europe discussed with surprise, admiration and even some alarm this remarkable success by the former Princess of Zerbst, who, not content with making herself Empress, had now made her lover a king.

What sort of king? Stanislaus at thirty-two still retained his high principles but since their midnight sleigh rides in St Petersburg he had lost rather than gained in strength. He referred to himself as 'Telemachus', the modest, justice-loving prince of Fénelon's book who invariably consults his mentor, in Stanislaus's case Catherine, and took as his motto 'Patience and Courage', with the emphasis on patience. Nevertheless he began reforming, as Catherine had done, and was even to call on Catherine's adviser Dumaresq, after the Englishman had finished in Russia, adopting towards him a typically modest tone: 'I am doing what I can for the schools of my country, but I shall do far better when you are willing to help.'

Every two years a Polish king submitted proposed new legislation to a Diet of magnates and gentlemen, proud of their right to wear blue jackets and spurs, but often so poor the spurs were strapped to bare feet. Each measure had to be passed unanimously and a single vote against it, known as the liberum veto, not only blocked the measure but ended the Diet. The liberum veto had caused 48 of the past 66 Diets to disperse in futility, and Stanislaus correctly identified it as the source of national weakness. Aided by a number of like-minded Poles, he prepared to abolish the crippling veto.

Catherine had given Poland a good king, but had no wish to see him strong. She sent her energetic young ambassador, Prince Nicholas Repnin, to warn Stanislaus that if he persisted he would lose his privy purse, which she provided, and all Russian support. At the same time Repnin warned the magnates that their king was plotting to subvert the republic. By this joint move Catherine easily secured retention of the liberum veto.

The next matter to occupy Catherine was the large minority of Greek Orthodox in Poland, who, with the Lutherans, were known as the Dissidents. For years they had been shamefully treated by the Catholic majority; they were denied ordinary civic rights, forbidden to build new churches and barred from high office. The Russian Church had long deplored their plight and urged Russian rulers to do something about it. After Catherine had installed Stanislaus the call became more pressing.

Catherine had just confirmed nationalization of Church lands and wished to do something to please the Church. Also she believed very firmly indeed in religious toleration. To these motives for intervening was added one still more important. Catherine sensed a growing national spirit in Poland, strongly Catholic, anti-Orthodox and therefore potentially anti-Russian. She decided she could best contain it by championing the Dissidents, and so acquiring, as Panin put it in instructions to Repnin, 'a firm and reliable party with the legal right to participate in all the affairs of Poland'.

Catherine received a letter from Stanislaus in which, quoting from Racine's *Athalie*, he gently warned her of the dangers of meddling in religion, about which his countrymen felt very strongly indeed. She disregarded his advice. She sent agents among the Dissidents, promising help if they demanded equal rights, and when the Diet met in October 1767 to consider this demand, she again stationed outside the assembly a Russian army, muskets loaded, bayonets fixed.

The Diet proved even rowdier than usual. When the papal nuncio made a speech against equal rights, delegates roared approval. Repnin forced a way in. 'Stop this uproar!' he cried. 'Or if you *will* have a row, I'll make a row too, and mine will be louder than yours.' Despite the threat Soltyk, Bishop of Cracow, and Zalusky, Bishop of Kiev, spoke against toleration, whereupon Repnin arrested both and sent them under guard to Russia.

Stanislaus found himself in a quandary. Many delegates looked to him to protest unequivocally against armed intervention in their Diet. Courage demanded that he should make the protest, and if Catherine would not heed him, to abdicate. But patience proved stronger than courage. Hoping for the best, Stanislaus decided to go along with his 'mentor'. He accepted Repnin's intervention with only a murmur, and the Diet, seeing no one to rally to and Russian bayonets glinting outside, agreed to a special commission of its members being chosen by Repnin which duly voted equal rights to the Dissidents.

Catherine savoured this new victory, but not for long. Two days after the Diet dispersed Stanislaus's warning was proved correct, when in the town of Bar, near the Turkish frontier, Catholic leaders banded together '*pro religione et libertate*' – to defend Catholicism and Polish independence. The Confederation of Bar declared Stanislaus deposed, won support from Austria and France, who sent money and military advisers, and began a bitter partisan war.

Instead of an easy diplomatic victory Catherine found herself having to send more and more Russian troops into Poland. In underestimating the strength of Polish Catholicism, she made her first diplomatic mistake. 'One would say that human nature is always the same,' she wrote crossly to Voltaire. 'The absurdity of the Crusades hasn't stopped the churchmen of Podolskiy, prompted by the papal nuncio, from preaching a crusade against me, and those so-called Confederate lunatics have taken the cross in one hand, and with the other formed an alliance with the Turks, promising them two of their provinces. Why? In order to prevent a quarter of their nation from enjoying civic rights.'

Catherine might abuse the Poles, but the urgent question remained, How could she extricate herself from her mistake?

The beginning of an answer came not from the impoverished plains of Poland but from a smart little baroque palace near Berlin. It was called Sans Souci and had been built by a man with many *soucis*. Now aged fifty-five, Frederick still sought the further aggrandizement of Prussia, and for long had cast covetous eyes on a strip of land, Polish Pomerania, which divided the main part of his realm, Brandenburg, from East Prussia. When he saw Catherine in difficulties, he suggested to her a plan which reflects his new brand of calculating power-politics: Russia should annexe the Greek Orthodox part of Poland and Frederick Polish Pomerania, while Maria Theresa would be offered as a sop part of Galicia.

When she came to the throne Catherine had recognized Prussia to be the strongest European power. Insecure herself in her military strength, she had decided to reaffirm her husband's alliance with Frederick. She did not like his militarism, but had to live with it. As regards his plan, it fitted in well with Russia's traditional attitude to Poland. Tsar Ivan the Third, in the fifteenth century, had declared that no peace with Poland could be permanent until the Orthodox population under Polish rule had been brought under the Russian empire. Frederick's plan would moreover satisfy both her first basic principle, of making Russia strong, and her second: 'We need population, not devastation.'

Catherine did not rise immediately to Frederick's bait. First she had to ponder Panin's view that Russia should continue to control Poland indirectly, as she controlled Sweden. Catherine decided that hatred engendered by the continuing war would render impossible peaceful coexistence between Catholics and Greek Orthodox, and she began to show Frederick interest. In 1770 Frederick's brother and Catherine's former suitor, Prince Heinrich, came to St Petersburg, where he and Catherine carried the plan further. Then Maria Theresa's scruples had to be overcome. Shedding tears, the Austrian Empress declared piously that she would never consent to so Machiavellian a plan; but, said Frederick, 'the more tears she shed, the more she wanted to grab.' Only in August 1772, when Russian troops had captured Cracow and the Confederation of Bar collapsed, did partition become feasible.

At Maria Theresa's request the document dividing one quarter of Poland between Russia, Prussia and Austria began with the traditional formula: 'In the name of the Holy Trinity . . .', causing foreign observers to make the obvious quip. Frederick obtained Polish Pomerania less Danzig and Torun, Maria Theresa Spis and Galicia; Catherine 88,000 square kilometres of territory in what is now Belorussia, the inhabitants of which were of predominantly Russian stock.

This first partition of Poland was confirmed by a Polish Diet in January 1773. By it Catherine not only retrieved her initial mistake but acquired valuable new provinces. Moreover, through King Stanislaus, she now controlled the foreign and domestic policy of Poland. Exhausted by war, that unhappy country settled down to a period of calm and reconstruction, which was to last well into the second half of Catherine's reign when once again the Polish problem would re-emerge.

On her south-west frontier Catherine faced the strongest of Russia's neighbours, the Ottoman Empire, which then stretched from the Adriatic to the Caspian and controlled, directly or indirectly, what is now Romania, Greece, Turkey, Arabia and Egypt. Off and on for the past century Russians and Turks had been making war, the cross against the crescent, and even Peter the Great had failed to master the formidable Turkish cavalry. The present Sultan, Mustapha III, scholar, poet and reformer, had modernized his army and navy, helped by a French artillery expert, Baron François de Tott.

In 1768 Russian troops pursued a group of Confederate Poles across the Polish frontier to the Turkish town of Balta, where in the fighting that ensued they killed a number of Turks. Prompted by Turkey's traditional ally, France, Mustapha decided to treat the small incident as an outrage and declared war on Russia.

Catherine had not wanted war but once it came she decided to pursue it with all her strength. She immediately set up a seven-man Council to advise her – it included Panin, Gregory Orlov, Zachary Chernuishev and Cyril Razumovsky – and presided over its twice-weekly meetings. With her Council's approval Catherine sent Field Marshal Rumyantsov to the Danubian provinces with a small army, where he made a good start by capturing Jassy. In letter after letter Catherine urged Rumyantsov to win fresh laurels: 'Europe is watching you,' she wrote, and the reference to Europe is typical of Catherine. To her intense satisfaction in summer 1770 Rumyantsov twice defeated a superior Turkish army.

Meanwhile Catherine was considering ways of using her navy. Born in one port, long resident in another, Catherine liked the sea and knew about ships. She had changed her 'herring fleet' into a strong force and added to the officers thirty Britons. She had done this with the Baltic in mind, Russia's traditional naval battlefield, but as the Turkish war dragged on she wondered whether she could not use it against the Sultan. With one eye as usual on Europe and with her admiration for England, which used the Royal Navy intercontinentally, Catherine herself was almost certainly the originator of a brilliant, daring plan to send the Russian fleet all the way round Western Europe, through the Strait of Gibraltar, into the Eastern Mediterranean, there to engage the Turks: from latitude 60 degrees to 36, a distance there and back of 10,000 miles. Nothing like this had been dreamed of before in Russia and the dream would never have been put into action so speedily save at the command of an energetic autocrat.

To execute her plan Catherine needed the help of a friendly power. She approached England, and the government in Whitehall gave their assent, hoping that the Russian effort would win England eastern Mediterranean markets, then dominated by France, and never supposing the Russians would score more than a minor success.

For weeks Catherine occupied herself with masts, yard-arms, bowsprits, anchors, sails and, not least, the crews who, for the period, enjoyed quite good conditions, eating meat and vegetables four days a week, salted fish, black biscuit and butter the other three. They got a daily issue of brandy and were paid eight roubles a year.

On 6th August 1769 Catherine watched the first Russian squadron, commanded by Admiral Spiridov, set sail from Cronstadt on the first leg of its long voyage. A second squadron, commanded by John Elphinston, followed in October. Spiridov's squadron touched at Hull, and wintered agreeably in Minorca, then in British hands. Elphinston wintered in Spithead, sailed again in April and on 20th May 1770 made Cape Matapan in the Greek Peloponnese.

Catherine had given command of the fleet to Alexis Orlov, with Captain Samuel Greig of Inverkeithing in Fife as his technical adviser. The colossal scar-faced Russian, who could down a whole bottle of champagne at a single gulp, made up in courage what he lacked in knowledge of the sea. Regrouping his ships, he began to scour the blue waters of the Aegean for signs of the enemy.

The island of Chios lies off the coast of Turkish Anatolia and it was in the waters of Chios, on 7th July, that the Turkish admiral sighted fourteen trim, newly-built ships approaching in line under full sail. One can imagine his surprise when he saw them flying at the stern the white ensign with the blue cross of St Andrew.

Orlov immediately engaged the Turkish fleet, numbering thirteen ships of the line, near the north entrance of Chesme Bay, an inlet on the coast of Anatolia opposite Chios. Admiral Spiridov's flagship led the attack but early on her starboard-main-brace and larboard-main-topsail-brace were shot away, she became unmanoeuvrable and fell with her broadside on board the *Capitana Ali Bey*, 100 guns. Russian and Turkish sailors grappled hand-to-hand on the jammed ships for fifteen minutes, then fire broke out and both ships exploded. The other Turkish vessels at once scurried into Chesme Bay.

The Turkish admiral thought he was safe in the narrow, shallow bay, which offered the Russians no room for manoeuvre. But next morning Orlov ordered a full-scale attack. Greig led three ships into the bay and engaged a 96-gun Turkish ship of the line, while under cover of the smoke and confusion three old Greek hulks were prepared as fire-ships. The first, commanded by Lieutenant Dugdale, ran on to rocks and did no damage; the second, commanded by Lieutenant Mackenzie, sailed straight into the Turkish fleet, a moving wall of flame. It set fire to one ship and, fanned by a stiff breeze in a constricted space, the flames spread, while the Russian guns bombarded with cannon balls, shells and small shot. Ship after ship of the Turkish fleet exploded. One only escaped; otherwise the whole Turkish fleet was destroyed that day. Thirty Russians lost their lives against nine thousand Turks.

Chesme Bay was a great achievement by any standard and Catherine, typically, put it into historical perspective: 'the first Russian naval victory for 900 years'. She awarded Orlov the Order of St George, which she herself had founded, and she was later to build a palace with the name Chesme.

The victory's immediate effects were two: it relieved pressure along the Black Sea front, where strong Turkish forces had been bearing heavily on the Russians, and it allowed Orlov to move at will, stirring up rebellion against Sultan Mustapha not only among the Greeks but as far south as Arabia Felix. It was in recognition of Russian help at this time that the ruler of Arabia Felix presented Orlov with a remarkable five-year-old bay pure-blood, Ali Bey, which became the chief stallion of Orlov's stud.

The final battles of the Russo-Turkish war were to be fought on land and will be described presently. Meanwhile Alexis Orlov, having completed his task, received orders to sail his fleet home. On the way he stopped at Leghorn. Catherine had commissioned Hackert to paint four pictures of the battle of Chesme Bay, and as the artist had never seen a ship blow up Orlov with characteristic bravado blew up an old ship for him, rocking the quiet Tuscan port to its foundations.

During his stay in Leghorn Orlov took the leading role in a second, much more important incident. It concerns a mysterious adventuress who first attracted notice in Paris in 1772. Aged about twenty, black-haired, brown-eyed, Italian-looking, she was probably the daughter of a Prague innkeeper, but she claimed to be the Dame of Azov, a town at the mouth of the Don disputed by Russia and Turkey. She explained that she had been orphaned at four, brought up by her uncle the Shah of Persia and that she possessed powerful connections throughout the Middle East.

Prince Charles Radziwill, leader of the anti-Russian Poles, then living in Paris, decided that this woman could be useful to him. He took her under his protection and persuaded her to pitch her claim an octave higher, to declare herself the Princess Tarakanova, a daughter of the Russian Empress Elizabeth by Alexis Razumovsky, a person of whom there had long been rumours.

The existence in Europe of a lady claiming to be the sovereign of Russia would in any circumstances have been a considerable embarrassment to Catherine. In 1772, with the Polish question unresolved and Turkish armies battering at her frontier, the Princess was potentially very dangerous. The chancelleries of Europe buzzed with stories of this dark attractive lady whose love life in no way fell short of Catherine's. Had her Polish friends – for she moved from one to the other of Radziwill's group – possessed more money and more political astuteness, she would have become a major threat to Catherine. As it is, she drifted uncertainly across Europe, then made a wild bid for the throne of Russia.

She wrote to Alexis Orlov, then being feted in Leghorn as the victor of Chesme Bay. Somewhat confused genealogically, she declared Pugachev, alias Peter III, to be her brother, and Sultan Mustapha her protector. She declared that she freed Orlov and all officers and men of the Russian Navy from their oath to 'the usurper' and commanded them to swear allegiance to her as their rightful sovereign. She signed the letter 'Elizabeth'.

The Princess received no answer to her letter, which Orlov forwarded to Catherine. With her current lover, Radziwill's aide Domanski, she then went to live in Rome and tried to borrow money from Sir William Hamilton. Hamilton, who had heard rumours of her pretensions, sent her letter to the British consul in Leghorn. The consul alerted Orlov and gave him the Princess's address.

When she received the Princess's letter from Orlov, Catherine was very angry indeed. Across the southern provinces Pugachev's Cossacks and serfs were burning, looting, killing, while the Turks still made war on Russia. In this crisis, when Orlov proposed trying to capture the Princess, who at the time he wrote was believed to be living in Ragusa, Catherine readily agreed. 'I permit you to use threats and even force if Ragusa does not yield the creature up . . . A few cannon balls might persuade them.'

Orlov had developed some unpleasant habits in his week at Ropsha. One of them was duplicity. He wrote the Princess a charming letter, inviting her to Pisa. The Princess accepted and took up residence at

Orlov's expense in a sumptuous apartment. Orlov gave her his portrait and pretended to be in love with her. The Princess doubtless imagined that she and Alexis were about to join destinies in order to outwit Catherine and Gregory.

After several weeks of attentive courting, Orlov invited the Princess to watch his fleet engage in mock combat. She accepted, little knowing that it was a mock invitation. After dining with the British consul, accompanied by the consul and by two Polish friends, the dark lady embarked on Greig's flagship. Hardly had she stepped aboard when Captain Litvinov of the Russian navy came up to her. 'You are our prisoner,' he said, then led her to a room in Greig's suite, turning the key behind her. The papers in the Princess's Pisa apartment were seized and next day Greig set sail for Cronstadt.

Catherine imprisoned the Princess in the Saints Peter and Paul Fortress, across the Neva from the Winter Palace. She was well within her rights in keeping under guard a pretender who by her own admission was in league with Russia's enemy. But the Princess was suffering from advanced tuberculosis. Six months later, still in prison, she died.

There is a sequel. Princess Tarakanova's legendary origins were matched by a legendary death. Two years after her actual death from tuberculosis a flood hit St Petersburg, inundating buildings near the river, including the Saints Peter and Paul Fortress, and a story arose, quite untrue, that the Princess, chained to the wall of her dungeon, had died of drowning.

Pretenders were endemic to Tsarist Russia. They had threatened the crown often in the past. But because of her foreign birth and the circumstances of her accession Catherine suffered more than most from plots by or on behalf of pretenders, the most dangerous being a conspiracy by a group of soldiers in Schlüsselburg to put Prisoner Number One on the throne as Ivan VI, which ended in Ivan being stabbed by his gaolers. Catherine knew that Russia could never be respected abroad as long as her crown was insecure; this helps to explain, if it does not excuse, the severity of her measures against pretenders.

The claim of Princess Tarakanova was only one of many threats that made life difficult for Catherine in the early 1770s. Plague decimated Moscow in 1771; Pugachev threatened the same city in 1774; and all the while she had to conduct war against the Turk.

She was fighting that war on three fronts: on the Lower Don around Azov; on the Dnieper, where the Tartars of Crimea, a protectorate of Turkey, had erupted, and on the Danube, where Rumyantsov had failed to follow up his victories of 1770. In 1772, hard pressed in Poland, Catherine opened peace talks with Mustapha but, unable to obtain the terms she wanted, broke them off. By 1773, having partitioned Poland, she was able to move to the Danube, most important of the three fronts, troops that had been fighting the Confederates and, in particular, a brilliant Russian general.

Alexander Suvorov was a thin, quick little man with puckish face and blue eyes, who had originally been rejected by the Cadet School because of poor physique. The setback served as a stimulus: young Suvorov built up his muscles, enlisted as a private, won a commission and soon distinguished himself by his Spartan habits and laconic speech, by his devoted care of his troops and his belief, repeatedly demonstrated, that battles are won with the bayonet. He was still a young man, the same age as herself, when Catherine singled him out for promotion. She gave him an independent command in Poland and saw him fully justify her confidence when he captured Cracow.

Never one to lose time, as soon as he reached the Danube front Suvorov with 3000 men attacked and defeated 12,000 Turks. In July 1774 he made a night-time bayonet attack on 40,000 Turks at Kozlodui, in what is now Bulgaria. This broke the Turkish lines and brought the Russian advanceguard to within 250 miles of Constantinople. Mustapha III's brother had succeeded to the Sultanate earlier in the year; recognizing the danger he decided to end a war he had not himself started.

By the peace of Kutchuk Kainarji, signed in August 1774, Catherine traded her gains on the Danube for more important acquisitions on the Black Sea. The Turkish presence in the Crimea had for long been a pistol thrust into Russia's underbelly; now Catherine removed it. Crimea was declared independent; the old Khan, who had enjoyed Turkish protection, went into exile and was replaced by a new one. Azov, Kerch and several other coastal towns passed to Russia, which now established itself definitely on the Black Sea, securing the right to send merchant ships through the Bosphorus and Dardanelles to the Mediterranean.

Catherine also obtained a number of concessions designed to please the Church. Persecution of Christians in the Ottoman Empire was to cease; Catherine became 'protectress' of the Greek Orthodox population in Moldavia; and a Russian Orthodox church was to be built amid the mosques and minarets of Constantinople as a visible symbol that the Sultan subscribed to Catherine's views on religious toleration.

Foreign affairs during this first half of Catherine's reign may now be briefly summarized. Her energetic action in Poland had won

Catherine valuable land and 600,000 inhabitants to work the land, but it had cost many Russian lives and led, indirectly, to war with Turkey. By her victories over the Turk at Chesme Bay and on the Danube Catherine had proved what had hitherto been in doubt: that Russia was superior to Turkey on land and sea, and she had gained Europe's respect for her army and navy. Finally, she had achieved on the Black Sea what Peter had achieved on the Baltic: providing Russia with a direct outlet by water to Europe, thus reaffirming in territorial terms her belief, expressed in the *Instruction*, that 'Russia is a European country.'

CHAPTER 17

PORTRAIT OF THE EMPRESS

By what means did Catherine achieve these things, and continue to achieve so much in so many fields? How did she stir a sleeping bear to such prolonged and diverse activity? What in short was the personal element in her political success?

Catherine used to say that she arrived in Russia without a dowry. That is not quite true. She did bring a dowry: her German sense of time. 'In the immensity of Russia,' Catherine once wrote, 'a year is no more than a day.' In the person of Catherine a day became the equivalent of a Russian gentleman's week, so thoroughly did she fill it. Not a moment was lost. Up at seven every morning, she consistently worked a ten-hour day and a six-day week. It was no affectation that made her choose as her emblem the bee, and the motto 'Utility' – to Russia, of course.

The second element in Catherine's success was the ability to choose able men. 'Search for true merit,' she wrote in a memo to herself, 'be it at the other end of the world, for usually it is modest and retiring.' By true merit Catherine meant an honest man who worked.

One such was Alexander Vyazemsky. The son of a lieutenant in the navy, Vyazemsky was born in 1727, two years before Catherine, attended the Cadet School and entered government service. He was a big man with a round face and strong chin, a self-effacing manner and simple tastes – a foe of luxury and wastefulness. In 1763 Catherine sent him to make peace between owners and employees in the troubled Urals manufactories. Impressed with his efforts, in 1764 she promoted him Procurator General of the Senate, with orders to end senatorial abuses that had developed under Elizabeth. What she wanted, she told him, was not servility, but honesty and firmness in dealing with public problems. She promised him that, whatever his detractors might say, he need not fear losing his post so long as he conscientiously performed his duties.

In 1768 Catherine made Vyazemsky a member of her War Council and in 1769 gave him powers to draw up the first centralized State budget.

Later she was to make him director of the Mint and of State banks, with powers even to issue paper money.

Catherine, who was young when she came to the throne, chose young helpers. Vyazemsky was thirty-six when he got his first big post, and others too whom Catherine entrusted with important tasks were young: Gregory Orlov, Nikita Panin, Prince Repnin, Alexander Suvorov, Alexis Orlov. This element of youth helps to explain the energy of the reign.

How did Catherine treat her helpers? Giovanni Casanova, who had four conversations with the Empress in 1765 and was something of a connoisseur of women, noticed that Catherine was sweet and affable, and held back her knowledge: 'she seemed to know less than she did'. 'With these qualities,' Casanova continued, 'and her undemanding manner, she could demand more than Frederick of Prussia, and obtain it.' Catherine put the same thing slightly differently. 'My first principle in dealing with men is to make them believe that they want to do what I tell them to do.'

Having chosen a man and tried him out, Catherine gave him a pretty free hand. She was particularly broad-minded about money. For instance, she fixed an annual sum for household expenses, and provided her meals, theatre and stables did not fall below a certain standard she was satisfied. 'It doesn't matter to me if officials stint or steal with more or less cunning; what matters to me is that the sum specified is not exceeded.'

Catherine brought the same positive approach to criticism. One day when a gentleman of the chamber, Chichagov, turned up late for his duties, Catherine launched into a eulogy of the man's father who, fifty years before, had been known for his punctuality. Those listening thought Chichagov was receiving marks of favour, but he declared afterwards that he had never felt so ashamed in his life. 'My technique,' said Catherine, 'is to praise in a loud voice and scold in a whisper.' Similarly, to show her displeasure with Count Roman Vorontsov, the father of Elizabeth Vorontsova and Princess Dashkova, who as a provincial governor-general accepted large bribes, Catherine simply sent him as a birthday gift an empty purse.

Catherine kept her chosen men; though a target for Court intrigues, Alexander Vyazemsky is typical in remaining in her service 26 years, until disabled by paralysis. 'When I have given someone a post,' Catherine declared, 'unless he commits a crime he is sure of keeping it. Should he prove incompetent, I work with one of his deputies, but I will not disgrace him, for the initial fault would have been mine, not his.'

Under Elizabeth, imperial orders were so tardily carried out that the expression 'They are waiting for the third ukase' had almost come to be a proverb, because the first and the second were never complied with. Catherine facilitated her helpers' task by restoring respect for the imperial ukase. It had to be executed exactly and if this proved impossible Catherine invariably employed saving tactics, as Casanova noticed in 1765. The Italian was crossing a wooden bridge over the Neva with some friends. 'One of them, hearing me criticize the meanness of the bridge, said that it would be built of stone by the day of a certain public function on which the Empress was to cross it. Since it was only three weeks to the day, I said it was impossible; a Russian, looking at me askance, said that it was not to be doubted, for there had been a ukase. I was going to reply, but Papanelopulo [Casanova's banker] pressed my hand and made me a sign to say nothing. In the end the bridge was not built, but that did not put me in the right for, ten days before the day, the Empress issued a second ukase in which she decreed that it was her good pleasure that the bridge should not be built until the following year.'

Another element in Catherine's success as a ruler is that she understood her limitations. She did not press things too far. For instance, the Russian Julian Calendar lagged eleven days behind the Gregorian, which was generally used in Europe and had been adopted by England in 1752. When a foreign visitor urged her to follow England's example, Catherine explained that she didn't dare. 'People would not complain aloud, for that is not the way here, but they would whisper to one another that I am an atheist and that I am clearly attacking the infallibility of the Council of Nicaea.'

When one turns to Catherine's daily life one finds great changes since her enforced idleness and semi-imprisonment as Grand Duchess. As Empress Catherine got up, as had been said, at seven, but if she had a lot to do, as early as five-thirty. On one of these early mornings in winter she was about to light the fire in her study when, to her surprise, she heard something moving in the flue. Interrupting her fire-lighting she investigated, and just as well, for the noise turned out to be a little boy chimney-sweep at work even earlier than she.

Catherine's breakfast consisted of a cup of black coffee, without anything to eat. She said her morning prayers and then sat at her desk to begin work.

Some rulers, such as Napoleon, feel the need to speak their thoughts to secretaries; others prefer to write their thoughts down, and to this category Catherine belonged. She was never happier than when dipping her quill pen into ink, indeed she confessed, 'I can never see a new pen without feeling an itch to use it.' In the early morning, when her mind was freshest, she drafted ukases, directives, projects, memoranda: these she passed to a secretary who corrected misspellings. She wrote letters in her own hand to provincial governors, ambassadors, generals, admirals. She conducted much of her foreign policy by letter, writing in her own hand to her fellow sovereigns, notably Frederick of Prussia, who over a period of 24 years received 180 letters from Catherine. Always her pen was busy, and if she had no one special to write to she would pen little memoranda to herself.

In mid-morning Catherine began to receive the men who helped her govern. Each came on a specified day, made his report and presented problems. Catherine discussed the difficulties, usually asked his advice and gave her decision. According to her secretary Gribovsky, Catherine 'liked to use simple and purely Russian words – that is, not of Latin or other Western origin – and she knew a great many of them.'

Catherine dined at two, usually with a number of invited guests, in the company of her son Paul and Gregory Orlov. The food in St Petersburg was accounted very good, though expensive, by foreign residents: there was caviar, oysters, a variety of fish, woodcock, duck, hare, plentiful fruit, and sour cream with everything. Only cheese was lacking. Catherine, however, ate little and was not specially fond of delicacies. She liked best a dish that recalled her girlhood: salt pork and pickled cabbage, and for dessert sour milk flavoured with nutmeg. She drank moderately too: sometimes a glass of wine diluted with water, sometimes water and redcurrant juice.

Catherine's health improved when she became Empress and continued good during the first half of her reign. But she did suffer from severe headaches of two kinds: one accompanied by spasms and vomiting – which she attributed to wind; the other followed by a deep lethargy. Probably both kinds of headache were caused by alcalosis, a condition arising from lack of sunshine and lack of butter and cream in the diet: insufficiencies that had already caused her girlhood scoliosis.

In the afternoon Catherine either returned to her desk or undertook a public engagement, such as visiting the State porcelain works or initiating a new project, a school, say, or a canal. 'I have a decided taste for the word *schaffen* [meaning to produce, do or make],' she told her German confidante Grimm. 'It seems to me closely linked with creation, and creation has always appealed to me.' She liked Russia, she said, because it was still in a formative period. 'Only in Russia am I good for something; anywhere else there is no more *sancta Natura*, everything is disfigured and mannered.'

Creativeness, as so often, went with a simple style of living. Catherine disliked the military pageantry which had so thrilled her husband, and when she drove out her carriage had no military guard, only the footmen behind. It was typical of the woman that she disliked opulent leather and gold book-bindings, and had only plainly-bound volumes on her shelves. Wigs she positively hated, so that the wig went out of fashion at Court. Cosmetics she rarely wore, so that among the Court ladies, their cheeks painted red in the Russian style, she stood out by her paleness.

On her return to the palace, Catherine went for a walk in the gardens. Then came supper, a light meal which she sometimes skipped. After supper she relaxed with a few close friends, including Leo Naruishkin and Leo's sister-in-law Anna, for whom Catherine felt a special sympathy, because Anna's husband never consummated their marriage. Catherine liked these evenings to be informal and even drew up a set of mock rules for newcomers to them. 'Your Order of Precedence and your arrogance and any other such qualities – leave them outside the door . . . Be gay – without, however, breaking or spoiling the furniture . . . Discuss anything, argue anything, but without bitterness or bad temper.'

Even after she became Empress, Catherine continued to amuse friends with her imitations of animals and of a cats' concert. She was full of fun during these intimate evenings, and would tease her friends for any affectation of behaviour or language: Admiral Knowles for his habit of saying '*Il vente aujourd'hui* – It windeth today', her German friend and correspondent Grimm for his snobbism – 'Gotha-Grimma'; while even Gustavus III of Sweden did not escape; when he fell from his horse while reviewing a regiment and broke his arm, Catherine remarked, 'Fancy doing a somersault in front of one's troops.'

Her Scots physician, John Rogerson, whom Catherine liked and entrusted with diplomatic tasks, also came in for teasing. Rogerson was not paid for his professional services outside the Court but each patient presented him with a silver snuff-box. This gift Rogerson sent down to the jeweller, who bought it from him and placed it ready for purchase by the next patient. Thus did he obtain the £130,000 with which, on retirement, he bought the estate of Wamphray and built Dumcrieff in his native Dumfriesshire.

The Meissen Room in the balconied pavilion, Oranienbaum.
ommissioned by Catherine and designed by Rinaldi, its colours are green, pink and yellow.
Some of the brackets are in the form of monkeys.

Prince Gregory Potemkin, by G.B. Lampi.

Catherine, by an unknown artist,
probably about four years after her accession.

A corner of Catherine's bedroom in Tsarskoe Selo, designed by Charles Cameron. This is the earlier of two bedrooms designed for Catherine by Cameron and the only one to have been restored after damage in World War II. Altogether the bedroom has fifty slender shafts of pistachio-green and white faience.

Catherine liked whist and often gave evening whist parties. An incident recorded by the English ambassador reflects her fondness for the game and her consideration for servants, noted by many observers. She did not play herself that evening but walked from table to table watching the different hands. Presently she turned aside and rang for a page. She rang three times and when no one answered left the room looking furious. On entering the ante-room she found the page playing whist and holding such a good hand that when she rang he could not bear to leave it. 'Now, what did the Empress do?' says the ambassador. 'She despatched the page on his errand, and then quietly sat down to hold his cards till he should return.'

Shortly before ten o'clock the whist or other amusement came to an end, and Catherine went to bed. She was very particular about getting a full night's sleep, and unless there was some important celebration the light went out in the palace soon after ten o'clock.

On Sundays Catherine attended Mass. Like an ordinary worshipper, she stood during the two-hour ceremony, but her gaze wandered. She exchanged glances with Gregory Orlov and with others she wished to favour. For Catherine had lost much of her early piety. She was moving towards a typically eighteenth-century belief in progress, in particular progress for Russia, and she saw herself as being helped by Providence to forward the well-being of the Russian people. It is symptomatic that she liked a priest not only to celebrate Mass but to be able to operate and mend a mechanical harrow.

On Sundays too Catherine had time for her pleasures. Reading was still a firm favourite. But she had turned from history to contemporary works from which she could draw information useful to Russia. She read agricultural treatises, geological reports, the latest journals of navigators and explorers, and even a code of Danish laws, so dull, she declared, that if she were to throw it into the crater of Vesuvius, it would extinguish the volcano. Even when she read Catherine had her pen handy, and annotated the margins.

One of Catherine's few outdoor pleasures in winter was going for a ride on the Toboggan Hills constructed by Elizabeth midway between St Petersburg and Tsarskoe Selo. From a fifty-foot-high platform cars on castors positioned in a groove raced down a curved, undulating wooden framework covered with ice. On one of these outings Catherine's car ran off the groove and an accident would have occurred had not Gregory Orlov been seated beside her. Gregory was strong enough to guide the careering car down to safety with his leg.

When she went for her Sunday walk, Catherine took with her Sir

Tom, an English whippet whose correct name was Tom Anderson. She was devoted to Sir Tom, knitted him a woollen blanket and allowed him to sleep in her bedroom. When he fathered a litter of puppies, they accompanied her on her walks also, and though only Sir Tom slept in her bedroom, all the whippets were allowed to attend their mistress whenever she went to the Court theatre.

Within the framework of this daily programme Catherine's son Paul naturally occupied an important place. For the first seven years of his life Paul had been fussed over and spoiled by Empress Elizabeth, and had grown into boyhood without the presence either of mother or father. When she retrieved him on her accession – small for his age, with fair curls and brown eyes – Catherine found, inevitably, that Paul was wilful. He resented the more regular, disciplined life he was now obliged to lead.

Catherine wanted Paul to have the best possible education. She invited Jean d'Alembert to be his tutor, but the Frenchman declined, explaining to Voltaire, 'I am too prone to haemorrhoids, which in Russia is a severe complaint. I prefer to have a painful behind in the safety of my home.' Catherine then chose her friend Francis Aepinus, a German-born scientist resident in Russia who had written an important work on the electrical properties of tourmaline, to give her son lessons in physics, astronomy, mathematics and history. Catherine selected three of her favourite works as basic text-books: Fénelon's *Telemachus*, Voltaire's *Philosophic Dictionary* and Buffon's *Natural History*. To these she added Racine's plays and William Robertson's *History* and biographies, which had been commended to her by her physician, Dr Rogerson.

As he grew up, Paul lost his looks. He had a small frail body; his head was unattractive, with receding brow and chin; his underlip protruded and he had a short-turned-up nose which gave him the appearance of a Pekinese. This nose must have been a daily reminder to Catherine of Paul's origins. Peter and Peter's father and mother had had long straight noses, whereas a number of the Saltuikovs had turned-up noses.

Catherine had made Serge Saltuikov her ambassador to France and helped him with gifts of money. But he proved so inefficient he had to be dismissed the Foreign Service. And Paul was like a caricature of Serge. He was a reminder of her adultery with a man who had quickly deserted her, and now become a failure. For these reasons Catherine felt little attraction to her son.

Paul for his part was learning certain facts not in Aepinus's curriculum, notably that Peter III – who, like everyone except Catherine and Serge, he believed to be his father – had not died naturally, but had been strangled by Alexis Orlov, and that his mother, instead of wearing widow's weeds and passing her days in grief and prayer, was sharing her bed with the brother of her husband's murderer.

The situation was not unlike that in *Hamlet*, but the Grand Duke in no way resembled the Prince of Denmark. He lacked the fibre and the muscle for revenge. Instead, his early wilfulness deteriorated into sombre moroseness, and his small features became increasingly darkened by sullen resentment. This resentment, it has to be emphasized, was directed exclusively against Catherine in her relations with the Orlovs. Catherine had not cheated Paul of the throne, for a son did not possess a legal right of succession, and Paul felt no resentment against Catherine on that score.

Catherine was saddened by this development in her son. The only way she could put things right would be to tell him who his real father was. But Catherine did not feel up to doing this. It would seriously weaken her position on the throne, for it was part of her political programme that she was preparing the way for the eventual rule of Peter the Great's great-grandson.

Catherine did what she could to bridge the gulf between her and Paul. She gave him lessons in politics; she confided in him certain of her plans; she associated him in her schemes for public welfare. She partly succeeded in her aim. For during her absence from St Petersburg in spring 1772 a group of NCOs in the Preobrazhensky regiment, discontented for some reason that is not clear, came to Paul's apartment and urged him, now that he had attained the age of eighteen, to oust his mother and rule as Tsar; Paul would have nothing to do with them, though they offered to lay down their lives for him; he at once informed Panin and the guardsmen were brought to trial.

This failed plot had the paradoxical result of turning Catherine even more against her son. She began to wonder when the next plot would break and how Paul would act then. Dark fears pressed on her. She became suspicious of her son and refused to allow him to have the independence of action that would probably have improved his character. And this in turn increased Paul's resentment.

Catherine withheld a trustful affection from Paul because she wanted to try to hush up part of herself: her adultery with Serge and her own plot against Peter. Like everyone who tries to hush up part of himself, Catherine was to that extent diminished. Her poor relations with Paul fell like a small shadow over these first splendid years on the throne, and the shadow was to lengthen with her reign.

By contrast Catherine's relations with her son by Gregory, Alexis Bobrinsky, were more straightforward. Aged two months when Catherine came to the throne, Alexis enjoyed an almost normal childhood, with Catherine and Gregory in their parental role. He received an excellent education in the palace and grew up to be good-looking and open. Then he travelled abroad, developed bad habits, consistently overspent the allowance Catherine gave him and became a wastrel.

The most important person in Catherine's life in the years after her accession was Gregory Orlov. His striking good looks, his courage and his generosity had from the first made him deeply attractive to her, and their liaison before the coup had been happy on both sides. Gregory the war hero had been the strong partner; he had stirred up the Guard, and Catherine had been dependent on him. When she became Empress, Gregory sensed that the balance of their relationship would suffer; as has been seen, he offered to withdraw. At Catherine's pressing request, he remained.

Gregory was not self-effacing like Alexis Razumovsky or Ivan Shuvalov. He found it unvirile to hang around the imperial bedroom like a second whippet. Catherine was free now; he wanted to marry her, and as soon as the coronation was over this is what he pressed for.

Catherine too wanted the marriage, from love and from a desire to make Gregory happy. But she met great opposition from Panin who, as usual, voiced the feelings of the influential gentry. A Tsarina, argued Panin, did not marry for love, she married in order to forward Russia's foreign policy.

Catherine had grounds for believing that her predecessor had secretly married Alexis Razumovsky. If she could obtain proof of this, she would be able to answer Panin's argument and provide a precedent for what she wished to do. So she sent Michael Vorontsov, then for a short time her Chancellor, to Alexis Razumovsky's house with an offer to raise him to the title of Imperial Highness as the widowed Prince Consort, provided only that he could show his marriage certificate.

The former chorister was then aged fifty-four, much in eclipse since Elizabeth's death but on good terms with Catherine. His handsome face was lined, his hair greying, he drank too much vodka, but one of the distinctive facets of his character remained unchanged. After listening to Vorontsov, he rose from his seat by the fireside and, unlocking an ebony chest, took out a parcel wrapped, curiously, in pink silk. Undoing it, he removed some papers, which he read in silence. When he had finished, he kissed the papers, put them back with the rest, made a sign of the cross and threw the parcel into the blazing fire. As they burned, he turned to Vorontsov, visibly moved. 'I have never been anything but the late Empress's most faithful slave. You can see for yourself I possess no documents of any kind.'

Unsuccessful in producing proof that Empress Elizabeth had married for love, Catherine had to listen to a second, even more telling objection from Panin. It was common knowledge at Court that Alexis Orlov had helped Peter to the grave; if Catherine married Alexis's brother she would seem to be associating herself in the murder; and that would be an outrage intolerable to public opinion.

Catherine was too astute a politician not to see the force of this argument. Doubtless it came as a surprise and a paradox to her that even as Empress of Russia she could not marry the man she loved, but reluctantly, sadly, Catherine accepted the fact that she and Gregory, like Elizabeth of England and Leicester, were kept apart by the body of a murdered spouse.

Catherine, however, had no intention of parting from Gregory – she loved him too much for that. She kept him as her lover – the polite term was 'general aide-de-camp'. She gave him apartments communicating with her own by a private staircase. She consulted him on all important matters, had him beside her on State occasions. She gave him large estates so that he would be financially independent. She appointed him to several senior posts, including Mastership of the Ordnance. In short, she did everything in her power to make Gregory contented.

Gregory by temperament and profession was a soldier. He did not take kindly to a life of ease. He wanted to achieve something positive, something that would win him honour and respect, and since he was interested in science, with Catherine's encouragement he began practical scientific work. He built a carriage gateway the base of which he embedded in ice instead of cement. Describing the gateway-in-ice later to Voltaire, Catherine proudly said that it had stood firm for four years. He also installed an observatory on the palace roof, and during the long winter nights General Gregory Orlov divided his time between watching the stars and making love to 'the star of the north', as the *philosophes* called Catherine.

But Gregory lacked the education to do more than dabble. And all the while he was incurring the envy of those over whose heads he had been promoted, and the silent rancour of those, like Panin, who disapproved of soldier-favourites. Expressions of this ill-feeling reached Gregory in curious ways. For instance, one day in October 1763 he received a parcel from Moscow accompanied by a blank letter. Undoing the several wrappings of the parcel, he found a large empty cheese filled with horse dung, and stabbed through the centre by a truncheon.

Gregory took these signs of enmity very much to heart, and there came uppermost in his character a latent instability. He would flare up into capricious ill-temper and take out on Catherine his sense of personal failure. He professed a contempt for Court life and announced his intention of settling in the remote countryside. Rousseau would join him, he hoped, and an invitation was sent to the Swiss sage. As though to justify his peculiar conduct Gregory began his letter: 'Men are inclined to be peculiar.' The people on his estate, Gregory continued, 'do not understand English or French, still less Greek and Latin . . . you will shoot your own game and catch your own fish.' The prospect of shooting his own game and catching his own fish made small appeal to the impractical Rousseau, who declined Gregory's invitation, saying, 'Sir, you expect a wit, but I am no talker; I commune in silence with plants.'

Foiled in his plan for rustic seclusion, Gregory started throwing even worse tantrums, and plunged into a series of affairs with various ladies of his acquaintance, including one of Catherine's maids of honour. A woman forgives such affairs more easily than a man forgives a woman's affairs, for she knows that his senses and not his heart are involved. Catherine showed patience, and even when Gregory's philandering became the talk of the Court continued to keep him as her favourite.

In 1771 a form of plague from the battlefields struck Moscow. It killed more women than men, and post-mortems showed the blood to be congested in the heart and lungs. The doctors tried various kinds of medicine in vain. Archbishop Ambrose, a good and sensible prelate, decided to reduce infection by removing a much-loved 'healing' icon of the Blessed Virgin, which Moscovites were flocking to kiss. The people misunderstood his action. In fury they attacked the Donskoy monastery, seized the archbishop and killed him: 'something for this famous eighteenth century to boast of' was Catherine's sickened comment to Voltaire.

Catherine sent Gregory to take charge of a highly dangerous situation compounded of disease and panic. This was the kind of task the war-hero excelled at. Showing great personal courage, Gregory imposed emergency measures, rigorously separated the infected from the uninfected, and eventually found that the only effective way of treating them was to wrap them in blankets and make them sweat profusely. Gregory soon had the epidemic mastered and when he returned to

St Petersburg Catherine erected a triumphal arch inscribed 'To him who saved Moscow from the plague'.

For a short time Gregory glowed in the favour won by his courage. Then the old instability returned, but worse. He felt he was being bypassed by Catherine. 'I could dethrone her in a month,' he boasted to Rumyantsov, to which the soldier replied, 'No. For in two weeks we should have hanged you.' Catherine found herself increasingly exhausted by Gregory's tantrums, which were to get even more irrational as he grew older and to end in madness. When Gregory told her that he had fallen in love with his thirteen-year-old first cousin, Catherine Zinovieva, and despite family opposition was thinking of marrying her, Catherine decided that this was the moment to separate from a man who was making her ill with his affronts and scenes. In summer 1772 she sent Gregory to distant Focsani, in what is now Romania, to take part in peace talks with Sultan Mustapha's envoys.

Gregory's departure relieved Catherine of nervous tension but it also left her painfully alone. The year 1772 was the most difficult of her reign so far: her country was at war; the situation in Poland still critical; she had been deeply shaken by the Preobrazhensky NCOs' recent attempt to make her son Emperor. When it became apparent that she had dismissed Gregory, he and his brothers, who commanded a strong following, might well turn against her, might even try to dethrone her.

In this situation any person would have sought strength, and Catherine, an unmarried woman with no family to support her, naturally sought the strength of a man. Close to despair, she felt the need of someone solid and uncomplicated, preferably a soldier, with a soldier's calm reassurance in face of danger: someone who would be a visible successor to Gregory and would help her to stand out against Gregory, should he demand reinstatement.

As a young woman Catherine had been rather thin and her face had had a pinched look. Now as then its main features were the arched eyebrows, large eyes and mouth turned up at the corners, but the cheeks had filled out and at forty-three Catherine's looks were in full bloom. With the mystique of monarchy about her and a mischievous smile on her lips, Catherine was still able to compete for the young officers at Court. Many were ready to succeed Gregory Orlov, and had only to be shown a mark of favour by Catherine to step forward.

The man Catherine chose was a twenty-eight-year-old officer of the Horse Guards named Alexander Vasilchikov. He came of a family of gentlefolk, was even-tempered – a desirable quality after Gregory's moodiness – and rather shy. If he did not speak wittily at least he had the wit to speak very little. In September 1772 Alexander Vasilchikov became Catherine's fourth lover.

Besides her need for protective strength, was there also in Catherine's behaviour at this point a strong element of sensuality? Was Catherine a lusty woman seeking sexual pleasure? – the question was raised by some during her lifetime. The answer must be sought in Catherine's character as reflected in other aspects of her life. Her early rising, indifference to comfort, frugality at table, the absence in her hundreds of letters of tactile imagery or indeed of more than a rare reference to pleasures of the senses – these are not the mark of a sensual woman. Catherine took pleasure in books, in being with friends and above all in ruling – building up Russia, modernizing it and governing it well; these again are not the kind of pleasure one associates with a sensual woman. What one does find in Catherine is a feminine need for tenderness and protection, and a preoccupation, mainly aesthetic, with the good looks of this or that man, especially with his eyes, these features being interpreted as signs of character. All the evidence suggests that what Catherine was seeking in Alexander Vasilchikov was the protective strength of an uncomplicated, handsome, brave young officer, who loved her and could be expected to continue loving her.

When he heard that Catherine had taken a new lover, Gregory Orlov came rushing back from the peace talks in a fury. Catherine was so frightened that he and Alexis might try to kill her that she changed all the locks on the palace doors. However, as he had come from the battle-lines, where the Moscow plague was believed to have originated, Gregory was obliged to observe four weeks' quarantine before entering St Petersburg, and this cooled him down. Catherine then gave him the title of Prince and persuaded him to retire to Revel, on the Baltic, pending a decision on his future.

Catherine came to the conclusion that the Orlovs, with their close connections in the Guards' regiments, were too powerful to be alienated. She therefore recalled Prince Gregory, as he now was, in March 1773. Her new attachment to Alexander Vasilchikov had extinguished the last embers of her love for Gregory and she was able to bear his presence at Court with equanimity. She restored him to his former posts, increased his allowance, made him gifts of money, and treated him with respect. Their sexual relations were at an end, but otherwise she readmitted Gregory to his former status.

Gregory, unpredictable as ever, was touched to the heart and decided to show his gratitude in a gesture of great extravagance.

Gathering together what remained of the money Catherine had heaped on him, he paid an Armenian merchant in Amsterdam a sum of about 400,000 roubles for a 199-carat diamond of bluish-green tinge, which had been discovered in the Golconda mines and acquired by Shah Jehan, who had it cut in the form of a high rosette, $1\frac{3}{8}$ inches long, $1\frac{1}{4}$ inches wide, and $\frac{7}{8}$ of an inch high. This diamond Gregory gave to Catherine.

Probably no woman has ever received so valuable a present from her lover. This diamond was to other diamonds what a comet is to stars. Catherine doubtless was deeply touched and pleased. But, typically, she did not keep the Orlov diamond, as it came to be called, for her personal use. She did not mount it in a tiara or necklace; she gave it to the State, and had it set at the top of the imperial sceptre.

The last scene in the stormy drama between Catherine and Gregory occurred in 1776. Catherine helped Gregory to marry his first cousin, though such marriages were not normally permitted by the Church, and to stem any hostility at Court, she made the bride her lady-in-waiting and gave her the Order of St Catherine, usually reserved for royalty.

In summarizing this account of Catherine's personal life during the first part of her reign, it may be said that Catherine fulfilled herself amply as Empress, but in her role of mother she met with disappointments for which she must be held partly to blame. She discovered that the roles of Empress and woman in love could conflict, and out of such a conflict she lost Gregory. But Catherine was still only in her early forties; it might well be that she could yet combine her duties as ruler with her aspirations as a woman.

CHAPTER 18

ENTER POTEMKIN

The Potemkin family had a name for devoted service to the Crown and for frequently odd behaviour. Peter Potemkin, born in 1617, went as Russian envoy to Copenhagen. There he learned that King Christian of Denmark, who was unwell and confined to bed, intended to receive him in the royal bedchamber. Get a bed for me too, said Peter Potemkin, explaining that the Tsar's representative could negotiate only on terms of absolute equality. His wish was complied with, and the diplomatic talks took place, in a smell of medicines but with honour satisfied, between the King in one bed and Potemkin, stretched out fully dressed, on a second bed opposite.

The oddness of Alexander Potemkin took a different form. After completing his military service as a colonel, he retired to a small estate in Smolensk. One day, while travelling near Kiev, he met an attractive widow, Darya Skuratova. Although she was twenty-nine years younger than he, Alexander proposed to, and married, Darya. All went well for a few months. Then Darya, by then pregnant and living in Smolensk, discovered that her husband had married her bigamously. Throwing herself at the feet of the first wife, by then an elderly lady, Darya poured out her sorrow: what was to become of her and her unborn child? The first wife, who had been unhappy with Potemkin, solved the dilemma by entering a convent. Darya remained with Potemkin, who turned out to be a bully, easily jealous, and she bore him four daughters and one son.

The son, Gregory Potemkin, was born in 1739. When he was six his father died; that loss and an upbringing by a tender mother, with four admiring sisters looking on, accustomed young Potemkin to getting his own way. At the University of Moscow he won a gold medal, but was expelled for laziness and not attending lectures. Despite the gold medal, he chose a military career and as a quartermaster in the Horse Guards helped Catherine to the throne. As a reward for what she called his 'discernment, courage and energy' Catherine gave the young man a present of money and the post of supplementary groom-in-waiting.

Potemkin swaggered into Catherine's Court: tall, handsome, brown-haired, strong. He loved feasting late at night on oysters, champagne and spiced dishes he cooked himself, then lying in bed till noon; he loved the feel of diamonds between his large fingers, and flashy military Orders, heavy with intricately-worked enamel and precious stones. He had a special fondness for goldfish and at his dinner parties would place tanks of goldfish here and there to decorate the table. He loved pretty women, especially those who were calm and majestic, associating them in his imagination with the bluish-white light of diamonds and his favourite colours, aquamarine, lilac and pale green. He loved life itself, was curious about everything and fired questions at new acquaintances as readily as he fired off his pistol, on summer nights, at clustering midges.

When this handsome young groom-in-waiting was first presented to her, Catherine asked him about his well-known impersonations. Could he do one for her? Without a moment's hesitation Potemkin answered Catherine in her own voice, cleverly imitating the pitch, the tone, and her slight German accent. It was a cocky thing to try but he pulled it off: Catherine laughed delightedly.

Catherine soon discovered that there was more to her groom-in-waiting than animal vivacity and fun. One day, as she met him in a palace corridor, he threw himself on his knees at her feet and, kissing her hand, stammered words of admiration and devotion.

Catherine was then deeply in love with Gregory Orlov. Probably she was mildly pleased and a little surprised by Potemkin's warmth of feeling for her – nothing more. But Gregory Orlov did not like the look of this pushing young courtier. He summoned Potemkin to his room and there he and his brother Alexis started beating up the newcomer. Chairs flew across the room, looking-glasses were smashed, and at the end Potemkin emerged bruised and bleeding.

Potemkin stood his ground: he did not leave Court, as the Orlovs had hoped. That came later, as the result of a misfortune. Potemkin contracted an eye infection and had it treated by a doctor who only made the infection worse. Finally he lost his left eye. His vanity wounded by what he considered a bad disfigurement, he disappeared to lead the life of a recluse.

Eighteen months later Catherine summoned the Legislative Commission. Remembering Potemkin's devoted words and discovering that an interest in religion had led him to study Russia's religious minorities, she had Gregory Orlov appoint him to the Commission as Protector of the Tartars and other alien races in the Empire, and to the

Civil and Religious Commission. Though not by temperament a committee man, Potemkin did useful work and, when war broke, served with distinction, first as Rumyantsov's aide-de-camp, then in the cavalry, where he rose fast to the rank of major-general. From the front he wrote to Catherine in the same devoted tone he had used in the palace corridor; she replied, and soon they were exchanging letters. Catherine was impressed now by his good sense and largeness of vision. In December 1773, when he was besieging Silistra, she took the unusual step of asking him not to expose himself to danger.

Meanwhile Catherine had seen Gregory Orlov become increasingly difficult, ended her physical relations with him and taken up with Alexander Vasilchikov. But the handsome officer with narrow horizons did not give her the comfort she had hoped for; on the contrary, his limitations pulled her down and she began to realize that she had made a bad mistake. She was later to tell Potemkin, with understandable exaggeration: 'All his caresses provoked nothing in me but tears, so that I believe I have never cried since my birth as I have in these eighteen months. I thought at first that I would get accustomed to the situation but things grew worse and worse; he for his part sulked sometimes for three months and to tell the truth I was never happier than when he got angry and left me in peace, for his caresses only made me cry.'

Because of his absence at the front Catherine had seen Potemkin only once in the past five years. Panin and others warned her that he had a difficult character – was proud and moody – but Catherine liked what she remembered of him and, from his letters and what friends told her, inclined to believe that he was attracted to her. In January 1774 she felt the need to see him again. She summoned Major-General Potemkin to St Petersburg 'with the secret intention, however, of not acting blindly after he did come, but of trying to discover whether he really had the inclination I wanted him to have.'

Potemkin arrived. He was now aged thirty-four and had put on weight. His cheeks and jowls were fleshy, his full, sensual mouth revealed strong white teeth, his long nose came down to near his upper lip, so that in profile he resembled a pouter pigeon. Full face, however, the missing left eye lent him a rough, almost savage quality. Still wrapped in himself, and with a new assurance born of achievement, he was like a big powerful animal.

Catherine loved this quality in Potemkin; that is clear from one of the names she chose to call him by: Lion in the Jungle. The other quality she responded to was his obvious sensuality. Though she kept a decorous Court and insisted on cuts in the French plays performed by the young ladies of her Smolny Institute, Catherine was no hypocrite about sex. She had a healthy attitude to the pleasures of the bed and her talk could sometimes be bawdy, as the French diplomat Corberon reports.

One afternoon, after a festive dinner at which everyone had drunk wine, Catherine visited the porcelain works. One of her suite, Prince Repnin, picked up a newly made, still unfired vase of soft paste and, flattening the opening with his hands until it was oval, murmured, 'What does this look like, I wonder?' Catherine overheard and replied, 'Three things: a chamber pot, a bonnet or – ' she lowered her voice – 'a vagina.' The French potter who had made the vase approached and asked Catherine whether there was anything she would specially like him to make for her. 'What does your Majesty command?' said Repnin, and Catherine made her suite laugh by replying, 'Since he's done the vagina, he had better make what goes inside.'

Catherine then was no prude and she found Potemkin, with his zest for the pleasures of life, extremely attractive. When he returned from the front, she quickly fell in love with him. She felt fairly sure that he loved her also, but she did not wish to take the first step. She wanted Potemkin fully to play the male role and to make a definite declaration.

The first person Potemkin met in St Petersburg was Gregory Orlov coming down the palace staircase. 'Any news?' he asked, to which Orlov replied coldly, 'Nothing special, except that you are going up and I am coming down.' Despite this promising remark, Potemkin did not like what he saw at Court: Gregory Orlov still in great favour, Alexander Vasilchikov general aide-de-camp. Why had the Empress summoned him from the battlefield? To play third violin? Potemkin's pride was hurt and he stalked off to the St Alexander Nevsky monastery, put on a cassock, started to grow a beard and announced his intention of becoming a monk.

Potemkin was probably not bluffing, for he had a strong religious side and could discourse for hours on the Councils of Nicaea, Chalcedon and Florence. But whether or not his retirement was sincere, it was the kind of strong independent action Catherine liked. At the same time it caused her considerable alarm. Informing Panin that Potemkin was too useful a servant of the State for her to allow him to become a monk, Catherine sent a friend, Countess Bruce, to the monastery with a message for the would-be novice. If he chose to come back, ran the message, he could rely on her 'greatest favours'.

Potemkin's pride was satisfied. Removing his cassock and shaving his beard, he returned with Countess Bruce and wrote to Catherine, asking to be appointed general aide-de-camp. This was the declaration Catherine had been awaiting. 'I am particularly pleased,' she wrote back, 'that your confidence in me is such that you addressed your request directly to me.' She gave Alexander Vasilchikov a large sum of money and a country estate which, it was suggested, he should go and visit forthwith. Alexander took the hint and on 1st March 1774 Potemkin moved into the favourite's apartment in the Winter Palace, from which a green-carpeted private staircase led to the imperial bedroom.

A new life opened for Catherine. Potemkin would arrive in her room wearing only a brocade dressing-gown, none too clean, his hairy chest visible between its lapels. He would be munching a radish, a turnip or an apple – he always seemed to be hungry – and if none of these were to hand, he would be biting his nails. He would throw himself into a chair, or on to an ottoman big enough to seat twelve which he insisted on moving into her daintily furnished room, and loll there for hours, talking with great assurance on important issues and on trifles, punctuating his phrases with sudden bursts of laughter. Now his mood was tender, and he would sing Catherine sentimental verses he had written when he had first seen her at Court; now his mood was jealous, and he would reproach her with having had fifteen lovers, to which Catherine replied that there had been only four, 'the first from compulsion, the fourth from despair'; now his mood was teasing, and he would pretend to appropriate for his vast body the little woollen blanket she had knitted for Sir Tom the whippet; and most often he was just a splendidly healthy animal, exuding vitality but wrapped in himself.

Catherine adored him: no other word will do. She who readily saw people in terms of animals gave Potemkin a whole range of such endearments: Lion in the Jungle, Tiger, My Golden Pheasant, Dearest Pigeon, Little Parrot, Little Dog, Kitten. But also she called him Cossack, Giaour, Daddy, Twin Soul, Dear Little Heart.

Even though she saw him almost continually Catherine poured out her feelings in love-notes. Here is part of one of them:

> There are few people with a will as strong as yours; few as handsome, intelligent and good company as you. I'm not at all surprised that you are said to have made so many conquests . . . How strange it is! The very things I've laughed at all my life have happened to

> me, even my being blinded by love for you. I am now experiencing feelings that I used to consider idiotic, exaggerated and unreasonable. I cannot take my stupid eyes off you; I forget everything reason tells me and feel completely dazed when I'm with you. If I can I must avoid seeing you for at least three days in order to regain my senses; otherwise you will grow bored with me, and rightly so. I am very annoyed with myself today and have given myself a good scolding; I have made every possible effort to become more reasonable and to find the necessary firmness and strength of character – qualities that you possess in abundance.

In another letter Catherine wrote:

> My Pigeon, my little Grisha, you went out very early this morning and I hardly slept all night. My blood was coursing wildly and I even thought of sending for a doctor to bleed me, but as morning approached I felt a little better and went to sleep again. Don't ask whom I'm thinking about. Know that you are always in my thoughts. I say 'always' but I don't know if you want to remain there or if you intend to abandon me to myself? My great love for you terrifies me. Never mind. I shall find a way of resisting that fear. For the moment I shall be, as you so often put it, your 'woman of fire'. I shall try to hide 'my flames' without being able to prevent my feeling them.

Catherine was more carried away by her love for Potemkin than by any of her earlier affairs; she was surprised, even – as she said – terrified at the depth of her feelings, the 'madness' that made her write a note like this: 'General do you love me? Me love General very much.'

What were Potemkin's feelings for Catherine? He certainly loved her: 'no one,' he writes, 'has ever loved you as much as I.' Catherine was still physically very attractive, more so than her portraits would suggest, according to William Richardson, who says that 'in most of them her features appear too strong, and her air too masculine,' so that Potemkin's feelings probably had a strong physical basis. He liked the exotic, and Catherine with her German background would have appealed to this side of his character. What played a very large part in Potemkin's love was admiration for Catherine's achievements. He recognized in the Empress a person who loved Russia as much as he did and was governing the country better than any previous ruler. In the letter just quoted, he goes on to say that he wishes her 'to find consolation in me for the great work you have to accomplish, because of your high calling'.

Paradoxically, this soldier whom Catherine found so strong had a distinctively Russian streak of passivity. He wrote like this to Catherine, and no Frenchman or German of the period would have used such words: 'I am the work of your hands, I wish that my repose should be the work of your hands, that you should find joy in being kind to me.' So Potemkin needed Catherine differently from the way she needed him but quite as much, and this mutual need underpinned their love.

Catherine liked tidiness in her life and as a lawgiver had a respect for legal forms. Potemkin, virile and proud, did not wish to be a mere favourite. Probably the idea of marriage occurred early on to both. Catherine would have seen the danger in their ten years' difference of age, but she was too much in love to be deterred by that, or indeed by Panin's warning that Potemkin was insufferably arrogant. By 1774, with the Turkish and Polish questions satisfactorily settled, Catherine had won for herself a much stronger position than she had had in 1762, and could take her own decision about marriage.

What that decision was has to be inferred mainly from Catherine's correspondence with Potemkin – his love letters to her, save for a very few, have not survived. In twenty-three letters Catherine referred to Potemkin, explicitly or implicitly, as husband. 'Dear husband', 'tender spouse' are phrases that occur, and one letter she signed 'your devoted wife'. In another note she said, 'What is the good of believing your feverish imagination rather than the facts, which all confirm your wife's words? Hasn't she been attached to you now for two years by sacred bonds?'

These words evidently mean what they seem to mean. If so, Catherine and Potemkin were probably married near the end of 1774 in St Sampson's Church, which stood in a distant poor quarter of St Petersburg. Catherine did not wish the marriage to be made public, for it would only arouse jealousy and faction. The witnesses appear to have been the Chamberlain, Eugraf Chertkov, and Potemkin's nephew, Samoilov, each of whom received a copy of the marriage certificate. Samoilov's nephew was later to assert that one of these certificates was placed in his uncle's coffin when he died in 1814.

If Catherine did marry Potemkin, what a contrast with her first marriage it must have been. The Church of Our Lady of Kazan had been crowded with Russian and foreign dignitaries, all St Petersburg had drunk wine in the streets; she was just sixteen and there had been doubt in her heart; now she was forty-five, the church was almost empty, no fireworks zoomed into the night sky, but she was full of love and confidence, as she joined herself before God to the man she called her hero.

Catherine settled down to a married life that was none the less satisfying for having to be kept secret. Potemkin continued to loll about her room at all hours in his dressing-gown munching some unexpected vegetable, and to make her laugh with his unpredictable behaviour and odd turns of phrase: 'I'm so frozen I cannot even get my teeth warm.' Like any wife, Catherine took care of his health and watched particularly his susceptibility to colds. 'Let me know,' she wrote, 'whether I can come to your room, for I don't want you venturing down cold corridors after a steam-bath.'

Catherine derived a new strength from her happy life with Potemkin, and this made the year 1775 the most productive of her reign to date. In the five months from January Catherine composed her important Fundamental Law on the Administration of the Provinces, which, as has been seen, began a process of civilizing.

In her first passionate love letters Catherine had spoken of how unreasonably she was behaving, and of her unsuccessful attempts to control her display of feeling. After the honeymoon period she had to face up to the question of Potemkin's liking for late hours and her own need to be up at seven. In short, she had to choose between sexual dalliance and her duties as ruler. At first she had been 'your woman of fire', but as she herself said in a letter to Potemkin, 'I have no leanings towards wantonness'; before long she had regained control and was choosing – with her usual strength of will – the second course. When Potemkin stayed in her room till after midnight several nights running, Catherine found herself feverish, and wrote, 'Please be good enough to leave me earlier, it is really bad for me to stay up so late.' Again, inviting Potemkin to her boudoir, 'the only place without a draught', she wrote as follows – and her words again belie the notion of Catherine as sensual or licentious: 'We'll read a book together and say goodnight at half past ten.'

It may have been Catherine's firmness in this matter that caused Potemkin to feel hurt, and to show his sense of hurt in jealousy of Gregory Orlov, still very prominent at Court. Catherine handled Potemkin's incipient jealousy with as much firmness as she had shown in the matter of late hours and with characteristic loyalty to friends:

> 'Don't try to turn me against Prince Orlov, for I should consider that a great piece of ingratitude on your part. There is no one in the world about whom the prince has told me so much good and whom he likes more than you. If the prince has his faults, it is not for you or me to criticize them and to draw people's attention to them. He has been fond of you and as far as I'm concerned he and his brother

[Alexis] are both great friends of mine and I shall never abandon them.'

Potemkin showed signs of another weakness too; it is well described by William Richardson: 'In moments of extreme good humour, a Russian will make ample promises; he is quite sincere, his feelings at the time interest him in your favour; but those feelings subside; other interests engage his heart; he never meant to deceive you; but his promises are not fulfilled. Rigid virtue may call this double-dealing; but the Russian neither intends deceit, nor thinks his conduct deceitful.'

Potemkin would promise to meet Catherine at a certain hour, then fail to turn up; he would promise to keep his door open so that she could visit him in his room, and when she arrived she would find it locked. Catherine was often irritated by Potemkin's broken promises, but like Richardson, she seems to have come to accept them as part of the Russian character. For one as orderly as herself, perhaps Potemkin's behaviour held the attractiveness attaching to mystery.

A third, more serious difficulty arose between Potemkin and Catherine. Potemkin's political views in many ways tallied with hers: he had largeness of vision, and a love of Russia combined with respect for Europe. But he lacked Catherine's judgment. He applied the fashionable views of Lavater to sum up a man's character instantly by his physiognomy, and this sometimes led him to propose rash policies. Moreover in money matters he was none too scrupulous.

When war broke out between England and the American colonists, the English ambassadors Robert Gunning and, later, James Harris tried to hire Russian troops. Potemkin took a liking to Harris and pressed the English case with Catherine. She, however, though sympathetic to a king dealing with 'rebels', declined military aid, and in this she certainly acted in Russia's best interests.

Again, Potemkin wrote a long memorandum for Catherine suggesting that an old friend of his, an army contractor named Faleyev, should be allowed to collect the tax on salt. One of Catherine's first reforms had been the ending of tax-farming, and she replied, 'As long as I live no taxes will be leased.'

Catherine treasured her new-found happiness and in making these decisions took care to spare Potemkin's feelings. Nevertheless, Potemkin felt hurt that his suggestions should be disregarded. Like his forebear, ambassador Peter Potemkin, he had a strong sense of what was his due, and as Catherine's husband he considered it his right to take an active part in government. His virility and his pride were offended, and he began to feel resentment. His attitude seems to have been:

You call me Lion of the Jungle, but when I wish to behave as such you shackle me.

Potemkin continued to press his political views, particularly in regard to an English alliance. Catherine listened to him. Sometimes she adopted a good suggestion, and she passed her papers to him so that he could correct her Russian. But she would not let love interfere with ruling. She made clear to Potemkin that she valued his advice, but that she alone would take the decisions. Elizabeth of England had said as much to the Earl of Leicester: 'I will have but one mistress and no master.'

Potemkin, hurt, began to quarrel with Catherine, and since he had a strong will the quarrels often proved bitter and protracted. After a particularly sharp exchange, Catherine waited two hours in the draughty palace library, hoping Potemkin would come and make it up. 'Towards eleven o'clock,' she wrote to him afterwards, 'I returned sadly to my rooms where on your account I had already spent four nights without shutting an eye.'

One quarrel led to another as Potemkin, hurt in his manhood, tried to humiliate Catherine. As in public affairs, Catherine felt surer of herself when writing than when speaking, and she now began to write to Potemkin, urging him to desist. In one letter she admitted how much strength she had gained from her Grisha, but added: 'Having given me the means of being an Empress you take all my force away from me by tormenting me with your insufferable and continually recurring caprices.' In another letter she diagnosed their trouble: 'For God's sake, please do all you can to avoid our quarrelling, for the causes of our quarrels are always insignificant. The essence of our disagreement is always the question of power and never that of love.'

Power was indeed the issue between them. Potemkin, brought up in a home with four admiring sisters, and in many ways Asiatic in his attitude to women, thought that he should be cock of the roost. Catherine, an early example of the career woman, maintained that there were certain areas of her life – the ruling of Russia but also her bedtime hours – over which he must have no control. So month after month the quarrels worsened.

Catherine came to see that she and Potemkin were slowly destroying each other. She was becoming exhausted by constant scenes with the man she deeply loved; Potemkin was becoming bitter, frustrated, cruel. What was to be done?

In this dilemma Catherine showed a positive, imaginative approach. She sensed that Potemkin possessed great potential gifts, both of intelligence and leadership. If he could only fructify those gifts, he would find fulfilment as a man. His great failing was laziness. To overcome that failing, he needed a motive. She recalled the protestations of loyalty to her in the palace corridor and in his letters from the front – he had expressed the wish of 'shedding my blood for your Majesty's glory' – Well, that might be the spring in his character to press. She could not allow him a share in the strategy of government or in foreign policy, but there were other areas calling for first-rate men, in particular those involving religious and political minorities. There she could give him a free hand.

But if she did that, Potemkin would have to leave St Petersburg. It was a condition of his fulfilling himself as a man that he should leave the enchanted palace.

It was not easy for Catherine to take her decision. She loved Potemkin and almost the last thing she wanted was to part from him. But she recognized that, given their characters and situation, their love could endure only if they separated. Only if she allowed Potemkin a certain autonomy would he continue to love her.

Catherine made the proposal as attractive as possible to Potemkin. He would go as a kind of roving viceroy, first to the Polish provinces, then to the Black Sea. He would conciliate religious minorities, he would build the Black Sea ports. Wherever he went he would be received as her special representative, with imperial honours.

Potemkin saw the good sense of Catherine's proposal. He did indeed feel constricted in St Petersburg. At heart he was a man of the open spaces, and he sensed that he would be able to do well the jobs she had proposed. He was bursting with ambition and only thirty-seven. With the enthusiasm he usually brought to new projects, he agreed to Catherine's plan.

Catherine would be the loser by her husband's departure. She would be deprived, at a stroke, of the strength he had brought her, and this at a time when her nerves were worn by quarrels and scenes. In the taxing task of ruling Russia Catherine had come to feel it an absolute necessity to have the physical support of a man. After giving orders all day, mastering opposition and inertia, she required in the evening to be treated as a woman, to lie in a man's strong arms, and to feel her nerves grow calm.

One last weight therefore required to be added to the mechanism if her complicated piece of clockwork was to turn correctly: a favourite to take the place of her absent husband. Catherine had learned from her mistake with Alexander Vasilchikov, and this time chose wisely: a good-looking, intelligent, happy officer of a family originally Polish but settled in the Ukraine, the same age as Potemkin and devoted to her; his name was Peter Zavadovsky. In November 1776, with the agreement of Potemkin, who had gone off on a preliminary tour of inspection, Catherine took Peter Zavadovsky as her fifth lover.

There was no question of his replacing Potemkin in Catherine's heart. Potemkin remained her hero, the great love of her life; Peter Zavadovsky merely provided the male presence she found essential if she, the autocrat, were to retain her psychological balance. And it was to Potemkin, as he set himself to justify the confidence placed in him, that Catherine continued to pour out her heart. When he sent her a big melon from the hot south, she wrote: 'Thank you, my master . . . I am burning with impatience to see you again; it seems a year since I saw you last. Goodbye and God bless you. I kiss you, my friend. Come back happy and in good health and we shall love each other.'

It was a strange proposed solution to the problem latent in every marriage between a powerful woman and a gifted man. Potemkin now went out to realize, so to speak in the field, the plans for good government and prosperity evolved by his wife. Catherine remained behind, giving him by letter love and encouragement, with Peter Zavadovsky to comfort her loneliness. Both Catherine and Potemkin were gamblers, and this curious plan was something of a gamble. It remained to be seen whether, in time, it would work.

CHAPTER 19

THE LITERARY SCENE

The improvements in government, growing prosperity and a sense of security which began to make themselves felt by the middle of Catherine's reign had their counterparts in intellectual and artistic achievements. A new spirit of confident experiment stirred, nowhere more strikingly than in literature. Almost all genres of fiction and non-fiction showed new activity and some produced distinguished results. It is possible to speak of a literary flowering at the centre of which, as patron and writer, stood Catherine herself.

It is first necessary to look, once again, at Russia on Catherine's arrival. In the preceding six hundred years only one Russian book of undisputed merit had appeared: the *Autobiography* of Archpriest Avvakum. As an Old Believer, Avvakum is persecuted mercilessly, exiled to Siberia, flung into prison, shipwrecked on river journeys; he is reviled and half-starved; his friends have their tongues cut out, and in one of the big scenes the archpriest is obliged to drive the Devil out of a fellow-prisoner by lashing him with his heavy-beaded rosary. One part xenophobia and three parts masochism, Avvakum's *Autobiography* is typical of the literary tradition Catherine found on her arrival. Apart from Church service books, about twenty books were published annually. When she wanted to read Plutarch's *Lives*, Catherine found that no Russian translation existed, and foreign books were so scarce it took her two years to get hold of a copy of Amyot's French translation. Ivan Shuvalov's literary patronage centred on persuading Voltaire – against his better judgment, after he learned that Peter had murdered his son – to write a *History of Peter the Great*; as for Empress Elizabeth, she considered reading bad for the health.

The most striking thing about the Russian literary scene was that the Greek and Roman classics were virtually unknown. Russia had never had a Renaissance, and it was part of the secret of her backwardness. So one of the first things Catherine did was to found, with a capital of 5000 roubles, a society for translating the classics, and other key books. It is an act that attracted little attention at the time, or indeed since, but it is of the first importance.

Homer and Plato now arrived in Russia, Virgil, translated by Catherine's librarian Petrov, Horace and Ovid and Cicero. Three centuries after Italy, under the impulse of one woman, Russia underwent the ferment of the Renaissance.

This in itself was an event of the first importance. But it occurred at the same time as a second event of equal importance – the Enlightenment. This too was made available to Russians by Catherine. It was she who sponsored translations of the leading champions of human rights, such as Montesquieu and Beccaria and the *Encyclopédie*, in a special three-volume Russian edition. While awaiting a Russian translation of Voltaire's *Portable Philosophic Dictionary*, Catherine imported 3000 copies of that work, which sold in a week. On a journey down the Volga in 1767 Catherine took along copies of Marmontel's *Belisarius* – conversations between General Belisarius, old and blind, Emperor Justinian and Justinian's son – and invited members of her suite each to translate a chapter, she herself translating chapter 9, which teaches that the only absolute power in a State is that of the laws.

Finally, Catherine's reign saw translations of modern works of literature: among those which met with success were *Robinson Crusoe* and *Gulliver's Travels*, Rousseau's *La Nouvelle Héloise* and Goethe's *Werther*, the poetry of John Milton, James Thomson and Edward Young. In the decade ending 1778 no fewer than 173 books, ancient and modern, were published in translation, bringing Russia at a single throw the accumulated pool of Europe's literary riches.

But in the field of literature Catherine did not wish just to Europeanize Russia. It would be nearer the truth to say that she wished to Russianize Europe, in the sense that she believed in the literary powers of the Russian people, and she told Princess Dashkova that 'our Russian language, uniting as it does the strength, richness and energy of German with the sweetness of Italian, will one day become the standard language of the world.'

Catherine's attitude and the translations themselves stimulated a new generation of Russian writers. The novel got going with *A Russian Pamela*, the story of a young nobleman's love for a beautiful peasant girl, modelled on Richardson's classic. Russian poets, influenced by Young's *Night Thoughts*, gave voice to a deep strain of melancholy in the national character. But perhaps the best poet of the reign is Gabriel Derzhavin who, freeing himself from youthful bombast, celebrated the Russia of his day and its notable men, including Potemkin, whom he compared to a mighty waterfall. Catherine honoured Derzhavin by appointing him one of her secretaries, but the Empress and the self-important poet were temperamentally unsuited, as Catherine found one day when, having asked him for a concise report on a certain subject, Derzhavin arrived in her study with two sacks of papers. After that she let him give all his time to poetry.

As her gift for mimicry and her liking of Potemkin's impersonation of herself would suggest, Catherine was very fond of the theatre and did a lot to encourage it. When a touring English company managed by a Mr Fisher performed Home's *Tragedy of Douglas* in an old barn, she went to see it, thought well of the actors and lent them a proper theatre. She founded a school of dramatic art for fifteen young men and fifteen young women of any class, including serfs. She had the best new plays produced at her Court theatre, stimulating the gentry to similar patronage, so that by 1793 St Petersburg had eight private theatres. Catherine particularly liked satirical comedies and encouraged two playwrights in this genre: Alexander Sumarokov and Denis Fonvizin. Both excelled at plays ridiculing dandies, misers and Frenchified aristocrats, Fonvizin producing in *The Adolescent* a minor masterpiece.

In the field of history, her favourite non-fiction subject, Catherine opened the imperial archives, where she herself sometimes worked, to scholars of all political persuasions, including a man she knew to be her enemy, Prince Michael Shcherbatov, the champion of serfdom. Drawing on manuscript sources, Shcherbatov wrote a seven-volume *History of Russia* to 1610, in which he painted Court favourites in the darkest tones – the nearest he got to openly criticizing Orlov and Potemkin, whom he detested.

The origin of political institutions in Russia was a question then very much in the air. According to some they originated with a group of Vikings who came from a place known as Russ somewhere in Scandinavia, probably Sweden. According to others the Vikings merely developed existing institutions. Leipzig-educated Gerhard Müller had upheld the first view; Lomonosov, expressing a national Slav consciousness, the second.

In this version of the old Europe-Asia conflict, Catherine stepped warily. She showed her appreciation of Müller's scholarship by making him superintendent of the imperial archives, but she ordered the publication, at government expense, of a two-volume historical study by Ivan Boltin, in which he attacks the theory of Scandinavian origins and also – incorrectly – equates Russian serfdom with European feudalism.

If there was much to discover and publish in early Russian history, even more remained to be done regarding contemporary Russia, where Catherine found herself almost in the position of a fairy-tale character: sending out explorers to tell her about, or actually to discover, territories that were unknown yet belonged to her. She sent Goldenstadt and Reinegg to study the Caucasus and Georgia, Johann Georgi the flora and fauna of the Urals, Dr Samuel Gmelin of Tübingen to explore the lands bordering Persia, Peter Simon Pallas, the brilliant Professor of Natural History in St Petersburg, to study the flora and fauna of Siberia as far as Lake Baikal and Kyakhta. Pallas found a wide distribution of mammoth and rhinoceros fossils, including some with their hairy hides preserved in the Siberian ice: these and other new species he described in a pioneer book, *Journey Through Various Provinces of the Russian Empire*.

Catherine pushed the search for new knowledge beyond the Russian mainland when she sent Captain Khrenitsin and Lieutenant Levashev to explore the Aleutians and coast of Alaska. She passed to William Robertson, principal of Edinburgh University, via Dr Rogerson, a new chart of their discoveries prepared by the Academy which showed that they were the first Russians to visit the American continent, and she gave Admiral Knowles the original journals of the expedition. Shelekov followed up by establishing a fur station on the mainland of Alaska, at Cook Inlet, the first permanent Russian settlement of Alaska. From the reports of these travellers and of a later expedition sponsored by Catherine and led by Joseph Billings, the Aleutian Islanders emerged from the Arctic mists that had hitherto enveloped them: a brave people who made fire by rubbing sticks together, needles from bones of birds and thread from whale sinews; who warmed themselves by burning whale fat in shells, and hunted in leather boats, firing from hand-boards stone-pointed six-foot harpoons.

Catherine's literary activities extended also to journalism. In 1769 she started Russia's first weekly magazine, modelled on *The Spectator* and called *All Sorts and Sundries*. The aim of the articles was to correct social defects by kindly humour. Catherine herself wrote articles for the magazine, which sold well and became 'the grandmother' – Catherine's term – for many other satirical magazines with a strong social purpose. The most outspoken of these was started by a young, well-educated, intellectual gentleman, Nicholas Novikov. *The Drone*, as Novikov's magazine was called, ran a famous article showing up a nobleman who orders his bailiff to punish a famine-stricken village in arrears with its *obrok*, mainly by flogging and fines.

The satirical magazines allowed Russians to express themselves freely on social issues for the first time. *The Drone* ran for fifty-two issues; it was not, as is usually said, closed by Catherine, but appears to have died a natural death of failing circulation. Other magazines continued to appear down to 1774. In that year the Pugachev revolt, which cost the lives of so many landowners, caused Catherine to reconsider her policy and she ended the publication of all magazines.

Catherine allowed Russians more freedom of expression than previous rulers, but she limited it to moral and social questions. She had learned from reading history that in Russia political opposition usually culminated in a change of ruler – indeed the structure of government was such that adverse political comment could hardly be other than revolutionary – so Catherine declined to allow freedom of expression in political matters.

In Catherine's reign, as in the past, the police censored books, but somewhat laxly, while plays were often referred to the Sovereign. When Nikolev's *Sorena and Zemir* was performed in Moscow, it was denounced to the Moscow commandant, who forwarded a copy to Catherine, saying that he found it unfit for the stage and marking certain lines, including these:

> For ever vanish thou, that fatal law
> That is derived from the imperial frown.
> Can bliss be sought where pride does wear the crown,
> Where hearts are chained with just the whim of one?

Catherine replied: 'I am surprised, Count Yakov Aleksendrovich, at the fact that you suspended the performance of the tragedy which, I understand, was well received by the public. The meaning of the verses you have noted has no bearing upon your Empress. The author challenges the despotism of the tyrants, whereas you call Catherine a mother.'

On the other hand, when Princess Dashkova printed in the Academy of Arts, *Bulletin* Knyazhnin's play *Vadim*, which contains the lines:

> Around the throne the censors of dishonest guile
> Exalt those gods with flatt'ring words and cunning smile,
> Comparing culprits crown'd with all that is divine,
> And drown their slaves in blood to make their glory shine.

Catherine evidently found 'culprits crown'd' too near the knuckle, for she informed the Senate, who had all copies of the offending *Bulletin* destroyed.

Catherine incidentally could be displeased with a play for a non-political reason. In 1777 she attended a private performance of *Le Médecin par occasion*, in which one of the actors, speaking of women in love, has the line: 'A woman of thirty falling in love – well and good; but a woman of sixty, that's intolerable.' The forty-eight-year-old Empress rose from her seat, saying, 'This play is stupid and boring.' She left the theatre, whereupon the performance stopped and was not repeated.

In the sphere of freedom of expression one of the most important movements Catherine had to deal with was Freemasonry. Though condemned by the Catholic Church, it was widespread in Europe, where it filled a vacuum left by declining religious belief, and it had swept into Russia mainly from Germany and Sweden. It was a multifarious movement, ranging from groups that combined secret passwords and medieval trappings with a quest for social justice and self-improvement, to the Rosicrucians who dabbled in occultism and alchemy.

As a girl Catherine had believed in fortune-tellers, such as the monk at Brunswick who had 'seen' three crowns on her brow, but her reading of Voltaire had made her ashamed of such credulity. Later she had seen the damage it could do, when her mother, in Paris, dabbled in alchemy, then became a prey to it, and finally lost what little gold she possessed trying to manufacture gold.

The latent streak of credulity in herself and her mother's ruin help to explain the extremely forceful critical stand Catherine adopted to Freemasonry. In a letter to Grimm she called it 'one of the greatest aberrations to which the human race has succumbed. I had the patience to plod through both published and manuscript sources of all the tedious nonsense with which they busy themselves. In disgust I came to the conclusion that, though they make fun of others, they are neither more enlightened nor any wiser than the rest of us . . . When they meet, how can they keep from splitting their sides with laughter?'

Catherine knew that the four thousand Freemasons in Russia – half of them foreigners – were more dangerous than her letter to Grimm suggests: for instance, the Berlin-appointed supremo of the Rosicrucians, Schwarz, confessed on his deathbed that the Order's secret purpose was subversion of the Orthodox faith. But Catherine did not ban Freemasonry, as the Kings of France had done. She allowed Masons to meet and express themselves freely, thus remaining true to her principle of toleration on social and religious issues. When Novikov joined the Rosicrucians, Catherine granted him a lease of the University of Moscow press, on which he printed Masonic books. Only at the end of the reign, in a changed political climate, was Catherine to harden her attitude to Freemasonry.

Catherine believed in the power of laughter to correct human folly, Masonic or otherwise, hence her admiration for Voltaire. The sage of Ferney remained her literary hero, his bust stood in her library, and she many times invited him to St Petersburg, but Voltaire recoiled from the long journey, and Catherine had to content herself with a lesser French writer and champion of Justice, Denis Diderot.

Diderot paid a six-month visit to St Petersburg as Catherine's guest in 1773. He had about sixty conversations with the Empress, ranging over politics, law, education and literature. Diderot urged the setting up of an English-style Parliament; Catherine replied that it was easy for him to reform on paper that did not answer back; as for her, she had to deal with human beings, with all their traditions and susceptibilities. On this point they eventually agreed to differ, and Catherine showed her respect for Diderot the writer, if not the politician, by having him elected to the Academy of Sciences.

Catherine bought Diderot's library, when financial difficulties obliged him to put it up for sale; her very generous terms allowed him to keep the books during his lifetime and to be paid for this 'curatorship'. She also bought Voltaire's books after his death. These two acquisitions and her private purchases increased the imperial library from a few hundred volumes to 38,000.

Catherine had parted company with Princess Dashkova after the coup, annoyed because the Princess wanted to claim more credit than Catherine thought was her due. Widowed at twenty-one, the blue-stocking Princess travelled in Europe and enlarged her views. Returning to St Petersburg in 1783, she met Catherine at a Court ball. Their differences now forgotten, Catherine invited this very able lady to become first Director of the Academy of Sciences, then President of a Russian Academy, whose interests would be literary and philological. The double appointment is important, for it marks the first occasion anywhere on which a woman held such influential posts. The Princess began compiling a Russian dictionary, to the first volume of which Catherine contributed notes on the language, so that their originally political collaboration continued at the level of lexicography.

Catherine brought to the literary scene the intuitive understanding of one who was herself an author. Some of her works are very slight, such as those she wrote for her grandchildren, the elder sons of Grand Duke Paul. *The Grandmother's ABC Book* teaches the alphabet through simple Russian sayings and proverbs, of which Catherine was very fond, particular emphasis being placed on the need to work hard and to be concerned for one's fellow creatures. It is the first children's text-book in Russian.

Catherine also wrote two fairy-tales for her grandsons, both about heirs to the throne. They are simple, and for present-day taste rather too didactic. 'Ivan Tsarevich, or the Rose without Thorns' goes like this: The Tsar's young son is kidnapped by the Khan of the Kirgiz who, wishing to test whether the boy is as wise as he is said to be, commands him to find, within three days, a rose without thorns. Guided by a young man, Rassudok, meaning Reason, the boy sets out on his quest. Resisting various blandishments and traps, he eventually learns from a wise teacher that the flower in question is virtue, and is to be found at the top of a steep hill, reached by a straight road. Supplied with staffs by Honesty and Truth, the boy and his guide Rassudok climb the hill, find the rose, pick it, and all ends happily.

More important than these writings for her grandsons, but animated by a similar didactic purpose, are Catherine's plays. She began, in the early 1770s, with five comedies satirizing failings in contemporary society. *A Prominent Boyar's Anteroom* brings on stage a medley of sycophants, French, German and Russian, who attend an influential nobleman's reception, hoping, with his help, to live off the Treasury. The best of this group of plays, *O, the Times!* is set in Moscow. Madame Khanzhakhina – the name means a specific type of Hypocrisy – is a Tartuffe-like figure who borrows at 6 per cent while lending at 16 per cent and who, when her creditors arrive with their bills, informs them that she is deep in prayer and cannot be disturbed. Other characters are Madame Vestnikova, a gossip forever telling exaggerated stories against the government, and Madame Chudikhina, who ties amulets into her handkerchief and has a morbid fear of crickets. The plot turns on Madame Khanzhakhina's attempt to marry off her grandchild without giving her a dowry, but the play's real purpose is to scoff at the vanity and prejudices of certain of the middle gentry.

Catherine found a new theme for plays with the arrival in 1779 of the Sicilian charlatan Cagliostro, self-styled son of Enoch, who conducted seances and alchemical experiments, and claimed to perform miraculous cures. At one of his public appearances Cagliostro proposed to cure a man of gout by bathing the affected foot in water and then draining off mercury from the foot, but was caught surreptiously introducing a spoonful of mercury into the water. This discredited him with some, but not with the Freemasons, who feted him and believed his claim that he could travel, angel-like, through the air and also back and forth between the centuries.

Catherine satirized Cagliostro, and the Freemasons who swallowed that sort of nonsense, in three plays, *The Impostor*, *The Victim of Delusion* and *The Siberian Shaman*. The latter Catherine described as 'a body-blow at enthusiasts. Imagine a man who has risen through 140 different grades, and achieved such a degree of intellectual beatitude that instead of replying rationally to people's questions he utters extraordinary phrases, miaows like a cat, crows like a cock, barks like a dog and so on. Yet underneath he's just a knavish pimp.'

Catherine's plays were performed and enjoyed a certain success. In most the characters' foibles or vices are too often described, too seldom conveyed through action. But the plays show a sense of fun and a considerable gift for satire.

For the sake of completeness, it is necessary to mention three lesser dramatic works by Catherine. One, a dramatic sketch portraying the monarchs of Europe, contains the following amusing exchange between the pious Empress of Austria and her free-thinking son:

MARIA THERESA: I have always placed all my hopes in Jesus Christ.
JOSEPH II: Yes, Mama. With that we have lost Silesia. Now we must have troops, money and a good general to work the miracle so that we can get it back.

The other two plays are adaptations of Shakespeare, whose works Catherine read in Eschenburg's German. With her liking for *outré* character, she chose to adapt *The Merry Wives of Windsor*, in which Falstaff becomes a Frenchified Don Juan just back from Paris, and *Timon of Athens*. The last act of Catherine's *Timon* is unfinished, but she evidently intended that he should marry and regain his place in society.

The next group of Catherine's writings are those which display her love of Russia. The first is *Notes on Russian History*, Parts I and II, a brief account of the period from 862 to 1161, when Russia was a small principality centred on Kiev and Novgorod. With a German appetite for even the dullest chronicles, Catherine drew on early annals, some in manuscript, for this history, in which she stressed the important role of Russia's rulers, from Ruric to Izyaslav III, and, with less justification, depicted the people as being at a stage of development equal to their contemporaries in Europe.

In the late 1760s Catherine read *Voyage en Sibérie, fait . . . en 1761; contenant les mœurs, les usages des russes*, by Abbé Jean Chappe d'Auteroche, published in Paris, as the title page explained, with the approval of the French Academy of Sciences. The abbé, an astronomer, had visited northern Siberia to observe the passage of Venus across the sun, and on his return written one more volume in the long series of French books damning Russia. It presented, as Samuel Bentham says, an unfair picture, and of course it made Catherine very angry indeed. So angry, in fact, that she answered the abbé's 'poisonous' book by writing a 300-page *Antidote*, or refutation.

One of the least read of her writings, the *Antidote* is very revealing of Catherine's character. It shows her love of Russia and her desire that Russia should be fairly understood abroad; it shows her impatience with factual errors and her desire to put the record straight; it shows the strong tendency to ridicule charlatans, found in her anti-Masonic plays.

Catherine argues that the abbé has missed the point about Russia. He has failed to perceive the fraternal spirit of the Russian people, the cooperativeness that keeps the country ticking over at village level in the absence of those sophisticated organs of government found for instance in France. That is one part of her criticism. The other is the singling out of particular errors. The abbé had fallen into the trap of supposing that Siberia embodied every imaginable evil. In Tobolsk, for instance, he writes of 'the difficulty of finding manual workers in this country where everyone is a serf obliged me to turn to the Governor.' 'How,' asks Catherine, pouncing, 'do you arrive at such odd conclusions? In all Siberia east of Solikamsk there are no estates belonging to gentry. Siberia is a domain of the crown, so the peasants can earn their living as they wish and as they can. Once they have paid their poll-tax, they can do as they wish with what they own, and should they decide to move they can obtain a passport valid for years.'

When the abbé argues that because Russia is a vast plain the people are stupid, Catherine rounds on him: 'Let it be known that the author has flattened my intelligence and pronounces me stupid because there are few mountains in Russia. This reasoning by the Lord d' Auteroche gives me boundless respect for the Swiss and the Savoyards. I am already fully convinced that they are Europe's most wonderful geniuses because they have been lucky enough to open their new-born eyes on high mountains. However, I am deeply saddened to find that in several countries these great geniuses are employed as janitors and boot-boys.'

The third in the group of Catherine's works relating to Russia is both the most ambitious and the most limited by virtue of its typically eighteenth-century belief that the babel of world languages has a common ancestry.

Catherine, who could speak four languages and understand two more, noticed the large number of words and place-names that seemed to her to have a Slav root. She decided to find out whether other languages showed a similar pattern and drew up a list of common words, as samples to be tested.

Though Professor Pallas said he did not believe in her theory, Catherine pushed ahead and sought information from foreign governments. Some such as Spain offered little help, while others, such as the United States, proved cooperative. For when Catherine approached Thomas Jefferson, then in Paris, asking him if he could kindly procure a translation of 300 important words ranging from God to grapes into the languages of the Shawnee and the Delaware Indians, Jefferson passed her word-list to George Washington with a letter dated 10th February 1786. In November Washington asked General Richard Butler to prepare the translation. Butler, a thorough man, did as he was asked, save for certain words such as eyebrow and eyelid, which did not exist in Shawnee. He also sent a complete vocabulary of the Shawnee language, and a list of important words in Cherokee and Chocktaw. These were forwarded to Jefferson on 10th January 1788, and by Jefferson passed to Catherine, who would have been well pleased with so full an answer to her questionnaire.

'I've got hold of as many dictionaries as I could find,' Catherine wrote to a friend, 'including a Finnish, a Mari and a Votic [Finno-Ugric languages]; from these I compile my word-lists. Also, I have collected a lot of information about the ancient Slavs, and I shall soon be able to prove that the Slavs named the majority of rivers, mountains, valleys and regions of France, Spain, Scotland and elsewhere.'

Catherine's comparative dictionary is typical of her wide range of interests and her desire to find Russian links with Europe. Though its basic principle is now known to be incorrect, the comparison of a great variety of words from three continents was something not hitherto attempted.

The last category of Catherine's literary works are her personal writings: her *Memoirs*, written at the end of her life, which will be considered in a later chapter, and her private correspondence. Certain letters, for instance to her father, to Voltaire and to Potemkin, have been quoted in part, and there remains the correspondence with Grimm, begun in April 1774 and continuing to October 1796, comprising 273 letters, filling 695 quarto pages and totalling 300,000 words.

Frederick Melchior Grimm was a poor Bavarian burgher's son who made his name by starting, in Paris, a private news-letter for foreigners to which Catherine subscribed. It printed reviews of books and plays, news of Paris and even current *bons mots*, such as Sophie

Arnould's 'Divorce is the sacrament of adultery.'

Catherine met Grimm when he visited Russia in 1774. A bachelor of fifty-one, he was by no means handsome, having big protruding eyes and a red complexion which he tried to tone down with ceruse. But he possessed an infectious enthusiasm for all the arts, a homely German common sense and a liking for jokes, qualities that endeared him to Catherine. The two became friends, and Catherine, who felt a need to tease all friends, teased Grimm about his predilection for the German aristocracy, and about his ceruse, nicknaming him Tiran le Blanc.

Catherine's correspondence with Grimm is, after Madame de Sévigné's, perhaps the most sustained and revealing ever written by a woman. It is remarkable for its range – upset stomachs to upset governments, latest lover to latest play – and for its buoyancy. The letters are shot through with playful humour, and sometimes with made-up words: '*Voilà mon dernier dernierissime mot*'; my 'epistle to the Grimmalians'. Re-reading a three-page letter Catherine finds she has forgotten to put 'Monsieur'; she thereupon adds a batch of 'Monsieurs' for Grimm to distribute as needed.

The letters reflect Catherine as she was: energetic, positive, on the whole happy. But the fact that they were written at all, and sustained for twenty-two years, points to something in Catherine which she probably did not even admit to herself. Surrounded by friends, collaborators and an admiring Court, the Empress of Russia nevertheless sometimes felt lonely.

A woman autocrat tends to feel lonely, because the woman longs to lean and the autocrat cannot. Catherine felt lonely too because her parents were dead, and she never saw her German family, because her relations with Paul were unsatisfactory, and because, from 1776, Potemkin toiled a thousand miles from her. She was lonely because, though she loved Russia, she was by heredity, instinct and upbringing European. From Grimm she got news of Europe; with Grimm she could behave naturally, as a European.

In this long series of letters Catherine revealed her literary tastes. She had a particular liking for Sterne's *Tristram Shandy*, and she liked too books of homespun philosophy such as Benjamin Franklin's *Poor Richard's Almanack*. She liked *Cinna*, Corneille's drama of a monarch's clemency which was also to be the favourite play of Napoleon. She disliked mannered writing of any kind and she particularly disliked tragedy.

Catherine's attitude to tragedy is interesting. It is true that most of her contemporaries disliked tragedy, and Catherine's *Timon* with a happy ending has a counterpart in Ducis's *Macbeth* with the Thane of Cawdor killing Duncan in self-defence. But her contemporaries disliked tragedy because they believed in the natural goodness of man, and that was a belief Catherine did not share.

Catherine's dislike of tragedy probably reflects a wish to forget her unhappy marriage and the murder of Peter, and its obverse is a very noticeable need to be surrounded by happy faces. Catherine keeps saying how gay she is – rather too often to be convincing: when seeking a wife for Paul she insists on a happy person: 'At the Russian Court we set high store by gaiety . . . I am by nature very gay and my son also.' All the evidence suggests that the last part of her statement is untrue. Paul in fact was a sombre young man, haunted by suspicions he termed 'black butterflies'. Catherine has altered the truth to suit her deep need for the reassurance of happy faces. This need has already been seen in her taking as lovers Alexander Vasilchikov and Peter Zavadovsky. Insofar as it embodies a refusal to face the realities of her life it was, in Catherine's otherwise healthy moral character, a potentially dangerous symptom.

Catherine did not intend her letters to Grimm for publication, and near the end of her life was to ask him to destroy them. Grimm declined to do so, and they found their way to Moscow, where they are today.

Catherine's other writings, combined with her literary patronage, acted both as example and stimulus. Seventy other women began to write in her reign, while the number of books published, other than Church service books, rose from 918 in the first half of the century to 8696 in the second half. Quite as remarkable as these figures is Catherine's prophetic belief in the coming greatness of Russian literature. Commenting to Grimm on a mannered French play 'as cold as ice', Catherine said: 'The scrupulously careful age of Laharpe and company will fade, and the star of the East will rise. Yes, yes, it is from that side that light will return, for here, in the embers, there is more intelligence and more vigour than anywhere else.'

CHAPTER 20

OF PALACES AND PAINTINGS

To the fine arts and music Catherine brought the same keen interest and discriminating patronage that mark her literary endeavours. Architecture in particular appealed to her, for in putting up a building she felt that she was *par excellence* carrying on the activity she had praised to Grimm: *schaffen*; and, with each range of stone or marble, she was, perhaps subconsciously, reassuring herself, the parvenue.

Catherine as Empress came into possession of three country palaces, two houses in St Petersburg, and various lesser houses in or near Moscow. She can scarcely have felt an urgent need for new accommodation; nevertheless she was to undertake not just one but two new palaces.

When she went to Moscow in 1775 Catherine avoided the cramped Kremlin and took up residence in three large houses belonging to the Golitsuin and Dolgoruky families, joined for the occasion by wooden galleries. Catherine promptly got lost for two hours in the maze of galleries, and wrote to Grimm: 'I've never seen so many doors. I've got rid of half a dozen, and still have twice the number I need.'

Unsatisfied with this arrangement, Catherine resolved to build a new palace near Moscow, to be called Tsaritsina. She chose a Russian architect, Basil Bazhenov, and, if one is to judge by her other projects, probably gave him fairly specific directives. It would appear that Catherine drew on her own architectural background, German Gothic, for the idea of detached brick buildings, many with towers; and she wished these to be linked by a colonnade with a central triumphal arch. After work had been going on for ten years Catherine took a dislike to the half-finished palace – she compared it to candelabra surrounding a coffin – and abandoned it, probably wisely.

For the site of her other palace Catherine chose a staging-post on the St Petersburg–Tsarskoe Selo road called Kekerekeksinen, a Finnish word meaning Frog Marsh. Since she intended the palace to commemorate the naval victory at Chesme Bay, Catherine adopted the mixture of Eastern and 'Gothic' forms then fashionable in Europe as the Turkish style. The ground-plan is an equilateral triangle, with a spacious round hall in the centre. Three towers, one at each corner, support smaller towers, topped with green domes *à la turque*. The walls have battlements and are pierced by Gothic lancet windows.

The most immediate difference between buildings in Russia and their European equivalents at that time was that the former were painted vivid colours, to give them some life during the long snow-bound winter; they were to European buildings what painted Greek statuary is to statues in museums. Catherine naturally subscribed to Russian practice and had her Chesme Palace painted green, yellow and cherry-red. In one of its rooms she hung portraits of all Russia's rulers and of all the crowned heads in the Europe of her day.

Most of Catherine's building for her own needs is on a smaller scale than Chesme and comprises additions to, or adaptations of, three existing palaces. The first relates to her usual winter residence, the 1000-room baroque palace in St Petersburg built by Rastrelli for Elizabeth, the façade of which was apple-green and white. Moved by her fear of draughts and her liking for intimate informal gatherings, Catherine made a threefold addition to the palace: a number of small tasteful rooms comprising, in the strict sense, the Hermitage; a series of more spacious well-lighted rooms to serve as a picture-gallery, and a neo-classical theatre, designed by Quarenghi on the lines of Palladio's Teatro Olimpico in Vicenza, copiously decorated with marble columns, statues and medallions of playwrights and composers. It was in this theatre, its curtains inscribed *Corrigat Mores Ridendo*, that Catherine's plays received their first performance.

At Oranienbaum, the seaside estate where she had spent happy days at the beginning of her marriage, and of which she continued to be fond, Catherine built a large balconied pavilion where, in winter, spectators could watch their friends swishing down the icy slopes of a switchback. The pavilion, in wood, consists of a circular hall surmounted by a conical cupola, with three projecting wings, giving on to wide balconies at three different levels. Painted pale blue and white, it is an unusual, very pleasing building. The most opulent of its rooms Catherine decorated in a German rococo so rich it becomes three-dimensional: the ornamentation of the walls includes brackets, several in the form of monkeys, on which stand pieces of Meissen china.

Also at Oranienbaum Catherine commissioned Rinaldi to build her a single-storey Chinese-style pavilion. Again she combined simple exterior lines with a very opulent interior. Her bedroom has white satin walls, rococo looking-glasses and Chinese-style gouache drawings.

For the small drawing-room Catherine chose a colour scheme of blue, mauve and pink, the walls being hung with silk sewn with two million beads of milky glass, to provide a shimmering landscape of trees, with flying birds. A feature of the pavilion was authentic Chinese wallpaper, which took twelve years to procure.

Though she did commission some beautiful rococo work, Catherine was not by temperament rococo. Orderly, controlled, balanced, she inclined more to the classical, and as neo-classicism gained ground in Europe, Catherine took to it and introduced it to Russia. In 1773, after reading Cochin's *Costume des anciens peuples*, she had the idea of building a house in ancient-Roman style. She approached Clérisseau, who conceived a house as big as Diocletian's palace in Split. Catherine, who had enough big palaces, rejected Clérisseau's plans. She continued, however, to follow the neo-classical movement, bought the first two parts of *Works in Architecture of Robert and James Adam*, and looked about for a suitable neo-classical architect.

In 1778 she found him. Charles Cameron, born of Scottish parents in London probably in 1743, had studied in Rome and written *The Baths of the Romans*. Catherine had romantic sympathies for the Stuarts, and perhaps Cameron played up to them, for Catherine informed Grimm that her architect was the nephew of Miss Jenny Cameron, and had been brought up in the Pretender's house in Rome; neither of these statements is true.

Catherine wished Cameron to redecorate in neo-classical style part of Tsarskoe Selo, the large green and buff country palace where she spent her summers. She tested him on eight small rooms including her bedroom and, pleased with the result, set him to decorate for her a new private suite. One of the problems facing Cameron was that wooden panelling could not be used in the window-recesses, because the severe climate split it; painted or gilded stucco had to be employed instead.

Catherine chose opalescent milky white, blue and green for her suite, and lilac for her bedroom. An unusual feature of the bedroom is deep violet slender moulded glass columns, on small bronze bases and topped by small bronze capitals. The marble overmantel is decorated in white, amethyst and gold and studded with Wedgwood medallions, including two Bacchanalian figures. Of the suite as a whole it may be said that only the lines are robustly classical, the general mood being one of feminine delicacy, lightness and grace.

Cameron's third commission was the building of an extension to Tsarskoe Selo, for which sixty masons, bricklayers and plasterers were recruited in Scotland. The extension consists of rooms copiously decorated with agate known as the Agate Pavilion, and a marble gallery 90 yards long, with a balcony of Ionic columns, above steam baths, and giving on to a double stairway leading to the park. This open gallery became one of Catherine's favourite spots for sitting. She placed nineteen bronze busts in it, eleven of them Greek or Roman writers.

Catherine in her prime used to walk ten miles daily during the summer, measuring the distance with a pedometer – a very German trait. Probably in order to vary her walks she wished to enlarge the park at Tsarskoe Selo by bringing into it an apple orchard belonging to the Crown but leased to a Crown peasant. She offered the man ten times the value of his orchard, but he did not want to sell because, he said, the trees had been planted by his father. Catherine yielded, and the wall of her new park turned at an angle to leave the orchard unenclosed.

Catherine had not done with chinoiserie, for within the park she got Cameron to build a small village of Chinese-style houses, complete with dragons on the roofs. She gave this village her original Christian name, Sophia. At first she used it to house serfs who had left their masters because they were oppressed; later she arranged for a priest, Samborsky, who had studied under the agricultural expert, Arthur Young, and brought back from Suffolk the latest in seed-drills and hay-rakes, to teach modern farming to the children of priests and selected peasants. Chinese Sophia became in effect an English-style agricultural college.

At various points in the park Catherine erected monuments or columns to her victorious generals, an Egyptian-style pyramid over the body of her whippet Tom Anderson, when he died of old age, and, spanning the lake, a Palladian bridge of grey Siberian marble modelled on the bridge at Wilton.

Catherine liked flowers and was particularly fond of the snowdrop, piercing the grass while ice still held the Neva immobile, the first grace-note of spring. At Tsarskoe Selo she planted flowers from all over the known world. Her roses did well but the tulips faded disappointingly fast, sometimes within the space of one of the very long summer days, in which case she had them removed at night and replaced with others in pots. She kept herself informed about newly discovered or newly developed species, and subscribed to the limited edition of the Earl of Bute's beautifully illustrated *Botanical Tables*.

The garden Catherine found at Tsarskoe Selo was the Dutch garden laid out by Peter the Great: fish-canals, straight neat paths and espaliers. Catherine wanted it changed into lawns, shady walks and unclipped trees: 'Anglomania,' she told Voltaire, 'rules my plantomania.' To do this she brought out an English gardener, John Bush of Hackney. He lived in a flat above the orangery, Mrs Bush fattened her turkeys on dried ants' eggs, one of their daughters, Catherine, married Cameron, and in 1789 the son, Joseph, succeeded his father, who was by then growing old.

So much for the building and landscaping Catherine did on her own account. She also built much for others. For Gregory Orlov she commissioned Rinaldi to build a town house which, instead of the customary brick and stucco, was faced with red granite and grey Siberian marble, hence its name, Marble Palace. On the façade Catherine inscribed the words 'In grateful friendship'.

Fifteen years later, when she built a town house for Potemkin, she chose a Russian architect, Starov, and the neo-classical style. A low central block has a portico of six unfluted Doric columns supporting a pediment; from it run single-storeyed wings terminating in two-storeyed pavilions with Ionic porticoes.

'The more one builds,' Catherine told Grimm, 'the more one wants to build, it is like drinking.' Certainly she indulged her constructive instinct to the full. For her son Paul she built the Kammeno-Ostrovsky Palace in St Petersburg, and Pavlovsk, an extremely beautiful country house designed by Cameron; for her eldest grandson, Alexander, she built the Alexandrovsky Palace. Add to these St Isaac's Cathedral, the immense Academy of Arts and Quarenghi's Academy of Sciences, and Catherine's building activities rival those of Peter the Great.

Yet the work of art by which Catherine is best known is not a building but a statue. Perhaps remembering the enigmatic bronze figure of the butter-girl in Zerbst, Catherine conceived the idea of a huge bronze statue of Peter the Great to stand in a position west of the Admiralty, beside the River Neva. The artist she commissioned was a fifty-one-year-old Frenchman named Etienne Falconet who had made porcelain figures and small frivolous statues for Madame de Pompadour's Bellevue. 'The least schoolchild knows more about sculpture than I,' Catherine said to Falconet, but she did know what she wanted, and she also knew how to handle an exceedingly touchy artist.

Falconet spent twelve years on the statue, which shows Peter reining in his horse on the brink of a rock, his face turned towards the Neva, one hand outstretched towards the city he had founded, while a serpent, symbolizing the difficulties he encountered, is trodden down by the horse's hind hooves. Falconet distributes the immense weight – sixteen tons – by varying the thickness of the bronze from one inch to a quarter of an inch, so that the centre of gravity lies immediately above the hind hooves. The granite pedestal weighs 1500 tons, and was brought from a nearby village by 500 men, who laboured five weeks. On the pedestal in gold letters Catherine placed an inscription that linked her name with Peter's and by its use of Latin reasserted a Westernizing policy: on one side PETRÙ PÈRVOMU – EKATÉRÍNA VTÓRAYA; on the other PETRO PRIMO – CATHARINA SECUNDA MDCCLXXXII.

When she honoured Peter by this fine statue it would not have escaped Catherine's notice that her predecessor had done little for the arts other than architecture, and had left hardly any paintings save scenes of himself winning the battle of Poltava. Elizabeth had acquired some dull German, Dutch and Flemish pictures, but the imperial collection ranked far beneath that of a lesser Italian duke. Since nations were now beginning to be respected by their artistic collections as well as by their armies and navies, Catherine decided to make good the deficiency.

She possessed a natural good taste, evident in her pleasingly-formed handwriting laid out gracefully on the page, but no expert knowledge. She accepted the view of Winckelmann and Mengs that Raphael and Michelangelo surpassed even the ancients, and heeded Diderot, when he praised the sentimental, story-telling Greuze. But since sales took place in Europe she could not herself see the pictures for which she bid.

Catherine's first acquisition, in 1766, was Rembrandt's *Return of the Prodigal Son*. Two years later, still feeling her way, she bought five Rubens and 41 other canvases from the Coblenz collection. The following year, when the collection of Brühl, a Dresden connoisseur, came under the hammer, she acquired four more Rembrandts, two more Rubens and two portraits by Lucas Cranach the elder. Then, in 1772, the second-best collection in France, that of Crozat, came up for sale, Catherine secured all the items save Van Dyck's *Charles I*, which Madame Du Barry bought, believing Stuart blood ran in her veins. Catherine doubtless felt considerable excitement when the crates arrived by sea and were unpacked before her in the Winter Palace. Here at last were prized Italian masterpieces: Raphael's *Holy Family with Beardless St Joseph*, and a *Judith* believed to be by Raphael, but now attributed to Giorgione, Titian's *Danaë* and *Portrait of a Young Woman Wearing a Hat*, Schiavoni's *Landscape with Jupiter and Io*, Tintoretto's *Birth of John the Baptist* and many others, altogether 400 works, for which Catherine paid 460,000 livres.

Catherine did not spend so lavishly again. In fact she enjoyed getting a bargain, especially against stiff competition. At the sale of the Duc

Catherine commissioned Rinaldi to build the Marble Palace, which she gave to Gregory Orlov, complete with furniture, silver and porcelain. It was the first Russian house to be built of marble, which came from recently opened quarries in the Urals.

Four of Catherine's lovers in later life.
Above: Ivan Rimsky-Korsakov and Alexander Lanskoy.
Below: Alexander Dmitriev-Mamonov and Plato Zubov.

de Choiseul's collection, with Diderot's help, she bought Flemish and Spanish pictures at low prices; in 1778 when the 3rd Earl of Orford sold the collection formed by Sir Robert Walpole, Catherine scooped the lot for £40,000, and was lucky to get them, for a question had been asked in the House about the propriety of allowing such riches to leave England.

With part of the money he received from Catherine the eccentric Lord Orford indulged his passion for hare-coursing. He bred a remarkable greyhound to which he gave the name Czarina – as Catherine's title was then transliterated – and raced her on the heaths around Swaffham. His Lordship coursed Czarina forty-seven times and she was never once beaten. In her last match he worked himself up into such a passion about her that he fell from his horse and died. Czarina is the ancestor of every true-bred greyhound in the world today.

In 1781 the collection of the Comte de Baudouin came on the market in Paris. Catherine bid for, and secured, nine Rembrandts, six Van Dycks and Claude Lorrain's sublime *Morning at the Port*. This might be bulk buying, but it was high quality bulk.

The most important of Catherine's commissions in the field of painting was the copying of Raphael's Old Testament scenes and 'grotesque' decorations in the Vatican Loggie. Catherine had the immense work shipped in sections and built a special gallery to house it. She may have found fifty-two religious scenes oppressive, for when her ambassador proposed copies of the Raphael Cartoons in London she replied: 'If their subject-matter is sad or too solemn, I am not interested.'

Among her contemporaries Catherine bought works from Mengs and Kauffmann, Greuze's *Filial Piety* and Chardin's *Grace before Meat*. Curiously, she disliked Madame Vigée Lebrun's gay portraits, perhaps finding the innocence overdone, and she preferred Richard Brompton as a portraitist of her grandsons. She would have liked Bellotto to come to St Petersburg and paint its waterfronts as he had painted Venice, but he chose instead to work for King Stanislaus in Warsaw. She paid Sir Joshua Reynolds 1500 guineas to paint a subject of his choosing, *Hercules Strangling the Serpents in the Cradle*, 'in allusion,' says Sir Joshua, 'to the great difficulties which the Empress of Russia had to encounter in the civilization of her empire': for one well-informed Englishman at least strangling in the context of Russia evoked no sinister suspicions. The same painter provided Potemkin with a not very good *Cupid Untying the Zone of Venus*.

Catherine built up the imperial picture collection from a few dozen works to 3926. It was less a private indulgence than part of her twin purpose of civilizing Russia and making it respected. Here too, her patronage acted as a stimulus. Young Russians began to interest themselves in Western techniques – Catherine gave them special permission to enter the women's bathhouses to sketch from life – while rich amateurs, including Count Sheremetev and Panin's successor as chief Minister, Bezborodko, formed collections and, like Catherine, patronized the slowly-forming Russian School. Here, as in the theatre, Catherine had thrown a stone into still water, the ripples from which were to spread in widening circles.

One last artistic acquisition by Catherine is of interest. When planning Chesme Palace, which Catherine called the Froggery from its Finnish name, she ordered a fifty-place dinner service from Josiah Wedgwood, to be decorated with the most remarkable buildings, ruins, parks, gardens and other natural curiosities of Britain, each piece to be marked not with the imperial crest but with a green frog.

Wedgwood sent all over England for views, which were copied on to the service in Chelsea, under Thomas Bentley's direction, by women who were paid between three and eight shillings a week. It took three years to paint 1282 views on 760 pieces, and after being exhibited for two months in Greek Street, Soho, the service was shipped out in 1774.

Catherine got for her £3000 a five-course geography lesson, a unique panorama of the land she had become fond of in the person of Charles Hanbury-Williams, ranging from Castle Howard and Fountains Abbey to views of Highgate and Hampstead, to Westminster Hall and a cottage in the Hebrides. Catherine used the service at the first dinner party for a new English ambassador, and for galas at the Froggery.

Catherine claimed she had no voice nor ear for music and that she was not in the strict sense a music lover. The latter statement seems to be true. But Potemkin loved music and had his own orchestra, and it was probably he who helped Catherine to appreciate Russian folk songs. Opera she always liked and she did much to encourage it.

The first composer Catherine invited to Russia was Baldassare Galuppi, well known for his comic operas. He arrived in 1766 and composed for Catherine an *Iphigenia in Tauris* – a topical theme, since Tauris is in the Crimea. Next came Tommasso Traetta who, at the first performance of his operas, when presiding at the harpsichord, as the custom then was, would turn from time to time to the audience and say, 'Ladies and gentlemen, look sharp and pay attention to this passage.' Galuppi had to leave because the climate did not suit him and was succeeded, in 1776, by Giovanni Paisiello. The son of a Taranto veterinary, Paisiello had trained in Naples; he was a robust man of thirty-six with a big jaw and nose, and he arrived with his timid little wife, Cecilia. One day, walking by a lake, and believing herself attacked by a swan, Cecilia threw herself into the water and had to be dragged out, drenched and moaning. Catherine was much upset but Paisiello explained, '*E niente, e solamenta la paura, la paura* – It's nothing really, just fright.'

'Paisiello gave us a treat the day before yesterday,' Catherine told Grimm, 'with a comic opera composed in three weeks that would make you die laughing. It is *The Ridiculous Philosopher* or *The Pretentious Pundit*; there's an aria where coughing is put to music and when one actor sings about pneumonia, the other replies in terror that he hopes Signor Agaphontidas hasn't come to *crepare in mia casa*.' Catherine saw this opera four times, 'split her sides' with laughter and at a masked ball singled out Paisiello and actually sang him the aria, which she had taken the trouble to learn. So despite her denials she did have a voice and an ear of sorts.

Paisiello's chief success in St Petersburg was a *Barber of Seville*, with libretto by Petrosellini. After eight years in the service of Catherine he returned to Mediterranean sunshine and was succeeded by Giuseppe Sarti. Gentle and kind, mathematician as well as composer, Sarti was fond of explaining to Catherine his theories of opera and of acoustics, and he showed her a machine he had invented for counting the vibrations of sounds, 436 being the number he assigned to the note A.

While listening to Sarti with one ear, so to speak, Catherine listened with the other to Potemkin and to her Court singer, Trutovsky, who in 1778 had published Part One of a *Collection of Russian Ordinary Songs with Music*. Accompanying himself on the *gusli*, a stringed instrument, Trutovsky provided Catherine with examples of Russia's rich heritage of folk songs, which he was the first to print, and which had never yet been drawn on in sophisticated compositions.

Catherine decided to try to knot the Italian and Russian strands. Using her story, 'The Rose without Thorns' as a basis, she wrote a libretto for a historical Russian *opéra comique*, *Fevey*, which received its first performance at the Kammenuy Theatre on 19th April 1786. The music was by Pashkevich, and the Kalmuik Chorus is one of the earliest examples of Orientalism in Russian music.

Catherine wrote four more operas, all about figures from Russian history: *Basil Boyeslavich, the Warrior of Novgorod*, music by Fomin, was produced in 1786; *The Brave and Bold Knight Akhrideich*, music by a Bohemian composer, in 1787; *The Doleful Warrior Kosometovich*, music by Martin-y-Soler, in 1789; and *The Beginning of Oleg's Reign*, music by Canobbio, Pashkevich and Sarti, in 1790.

Of these operas *Oleg* is the most interesting. Act I shows Oleg, who ruled Russia at the end of the ninth century, laying the foundations of Moscow; in Act II Oleg arranges the marriage of his nephew, Prince Igor, and Olga, who came of a Scandinavian family established in Pskov; in Act III the marriage takes place; Act IV shows Oleg about to attack Constantinople in order to redress an injury to Russian honour, and being offered a desirable peace by Emperor Leo; the implications of Oleg's march to Constantinople would not have been lost on Catherine's audience. The final act is festivities given for Oleg by Leo, including a performance of three scenes from Act III of Euripides' *Alcestis*, and a ballet representing the Olympic Games. 'The words,' said Catherine, 'are all drawn from authentic historical sources; only the choruses have been adapted, and the scenes from Euripides; the choruses in the last act are based on Lomonosov's odes; those in Act III when Bekray is dressing are old Russian folk songs.'

Of *Akhrideich* an English traveller who saw the first performance said, 'The Scenery was very fine, the music and dancing excellent; at the head of the dancers are Lepisq and Rossi, but as the dancing was comic, it was not well calculated to display their talents.'

Charles Lepisq, or Lepicq, one of the two greatest dancers of his day, had been invited to Russia by Catherine in 1786. There he did much to form a native school of ballet dancers, the most talented of whom, Anastasiya Berilova, made her debut at the Court theatre during Catherine's reign and quickly rose to be a star. Dying while still in her twenties, Berilova was buried, it was said, in a grave lined with furs and covered not with earth but with flowers.

The best of the singers employed by Catherine was *la belle* Gabrielli. Born in Rome, she became, as Mozart discovered, an adept in runs and roulades, and was singing in Milan when Catherine invited her to Russia. She demanded 7000 roubles a year, a house and a carriage; when told a Field Marshal had no more, she replied, 'Then I would advise her Majesty to make one of her Marshals sing.' She spent four years at Catherine's Court, creating among other parts Traetta's *Antigone*, but proved very difficult. Whenever she was occupied with the latest in her string of lovers, she would plead a cold. Catherine remarked in exasperation, 'When I send an order to my Field Marshal, he comes, but when I call Gabrielli, she is never ready.'

Catherine's energetic patronage of the arts was more than an importation of foreign talent. As her opera librettos show, she sought also to develop specifically Russian gifts. Like a trainer with inexperienced athletes, Catherine gave the Russians what they then needed: self-confidence. Perhaps the most perceptive comment on Catherine's role is Buckinghamshire's: 'The Empress has laboured by magnificence, expense and her own example to teach her subjects to divert themselves. They are a little awkward at first, and tread the paths of refin'd pleasure with the same caution that the forest deer first enter an inexperienced pasture – but they will graze in time.'

CHAPTER 21

POTEMKIN PREDOMINANT

'Before it can be governed, a nation has to have its edges smoothed,' Catherine once wrote in a memo to herself. In St Petersburg smoothing the edges meant fostering the arts; elsewhere, particularly in the South, which began increasingly to occupy Catherine's attention, it took the more rudimentary form of colonizing, settling and building.

In 1776, we have seen, Catherine wished to employ Potemkin on important affairs of State. By the treaty of Kutchuk Kainarji with Turkey, new territory near the Black Sea had come into Russian hands, and Catherine decided to send Potemkin there as Overlord of Novorossisk and Azov, with orders to develop land between the Bug and Dnieper rivers and between the lower Don and Yeya, as well as the corn-fields and sheep-pastures of the former Zoporozhian Cossacks, whose autonomy Catherine ended in 1775.

Potemkin was a man who found it difficult to get out of bed in the morning but, once up and his imagination fired by a challenging task such as this, he could do the work of ten. Exchanging his brocade dressing-gown for an open-necked blouse, riding breeches and boots, courtier turned frontiersman, he got to know personally every mile of the area entrusted to him. First he dealt with the Cossacks, settling a few in villages, where he could keep an eye on them, but banding most into a new army, the Kuban Host, to defend the area north-west of the Caucasus. The vacuum so created he filled by bringing in colonists: State peasants and former Church peasants from areas where land was scarce, fugitive serfs, convicts, deserters from the army and runaway peasants, who received pardon for any crime save murder. But to fill these vast spaces still more men were needed. After trying unsuccessfully to get convicts from England, Potemkin drew on two other sources of manpower – Germany, which supplied 32,000 immigrants, and the Crimea, from which came 30,000 Christians of Greek, Albanian and Georgian stock.

Each settler received 142 acres and was classified as a State peasant, though he paid not *obrok* but a lighter form of land tax. He was allowed to trade freely in salt and vodka. Settlers of proved capacity received larger estates, of up to 32,000 acres where the soil was poor, provided they agreed to parcel out their estate to others within ten years. With Catherine's approval Potemkin disregarded the legal monopoly of the gentry in rural landownership, and allowed such estates to be held by men who were not gentry.

Potemkin set an example by himself developing several estates on the Dnieper, and employing capable Samuel Bentham to manage one of them. Like Cameron, Bentham brought over Scottish artisans, with their wives and children, 139 persons in all, to set up workshops for leather and glass-making, a smithy, a millwright's establishment and a rope-work. Bentham noted: 'The Prince wants much to introduce the use of Beer in his governments and permits the sale of it without any excise;' again: 'the Prince will have a Botanical garden . . . in which all the vegetable productions of the world are to be collected . . . He means also to have an elegant Dairy in which the best of Butter and as many different kinds of cheese as possible should be made.'

Happy only when he was doing a dozen things at once, in 1778 Potemkin began building, on the Dnieper, the port of Kherson, which four years later was described by Cyril Razumovsky: 'Imagine on the one hand a quantity, increasing hourly, of stone buildings; a fortress, which encompasses a citadel and the best buildings; the Admiralty, with ships being built and already built; a spacious suburb, inhabited by merchants and burghers of different races; and, on the other hand, barracks housing about 10,000 soldiers. Add to this, almost opposite the suburb, an attractive-looking island with quarantine buildings, with Greek merchant vessels, and with canals constructed to give these vessels access. Imagine all this and you will understand my bewilderment, for not so long ago there was nothing here but a building where beehives were kept for the winter.'

Few tasks are more difficult than clearing virgin soil with immigrant labour and building towns with improvised tools. At a distance of one thousand miles from base it becomes in the literal sense a Herculean task. Almost certainly it would have proved beyond Potemkin, had he not had Catherine. She was in front of him as an ideal and behind him as a support. Bullying, hectoring, pleading and sometimes cheating, Potemkin toiled year after year in the South, striving to overcome his compatriots' inertia, bypassing the usual administrative channels, writing direct to Catherine, for example in order to get money to buy wood for shipbuilding in Kherson, and receiving by return the necessary letter of authorization in Catherine's own hand.

At the end of seven years Potemkin had transformed much of the south from a turbulent frontier area of bandits and pirates into a fairly settled integral part of Russia. This allowed Catherine to take her next step: a momentous one. Protecting herself from Turkish or French retaliation by exchanging her alliance with Prussia for an alliance with Austria, in 1783 Catherine annexed the Crimea.

The Crimea, though described by Potemkin as 'the wart on Russia's nose', was in fact a region of great interest and importance. Colonized by the Greeks, occupied by the Romans, and visited by Ovid in exile, it was that part of the Russian mainland which had earliest been in touch with Europe. Later it had been occupied by Genghis Khan's Mongols, and its present population was mainly Moslem Tartars speaking a Turkic language, with sizeable minorities of Kalmuiks, Greeks, Armenians and Georgians. Having annexed it, Catherine instructed Potemkin to do there what he had done in the Ukraine: to develop, to establish order, roads and food supplies, and to modernize the ports.

Once again Potemkin acted with verve and imagination. He moved in thousands of colonists, providing them with cattle and ploughs, melon seeds, mulberries and silkworms. He established a measure of control over the nomadic Kalmuiks, whose women softened horseflesh under their saddles and made beer from mares' milk. He chose Sevastopol to be the site of a big new port and Admiral Thomas Mackenzie, who as a lieutenant had commanded a fire-ship at Chesme, to build it. The region being bare of good timber, Potemkin conceived the idea of bringing bargeloads of oak down the Dnieper from Poland.

As Sevastopol began to take shape Potemkin planted botanical gardens and vineyards, he set up another dairy, he built himself a fine house, where he took brief rests from his exertions, listening to concerts by his 65-piece orchestra, each player of which, says a visiting Spaniard, Francisco de Miranda, sounded only one note on a hunting horn: 'The horns range from twelve feet long to less than one foot, and the ensemble sounds rather like an organ.'

All the while Potemkin kept Catherine informed of progress and begged her to come and see what he had been achieving for her. Advisers warned the Empress that roads were impassable, that she would tire herself and fall ill. But Catherine wanted very much to go. Finally she set a date – 1787, her jubilee year.

The starting-point for the journey was Kiev. Potemkin, showman supreme, had had seven Roman-style galleys specially built. Catherine's was fitted in red brocade and gold, and had its own orchestra, conducted by Sarti. Staff, servants, including thirty washerwomen, food and fine wines would follow in eighty smaller craft, manned by 3000 sailors. After Easter, as soon as the ice on the Dnieper had melted, the galleys cast off, and Catherine began the long voyage south.

At one of the first stops, King Stanislaus of Poland came aboard to pay his respects. Thirty years had passed since he had taken Grand Duchess Catherine for midnight sleigh rides, and been loved and esteemed by her 'above all the rest of the human race'. He still loved Catherine, and though there were occasionally other women in his life none meant as much to him as she.

Catherine's feelings when she met her former lover can only be conjectured. Stanislaus was still a fine-looking man, and that was something she always responded to. But their positions had changed so much, it was she now who drove the political sleigh. Though she still felt a warm sentimental attachment to Stanislaus, it was eclipsed by the political facts. It would not do for the Empress of Russia to show undue affection to the King of Poland, who acted a trifle too independently for Russian liking. So Catherine gave Stanislaus dinner on her galley, and the blue ribbon of St Andrew which, with a nice touch, she unpinned from her own breast, but she declined his invitation to a dance.

Catherine had invited on the journey Emperor Joseph II of Austria. He had a dry, cutting manner, and like Peter III was constantly aping Frederick of Prussia. Nevertheless he was working hard for Austria's welfare, and Catherine, if she did not specially like him, found him 'very well read' and was glad to have him as her ally.

Catherine met Joseph in a place called Ekaterinoslav. To the visitor it looked like a scattering of wooden houses, but to Potemkin, who had conceived and named it, it was a beautiful city, the St Petersburg of the south, complete with university, law courts, conservatory of music, shops approached by an Acropolis-style porch, and a great cathedral on the scale of St Peter's in Rome but a few feet longer.

À propos the future cathedral, Joseph wrote to a friend: 'I performed a great deed today. The Empress laid the first stone of a new church, and I laid – the last.' His sarcasm was justified, for Ekaterinoslav proved to be one of Potemkin's mirages; its church was completed only many years later, and on a much reduced scale.

Having performed this ceremony, Catherine and Joseph went on board the luxurious galley. There Joseph met others of the company: Potemkin, the sylph-like French ambassador Louis Philippe de Ségur, who wrote fables, the Prince de Ligne, always cheerful and therefore specially liked by Catherine, and Charles de Nassau-Siegen, a Dutch-born collaborator of Potemkin who had circumnavigated the globe.

At each stop Catherine went ashore and questioned landowners, merchants, clergy and others about their work, aspirations and needs. She took careful note of injustices and abuses. Sometimes she slept in a fine house built for the occasion by Potemkin, at other times she remained afloat. One day, with Ségur, she read Lucian's *Zeus Catechized*, in which a cynic interviews the god on predestination and free will; another day Ségur tried, unsuccessfully, to teach her to write French verses. She was particularly anxious that her guests should enjoy themselves and one evening when the catering barges came up late with their supper she stormed off very peeved. She got over her mood by reappearing at nine wearing an apricot taffeta peignoir with blue ribbons, her hair unpinned and down to her shoulders, and in this flamboyant dress, which must have clashed with the galley's red brocade, she was once again her gay self, staying an hour and a half to watch Nassau and three others play a rubber of whist.

If Potemkin had had little tangible to offer at Ekaterinoslav, he made amends at Kherson. This port, which Potemkin had built virtually from scratch, was now under the command of General Hannibal, born in Russia of a black father and white mother. Hannibal had further developed the docks and shipyards since Razumovsky had seen the town in 1782; and when Catherine arrived by galley, she found two hundred merchant ships, many of them Russian, riding at anchor.

Having toured the town, which she liked to call by its classical name, Borysthenes, Catherine watched the launching of two ships of the line and a frigate – again carefully timed by Potemkin to coincide with her visit. When the moment came for her to resume her journey by land, Catherine left Kherson by a gate on which Potemkin had placed an inscription, in Greek: 'This is the way to Byzantium.'

The inscription had great significance for Catherine; indeed it summed up a new foreign policy, the first glimmerings of which had appeared in 1778. In that year Catherine's second grandson was born; she named him Constantine, after the last Greek emperor, Constantine Palaeologos, and struck medals showing Hagia Sophia on one side, the Black Sea with a star rising over it on the other. In 1781 Catherine replaced the cautious Panin by the more enterprising Alexander Bezborodko; with him and Potemkin Catherine evolved her full-blown 'Greek plan'. In alliance with Austria, Russia would free Bessarabia, Moldavia and Wallachia from the Turk, and combine them into 'Dacia', independent of Russia but governed by an Orthodox prince; Austria for her help would receive Serbia; meanwhile a new Russian navy, based on the Crimea, would spearhead an attack on Constantinople, free the Greeks, and revive the Byzantine Empire, with Catherine's grandson Constantine as Emperor. This was the dream that united Catherine and Potemkin, and gave an added thrill to the present grandiose journey.

Catherine crossed into the Crimea. She did not linger on the wind-swept north coast, but hurried to Bakhchisaray, former seat of the khans, successors of Genghis, beautifully set at the foot of mountains. Catherine had sent Cameron ahead to do up the palace, where fountains played amid jasmine and pomegranates, and the walls were decorated with fine Turkish paintings of Constantinople. In the palace Catherine discovered some wax fruit and flowers made by the Sultan's French adviser, Baron de Tott. The adulation she had been receiving seems to have gone temporarily to her head, for referring back to the Turkish war, Catherine said with unpleasing smugness: 'Tott cast 200 cannon in Constantinople; I captured them all; he decorated this palace with flowers, and these too I capture. Life is very odd.'

Catherine spent three days in sunny Bakhchisaray. Though the 5000 inhabitants already possessed nineteen mosques, Catherine thought it politic to endow two more; indeed she now favoured Islam, because polygamy produced lots of the children Russia so badly needed. Then she went on to the south coast, where steep headlands of red marble, crowned with pines and cypresses, reminded those who knew Italy of Amalfi, and where vines and traveller's joy – flowering viorna – twined round the trees and hung down to form bowers.

At Inkerman Catherine was lodged by Potemkin in a fine newly-built house and there, at a sign from the showman prince, the curtains of the main window were suddenly pulled back, revealing Sevastopol Bay, with a fleet of warships, which fired a roaring salute to Catherine. She continued to the town of Sevastopol, which in only three years Potemkin had built into a thriving port of 400 houses. Here Potemkin presented his Empress with her Black Sea Fleet: three 66-gun ships, three 50-gun frigates and ten smaller vessels. Catherine thanked him and remarked to her suite, 'I hope no one will ever again say the Prince is lazy.'

On the River Karasu, beyond Sevastopol, Potemkin had built a palatial house complete with garden, the scene of a finale to mark the twenty-fifth year of the Empress's reign. He offered her a concert and a banquet with local delicacies and the wines he had developed: a Burgundy-like red from the Don and a white Sudak from the Crimea.

As darkness fell, at a signal from Potemkin, 120 cannon fired jubilant salvoes and a display of fireworks began. In the long history of the Crimea there had been nothing like this. Thirty thousand rockets filled the warm night sky with coloured stars and, later, when she went to bed, Catherine could see from her window on the nearby mountain a huge 'E' for Ekaterina, spelled out by 55,000 lights.

Potemkin was feting a ruler he deeply admired and thanking her for the trust she had placed in him. It was the climax of Catherine's journey. She turned back and, again visiting new villages on the way, said goodbye to Potemkin on the field of Poltava, after he had staged a re-enactment of Peter the Great's victory.

While Catherine struck a medal to commemorate her three-month journey, the Saxon ambassador, who hated Potemkin and had stayed behind in St Petersburg, circulated a story that Potemkin had run up cardboard villages and populated them with neatly-dressed peasants driven on purpose from one place to the other. The ambassadors accompanying Catherine give no hint of this; while Jeremy Bentham, who was visiting his brother Samuel, on the spot and well placed to detect any dissimulation, says only that 'The streets through which she passed were edged with branches of firs and other evergreens, and illuminated with two barrels, alternating with rows of lamps, formed by earthenware pots filled with tallow and a candle-wick in the middle.'

At Ekaterinoslav Potemkin had planned far more than he achieved; at various points on the journey he had put up decorations and built a house suitable for an Empress to spend the night; and as favourite-in-chief he had many enemies – for these reasons the Saxon ambassador's libel stuck, and sticks a little today. But it contains no truth. As a leading authority on Catherine's Russia says, Potemkin's cardboard villages belong with 'Let them eat cake' in the waste-paper basket of history.

Potemkin's achievements in the south and in the Crimea are less than he described in letters to Catherine, but none the less solid. The creation of security in the steppes and the Crimea, annexed only four years earlier, the towns he founded, the villages built every twenty miles in open country, the construction of a fleet in the Black Sea – all these are facts, about which there can be no argument.

During the 1780s Potemkin was the most important man in Russia. How did this access of power affect his character? He became if anything more ebullient. In 1780 when Joseph II arrived incognito and announced stiffly that he would stay only in simple inns, never in palaces, Potemkin delighted Catherine by furnishing the Upper Bath-house at Tsarskoe Selo, sticking up a sign marked 'Inn' and installing Bush the gardener as 'mine host'. Ebullience led to heavy spending. If he felt like oysters or woodcock, he would send a courier thousands of miles to obtain them. When tradespeople presented overdue bills, he would call his secretary Popov and pretend to be angry with him. 'Why don't you pay this man?' Then he would make a sign with his hand. If he opened it, he allowed payment; if he closed his fist, the creditor got nothing.

He became overweening. He bought himself a silver bath and when two important courtiers stopped to admire it, he said, 'If you can excrete enough to fill it, I will give it to you.' He would send urgently for twenty aides-de-camp, and when they arrived say nothing to any of them. When his favourite niece, Alexandra Branicka, behaved impolitely to Count Stackelberg, Russian envoy to Warsaw, Potemkin seized the young lady by the nose and led her into the presence of King Stanislaus in order that she should apologize for her discourtesy.

His world-weariness increased, as an incident in Mogilev shows. Potemkin had done much to further the interests of the Jews in that town and one day he was feted by his grateful beneficiaries. They had built a platform covered with foliage and adorned with a banner inscribed 'Rejoice, O Israel, as in the days of Solomon.' They danced to flutes, cymbals and fiddles, and presented their protector with a pair of massive gold scales mounted on a diamond. After the reception Potemkin repeated impatiently, 'Coffee! I want some coffee.' Everyone ran to gratify his wish. Finally it arrived. Potemkin glanced at the coffee-pot on a golden plate and heaved a sigh: 'You can take it away. I only wanted to long for something and even here I have been done out of my pleasure.'

He propounded ideas almost of genius, such as forming the Jews into an 'Israelovsky' regiment, armed with huge lances, to regain and resettle the Holy Land; and another plan of uniting the Roman Catholic and Orthodox Churches. 'He is colossal, like Russia,' wrote Ligne. 'He embodies both desert wastes and gold mines', a comparison carried further by Ségur, who likened Potemkin's good eye to the Black Sea, his blind eye to the Baltic, blocked for much of the year by ice. 'He looks idle yet he works unceasingly, he is always lying on his couch yet never sleeps, he craves amusement and is sad in the midst of his pleasures, he is a sublime politician yet unreliable and capricious as a child.'

Towards Catherine Potemkin felt in equal degrees admiration, affection and gratitude. 'You are more than a real mother to me,' he wrote after the Crimea journey, and he thanked her 'that malice and envy could not prejudice me in your eyes and all perfidy was devoid of success. That is what is really rare in the world, such firmness is given to you alone.'

Yet, as Ligne noted, Potemkin could be capricious, and he sometimes showed that trait in his relations with Catherine. He was less loyal to her than she was to him. For instance, he promised the British ambassador, Harris, that he would persuade Catherine to accept England's offer of Minorca in exchange for Russian help against America. He failed to do so and then put the blame on Catherine, explaining to Harris that 'she has become suspicious, timid and narrow-minded.'

From the end of 1776 Potemkin ceased to have sexual relations with Catherine. He loved her still, but no longer felt sexually attracted to her. He transferred his sexual activities to three of his young Engelhardt nieces in turn, and to the eldest, Barbara, he wrote endearments more passionate than those he had used to Catherine: 'My dearest goddess, I kiss you all over.'

It is time now to look at Catherine's feelings for Potemkin. Catherine had originally sent her husband south in order that he should fulfil himself and in so doing continue to love her. Her plan had only partly succeeded. Potemkin had indeed fulfilled himself and he still loved her – but as his Empress, not in the tender way a husband loves a dear wife. Catherine had to face the fact that she had lost the sexual love first of Gregory Orlov, and now of Potemkin. Perhaps the double loss followed inevitably from her position as Empress, but it was none the less extremely galling.

Catherine felt for Potemkin first of all a gratitude similar to his for her. Replying to the letter he wrote after the Crimean journey, she said, 'Between you and me, my friend, everything can be said briefly: you serve me, and I am grateful, that is all. As to your enemies, you have slapped them on the fingers with your devotion to me and with your toil on behalf of the State.'

Over and above this current of gratitude Catherine continued to feel sexually attracted to Potemkin. She still considered him her hero. This is clear from the tone of her letters and the numerous presents she made him: for instance, she embroidered with her own hands a rich material sufficiently large to cover a sofa in the town house she had given him.

That was the position in summer 1777. Potemkin was then working in the south; Catherine had been for some months the mistress of Peter Zavadovsky. Suddenly Potemkin arrived in St Petersburg, having heard that Zavadovsky was working with the Vorontsovs to bring about his fall. He was met by Zavadovsky and told that the Empress refused to see him. Potemkin, furious, ignored Zavadovsky, forced his way into the palace and berated Catherine. 'A violent altercation is said to have happened between them, in course of which Potemkin threw a candlestick at her head.'

Potemkin asked Catherine to dismiss Zavadovsky and to let him find her another lover, whom he could trust. That a subject should seek to choose his Sovereign's favourite is, on the face of it, astonishing, and it is a measure of Catherine's love for Potemkin that she took his request seriously. It is probably true that Zavadovsky had been intriguing against Potemkin, and Catherine faced a clear choice: either Zavadovsky or Potemkin. She did not hesitate. Potemkin loomed incomparably larger in her life than the young officer. She agreed to send Zavadovsky away.

Potemkin proposed, and Catherine accepted, a tall, good-looking hussar, Simon Zorich, four times wounded, five years a war prisoner. He held the position of favourite eleven months. Then, quite naturally resenting Potemkin's hold on Catherine, Zorich began to turn against the older man, criticized him and provoked him to a duel. After the duel, in which neither was seriously wounded, 'Potemkin ordered him in a very cavalier style to take himself off and find another Empress if he could that would pay him so well for etc.' Potemkin replaced Zorich in June 1778 with Ivan Rimsky-Korsakov.

The most important thing about Rimsky-Korsakov is his age. Zavadovsky had been ten years younger than Catherine; Zorich sixteen years; while Rimsky-Korsakov, aged twenty-four, was twenty-five years younger than Catherine. The pattern of young lovers was to continue and since it reflects Catherine's own preference, it requires explanation.

Human beings divide into those who prefer older people, those who prefer their contemporaries, and those who prefer young people. Catherine belonged to the last class. She gravitated to an age group younger than her own; among her women friends Princess Dashkova was fifteen years her junior, Anna Protasova sixteen. The reason for this is probably to be found in Catherine's childhood. Without brother or sister of her own age at home, she had spent an unusually mature childhood, first fighting scoliosis, then spending much time with her mother and her mother's friends, and thinking like a grown-up. This may have left her hankering after the spontaneity, insouciance and idealism of youth.

To the question then why Catherine chose so many *young* lovers, the answer I think is not that she was seeking men who were more pliant to her will or more vigorous sexually than her contemporaries but rather that such a choice followed naturally from her general preference for young people.

Ivan Rimsky-Korsakov belonged to a collateral branch of the family that was to produce the famous composer, and he too was musical, singing well and playing the violin. His other attribute was a Greek profile, then very fashionable, because of Catherine's 'Greek plan', but his intellectual calibre may be gauged from the way he went about assembling a library, which he thought his new rank demanded. He went to St Petersburg's leading bookseller and told him he wanted books put up in the big house Catherine had given him. 'Which books exactly?' 'You understand that better than I. Big books at the bottom, then smaller ones and so on up to the top – as in the Empress's library.' The bookseller understood and unloaded in the new library unsold sheets of German Bible commentaries bound up in fancy leather.

Catherine loved Rimsky-Korsakov for his profile. She called him Pyrrhus, King of Epirus, after one of the youngest and most eminent of classical Greek princes. But Catherine was more than twice his age and such an affair, lacking intellectual links, could not last. One day, after he had been favourite fifteen months, Catherine caught Rimsky-Korsakov in the arms of Countess Bruce. It came as a doubly disagreeable shock, for Countess Bruce was one of Catherine's closest friends. Catherine immediately had a heart-to-heart talk with Rimsky-Korsakov and discovered that, though Countess Bruce was in love with him, he loved someone else: Countess Stroganova, a married woman. So tenacious in everything else, Catherine never tried to hold a lover who had stopped loving her. She dismissed Rimsky-Korsakov with her usual generous provisions for ex-favourites, and Countess Bruce also.

Once again Potemkin chose as favourite a man whom he knew would not work against him. Alexander Lanskoy was one of seven children born to parents of the provincial gentry, so poor they could not afford to send him to school. Alexander joined the Izmailovsky regiment at fourteen, then transferred to the Horse Guards. He took French lessons at this time and was said by his teacher to have had only five shirts to his name. On his appointment as general aide-de-camp he received from Catherine 100,000 roubles to buy clothes.

Alexander Lanskoy was the youngest of Catherine's lovers: twenty-one. He had a good intelligence, which Catherine trained by super-

Catherine's son, Paul, succeeded to the throne in 1796.

Catherine, aged 57, painted by Shibanov in Kiev
at the start of her silver jubilee journey to the Crimea.

intending his reading: one of the books she made him read was Cicero's Letters. He had a bent for art, drew well and made a profile portrait of Catherine which the Mint used on an issue of roubles. Of all her favourites in middle age Lanskoy – young enough to be her son – was the one Catherine loved most. She told Grimm that he worked hard, learned quickly and had come to share all her tastes; she hoped he would 'become the support of my old age'.

Even to Grimm Catherine was rather reticent about Lanskoy, and this suggests that he meant more to her than she cared to show. After a great many disappointments with men, and having experienced the whole spectrum of male misconduct, from Serge Saltuikov's weakness to Gregory Orlov's tantrums and Rimsky-Korsakov's unfaithfulness, Catherine had at last found a young man of unusually sweet character who loved her, who was content to be with her, learning from her wide experience of government, and sharing an enjoyment of art. In a few lines of one of her letters to Grimm Catherine reveals a little hieroglyph of her happiness: she and Lanskoy looking together at her collection of classical intaglios, passing the cut stones from hand to hand, admiring their beauty and speaking about their Greek and Roman makers.

In his fourth year as favourite Lanskoy was out riding when he fell heavily from his horse. As a result of the fall he developed chest pains, then contracted diphtheria, from which, on 14th June 1784, he died.

Not since the death of her mother in 1760 had Catherine experienced such a blow. She thought she would die of grief. She buried Lanskoy in Sophia and built a church over his grave; in Tsarskoe Selo park she erected a funerary urn in his memory and even two years later was seen to weep beside the urn, inscribed 'To my dearest friend'.

Potemkin had by then begun his exacting task in the Crimea, for which he urgently needed Catherine's support. Still working on the principle that unless he gave her a lover one of his enemies would do so and contrive his downfall, Potemkin waited eight months for Catherine to get over the shock of Lanskoy's death, then, in February 1785, chose a new favourite for her. Alexander Ermolov, aged thirty, blond, tall and with a flattened nose, is one of the most colourless of Catherine's favourites, little being known about him save the manner of his fall. He discovered that Potemkin was withholding for his own use the pension payable to the ex-Khan of Crimea, and told Catherine, who became very angry. Potemkin kept out of Catherine's way for a while, then suddenly arrived in the palace; repeating the tactics he had used against Zavadovsky, he gave Catherine a choice: either Ermolov or himself. Again Catherine chose her Lion of the Jungle, dismissing Ermolov, who had been favourite for only eighteen months.

Potemkin replaced Ermolov by one of his own aides-de-camp. Alexander Dmitriev-Mamonov, aged twenty-eight, was Asiatic-looking, with flattish face, high cheekbones, and attractive slanting black eyes. He had a good education and could speak French and Italian. On 16th July 1786, according to the diary kept by Catherine's secretary, 'Mamonov goes up the iron staircase and through the domed drawing room.' Next day the diary records that, contrary to her almost invariable habit of rising at seven, 'She slept until nine.' Three days later the new favourite gave Potemkin, who was his distant cousin, a gold teapot inscribed 'More united by love than by blood'. Mamonov accompanied Catherine to the Crimea and sometimes held up a game of whist by drawing amusing sketches in chalk on the baize table. He was Catherine's penultimate lover.

It is time to situate this series of favourites within Catherine's love-life as a whole. During the period of her first marriage Catherine took three lovers, to the last of whom, Orlov, she remained faithful until in effect he left her. In fact during the twenty-seven years 1745–1772 Catherine had no more than three lovers. After consoling herself for the loss of Orlov by a brief affair with Vasilchikov, Catherine took Potemkin as her lover, and probably married him. Thereafter he dominated, and changed the character of, her lovelife. He gave Catherine five out of her six lovers between 1776 and 1786; and of these five, two were badly chosen in the sense that they turned against Potemkin and had to be replaced by him. If her last favourite, Mamonov's successor, is included, Catherine had a total of two husbands and eleven lovers, of whom she chose five, Empress Elizabeth one, Potemkin the rest.

Potemkin was not Catherine's pander. He considered not her pleasure but his own power. Nonetheless, in choosing a new favourite, he naturally had to consider Catherine's taste for young men.

By taking lovers half her age Catherine kept in touch with the rising generation, but in every other respect this new tendency had a harmful effect on her character. It led her to attach importance to unimportant traits, such as her lover's profile or beautiful eyes. It encouraged her to mould rather than to adapt; indeed in her relations with these young men she shows herself less a mistress than a schoolmistress. It increased a tendency to selfishness, illustrated for instance in her description of Alexander Lanskoy as a 'young man I was forming; he was grateful, sweet-tempered and honest; he shared my sorrows when I had any and rejoiced in my pleasures.' We notice the unfeminine way in which Catherine now speaks of Lanskoy sharing her experiences, not of her sharing his.

'God, grant us our desires, and grant them quickly,' was Catherine's favourite toast. In changing lovers Catherine certainly acted quickly. The speed with which she ended a liaison and embarked on a new one suggests that she could not bear loneliness for long. Probably she found it increasingly difficult to face the fact that she had lost the sexual love of the two men she had idolized, Orlov and Potemkin. Whatever the reason, this game of musical beds arranged by Potemkin during her middle age deprived Catherine of the fructifying experience of periods of loneliness, of facing up to her double loss, of seeing herself as she really was, and in the long run it would be bound to diminish her. Potemkin by his activities in the South did a great deal for Catherine as Empress, but by bolstering his power through a series of lovers he unwittingly harmed her as a woman.

CHAPTER 22

THE LATER ACHIEVEMENTS

The development of the South by no means absorbed all Catherine's energy during the second half of her reign. She gave much attention also to supervising the education of her eldest grandson, to continuing her reforms at home and to pursuing a vigorous policy abroad. In these activities, diverse though they be, she sought, literally or metaphorically, to bring Russia closer to Europe.

Grand Duke Paul lost his first wife, Princess Wilhelmina of Hesse-Darmstadt, in childbirth, and in 1776 married Princess Sophia Dorothea of Württemberg, a plump kindly girl from a family of nine, who in 1777 bore him his first surviving child, a son. This was an important event in Catherine's life. Frustrated in her relations with her own three babies, from the first Catherine took extreme pleasure in this first grandson and she, who seldom showed her feelings in public, on the day the boy was christened shed tears of joy. 'Monsieur Alexander', she invariably called him, 'not Alexander the Great,' she specified to Grimm, 'but a very, very small Alexander.'

Without going so far as the Empress Elizabeth had done, Catherine took an almost possessive interest in the boy. She designed for him a loose-fitting nightdress which had the advantage – unusual then – of closing at the back with five hooks. She had him in her study four hours a day, taught him games and was delighted when, as she had done, he could amuse himself with just a handkerchief. It was Catherine who chose for him a 'tidy, clean, simple and sensible' nurse, not a great lady but Pauline Hessler, English wife of a palace footman, and instructed her to develop early the boy's self-respect and compassion.

Catherine was very much the doting grandmother. She considered Alexander at twenty months more knowledgeable than a three-year-old, and with his blue eyes and fair brown hair as pretty as Cupid, whereas his uncouth younger brother Constantine was merely 'a little Vulcan'. She was delighted when Alexander showed a taste for books and soon had him reading her *ABC Book*. There he learned that 'he had come into the world completely naked, like a hand that knows nothing, that all children are born thus, that by birth all men are equal, and that by learning things they come to differ enormously one from another.'

In the twenty years since she had supervised Paul's education Catherine had built up her authority to a point where she could choose no matter who to be Alexander's tutor. Her choice fell not on a Russian, a German, or a Frenchman, but on a young French-speaking Swiss of strongly republican views. Frédéric César Laharpe was a barrister who had so vigorously attacked the administration by Bernese aristocrats in his native Vaud that he had been obliged to leave Switzerland for a year; during that time he came to Grimm's notice. Catherine invited him to St Petersburg, thought well of him and his principles, and in 1784 appointed him tutor to her grandsons.

Catherine appointed some Russian teachers also – she jestingly calls herself *Universalnormalschulmeisterin*, Directress of the Teachers' Training College – but it was Laharpe who taught the future Tsar the key subjects of history and philosophy. With Catherine's approval he impressed upon Alexander that a prince must be the first subject of the State, and that 'liberty and independence are the most precious things in the world.' This Swiss who was to become a central figure in the creation of the Helvetian Republic deeply influenced the Russian boy by his amiable character, moral rectitude and championship of the common people. But of course he attracted opposition from the xenophobes and traditionalists. What, they asked, was the Empress about with her Alpine yokel?

Catherine knew very well what she was about. At this stage in the eighteenth century 'republic' meant what it meant for Dr Johnson, a 'state in which the power is lodged in more than one.' Catherine was already planning to lodge a measure of power in others than herself, so that Laharpe's appointment tallies with her later domestic reforms.

Between 1785 and 1787 Catherine organized the Russian nation in permeable corporate groups with definite legal powers to protect them against the crown or its bureaucracy. She chose to allot 'privileges' or in more modern terminology 'civil rights', not individually but by social function, a procedure in harmony with the 'estate' thinking of European writers.

Catherine began in 1785 by issuing a Charter of the Gentry. This for the first time recognized that land held by the gentry was legally their property, and removed long-standing restrictions on travel abroad. It organized the gentry into six classes – hereditary nobles at the bottom, gentry who had attained their rank by service to the State at the top –

and corporately by district. Each group was allowed to elect its own assembly.

In the same year Catherine issued a Charter of the Cities. The business of city or town government was entrusted to an executive board of six members, one from each of six groups: property owners, merchants, artisans, non-resident merchants, small traders, and 'distinguished citizens', a group ranging from bankers to former municipal officials and including artists.

In 1787 Catherine extended this principle of limited self-government to the State peasants in those southern provinces known collectively as the Ekaterinoslav Viceroyalty. Catherine defined the responsibilities of the village and of each type of elected official, enjoined elected village assessors to divide the tax burden fairly according to capacity to pay, and conferred on villagers the right to appeal to the Governor or to the provincial Director of Economy. Her act covered such matters as fire protection and schooling, and showed particular sympathy for the plight of unmarried mothers. Catherine later extended this act to two other Viceroyalties and from papers found in her study after her death it is clear that she was planning to apply the act to all State peasants – forty per cent of the population.

Catherine intended to top off these reforms by establishing a Chief Executive Chamber composed of one elected deputy from the nobility, from the townspeople and from the free peasants of each province. Her drafts for this project, which have only recently been discovered, suggest that she intended the Chamber to combine the best features of a French *parlement* and of the English Parliament, with powers both judicial and legislative. Catherine was prevented from realizing this project by events in Europe in the last years of her reign, but the Chamber remains an important statement of her political intentions for Russia.

What of the serfs? Catherine's ameliorative ukases were having an effect. Although it is often said that her reign saw the high point of serfdom, in fact a downward trend began in the decade 1772–82. In 1762–4 serfs had represented 52.17% of the total male population; in 1795–6 the percentage in the same area had fallen to 49.49.

Nor had Catherine dropped her hopes of eventual emancipation. Among the papers found at her death was the following: 'Here is an easy . . . means [towards emancipation]; to decree that with each sale of an estate to a new owner, the serfs are declared free. In a hundred years all or most lands will have changed owners. *Voilà*, the people are free.'

From what Laharpe taught Alexander with his employer's encouragement it is plain that Catherine hoped that her grandson, whom she called 'my legacy to Russia', would by virtue of his stronger position as a true-born Russian undertake abolition of serfdom. For herself, she continued to prepare the way for him by combating the attitude behind serfdom. In 1786 she changed the formula for petitions from 'Your Majesty's slave, brow prostrated to the ground, begs . . .' to 'Your Majesty's subject begs . . .'

Catherine continued also to help the poor and underprivileged. According to a courtier, Sumarokov, 'One day, early in the morning, she saw an old woman in the square opposite the palace, trying to catch a hen; the old woman was running after it, and was worn out by her lack of success. "Give orders that the poor creature should be helped, and find out what this means," she said to her footman. Inquiries were made, and it was reported that the old woman's grandson was the kitchen-boy to the Court, and that the hen was State property which was being stolen. "Make it a rule for ever," said Catherine, "that the old woman should be given a hen every day; only, not a live one, but a dead one. In this way we shall deter the young man from crime, and relieve his grandmother from her efforts and help her in her poverty." So from then on the old woman received a chicken as her right.'

From a thick sheaf of ukases designed to help the underprivileged two may be cited by way of illustration. In December 1792, according to the Swedish ambassador, 'Her Majesty has given 100,000 roubles for wood, so that everyone in need in St Petersburg, especially the poor, can buy a supply at the lowest going price.' At the same period John Parkinson, an Oxford don on the Northern Tour, says that when the thermometer fell to 15 degrees below freezing the Empress ordered all public places such as theatres to be shut so that coachmen, accustomed to wait long hours for their masters, would be spared undue suffering.

In another field also, religious affairs, Catherine pressed on with her earlier policy. She now gave every year what she called a dinner of toleration for members of different or opposed sects. In 1783 the dinner, at which Catherine presided, brought together the Catholicos of Georgia and the Russian Bishop of Polotsk; a Greek archimandrite found himself sitting next to a Catholic bishop, Franciscans next to Lutheran Pastors, the Anglican chaplain of the English merchants beside a German-born Calvinist. Catherine told her secretary Khrapovitsky, somewhat over-optimistically, that thanks to education in a few years all sects would disappear.

Catherine let it be known that she carried a snuff-box portraying Peter the Great and in moments of dilemma took it out and asked herself what Peter would do. That may have been true in military affairs or it may have been just a tactful tribute to a much-respected predecessor, but it certainly does not apply to Catherine's treatment of the Polish Jesuits who, on partition, became Russian subjects. Peter had detested the Jesuits – 'ambitious, subversive intriguers'; Catherine considered them excellent teachers and allowed them to keep their schools. Moreover, when Pope Clement XIV suppressed the Society of Jesus in 1773, Catherine declined to promulgate his Brief in Russia, partly on the grounds of toleration, partly to take an independent line with the Pope. She allowed the Jesuits to continue to exist as a corporate body on Russian territory, thus ensuring their survival until the time, much later, when they would be restored by Pius VII. Catherine even invited Jesuits to her dinners of toleration. To Orthodox critics who deplored her attitude Catherine quipped; 'Heretics are to suffer so much in the next world, we really ought to be kind to them in this.'

Abroad, during the second half of her reign, Catherine reaped both the cockle and the wheat of her earlier vigorous sowing. The chief cockle was the deterioration of Anglo-Russian relations. In 1765 Macartney had laid it down as axiomatic that the Russians could never become a formidable naval power, but Catherine proved him twice wrong, first with her Mediterranean victory at Chesme Bay and again, three years later, when she met England's claim to stop and search Russian ships that might be heading for France by successfully forming an 'armed neutrality', a kind of third force of Catherine's own invention, which grouped seven neutral nations under Russia's protection to resist any interference by foreign navies.

The British government resented Catherine's determination, if not to rule the waves, at least to prevent Britannia ruling them. They also looked askance at Catherine's annexation of the Crimea, and her secret plans for breaking up the Turkish Empire. When Catherine began a diplomatic offensive to annex the Turkish vassal state of Georgia, England decided that such an advance by Russia across the Caucasus must be prevented, and began putting pressure on Turkey. The Sultan, already alarmed at Russia's movements in the Caucasus, was stirred by this intervention to act, and in August 1787 declared war on Russia.

Catherine, who could boast of only six years' war in twenty-five years, deeply regretted the resumption of hostilities. She had not wanted more fighting, but her Greek plan made it sooner or later almost inevitable, and this time she had Austria as an ally. While Joseph II honoured his word by invading Serbia, Catherine appointed Potemkin commander-in-chief of the Russian army on the Black Sea.

Suvorov of the impish blue eyes and sharp nose was now fifty-nine and had been wounded so often he had been removed from the active list, to his great sorrow. One day he turned up at Tsarskoe Selo and took Catherine rowing on the lake. Half-way across he began to rock the boat with such force that Catherine had to admit he was still fit for action, and she sent him to command Potemkin's third division. Suvorov had become more Spartan than ever, indeed rather self-consciously so: asked by Ségur whether the stories were true that he always slept in his clothes, he replied, yes, but if he really wanted a comfortable night he took off his spurs. From the Turkish front he sent Catherine succinct bulletins – in verse.

Catherine ordered Potemkin to capture the extremely powerful fortress town of Ochakov, on an estuary of the Black Sea between the Bug and Dniester rivers. This in itself was a formidable task, since Ochakov was defended on land by 15,000 Turks, and from the sea by a strong navy under an intrepid admiral, Gazi Hassan, but Catherine made it even more formidable by asking Potemkin to be sparing of Russian lives: in other words, not to mount a frontal assault.

Potemkin had last seen military action eleven years before. He was out of training. By temperament he was suited for daring cavalry charges, not for the long haul of a siege. Ochakov was low-lying and unhealthy, the sandy soil made entrenchment difficult, and on top of everything, he hated the noise of gunfire.

Potemkin shut himself up in his tent and sank into a deep gloom. He did not even reply to Catherine's letters and she became worried. 'For God's sake and for mine take care of yourself! Nothing makes me more wretched than the fear that you may be ill . . .'

Potemkin was not ill. He had begun to while away the time with champagne parties and bevies of attractive women. Then the Black Sea fleet which had been helping in the siege was damaged in a storm, and Potemkin decided everything was lost. He actually wrote to Catherine saying he planned to evacuate the Crimea. Her Majesty's anger may be imagined. 'Where,' she replied, 'shall we dispose the remainder of the fleet if we evacuate Sevastopol? For heaven's sake think no more of this. A man who sits a horse does not climb down in order to cling to the animal's tail!'

Potemkin obeyed. But he did not see how he could capture Ochakov. When the Prince de Ligne hinted that he was doing less than he should, Potemkin would arrange for a breathless messenger to arrive with news of a fictitious victory in the Caucasus. But Catherine he could not gull. Finally he begged her to relieve him of his command and let him retire to a monastery.

Catherine found Potemkin more difficult to manage even than fierce little Constantine, who once bit Laharpe's finger to the bone. 'You are my friend, my dearest pupil,' she wrote back. 'You often give me better counsel than I can myself provide. But you are as impatient as a five-year-old, while the business entrusted to you demands patience, infinite and unshakable patience.'

For more than a year Catherine urged on her reluctant Field Marshal by letter and also supplied him with able officers. John Paul Jones, Scottish-born hero of the American War of Independence, was one of those who applied for service in Catherine's navy. James Brogden, an Englishman visiting St Petersburg, was expecting a desperado but found Jones 'a very good-looking man: he was dressed in a French uniform and was neither covered with blood nor armed with pistols.' Catherine sent him south with the rank of Rear Admiral and thought he would 'work wonders'.

He did. In June 1788 he and Nassau-Siegen led the Russian Black Sea fleet against a superior Turkish force, and with the help of 13-inch mortars designed and cast by Samuel Bentham won a notable victory, destroying fifteen ships and taking 1600 prisoners. Unfortunately Jones and Nassau-Siegen were temperamentally unsuited; they quarrelled; Catherine took Nassau-Siegen's part and Paul Jones left Russia somewhat bitter. But his victory proved precious to Catherine, for it allowed Potemkin's troops to surround Ochakov. On the feast of St Nicholas, 6th December 1788, Potemkin finally attacked from two directions, and despite heavy losses – Suvorov got a bullet wound in the neck – captured Ochakov.

'I take you by both ears,' wrote Catherine delightedly, 'and kiss you in my thoughts, Grishenka, dear friend of my heart.' She gave him the long-coveted St George's Cross and to every soldier who had entered Ochakov a silver medal. Sarti she commissioned to write a *Te Deum*, which includes one hundred cannon salvoes to be rendered by the organ.

Catherine's joy was purely relative, and short-lasting too, for her attention now was focused on the North. Since Peter the Great's crushing victories over Sweden, Russia's influence had kept that country weak until 1772, when Gustavus III, the homosexual son of Catherine's uncle Adolphus Frederick, effected a coup and re-established a strong monarchy. Behind professions of friendship Gustavus had long been seeking an opportunity to avenge Poltava, and in the summer of 1788 he thought he saw his chance. Taking advantage of a promise by England of money and military help, he invaded Russian Finland at a point barely a hundred miles from St Petersburg.

This was extremely serious. With most of her troops in the South, Catherine raised a peasant home guard and sent old Admiral Greig to blockade the Swedish fleet. But these measures could provide at best but temporary relief, and the two years following Gustavus's attack were the most harrowing of Catherine's reign, not only on account of the two-front war but because of domestic misfortunes.

Forgetting the frustrations Grand Duke Peter had suffered at the hands of Elizabeth, Catherine gave her son Paul no political power. As a result he made a cult of his supposed father and, through him, of Frederick II and Frederick William, spending much of his day on the parade ground, drilling soldiers. When the Turkish war broke out he pleaded with Catherine to let him go to the front: 'What will Europe say if I don't go?' Catherine replied, 'Europe will say that the Grand Duke is a dutiful son.' But Paul, with ample justification it must be said, resented this decision, and relations between mother and son worsened.

As though this were not enough, Alexander Mamonov, her current favourite, of whom Catherine had grown very fond, chose the summer of 1789 to fall in love with a Court lady. Once again Catherine made no attempt to fight a younger rival. She gave her sanction to their marriage, dressed the bride with her own hands and loaded her with presents. Nevertheless she wrote, 'I have received a bitter lesson.'

The following year, 1790, was to prove even more bitter. In May the Swedish navy slipped out of harbour and was engaged by the Russians off Cronstadt. The news of this engagement, little more than a skirmish, was brought to Catherine at Tsarskoe Selo by one of the junior officers, Lieutenant Elphinstone. The ensuing scene reveals Catherine in a new role, personally handling the defence of Russia.

Young Elphinstone arrived late at night in his fighting clothes, covered with dust and gunpowder, and exhausted. His despatches were instantly carried to Catherine, who ordered her page to give Elphinstone refreshments and a bed, and requested that he be on no account disturbed. Catherine sent three times, but still he slept. At length Elphinstone, in deshabille, was conducted to her presence by her secretary, when Catherine began a conversation in which she complimented the gallantry and many naval achievements of his family, calling him 'My son'. 'Now let us proceed to business: I have received the despatches . . . I thank you for your bravery and zeal; I beg you will describe to me the position of the ships.' While Elphinstone did so Catherine wrote notes in a pocket-book. When he had finished she personally gave her orders to the commander-in-chief; Elphinstone she presented with a *rouleau* of ducats, a beautiful little French watch, and, although very young, promoted him to the rank of Captain.

The skirmish at Cronstadt was followed later in the summer by a full-scale battle at Svenskund, in which the Russian navy under Nassau-Siegen suffered a crushing defeat. The Russians lost some of their best ships, and 9500 casualties and prisoners. Catherine wrote to Potemkin, almost in tears, that Svenskund had practically broken her heart.

Catherine could now hear Swedish gunfire from the palace windows. The situation was so serious that she was advised to leave for Moscow. In the South things were bad also, for Joseph II had died and his successor Leopold II had begun peace talks with Turkey. Catherine lived on coffee and rusks, and lost weight so rapidly that her women had to take in all her dresses.

But she remained in St Petersburg. She had once been told by Ligne that she was imperturbable – in modern idiom, unflappable – and she resolved now to deserve the compliment. In a letter to Ligne she referred to herself as 'Votre imperturbable' and, when things were at their blackest, would repeat aloud to herself very slowly, '*J'ai donc de l'imperturbabilité.*'

While the Swedes advanced, it was Catherine who bade tearful Bezborodko imitate Frederick the Great, who never lost his head even amid the most terrible disasters, and to her defeated admiral, Nassau-Siegen, who, full of shame, had returned all his decorations and begged for his discharge, she wrote a letter of consolation and encouragement.

Catherine succeeded in rallying the forces that remained to her, while Gustavus not only failed to follow up his naval success but by tactlessness lost the support of his nobles. He believed he could retain his throne only by making peace, and a treaty was signed at Verela in August 1790, confirming the position which existed before the war. Proposals were also made for a marriage, at some future date, between Gustavus's son and one of Catherine's granddaughters. Catherine was intensely relieved at the end of hostilities and indulged in a quip to Grimm: 'This morning four troublesome corns dropped off my feet;

what with that and the peace, I reckon today among the propitious days.'

For another propitious day of this kind Catherine had to wait a further seventeen months. Successes on land by Suvorov and a naval victory in the Black Sea by Ushakov finally brought the Turks to the peace table. By the terms of the treaty of Jassy, in January 1792, Catherine gained all the territory between the Bug and the Dniester, thus rounding off her earlier acquisitions on the Black Sea.

The ending of the Second Turkish War, though important to Russia, was hardly more than a minor event in the greatly-changed context of European politics, dominated now by the French Revolution. What were Catherine's reactions to the storming of the Bastille, the National Assembly and the Tricolour? Not, as is often said, the unreasoned prejudice of an ageing despot, but an attitude that followed logically from her beliefs.

Catherine believed in monarchy and defended her belief on grounds of efficiency: 'Tell a thousand people to draft a letter, allow them to debate every phrase, and see what you get.' She believed in the equality of all before the law, and in a permeable society where talent, stimulated by honours, could rise to the top. As early as 1779, when reading about Denmark, an early version of a bourgeois society, she had found that last element lacking: 'Everything is predictable, so no one thinks and you get a nation of sheep.' Catherine believed the imposed equality in France would stifle talent. To Ligne she proposed a prize essay on the theme: Do we need honour and courage? 'If we do, we mustn't forbid competition or hobble it with its arch-enemy, equality.'

But Catherine's main objection to the Revolutionaries followed from their stifling of all contrary opinions, religious and political. 'Since these gentlemen,' she wrote to Grimm, 'are convinced republicans, they ought to love, respect and encourage the truth, and if they don't, I shall declare them to be nothing at all, since they break with their own principles. In my view they are likely to discredit liberty for a long time and to make it hateful to every nation.' Catherine was saying in effect that her own work of reform, and Alexander's later, had been rendered much more difficult, first by the betrayal of republican principles, and secondly by their campaign against Christianity, which had hardened opinion in Russia against Europe.

Another article in French Revolutionary principles – independence for all nations – concerned Catherine most urgently of all, for it erupted so to speak on her doorstep. In 1791 the Poles, profiting from the Second Turkish War, decided to establish a new constitution, guaranteed by Austria and Prussia. It ended the liberum veto, strengthened the crown, and made it hereditary, after Stanislaus's death, in the House of Saxony. This amounted to a declaration of intention to leave Russia's orbit.

By the time Catherine had concluded peace with Turkey and was free to act in Poland, Austria and Prussia were at war with France and no longer in a position to help the country whose constitution they had guaranteed. Catherine sent in a very strong army – 65,000 men – which convened a Diet at Grodno, to which she virtually dictated terms. In a period of revolution, Catherine had decided, Russia must have a stable western frontier, and hence Poland must be rendered weak. Under duress in summer 1793 the Diet agreed to submit all future domestic and foreign policy to Russia's approval and to a second partition, whereby Catherine gained the Polish Ukraine, Minsk and Vilnius, with a population of three million, while Prussia, as a gratuity for lending diplomatic support, was given Torun and Danzig.

This, however, did not end the Polish question. In March 1794 Thaddaeus Kosciuszko, a young Pole who had fought beside Lafayette in the American War of Independence, hoisted the standard of Polish freedom, and roused a new national spirit by promising to emancipate the serfs and expunging from the coinage the effigy of King Stanislaus, who had acquiesced in the recent partition.

King Frederick William II of Prussia dispatched an army to check Kosciuszko's movement but it failed to take Warsaw. Catherine thereupon sent in Suvorov, who captured the city in November 1794, and thus regained the initiative. Catherine was determined now to erase Poland from the map and, playing off Prussia against Austria, it was she who laid down terms for the third and final partition. Austria got Cracow, Sandomierz and Lublin, Prussia got Warsaw, Russia took Courland and the rest of Lithuania. Poland ceased to exist, and the unfortunate Stanislaus, a king who had outlived his country, retired to take up botany.

In one sense the dismemberment of Poland marks the failure of Catherine's concept of a puppet-kingdom; in another it marks a success, since it removed a long-standing barrier between Russia and Europe. Henceforward, with her frontier contiguous to Prussia and the Austrian Empire, Russia would be geographically as well as ideologically involved with the nations of the West.

Catherine's dealings with Poland have one interesting footnote.

She once remarked that she had arrived dowerless but had given Russia a dowry in the shape of Poland. This is true in an almost literal sense, for it was mainly in Poland that Catherine found the estates which she lavished on those of her favourites who served Russia well, such as Potemkin and Orlov. In a country permanently short of capital in the form of cash it was traditional for a ruler to reward merit with gifts of land, including the serfs who worked the land, and it was obviously sound policy to introduce Russian landowners to newly-annexed regions. This explains why, of 398,973 male peasants transferred by Catherine to private ownership, 314,226 came from former Polish territories.

To complete this survey a word is required about foreign policy in other areas. In the Far East whenever an opportunity presented itself Catherine seized it. When a Japanese ship was wrecked on Russia's coast, Catherine arranged for the captain to be taught Russian and then to teach his masters Japanese. She then had him escorted home, and in return secured permission for one Russian ship a year to trade with Japan, where previously the Dutch held a monopoly.

In 1792 Catherine granted further financial support – and ten missionaries – to Shelekhov in his Alaskan colony, and she vied with the Dutch, the French, the English and Yankees from Salem, Boston and New York, in exploring the coast south from Alaska. In 1794 the British ambassador brought to Lord Grenville's attention 'a new chart of the Russian Empire, in which a considerable tract of the North West Coast of America, to the northward of Nootka Sound [Vancouver] is found to be part of Her Imperial Majesty's Dominions'.

On the mainland of Asia Catherine reacted vigorously to China's occupation of an island in the Amur River by bringing up 30,000 troops. When Persia attacked Russia's new protectorate, Georgia, and blocked Russia's attempts to trade with India, Catherine sent into Persian territory an army ably commanded by General Valerian Zubov, which captured Derbent and Baku. 'I will not die,' she told Derzhavin, 'until I have driven the Turks out of Europe, until I have brought low China's pride, and until I have established trade with India.'

The results of Catherine's foreign policy may now be briefly summarized. Russia acquired, in Poland, the Crimea, on the Black Sea and the Alaskan coast, territory equal to the whole of France, a population of seven million, and annual revenue of 10 million roubles, about a quarter of her total. No less important for the future, by her victories on land and sea Catherine laid the foundations of a new national spirit which was to stand her grandson Alexander in good stead when the French Revolution, in the person of another remarkable foreign-born ruler, eventually erupted on to Russian soil. Unlike Austria, unlike Frederick the Great's Prussia, Russia would then be ready, morally and militarily, to resist and eventually to triumph.

CHAPTER 23

LIKE A FLY IN SPRING

In the spring of 1789 a young officer in the Horse Guards arrived at Tsarskoe Selo to take up the post of duty captain. Plato Zubov was the third of four sons of Alexander Zubov, the governor of a province, and after active service against the Swedes he had applied for his present post, probably well aware that it had led Vasilchikov and Lanskoy to become favourites.

Plato Zubov was of medium height, with broad shoulders and an athlete's body. His features were regular, rather on the small side but redeemed by magnificent eyes. He was twenty-one years old and in many ways still boyish: one of his amusements at Tsarskoe Selo was flying a kite. He loved music and, like Rimsky-Korsakov, played the violin.

That summer Catherine learned that her favourite, Mamonov, had fallen in love with another woman. She at once had a long talk with her old friend Anna Nikitichna Naruishkin. Next day her faithful footman, Zachary Zotov, told Catherine's secretary Khrapovitsky that he 'suspected the duty captain, Plato Zubov'.

On the day after Mamonov's engagement took place, according to Khrapovitsky, 'Zubov was brought in by way of the upper floor and remained after dinner, as well as Anna Nikitichna, and again in the evening until eleven.' Three days later Catherine ordered Khrapovitsky to bring from her study some rings and 10,000 roubles. Next morning he put the 10,000 roubles behind one of the sofa cushions; Catherine gave them to Zubov, and a ring with her miniature in it. Another of the rings, worth 1000 roubles, Zubov gave to Zotov the footman. A week later Zubov was appointed Catherine's aide-de-camp and a couple of days afterwards, according to Khrapovitsky, 'gave Anna Nikitichna a watch worth 2000 roubles'.

At the beginning of their relationship Catherine referred to Zubov in her letters as a child. 'I love this child very much, and he is devoted to me, crying like a child if he is not allowed to come to my room.' She also called him 'the most innocent soul in the world', evidently confusing, as do many who are no longer young, youthful freshness with moral innocence. She treated Zubov, even more than previous favourites, as a pupil to be educated – they translated Plutarch's *Life of Alcibiades* together – and she informed senior statesmen that she was doing estimable work forming a valuable servant for the State. Nevertheless there is little doubt that Catherine and her young favourite had sexual relations. On 5th August 1789, à propos Zubov, Catherine wrote: 'I am keeping well. I am gay and I feel I am being reborn like a fly in spring.'

Plato Zubov was an agreeable young man who, according to Bush the gardener, 'never was known to do any harm to anybody and whenever it is in his power he is glad to do a service.' It is unlikely that he felt any strong physical attraction to Catherine, although she was a well-preserved lady with sound white teeth. Zubov, Parkinson noticed, 'behaves with no small degree of hauteur, which in a person from the dust as he is gives no small offence.' He spoke little and very drily; he would keep fifty gentlemen waiting in his ante-room before receiving them in an off-hand manner. Only Suvorov would not stand for it. Once having been received by Zubov in incorrect dress, the veteran got his own back by having the favourite shown into his room when he, Suvorov, was wearing only a shirt. On another occasion when dining with Zubov and her son, the Empress asked Paul his view of a certain question. 'I share Plato Aleksandrovich's opinion,' replied the Grand Duke. 'What?' said Zubov drily. 'Did I say something silly?'

The news of this tendency to arrogance got around, and eventually reached Potemkin. Catherine from the first had been worried what Potemkin's reaction to Zubov would be. In her letters she referred to Zubov as 'your cornet' because Potemkin had originally given Zubov that rank in the Horse Guards, and she repeated any complimentary remarks made by Zubov about the Prince.

Potemkin declined to be mollified. This new favourite had not been chosen by him, he had done nothing remarkable, he was a potential rival, and his behaviour was such as might alienate important persons of State. As soon as the war allowed he hurried to St Petersburg. 'Zub' is Russian for tooth, and in his carriage Potemkin could be heard muttering, 'I must pull this bad tooth. I must.'

So the man she had built up into the most powerful in Russia, the Prince of Taurida, arrived to scold Catherine, not with the old violence – there seems to have been no throwing of candlesticks – but with the common-sense arguments of middle age that hurt quite as much. Catherine needed Potemkin: she had once written that without him she was like a person without arms. He was the one continuous strand in her otherwise variegated personal life. She particularly admired his exceptional 'courage of heart, spirit and soul'; indeed, he was still the only man she looked up to, and at the time of the Swedish War she had sent him her plan for defending St Petersburg with the words, 'Have I done right, my master?' Also, according to Zubov, she was afraid of him 'as of an angry husband'.

When Potemkin strode into the Winter Palace like an angry Polyphemus bent on 'extracting' Zubov, Catherine suffered mentally almost as much as when years ago the surgeon Gyon had struggled to pull out her wisdom tooth. As she listened to Potemkin's reproaches, some of which she deserved, Catherine shed tears. 'You have plunged a dagger into my breast,' she afterwards wrote to Potemkin, 'by saying that what I have done has made you love me less. Heavens, your love must be pretty faint, for I did nothing to offend you, nor will I ever do or think of doing such a thing, whatever your suspicious mind may imagine . . .' Then comes a phrase that reveals the deep anguish behind her disclaimers: 'Only one thing I could not bear, that is if you were really to stop loving me.'

Yet despite her fear that Potemkin might stop loving her, Catherine resisted this first attempt to make her give up Zubov. She tried to turn aside Potemkin's anger by making a great fuss of him as a war hero. She declared his successes had made him handsomer than ever and persuaded him to have his portrait painted by Lampi.

Installed in the Taurida Palace, Potemkin brooded on what to do next. On such occasions it was his habit to shut himself up in his room and ceaselessly clean the bezels of his rings with a little brush. From this period of pondering he emerged with a plan. He would throw a party in honour of Catherine more lavish than any given before in Russia, a party such as only he could imagine and devise, so dazzling that young Zubov would be eclipsed and Catherine, in a daze of admiration, gratitude and who knows what – probably Potemkin did not pinpoint Catherine's motives – would again make him master of her life.

Potemkin had lost none of his eccentricity and extravagance. He had recently ordered an immense organ costing 50,000 roubles, and according to Parkinson 'he would place himself under a fountain and suffer the water to come all over him without changing his clothes.' To his party for Catherine, he decided, he would invite two thousand guests; it would cost half a million roubles, it would incorporate theatre, ballet and music. Rehearsals were required for weeks before, and every day while they were going on Potemkin had his favourite very expensive sterlet soup, made from small sturgeon found in the Black and Caspian Seas, served to the various performers from a large silver tub.

At seven in the evening of 28th April 1791 Catherine arrived at Potemkin's house and was received by her host wearing red silk trousers and tail-coat, the gold buttons of which were each set with a large diamond, and a black laced cloak. The neo-classical Taurida Palace, her gift to him, was lit by 20,000 candles, its gardens with 140,000 lanterns, for which a special consignment of wax had had to be rushed from Moscow. As she entered the hall, a choir in the gallery, accompanied by an orchestra of three hundred, sang a specially-composed anthem in her honour. She was then led to a seat at the head of the ballroom, its great length of two hundred and fifty feet marked off by the converging lines of a double colonnade of Ionic columns.

Twenty-four couples, including the Grand Dukes Alexander and Constantine, half of them dressed in rose-red, half in blue, danced a carefully-rehearsed quadrille. Catherine was then escorted to the private theatre, where two short comedies and two ballets were performed. Next a huge clockwork-driven elephant, studded with emeralds and rubies, ambled in, and the elephant's Persian sadu beat a drum to announce that dinner was served.

The dinner consisted of choicest delicacies and vintage wines. When they rose from table Potemkin led Catherine to a winter garden adjoining the ballroom, where fountains played between sub-tropical trees and flowers. Here he showed her an agate obelisk on which the first letter of her name was picked out in precious stones, and a statue of white Paros marble depicting the goddess of friendship holding a bust of Catherine. It was inscribed with words which that evening held a special poignancy: 'To one who is Mother and more than Mother to me'.

Potemkin's generosity, his lavishness, his showmanship, which doubtless reminded her of his brilliant arrangements for her jubilee journey to the Crimea – these were admirable. But Catherine knew that basically the party was the flamboyant display by one male seeking to displace a rival – and here Potemkin had failed to read her heart.

Plato Zubov was not just a rival as at an earlier stage Zavadovsky and Ermolov had been rivals. He was a new kind of man in Catherine's life, because he was so very young – young enough, since she was now sixty-one, to be her grandson. Youthfulness had been a factor in her other loves, but with Zubov it becomes dominant.

Catherine prized Zubov's youthfulness not only for itself but because of what it could do to her. She very much wanted to have a long life, and had once written to Voltaire wishing that she might live to be 169, like a contempotary Englishman, John Kings – 'What a splendid age!' she had exclaimed. But Catherine wanted also to go on being young. When she played with her grandchildren, she told Grimm with relish, it was she who was the life and soul of their games. The key to Catherine's relations with Zubov is to be found in her phrase: 'I feel I am being reborn like a fly in spring.' Though she may not have been fully aware of it, Catherine loved Zubov because he was the instrument of her rejuvenation.

Put into cold arithmetic, Potemkin was fifty-one, Zubov twenty-three, and for someone seeking what Catherine was seeking there could be no hesitation between such figures. So when she said good-night to Potemkin and before returning to her State carriage, the spokes of its wheels gleaming with diamonds, and thanked him for so memorable an evening, Catherine made no sign of granting his request that she dismiss her young favourite. Potemkin understood. He knelt at her feet and in a symbolic gesture of defeat and acceptance of defeat covered Catherine's hands with kisses and tears.

Her desire to remain young through Zubov was a weakness on Catherine's part, yet surely an excusable one. She who embodied a vigorous young nation, how, she may have thought, could she ever grow old? Also, all day and every day she had to resist pressing officials, governors, ambassadors, using every trick in the book to make her accede to this or that request – could she not allow herself in this one area of her life to yield? It was after all a small weakness, indeed it may have been the condition of her continuing resolute strength in public life.

Catherine's affair with Zubov also contains a measure of self-delusion, for the Empress continued to assert that she was doing estimable work by training this child for the State. Long ago she had chosen to overlook certain differences between her Lutheranism and the Orthodox religion, and to that girlish blurring of the truth may be traced her refusal now to recognize the true nature of her affair with Zubov or to admit that she was transgressing, at the very least, her own principle of common sense.

One thing is clear: Catherine was happy with Zubov. She found him good company and very attentive. 'He takes such good care of me,' she told Grimm, 'that I don't know how to thank him.' Her feelings of happiness found expression in a little incident which she reported with gratification to Grimm. A distinguished Persian, visiting St Petersburg, was admiring her reproductions of Raphael's *loggie*. Coming on 'Adam and Eve being driven from Paradise', the Persian turned to Catherine with a puzzled look. 'That can't be true,' he said, 'for here in this palace we're in Paradise.'

Potemkin took Catherine's decision surprisingly well. Indeed his increased self-control, even the fact that he no longer bit his nails, worried Catherine a little for she had a theory that a man's faults are part of his vitality. They dined together once again before Potemkin, in July, said goodbye to Catherine for what was to be the last time.

The Prince travelled to Jassy and peace talks with the Turks. There, in mid-September, he had an attack of shivering fever – probably a recurrence of malaria contracted years before in the Crimea – wrapped wet towels round his head and had his servants spray him with eau-de-Cologne. 'Am very weak,' he informed Catherine. 'Please choose and send me a Chinese dressing-gown.' When she received this note, Catherine wept. She immediately sent the dressing-gown and two doctors as well.

Potemkin grew worse. Seized with sudden acute pain, he would jump out of bed and fall back writhing. The doctors suspected gall-stones, others poison from the hand of Zubov's family. Potemkin was prescribed liquids only, but he had as little confidence in doctors as Catherine and continued to wolf huge meals, including breakfasts of smoked Hamburg goose and slices of ham, wine and liqueurs. In intervals between pain he composed ten Canons to the Saviour, religious songs reminiscent of the Psalms, and conversed with his confessor, an archbishop, expressing not sorrow for his sins, but in true eighteenth-century style a conviction that all his life he had acted to make people happy. His greatest comfort was to receive letters from Catherine, which he would read and re-read and cover with kisses.

At the beginning of October, in increasing pain, Potemkin decided to move from low-lying Jassy to Nikolaiev, a town amid woods on the Black Sea which he had founded to commemorate the capture of Ochakov on St Nicholas's day. He had now been joined by his favourite niece and long-time mistress, Alexandra Branicka, who was on her way to Warsaw with her Polish husband when she heard the news of his illness and raced to nurse him. In the company of Alexandra and a few close members of his suite Potemkin was carried to a carriage and set off for Nikolaiev. At noon on the second day he suddenly cried out, 'I'm on fire, I'm dying.' The carriage was stopped, a carpet laid under a tree and there, in territory he had tamed and then defended against the Turk, his Serene Highness Prince Potemkin died at the age of fifty-two. As his friends looked for a gold coin to shut his one good eye, a Cossack proffered a five-copeck piece, and with this copper the soul of the richest man in Russia was speeded to the next world.

Potemkin may or may not have been Catherine's husband in the eyes of the Church but he had meant more to her than most husbands do to their wives: he had been an admired collaborator on the grand scale, a source of strength and encouragement. When she heard the news of his death Catherine fainted three times and had to be bled. For days afterwards Khrapovitsky's diary conveyed her grief: 'Tears and despair', 'She wept', or just 'Tears'.

'Now I have no one left on whom I can rely,' said Catherine, as she recovered from the blow. She had plenty of able civil servants, but she was thinking of her need – it really had become a need – for a handsome, honest, 'hero-like' collaborator.

Zubov was the likeliest candidate, though he lacked Potemkin's physical and intellectual largeness, and Catherine began to press forward with his education. She wrote memoranda on the situation in Europe, to train him in foreign affairs; she asked him for reports on Poland. Zubov had a good memory and was keen to learn. He was entrusted with more and more important business until he came to occupy the position formerly occupied by Panin, then by Bezborodko.

In no sense did Catherine allow Zubov to dominate her. Khrapovitsky's diary often mentions Catherine's impatience with an incomplete report by Zubov; and in June 1792 à propos a request by Zubov: 'Refused, angrily.' Nevertheless, the young favourite advanced. Catherine made him president of the College of War, Governor-General of the Taurida, and commander of the Black Sea fleet. That so many honours should have been granted to a man who had done so little angered Catherine's older advisers, and Zubov was not popular. But neither had Potemkin been popular. Catherine handled the relationship with such tact, dignity and decorum that Zubov came to be accepted for what in fact he had become: the Empress's trustworthy chief helper in ruling Russia.

CHAPTER 24

CRITICISM AND SEDITION

One of the officials Catherine received every morning was the chief of the St Petersburg police, who told her which notable persons had been entering or leaving the capital. This was standard practice in Continental Europe, indeed the Encyclopedists' complimentary phrase for a civilized country, where one could travel in safety, was *'un pays policé'*.

Catherine had also inherited the Secret Chancellery, or Secret Bureau, which controlled the political police. This was a long-standing Tsarist institution. The Empress Elizabeth had had personal charge of the Secret Chancellery, but Peter III put it under the control of the Senate. Catherine respected this arrangement and confirmed in office the head of the police, Sheshkovsky, who had received his appointment before she came to power. Sheshkovsky got a bad name for losing his temper when interrogating prisoners, but there is no evidence that Catherine employed the political police more often or more harshly than her immediate predecessors. The Secret Bureau continued, as before, to exist, but it played a minor role in her reign. Catherine helped to make Russia *un pays policé*, but it was never, under her, a police state.

One of the few occasions when Catherine made use of the secret police was in the early 1780s, during her affair with Lanskoy. Catherine instructed Sheshkovsky to discover the authors of caricatures and lampoons against her. There is evidence that Catherine instructed Sheshkovsky to apply 'gentle corporal punishment' to Madame Kozhina, wife of a major general, probably for circulating lampoons. The probable nature of that punishment will be considered in a moment.

When Catherine took Zubov as a lover the gossip became more malicious. In particular, the wife of Alexander Mamonov, Zubov's predecessor, began circulating stories about her husband's experiences in the Empress's bed. In a book about Russia by a minor French diplomat named Castera containing many falsehoods designed to please his anti-Russian French readers, the following story about Catherine's reaction to Madame Mamonova may be true, since it tallies with what Parkinson heard at the same period, and if it is true, it throws light also on the probable nature of Madame Kozhina's punishment:

> When Mamonov and his wife had gone to bed the chief of the Moscow police entered their apartment and, having shown them an order from her Majesty, left them in the hands of six women and retired to an ante-chamber. Then the six women, or rather the six men dressed as women, seized the babbling lady, and having stripped her of her nightdress, beat her with sticks in the presence of Mamonov, whom they forced to kneel. When the chastisement was over, the police chief re-entered the room and said: 'This is the way the Empress punishes a first indiscretion. For the second, people are sent to Siberia.'

A third occasion when Catherine faced criticism is recorded by Sumarokov.

> Amongst other petitions, Catherine's secretary Teplov received a very vicious lampoon against Catherine. In the chancellery the handwriting was recognized, the slanderer was summoned to St Petersburg, he confessed, and Teplov, wishing to show him his protection, waited for a suitable occasion to ask for mercy for him. It must be mentioned that the Director of the Postal Services always gave the Empress information as to how many papers each of the secretaries received by each post. One day, when Teplov had finished making his reports and was taking his leave, the Empress said to him: 'Stay here a little, we'll have a talk.'
>
> Going over various subjects, perhaps by chance, perhaps because she really knew the number of papers he had received, she asked: 'Haven't you got another report?' He was in confusion, did not want to lie, and was obliged to reveal the mystery. Irritated by this, Catherine demanded the lampoon. Teplov objected, because of its vile style, and did not want to show it; but 'I order you to,' threateningly uttered, made him obey, and he went home to fetch it. Teplov returned, went down on his knees, and asked for mercy.
>
> 'Get up,' said Catherine. 'I don't like people putting on an act; in the past people were hanged for that, and I myself can punish sternly.' She was flushed from emotion, walking swiftly about the room, her sleeves rolled up – all this showed great anger. Everything presaged the inevitable ruin of the sinner, the Empress's strong vexation already spoke of it; but suddenly her animosity vanished, little by little her peace of mind returned, mercy began to show on her face, and instead of the promised vengeance, an unexpected

decision followed. 'I don't even want to know who reviles me,' she said. 'Here's my revenge on him,' and she threw the paper into the fire.

As she aged Catherine grew more tolerant of criticisms of her love-life, perhaps because her relations with Zubov had by then become platonic. One day Countess Golovina brought her a copy of the Paris newspaper, *Le Moniteur*, which the Governor of St Petersburg thought should be seized. It contained an attack on Catherine headed 'Messalina of the North', an allusion to Emperor Claudius's lascivious wife. 'Couldn't they invent some new label for me?' Catherine remarked. She then read on, about 'infamous orgies in the cellars of the Winter Palace and the alcoves of Tsarskoe Selo'.

'Just fancy,' said Catherine, smiling, 'I've never been down to the palace cellars. What a splendid time we might have had there if only we'd known!' She ordered that number of *Le Moniteur* to be sold without restriction, explaining that it was right that her people should learn how deep was the pit into which French public opinion had fallen.

By far the most important written criticism which Catherine had to face during her reign was published at this time, and it came from an unexpected source: a senior civil servant and former protégé.

Alexander Radishchev, the eldest of a rich landowner's eleven children, was born in 1749 and received a scholarship from Catherine to study law at Leipzig University. During his five years there Radishchev came under the influence of a fervent champion of freedom of speech, Ernest Platner. On his return he entered government service, discharging his functions honestly, but his main attention was given to French thinkers, notably Rousseau, Mably, whose *Observations on the Greeks* he translated, and Raynal, who attacked both throne and altar. In appearance Radishchev was slim and gaunt, hair carefully brushed back from a high forehead, large dark eyes and an expression of hauteur. He is described as 'introspective, a man who takes no notice of what is going on around him'.

Radishchev's father had excellent relations with the peasants, and during Pugachev's revolt he and his family had been hidden by their serfs and so escaped massacre. Radishchev was less impressed by this real-life event than by his French books. In 1788 he decided to write a book himself attacking serfdom and other aspects of Russian life of which he disapproved.

Radishchev called his book *Journey from St Petersburg to Moscow*, and gave it the form of encounters with people in various walks of life. Officials turn out to be corrupt, priests power-hungry, parents motivated by vanity in bringing up their children. Above all, landowners turn out to be wicked, grasping and cruel.

The tone is Rousseauish. Merely drinking a cup of coffee makes the narrator weep, because he is reminded of slavery on coffee plantations. On another occasion the narrator indicates a group of peasant women. 'Come hither, my dear Moscow and Petersburg ladies, look at their teeth and learn from them how they keep them white. They have no dentists. They do not scour away the gleam of their teeth with toothbrushes and powder.'

Despite such mawkish passages, Radishchev has a strong and important central theme. All authority, he says, corrupts; and those it corrupts most are owners of serfs. In six separate passages he incites his readers to rebel against a government that permits serfdom.

It says much for the easy-going nature of censorship that Major General Ruileiev, Chief of Police in St Petersburg, simply read the title and glanced at a few passages before issuing a licence for publication. But no printer would touch the book, and Radishchev had to set the 453 pages himself. In May 1790 he put 625 copies of the book on sale.

Within weeks Catherine had begun to read the *Journey* and on 26th June spoke to Khrapovitsky. 'Conversation about the book *Journey from St Petersburg to Moscow*: the French plague disseminated therein, revolution from authority; the author is a Martinist; I have read [she said] thirty pages; suspicion points to Radishchev; Ruileiev sent for.' When Ruileiev arrived Catherine scolded him, then sent him off to arrest Zotov, a bookseller selling copies of the *Journey*, and to establish the identity of the author.

The notes Catherine took on the *Journey* reveal her attitude to it. 'Pages 254 and 255 are filled with abuse of victory, conquests and settlements . . . What do they want, to be left defenceless to fall captive to the Turks and Tartars, or to be conquered by the Swedes?' She noted that blame was thrown on the government even for syphilis, on the grounds that the government licensed prostitutes. Sometimes she thought well of a passage: for instance, in educating young people control of sensual impulses is commended; these passages, Catherine noted, 'are very well thought out'.

In another chapter a parvenu master rapes the prospective bride of one of his serfs; he is murdered, but the murderers are caught and sentenced to death. Catherine commented: 'This whole argument can easily be overthrown by one simple question: if someone does evil, does that give someone else the right to do even greater evil? Answer: of course not.'

'Pages 350 to 369 contain, in the guise of a discussion of prosody, an ode most clearly, manifestly revolutionary, in which Tsars are threatened with the block. Cromwell's example is cited and praised. These pages are of criminal intent, completely revolutionary.'

Like many a woman reader Catherine thought of a book less as a statement of ideas than as an expression of its author. So now. She decided that Radishchev had a 'bilious black and yellow view of things', and on 7th July told Khrapovitsky that Radishchev 'is a rebel worse than Pugachev, and showed me how at the end of the book he praises Franklin as a rabble-rouser, and sets himself up as another one. She spoke with heat and emotion.'

What was Catherine to do about such a book? In the first part of her reign she had encouraged freedom of thought – which was why Radishchev studied in Leipzig. She had allowed critical writing – though not on politics. In her *Instruction* of 1767 she had written: 'If they do not lead to the crime of high treason writings cannot, of themselves, constitute the essence of high treason.' Underlying that policy had been her sufferings as Grand Duchess. But lately Catherine had been changing. She wished to see only happy faces around her; Radishchev's was unhappy, and he wrote about faces still unhappier than his own. Had Catherine grown old with a man of her own age she would probably have understood the value of dialogue between equals, but in choosing a series of young lovers she had bent her own character; now she always had to be top. Though Radishchev was putting a point of view about serfdom, Catherine saw him challenging her authority.

Radishchev's book had appeared at a time of national danger, with Russia fighting a two-front war. Even so, Catherine could have allowed it to continue on sale and have answered it, perhaps anonymously, with another *Antidote*. In so doing she would have lived up to her own best principles.

But Catherine chose to act as any other Continental ruler would have acted. She forwarded her comments to Sheshkovsky as a basis for his interrogation of Radishchev, and with a view to drawing up a formal indictment.

The day after his arrest Radishchev wrote a confession: 'Raynal's style, drawing me from delusion to delusion, led to the completion of my insane book.' Tried by the Criminal Court of St Petersburg province on several charges, including conspiring against the Sovereign, he was found guilty and sentenced to death. The sentence was confirmed by the Senate and then referred to the Council of State by Catherine, who told members 'not to pay any heed to the personal allusions to myself, since I disdain them.' The Council of State commuted the sentence to ten years' hard labour at Nerchinsk in Siberia, but two weeks later, on conclusion of peace with Sweden, Catherine changed it to ten years' exile.

On 8th September Radishchev began his journey to Siberia. He left in chains but by special order of Catherine these were removed. He was accompanied by his sister-in-law, who later became his common-law wife. He lived first at Ilimsk, where he occupied a house with five large rooms and was waited on by eight servants. He was invited to all dinners, celebrations and theatrical performances, and allowed to continue writing.

In the narrow legalistic sense Catherine may have been right in her handling of Radishchev. Six incitements to rebellion did constitute high treason. But in the larger sense she was wrong, indeed badly wrong. She knew that she could not abolish serfdom in her lifetime, and all the evidence suggests that this caused her anguish. But even so, she should not have prevented a writer from depicting the hard life of certain serfs, however over-shrill his tone. This was carrying too far her taste for happy endings.

Just as the Radishchev case can be properly understood only in the context of national danger, so the Novikov case, which followed it, has to be seen against events in 1792. The French Revolution had entered a more violent phrase. Opposition to the King, centred on his cousin the Duc d'Orléans, expressed itself in the storming of the Tuileries, and the imprisonment of Louis XVI, who, as Catherine foresaw, would soon be guillotined. Violence spread to Sweden, where Gustavus III was assassinated at a masked ball and his brother the Duke of Södermanland became Regent.

Now many intelligent people in Europe saw behind these events a single force: Freemasonry. Catherine's Procurator General, Ivan Gagarin, was one of them. According to Parkinson, 'Gagarin having been Grand Master of the Free Masons at Moscow pretends to know for certain that the Jacobin Principles had their origin in the meetings of that society. Cagliostro had been by this means enabled, he thought, to foretell the fall of the Bastille. The Duke of Orleans was Grand Master at Paris and the Duke of Södermanland at Stockholm.'

Catherine had long adopted a tolerant attitude to the Masons. She had laughed at them in her plays but allowed them to reply. Now however she took a sharper look at the 145 Russian lodges and the activities of their most eloquent associate, Nicholas Novikov.

Novikov was now aged forty-eight. Since the days when he had edited *The Drone* he had turned from social criticism to the higher flights of Rosicrucianism. He had published the chief Pietist and mystical books of the past two centuries, from Boehme to Saint-Martin, thereby provoking criticism from the Orthodox Church, and had travelled much abroad, seeking more and more esoteric ways of attaining Deeper Peace and Higher Truth.

Catherine discovered that Novikov had been a friend of Radishchev and had paid him to translate Mably. She discovered also that he associated with a Freemason architect – the same who had designed her abandoned 'coffin-like' palace – Basil Bazhenov, and Bazhenov sometimes saw the Grand Duke Paul.

Paul was living a retired life at his country estate, Gatchina. Every day, wearing high boots and elbow-length gloves, he would drill his two battalions of personal troops and fuss over their buttons and bandoliers. He was still morose and had sudden rages when he would lash out with fists and cane. Relations between him and his mother were increasingly strained: he openly criticized her switch of alliance from Prussia to Austria and her love affairs, while Catherine was seriously thinking of passing over her unstable son and naming Alexander her heir.

Lately Paul had found a new interest. Dissatisfied with real life – 'What have I ever done except produce children?' – he readily turned to the secret world of Freemasonry and Rosicrucianism. He began to attach importance to his dreams, to spend much time in prayer, and his easily excited imagination opened up vistas of harmony within himself and within the world at large. He corresponded with Lavater and probably also, secretly, with Frederick William II of Prussia, an ardent Freemason. He began also to meet Russian Freemasons.

In 1792 the Moscow authorities ordered a police raid on Novikov's house. Found there was a memorandum by the Freemason Basil Bazhenov. It described a meeting between Bazhenov and the Grand Duke, during which Paul had accepted a gift of books by members of Novikov's circle.

That the quixotic Novikov and his associates had been trying to influence the heir to the throne would in normal times have aroused little concern, but events in Europe suggested that this was the way Freemasons prepared a *coup d'état*. Catherine had Paul questioned but discovered no definite evidence to suggest that he had behaved culpably.

Some at least of the Russian Freemasons were working to overthrow the Church: of that there is no doubt. Probably also a few wished to overthrow the monarchy. But because of inbuilt Masonic secrecy definite evidence of subversive activities was hard to come by. What has only recently become clear, with the publication of Parkinson's diary, is that Catherine stood in much greater danger from the Freemasons and the French Revolutionaries or from an alliance of both than has hitherto been realized. 'About eight months ago [i.e. in April 1791],' wrote Parkinson, quoting Gould, a well-informed English resident, 'it was known for certain that three men set off for Paris with a determination and after having bound themselves to assassinate her [the Empress]. They were stopped, however, on the frontiers. Yet Gould says that one of them had escaped all the vigilance of the police.'

With this and possibly other classified information at her disposal Catherine ordered the Governor-General of Moscow to question Novikov. The Governor-General found Novikov 'guilty'; he does not say of what: probably of no more than trying to induct the Grand Duke into a secret society with foreign links. Catherine thereupon ordered Novikov to be imprisoned in Schlüsselburg Fortress. According to Rostopchin, when he reached his cell Novikov knelt on the stone paving and thanked Heaven for sending him such chastisement. To a questionnaire drawn up by Catherine, Novikov replied, à propos Bazhenov's memorandum, that he threw himself at 'her Majesty's feet as a thoroughgoing criminal, filled with genuine and tender repentance and contrition'. Catherine took this as a confession of guilt and her opinion, as always, carried very great weight. Novikov was sentenced to fifteen years in Schlüsselburg.

In acting against Radishchev and Novikov Catherine believed she was protecting Russia from the principles of the French Revolution, yet she was also doing what she condemned in the revolutionaries: stifling opinions opposed to her own. There were undoubtedly extenuating circumstances, but the two cases are not to Catherine's credit.

When she came to deal with followers of revolutionary fashions Catherine adopted a lighter touch, described by Matthew Guthrie, Scots physician to the diplomatic corps: 'We could not help smiling at seeing the dark-coloured *Lacerna* banished [from] Rome by Augustus, appear in Petersburg in the reign of Catherine under the new name of Jacobin cloak which that sagacious Princess got rid of without an Edict, by only ordering the city watchmen with their long beards to put on the same kind of wrapper and strut alongside of the fantastic young men who were so attired in the Imperial gardens and public walks, always open to the public. They took the hint and we saw no more Jacobin cloaks during her reign.'

In corresponding with Novikov and in describing Radishchev's book Catherine had employed the word 'bilious', using it in the literal sense. She believed that anyone who held revolutionary views must be 'disordered' either physically or mentally. So when it came to purveyors of French revolutionary propaganda Catherine dealt with them as follows:

'The propagandists made us but short visits [wrote Guthrie], as they did not like Catherine's jokes, who used to send the physician of the madhouse to feel the pulse of all those who were found preaching *holy insurrection the most sacred of duties* to her subjects . . . the doctor was commonly accompanied with a couple of stout keepers from Bedlam who immediately carried the patient there.'

By ordering the seditious propaganda agents to be carried to the madhouse, Catherine evidently intended to ridicule them out of their 'disorder', much as her satirical plays ridiculed fops and scroungers. She succeeded. 'A blister on the head,' says Guthrie, 'with a few purges and water gruel soon brought him to his senses and made him as harmless as a child.'

Catherine seems to have been the first to use this method of correction, and in a jocular spirit. There is no means of knowing whether it was in imitation of her that a similar method was used, in earnest, by Nicholas I in his treatment of the writer Chaadayev. Later still, of course, and to a degree unthinkable in the eighteenth century, the madhouse was to be used by Soviet authorities in dealing with some political dissidents.

On his release the propaganda agent, continues Guthrie, 'was so laughed at by his disciples on reappearing in public that he quickly took the road to Prussia there to write secret memoirs of the Court of Russia and to abuse the whole empire by every possible falsehood that rage could invent. Even we English had our full share of abuse, as we happen to predominate in the administration of medicine in Russia, and were suspected to have prescribed the mode of cure for enraged Jacobins, whilst they hoped to be persecuted to gain proselytes and become men of consequence!'

CHAPTER 25

THE DREAM OF A RUSSIAN EUROPE

As she entered her middle sixties Catherine put on weight, her grey frizzy hair became touched with white, her lower cheeks filled out, but the intelligent eyes still looked directly at whomever she was speaking to. As described at sixty-five by Adrian Gribovsky, one of her secretaries, she still had 'a fairly fresh complexion, beautiful hands, and all her teeth intact. She spoke firmly, without mumbling, only in rather a masculine way.' She was subject to high blood pressure and swellings on her legs, and she had just got over an attack of erysipelas, for which she found relief in the drops invented by her old friend Bestuzhev. Despite such ailments, Catherine enjoyed fairly good health and her manner was lively.

She got up at eight, Gribovsky continues, drank one cup of coffee without cream, and worked in her study for an hour writing.

> At nine she went into her bedroom, where she sat down in a chair by the wall almost immediately by the entrance into her closet; before her stood two kidney-shaped little tables, with the concave side facing her, and a chair in front of one of them. She usually wore a white heavy silk dressing-gown or capote, and on her head a crêpe mob-cap, also white, tilted slightly to the left . . . She read with spectacles, using at the same time a magnifying glass. Once, when I was summoned to her with reports, I saw her reading in this manner. Smiling, she said to me: 'You probably don't need this contrivance yet? How old are you?'; and when I told her that I was twenty-eight, she added: 'But our sight has been blunted by long service to the State, and now we have to use spectacles.' And it seemed to me that 'we' was not said as an expression of majesty, but in a simple sense.

Having finished her written work the Empress rang a little bell, and when the lackey who always stood outside her door appeared, she told him to show in the first of her daily visitors, the chief of police in St Petersburg.

He gave her a verbal report of the state of the capital and of happenings there, and notes on a small piece of paper, written – badly and ungrammatically – by the police, about those who had entered or left the city the previous day . . .

After the departure of the chief of police the secretaries were summoned one by one, including me. When I entered the bedroom I behaved as follows. I made a low bow to the Empress, to which she replied by inclining her head and extending her hand. I kissed it, and felt my hand squeezed by hers. Then she said to me, 'Sit down.' Taking the chair opposite her I placed on the kidney-shaped table the papers I had brought and began to read. I suppose others did the same and were received in the same way, but as soon as Count Zubov appeared through the door opposite we all immediately went out into the closet.

At this time of day Zubov wore morning dress: a silk coloured frock-coat, sewn at the edges with broad shiny brilliants, white satin trousers and green half-boots. His hair was not yet powdered. He always brought papers for signing.

Prepared under Catherine's direction, the papers do not imply that Zubov had political power. At the period described by Gribovsky they would have dealt with preparations for the Alliance of St Petersburg, signed in autumn 1794, when Russia allied herself with Britain and Austria against France. As well as being flashily dressed, Zubov was usually accompanied by his pet monkey. This little animal was not house-trained, and once thought fit to urinate on the cordon bleu of Count Esterhazy; although Esterhazy was an impoverished and unimportant refugee, Catherine took pains to find him a new blue silk ribbon.

At eleven o'clock Catherine would have finished seeing Zubov, and received Count Bezborodko and other important officials or visitors, including the eccentric Suvorov, on leave after successes in Poland.

When he entered the bedroom, Suvorov made three bows to the ground in front of the icon of Our Lady of Kazan which hung in the corner to the right of the door, and in front of which a lamp burned. Then he turned to the Empress and made one bow to the ground to her, though she always tried to stop him, and, raising him with her hand, said, 'For goodness sake, Aleksander Vasilievich, aren't you ashamed to do that?' But the hero adored her and considered it his sacred duty to show his respect for her in this way. The Empress gave him her hand, which he kissed as though it were a holy relic. Then she asked him to sit down on the chair opposite her . . .

The Empress worked at affairs of State until twelve. After that in the inner closet her old hairdresser Kozlov did her hair in a very old-fashioned style with small curls behind the ears. It was not a high style and was very simple. Then she went out into the other closet, where we were all waiting to see her, and by this time her company would be joined by four elderly maids who came to help the Empress make her toilet. One of them handed her ice, with which she wiped her face, perhaps to show that she disdained facial cosmetics. Another put on her head a crêpe headdress and the two Zveryovuy sisters handed her pins to fasten it. Her toilet lasted not more than ten minutes, and during it the Empress chatted with one of those present, very often Leo Naruishkin and sometimes Count Stroganov, two men she particularly enjoyed talking to.

Then she would bow to the people there and retire into the bedroom with her ladies, with whose help and that of her personal maid, Maria Perekusikhina, she dressed. On ordinary days she wore a silk dress, Moldavian style [characterized by wide pleated sleeves and, behind them, a second pair of sleeves which were drawn behind the back and knotted]. The outer part of the dress was usually mauve or dark grey, without orders, and the under-part white.

On two occasions in the previous year Catherine's dress had been black: first, for three weeks, when Louis XVI went to the scaffold, and again, for double that period, when the guillotine blade fell on Antoinette, as Catherine, correctly, called the Queen of France.

At two o'clock Catherine dined with Zubov, her ladies-in-waiting and a few invited guests. She ladled out the soup herself, and each person on receiving it rose from his seat. The meal lasted under an hour. 'She was extremely frugal. She never had a morning collation and she never ate more than small helpings from three or four dishes. She drank one glass of Rhine or Hungarian wine, and she never had supper.'

In summer after her midday meal the Empress usually had a nap, but at the time Gribovsky is writing about Kosciuszko's rebellion in Poland was causing her concern and, forgoing her nap, Catherine worked twelve hours a day. At other times she might go for a walk or drive, and on these occasions, according to Esterhazy, she never saw a peasant without nodding to him or saying good day, 'and so the people adore her'. In the event of rain or snow she would embroider or read, her taste now being for medieval Russian history. Twice a week she listened to the foreign mail, read to her by Zubov or Count Markov or Count Popov, 'who however had a bad French pronunciation and was rarely asked to read'.

The high point of Catherine's day came at six o'clock, when her grandson Alexander arrived. He would be seventeen this December and had been married for a year to pretty, sweet-tempered Louisa of Baden. Under the guidance of Catherine and Laharpe, he was shaping well: dutiful, charming, considerate for others, and – Catherine's comparison – handsome as the Apollo Belvedere. He would be a much better man than Paul, Catherine thought, to continue her work, but she was waiting until he was a little older before doing anything definite about the succession.

With Alexander came Constantine, still 'an unlicked bear cub', and sometimes their four sisters. On a Hermitage day – usually a Thursday – Catherine would take them to a play or opera. On other evenings they and privileged guests would assemble in Catherine's private apartments for whist. Catherine usually played with Zubov, Chertkov and Stroganov. At ten o'clock she withdrew to her private closet, and the guests left. 'At eleven she was already in bed and total silence reigned.'

'Fifty years have passed since I arrived in Moscow,' Catherine wrote wistfully the previous February to Grimm, adding that few who had met her then survived. Betskoy lingered on, ninety years old, half blind and asking young courtiers whether they remembered – as he did – Peter the Great. Leo Naruishkin was still his amusing self and still loyal to her – she had not had to repeat the lesson of the stinging nettles – but Bestuzhev was dead, and Panin, and Countess Bruce, with whom in later life Catherine had become reconciled. Poor Gregory Orlov had ended tragically. He lost his young wife to tuberculosis, then he believed himself pursued by the bleeding ghost of Peter III, and died in the terrors of insanity.

Catherine was not a great person for looking back, but as she aged and ailments reminded her that she was mortal, she did sometimes recall Russia as it had been when she took power. Then the Empire had been a loose-knit grouping of unruly provinces; now you could travel without molestation through a series of uniformly administered provinces as far as the Pacific. Then, among Cossacks, Church serfs and factory serfs, there had been widespread unrest, with perhaps 200,000 in semi-rebellion; now for twenty years there had been no disturbances among those or other groups. Then, the population had been nineteen million; now, it was twenty-nine million. Then, there had been few schools, even fewer hospitals and orphanages; now every big town had its quota of all three; then, bribery had been rife among governors, now it was rare; then, all officials had been appointed from above; now many were elected and, exception made for the serfs, Russia had become a more permeable society than Prussia or Austria. Then, Old Believers had been persecuted; now they practised their rites in peace. Then, there had been a penury of specie and few credit facilities; now Russia had banks and, in line with leading commercial countries, an adequate money supply, much of it in banknotes. More metals were being mined than ever before, more timber grown and felled, more goods being manufactured. During 1794–8 Russia's annual exports were running at 57 million roubles, four times the rate when Catherine had come to the throne, and each year they exceeded imports by more than 3 million roubles.

These were measurable achievements. As for the imponderables, Catherine wrote that she had tried to bring her people happiness, liberty and prosperity, using the second word as defined in her *Instruction*: 'the right to do whatever the laws allow'. She had certainly done more to achieve these aims than any previous Russian ruler and though much remained for her successors to do, Catherine's improvements were sufficiently impressive to have won respect from her contemporaries. This can be seen, for example, in the number of English visitors. Formerly Russia had been considered barbarous ground, now it had become almost part of the Grand Tour, and among those who visited it in Catherine's reign, and were impressed, were Lord Barringdon, James Brogden, Lord Dalkeith, Sir Gilbert Eliot, Lord Grenville Leveson-Gower, Sir Richard Worsley, Lord Wycombe, Sir Watkin Williams Wynn and George, Lord Herbert, who as Earl of Pembroke was to marry a Vorontsov.

Catherine had become famous in three continents but, as Gribovsky's pen-portrait shows, she did not give herself airs. When Voltaire addressed her 'idolatrously yours, the priest of your temple', she laughingly answered that she preferred not to join the ranks of sacred cats, snakes and crocodiles; and when Grimm sent her a German book extolling her reign, she told him she found it boring and preferred criticism: 'Then I can say to myself, "Avenge this, prove them wrong!"' She boasted of little things, such as the nightdress she had designed for Monsieur Alexander, but not of her political successes. In 1788 when Grimm called her Catherine the Great, she told him not to do so again: 'My name is Catherine the Second;' and near the end of her reign she said to the same correspondent, 'All I can do for Russia is never more than a drop in the sea.'

When she thought of the past, her mind turned less often to the glorious years than to her unhappy marriage. Long ago she had felt a compelling need to set down on paper, for a few intimate friends such as Charles Hanbury-Williams, the true facts about her life as Grand Duchess. As she entered old age, Catherine decided to expand those earlier confessions into full-length Memoirs covering the years from her birth up until 1757, when she had succeeded in making Empress Elizabeth understand the true nature of her life with Peter. She intended these Memoirs in the first instance for Paul. After her death, he would read them, learn that Saltuikov was his father, and so, she hoped, free himself from his cult of Peter, and from his subconscious hatred of herself. But the care with which she wrote them suggests that she intended them also to be read by posterity.

The Memoirs make a book of 160,000 words. The early part, describing childhood and family, is candid, but after her engagement to Peter the book reads like evidence by an ill-used wife in a divorce case. In order to justify her infidelity Catherine piles on the humiliations Gothic-style. Catherine was good at loving, but she was also a good hater, and it is clear that, thirty years after his death, she still hated Peter. Allowance for this bias has to be made by the historian using them as a source, but the Memoirs, all the same, constitute a revealing self-portrait of a brave young woman. Also, the concatenation of hundreds of details regarding the non-consummation of her marriage and her first love affair is so coherent that it is extremely doubtful whether it could have been invented; and it provides very strong evidence that the father of Paul was Serge Saltuikov.

Partly because her own arranged marriage had been so disastrous, Catherine took great pains to arrange good marriages for her grandchildren. Constantine she married to Princess Julie of Saxe-Coburg, and the next on Catherine's list was her granddaughter Alexandra. For this clever, charming but not very pretty girl Catherine conceived a marriage to her cousin King Gustavus IV of Sweden, putative son of the assassinated Gustavus III. If she could pull it off, the marriage would be a brilliant diplomatic coup, drawing Sweden back into Russia's orbit, and strengthening Russia's northern frontier for the war against France. True, Gustavus had recently announced his engagement to Louise, daughter of the Duke of Mecklenburg, but Catherine at sixty-seven was not one to be deterred by a trifle like that. If she wanted a marriage, marriage there would be.

At Catherine's invitation Gustavus arrived in St Petersburg on 15th August 1796: a silent, serious, Bible-reading youth of seventeen, quite good-looking, with prominent eyes and fair hair down to the shoulders of his black suit. With him came his uncle, the Duke of Södermanland,

Regent of Sweden, a tiny man with a squint and 'legs like toothpicks'.

Catherine showered the boy King with charm and hospitality. Every night there was a ball in his honour. She noticed with satisfaction that after the first few evenings he lost his stiffness and spoke in a low voice to thirteen-year-old Alexandra. In the third week of his visit, during a dance, he went so far as to squeeze Alexandra's hand. 'I didn't know what would become of me,' she whispered afterwards to her governess. 'What did become of you?' 'I was so frightened I thought I would fall.'

Catherine took pleasure in watching the romance develop and two days later, after dinner in the Taurida Palace, Gustavus joined her on a bench in the garden. He confided that he was in love and wished to marry Alexandra. Catherine looked cold. He had no right, she said, to make such a proposal, nor she to listen to it, seeing that he was already engaged to someone else, and that prayers were being said throughout Sweden for Louise, the future Queen. As Catherine expected, Gustavus was brought up sharp. Since he did not specially care for Louise, he promised to send a messenger to the Duke of Mecklenburg breaking the engagement. Catherine, thawing, said she would speak to Alexandra's parents and give him an answer in three days.

Once Gustavus had broken his engagement Catherine tackled the second hurdle. Gustavus, pious by temperament, had received a rigorously Lutheran upbringing and been taught that his subjects would never forgive him if he took a wife belonging to any Church but the Lutheran. Gustavus and his suite had made clear that if an engagement were entered into Alexandra would be expected to renounce the Orthodox Church.

In face of the excesses of the French Revolution Catherine had revised her opinion of religion and now believed that only the Orthodox Church, 'a deep-rooted oak', was sturdy enough to resist subversion and such pseudo-cults as Swedenborgism, so fashionable in Stockholm. Also, Catherine wished Alexandra to go to Sweden as a Russian princess, Russian in her religion, Russian in her loyalties, serving Catherine as Stanislaus had served her in Poland.

So Catherine took a strong line with Gustavus. When he said he did not see how it would be possible for Alexandra to retain her religion, she plied him with forceful letters. 'Here is my final word,' she concluded. 'It is not fitting for a Russian princess to change religion.'

Catherine treated Gustavus less as a king than as a Lanskoy or Zubov. Where Gustavus's scruples called for discussion between equals, Catherine chose to be domineering. She thought she could afford to be, since the marriage alliance would bring Sweden generous Russian subsidies. Finally Gustavus committed himself to saying that he would do nothing to hurt Alexandra. Interpreting this as a pledge, Catherine suggested to the Regent that the young couple should be formally betrothed. After consulting Gustavus the Regent agreed. 'With the Church's blessing?' asked Catherine. 'Yes,' said the Regent. 'According to your rite.'

On the day set for the betrothal, Thursday 11th September, while Russian and Swedish officials prepared the final documents, Catherine contemplated with satisfaction this latest success. Only a week ago she had written to her cousin, the ruler of Anhalt-Zerbst, expressing her imperial wish that he should lodge Louis XVIII in the family palace in Zerbst. From there, at the head of 60,000 Russians, Suvorov would sweep the French King back to his throne, while Sweden, become Russia's submissive ally, defended the Baltic. Really this marriage was the coping-stone of a triumphal arch through which Russia would one day march west and resolve the old tension between Europe and Asia by absorbing Europe. 'If I were to live 200 years,' Catherine told Derzhavin, 'then of course all Europe would be subject to the Russian sceptre.'

Count Markov, handling the negotiations, unexpectedly asked her for audience and, entering Catherine's room, handed her a note. It was a reply by Gustavus to an article, drawn up by Catherine, which she wished inserted in the marriage contract. Gustavus wrote that Alexandra would not be hindered in the practice of her religion, he gave his word of honour, but he would put nothing in writing.

When she read this, the blood rushed to Catherine's head and she remained as though stunned, with her mouth open and twisted to one side. For some minutes she was unable to speak. A servant handed her a glass of water. Catherine drank it with difficulty and, very slowly, began to regain her composure. She had suffered a slight stroke, brought on by the shock of someone daring to thwart her.

Catherine, however, refused to let herself be beaten. Without delay she drafted a guarantee of Alexandra's religion and sent it to Gustavus, saying if he signed it all would be well; if not, the consequences would be grave. She then ordered the betrothal ceremony to be held as planned.

Catherine put on a rich brocade dress, the three stars of St Andrew, St George and St Vladimir, and on her head a small crown. Attended by her family and senior officials she took her seat in the palace throne-room. Beside her stood the Metropolitan of St Petersburg in ceremonial copes; on a table lay two rings. Two armchairs, upholstered in sapphire velvet, awaited the King and his bride-to-be.

Minutes passed, a quarter of an hour, half an hour, a full hour. Puzzled by so long a delay, officials exchanged anxious glances. At last the double doors opened. But it was not Gustavus, only Count Markov, who handed Catherine a paper and whispered some words in her ear. After reading the paper Catherine said to the assembly, 'His Majesty Gustavus IV has been taken unwell. The ceremony is postponed.' She then left the room on the arm of Alexander, seemingly unperturbed but in fact furious. Gustavus had refused to sign the guarantee.

Catherine was deeply shaken, physically by her stroke, mentally by her public humiliation. Though the Regent sent an apology for his nephew's foolish behaviour, Catherine refused to be appeased and hastened the Swedes' departure. A few days earlier she had been describing Gustavus to her friends as 'the most promising Sovereign in Europe'; now she loaded him with reproaches. He is stiff as a post, stubborn as a log, vain and Jesuitical: 'he thinks he's another Charles XII.' Near hysterically Catherine poured ridicule on the welcome awaiting him in Sweden: a gala at Gripsholm theatre, where 'the benches are half eaten away by rats and mice' but which the Swedes were fatuous enough to compare to her Hermitage theatre. Catherine painted a morbid picture of the Stockholm celebrations: Gustavus would see 'sibyls coming out of Zoroaster's grotto to predict the future' and dances by grotesque-looking very fat nymphs, at least one of whom would give birth to a child before the evening was out.

Abusive language helped to relieve Catherine's feelings but did not resolve her deeper tension. Her habit of getting her way, built up over a period of twenty years with very young favourites, had been shaken by the young King, precipitating recurrent anger, dangerous to a person with high blood pressure. Immediately after her stroke Catherine began to sleep little and badly, she lost her usual energy and found it an effort to attend Mass and dine with her family on Sundays. Her physician feared a second stroke.

It was probably during these ominous days that Catherine wrote her will. No time remained to prepare and name Alexander as her successor, but she left him all her books and papers, save the Memoirs, almost complete, which she set aside for Paul. She wrote instructions for her funeral and specified that 'marriages and music' should be permitted as soon as she had been buried. Catherine had done very well without marriage but she meant this as a final posthumous assertion of *joie de vivre*.

On the evening of 4th November 1796 Catherine appeared in quite good form. Though the clash with Gustavus still rankled deeply, she laughed when Leo Naruishkin, to cheer her up, dressed as a pedlar and proposed to sell her little models of the world's seas, mountains and continents. She received news – later to be proved unfounded – of an Austrian victory and wrote a jocular note to Count Cobenzl – the last of many million words that had flowed from her pen: 'I hasten to announce to your excellent Excellency that the excellent troops of his excellent Court have completely trounced the French.' After chatting a little with her ladies she went to bed.

Next morning Catherine was wakened at eight. She told Maria Perekusikhina that she had slept well and felt twenty years younger; she added that she was about to make plans for another visit to the Crimea in the spring. She put on her dressing-gown, drank a cup of coffee and, as her habit was, went into her water-closet.

Catherine usually spent about ten minutes in that room. Zotov, her footman, waited for her to come out. When half an hour elapsed and there was no sign in her apartment of the Empress, Zotov thought she might have gone for a walk, but when he opened her cupboard he found that none of her furs or shoes had been taken out. After waiting a few more minutes he decided to open the water-closet door. He found Catherine huddled on the floor. Gently raising her head, he saw that her face was dark red and her eyes closed. A rattle sounded in her throat.

Zotov called for help and with the assistance of other servants managed with difficulty to carry Catherine from the narrow closet into her bedroom. She was too heavy for them to lift on to her bed, so they laid her on a leather mattress on the floor. Then they sent for the doctors.

Zubov was the first to be told and the first to lose his head. Despite the entreaties of Zotov and Maria Perekusikhina, he would not let the duty doctor bleed Catherine. So a whole hour passed before Rogerson arrived and took things in hand. He bled Catherine and applied to her feet Spanish blister-flies.

Alexander, who loved his grandmother dearly, wept when he heard the news but kept his presence of mind. He asked Theodore Rostopchin, a trusted adviser, to go to Gatchina and inform Grand Duke Paul officially, in his son's name, of what had happened.

Grand Duke Paul, half a day's drive away, had spent a troubled night. He was subject to dreams and that night he had dreamed not once but several times that a mysterious force had swept him up to the skies. As soon as he woke he told his wife and learned that she had

had exactly the same dream. They spent a routine day until three in the afternoon when Zubov's brother Nicholas arrived with the news that Catherine had had a stroke. They left at once by seven-horse sleigh and at a staging-post half-way met Rostopchin.

'*C'est vous, mon cher Rostopchin*,' exclaimed Paul, getting out of the sleigh and embracing his friend. As usual, he wore military uniform and high leather boots.

When the horses in both sleighs had been changed, Paul asked Rostopchin to follow him.

> As we passed Chesme Palace [Rostopchin was later to recall], the Grand Duke got out of his sleigh to satisfy a need of nature. I got out too and drew his attention to the beauty of the night. It was extremely calm and light, with a temperature of about three degrees; the moon was visible through clouds. It seemed as though in expectation of such an important change in the world every sound was muffled and silence reigned. When I spoke of the weather I saw the Grand Duke fix his gaze on the moon; tears filled his eyes and flowed down his face . . .
>
> Unable to restrain myself I seized his hand. 'My lord, what a moment this is for you!'
>
> He pressed my hand. 'Wait, my dear friend, wait. I have lived forty-two years. God has given me strength. Perhaps he will give me the strength and good sense to bear my appointed destiny. Let's hope for the best from his goodness.'
>
> Then he re-entered his sleigh and at half past eight at night we arrived in St Petersburg, where as yet few people knew what was happening.

Paul found his mother still lying on the leather mattress, from which her doctors feared to move her, motionless, eyes closed. 'When my turn comes,' she had once said, 'I'll drive away all the weepers and I shall want only stout souls and professional laughers.' Professional laughers there were none. Family, friends, favourite – all were in tears.

The vigil lasted all through that night. At dawn the doctors examined Catherine again and told her son there was no hope. Metropolitan Gabriel was instructed to perform the last rites. He anointed Catherine on the forehead, nostrils, cheeks, mouth, breast and both sides of the hands. 'Holy Father, you the Physician of souls and bodies, who sent your only Son Our Lord Jesus Christ, who heals from every sickness and saves from every death, heal your servant Catherine of the bodily and spiritual sickness of which she is afflicted and give her the fullness of life through the grace of your Christ.'

Summoning Bezborodko, Paul told him to prepare a manifesto about his accession. He was already being treated as Emperor; symptomatically, both Alexander and Constantine had changed into military uniform like their father's. The most pathetic figure in the palace, thought Rostopchin, was Plato Zubov. Formerly just a smile from Zubov had made a person's happiness, but now he sat alone in a corner shunned by all, 'as though he had an infectious disease'. He was thirsty but did not dare even to ask for a glass of water; Rostopchin, who had a kind heart, told a footman to look after his needs.

At five that afternoon Catherine's pulse became much weaker. Three or four times the doctors thought her last moment had come, but they underestimated the strength of her constitution. Her face changed in colour from purple to dark brown. The doctors took it in turns to wipe from her mouth a liquid which was at first yellow, then black. The rattle in her throat grew louder until it could be heard two rooms away.

At nine in the evening Rogerson informed Paul that the end was now very near. All those who had been waiting outside went into the bedroom, members of the family standing on Catherine's left, officials, doctors and servants on the right. Catherine was struggling now for every breath. As her blood flowed to her head it distorted her features; as it flowed back, her face regained its natural look. The light was dim, no one spoke, two hours passed. As the clock struck a quarter past eleven on the night of 6th November 1796 the Empress of all the Russias sighed, drew a last breath and then fell still.

'It seemed that death,' says Rostopchin, 'cutting off a great woman's life and putting an end to her great works, left her body in a sweet sleep. Their pleasantness and greatness returned to her features, and she seemed again to be an Empress, full of the glory of her reign.'

Paul left the room in tears. To courtiers assembled in an antechamber Count Samoilov announced, 'Gentlemen, the Empress Catherine is dead, and his Majesty Pavel Petrovich has deigned to mount the throne of all the Russias.'

As the church bells of St Petersburg began to toll, the Winter Palace, says Derzhavin, suddenly took on a completely different aspect. 'There was a rattle of spurs, jackboots and broadswords, and military men burst into rooms all over the building with a great deal of noise, as if the city had been conquered.' A soldier now was Tsar.

Doctors removed the vital organs from Catherine's body, which was then embalmed and placed in an open coffin to lie in state. Paul had long been planning a petty revenge on his mother. Evidently he did not take time now to read the Memoirs she had left him, for he ordered Peter III's tomb to be opened, and the coffin containing his remains – a few handfuls of dust, tattered leather boot-soles and buttons from his uniform – placed beside Catherine's coffin. So even in death Catherine did not lie alone. To add an even grimmer note, the imperial crown was hurriedly fetched from Moscow and laid at the head of the coffin containing Peter's pitiful remains.

For three weeks members of the family, priests and courtiers kept vigil day and night beside Catherine's body, as she once had kept vigil beside Elizabeth's, while at each corner stood a silent guard, head bowed, arms reversed. Russians of every walk of life came to the palace to file silently past. As a girl, when Frederick William died, Catherine had decided that a ruler should try to win his people's respect and affection. The tears and the numbers of her mourners showed that Catherine had at least done that.

The funeral took place on 5th December and despite very cold weather, according to an English eyewitness, 'the concourse of people was prodigious'. Having sent Zubov to his country estate Paul brought forward Alexis Orlov, now an ageing grey-haired private citizen, to walk at the head of the procession, carrying on a cushion the gold crown of his victim Peter. Catherine's coffin, covered with wreaths of myrtles, and that of her husband Peter were followed by her family, by courtiers, by the diplomatic corps and by the now ubiquitous military, as they were drawn in procession across the frozen Neva to the Cathedral of St Peter and St Paul, topped by its pyramidal spire. Here, in marble tombs, lay the Sovereigns of Russia since the city's foundation, except Peter II, who had died in Moscow, the tomb of Peter the Great, near the south door, being a foot longer than any of the rest.

Requiem Mass was sung for the repose of the souls of Catherine and her husband Peter. High on the walls captured enemy flags bore silent witness to the military glory of a reign that had lasted thirty-four years. When the last blessing had been given, Peter's body was buried on the right of the iconostasis, near the tomb of his aunt, Empress Elizabeth, and Catherine's body was laid to rest in a tomb close to her husband's. The Metropolitan blessed Catherine's remains for the last time, earth was scattered on the coffin, then the tomb was sealed with a slab of highly-polished unflecked white marble, ornamented with a single large gold Greek cross.

CHAPTER 26

CATHERINE THE GREAT

One of her first obituaries, in the *Gentleman's Magazine*, described Catherine as a 'great princess', who effected 'that most important of all revolutions in the history of human kind, the civilization of so large a portion of the human race, and the cultivation of the wildest and most untrodden deserts'. Rostopchin in his *Memoirs* called Catherine great; Radishchev in his poem 'The Eighteenth Century' linked her name with Peter the Great's; while the Prince de Ligne, in a justly famous essay, wrote: 'Catherine the Great is no more. The most brilliant star in our hemisphere has disappeared.'

As early as 1767 the Commission on Laws had offered the woman who had called them into being the title of 'the Great', but Catherine had declined it, saying 'I shall leave it to posterity to judge impartially what I have done.' Except in France, which was at war with Russia, the immediate judgment of posterity was to confirm the opinions quoted. So Catherine joined the small group of rulers known at least in their own lands as 'the Great': Alexander of Macedon, Alfred of England, Charlemagne, Pope Gregory VII, Henri IV and Louis XIV, Peter I of Russia, and Catherine's contemporary Frederick II.

The list might be contested or added to, but it gives an idea of the company into which Catherine was, on her death, admitted by general acclaim. The men in it had been adjudged great first as persons of outstanding character, and secondly as rulers who had aggrandized, civilized or otherwise improved their State or institution. So in deciding whether Catherine deserves the title she was accorded, we have to consider her first as a person. What in brief were her distinguishing characteristics?

Vitality is the first that has to be mentioned, since it underlay so much else. Catherine had frequent indispositions and in her youth was hypochondriac, but she possessed a strong constitution. Her exuberance and endurance, directed by the habit of hard work learned in childhood, made possible the long productive hours in her study and a host of demanding relationships.

Vitality too coloured her views of the world. Catherine expected the best from people, but unlike so many in the eighteenth century did not expect too much. She was a qualified optimist.

Catherine was not an original thinker. But she had much good sense and grasped essentials quickly, nearly always from the practical side. When she came to take major decisions she liked to go slowly. She once told Potemkin that she wanted a week, preferably two, to make up her mind on a certain issue, 'so that my ideas, like beer, have time to ferment'.

Catherine who built the Hermitage was far from being a hermit. She enjoyed being with others, and this was one element in others' enjoyment of her company. She had many friends, valued their friendship and was loyal to them, Leo Naruishkin, for example, being her friend for almost fifty years. If there are more men than women among them, there is no reason to think that Catherine disliked women or was disliked by them, but only that there was in Russia a lack of educated women.

Catherine possessed majesty, but was not pompous. To the stiff exchanges of public functions she preferred informality and joking. Indeed, one of the most attractive things about her is her persistent sense of humour.

The quality which combined with all the others to make Catherine so outstanding a person was undoubtedly her strength of will. 'My head is made of iron,' she had written at the age of twenty-two to Zachary Chernuishev, 'and very resistant. You might succeed against other wills but not against mine.' It was that quality in the form of dogged endurance that carried Catherine through the agonizing early years of her marriage, trapped between Peter and Elizabeth, and later, in the form of stirring leadership, was to make possible her achievements as Empress.

'Yet that will,' Catherine continued to the same correspondent, 'left to itself, becomes wax when it is a question of pleasing someone I love.' The image is exaggerated if applied to Catherine's life as a whole, but in her youth it is quite true that Catherine presented a paradoxical mixture of iron strength and wax-like susceptibility to handsome men. When it came to her affair with Poniatowski, Catherine's waxen will nearly cost her the throne.

People liked Catherine, observers are agreed on that; how then did she come to lose the love of six out of the eleven men in her life: Peter, Saltuikov, Orlov, Potemkin, Rimsky-Korsakov and Mamonov? In each case there were special contributory factors, and even when he had fallen in love with his niece Potemkin retained a deep affection for Catherine, but the remarkable fact remains that Catherine, for all her advantages, lost the undivided love of six men.

In seeking an answer we would do well to recall Catherine's decision to marry Peter. In choosing Russia and not love she showed that love was not of the first importance to her. Later, when she did become deeply attracted to this or that man, the same principle applied. With the exception of Potemkin in the early stages, and whatever her occasional words to the contrary, Catherine did not treat any man as a world's wonder, an all-important being with whom she could forget herself. The explanation is that she was not a passionate woman. She always put something else, often the interest of the State, before the man she loved, hence her request to Potemkin not to come to her room after ten-thirty. And because she was not passionate Catherine changed lovers, if not lightly, at least without the heartache a woman more deeply engaged would have felt.

Secondly, Catherine was by nature inclined to tell people what and what not to do. She carried this trait into her love affairs. Eighteenth-century Russia was decidedly a man's world, and her lovers were bound to resent it. Mamonov at the end went so far as to use the word 'imprisonment'. These two factors are, I think, sufficient to explain why Catherine failed to retain the love of so many of the men in her life.

The next question is why did Catherine go on taking lovers well into her fifties and sixties? It could be argued that coming late to sexual pleasure Catherine wished, so to speak, to make up for lost time. I think such an argument rests on a mistaken reading of her character, like the argument that she chose young lovers because her contemporaries could not satisfy her physical demands. If we look back again to her marriage to Peter, we see that Catherine's choice of Russia instead of love suggests that the sexual element in her character was not very pronounced. Everything she is known to have said and written confirms that. Catherine took lovers into her fifties and sixties because she was a careerist wanting affection, and if she quickly replaced a departing lover, she did so in order to forget a set-back, as a rider having been thrown will at once remount.

If we turn from her relations with men to Catherine herself, what of the question sometimes asked, Was Catherine a masculine type of woman? Put like that the question is meaningless, for we know that a woman can possess so-called masculine traits yet remain essentially feminine, indeed the so-called masculine traits may elicit from her otherwise dormant feminine traits. Remarkable people, whether men or women, very often possess these traits of the other sex; it is part of the secret of their exceptional insights and capabilities.

Catherine possessed at least two traits found more often in men than in women: an ability for large-scale organization and a strong drive to power. It was probably these traits – her 'masculine side' – that attracted her young lovers, but Potemkin was undoubtedly drawn by her feminine side. The general 'relief' of her character is in my view decidedly feminine. One has only to think of the chit-chat in her letters, her tears, such a constant factor as late as 1793, when she wept at the news of Louis XVI's execution, and her grandmaternal feelings.

If the original question is re-worded as, Did the masculine elements in Catherine habitually become uppermost? my answer would be no. Catherine was not aggresive or bellicose, nor did she constantly feel a need to assert her power. As a person she was not in the strict sense masterful. One could not have said to her with justice, 'Bring forth men-children only.' She did not domineer. Indeed her private life is remarkable for the grace with which she relinquished those whose affections were drawn elsewhere.

Another aspect of Catherine's character that must be mentioned is the astonishing range of her activities. She was not a blue-stocking, being more interested in people than in ideas, but she could discuss knowledgeably and wittily almost any subject of contemporary interest, from philology to philosophy, iron-works to intaglios, China to chinoiserie. She mastered the intricacies of diplomacy and naval warfare, town-planning and criminal law, agriculture and banking.

Multiple interests make for a rich but often static character; with Catherine the richness was always dynamic. Knowledge with her was always to a purpose, and her choice of the bee as an emblem wholly appropriate.

Can the autocrat of all the Russias be described as an egoist? Catherine was interested in so many people beyond herself and took so much pleasure in almost everything going on around her that egoism would be a wrong description. She was decidedly not one of those people who bring everything back to herself. Indeed, if one is looking for the less satisfactory side of her character, it is to be found precisely in her lack of self-awareness.

Catherine gave little time to introspection. In her later years especially she preferred not to be alone – according to Parkinson, 'she must always have some living creature with her; at least a dog' – and the probable reason is that she did not care to think about herself. This suggests a character that is materialistic and unspiritual, and such an interpretation is borne out by Catherine's attitude to religion.

In deciding that Moscow was worth a Mass, Catherine sloughed off the tight skin of Lutheranism, and put on a religion that upper-class Russians wore very loosely indeed. She who spent so many hours in church had very little understanding of Russian spirituality. She once told her secretary, rather indignantly, that her confessor had been asking her whether she *really* believed in God. Had she met her contemporary, Tikhon Zadonsky, the model for Dostoievsky's saintly Father Zosima, probably Catherine would have found nothing to say to him. A whole dimension of Russia – what is sometimes called 'Holy Russia' – was hidden from Catherine, as under the influence of Voltaire Catherine moved from Christianity to Deism, and chose a benevolent, even beaming God, who demanded neither humility nor the rendering of accounts.

Yet Catherine did have an account to render. She had been guilty of at least one grave sin. She could not pretend that Peter's murder would not have happened if she had acted differently. Politically she had to keep silence about the murder and her part in it, but for that very reason at the deepest level of her personality there was all the more call for her to kneel before a redeeming God, to confess, and to receive forgiveness. But her religion or rather the absence of it precluded not only the requisite humility but also the resultant reconciliation. Catherine forgave easily, and perhaps she did forgive herself but that kind of absolution is not enough. Catherine was of stronger fibre than Gregory Orlov, who felt himself pursued by Peter's bleeding ghost to insanity and the tomb, but at the very least she would have felt a vestigial sense of guilt. It is noticeable how such people, those who carry with them a hidden sense of wrong-doing, try at every point in other fields to justify themselves. Sure enough, we find this characteristic in Catherine's Memoirs. In the course of that long work Catherine never once says: 'I did such and such, and was wrong to do it.' Peter is often wrong, Elizabeth, the Choglokovs, the Shuvalovs, but Catherine never.

If self-justification was Catherine's usual way of thinking about herself after 1762, she would have carried it over to her love affairs, and it is quite possible that this 'pure as snow' attitude was a third factor in alienating some of the men in her life.

Catherine was not the only monarch to lack a just understanding of herself. It is the occupational hazard. Usually, in the lives of the very powerful, some disaster occurs which acts as a corrective. Defeats and famine gradually led Louis XIV to his deathbed admission that he had loved war too much, and in St Helena Napoleon intermittently glimpsed that there was more to life than the destiny of France. But Catherine experienced no such disaster, for the challenge implicit in the excesses of the French Revolution was one she believed she could meet, and no such illumination followed. Until her sudden death she continued working hard and smiling brightly. The *allegro* gave way to no reflective slow movement.

When we turn to Catherine the ruler, the underlying remarkable fact is that she survived. At the time of her *coup d'état* diplomats in St Petersburg gave her at most six months, yet this young inexperienced German-born lady held on to the throne in a country hostile to Germans, weathered the Pugachev rebellion and various plots, reigned thirty-four years and died in her bed.

A good ruler, Catherine used to say, should act according to 'circumstances, conjecture and conjuncture'. Those are the words of a pragmatist. Catherine brought to her diplomacy and political decisions a notable absence of preconceived theory; she distrusted any philosophy or creed that laid down *a priori* what a man must be or do. If it be asked whether Catherine's pragmatism was sound sense or lack of principle, the answer is, a bit of both, for the very lack of strong Christian principles meant that she could act vigorously from the lesser principle of what was good for Russia.

Pragmatism directed her attitude to the Church. She came to power with the support of the clergy, but very soon displeased them by confirming Peter's nationalization of monastic lands and by her unprecedented tolerance. John Parkinson, questioning senior clergy in the last years of her reign, found some of them extremely critical of the Empress. But Catherine carried the Church with her by continuing to attend Mass, to receive the sacraments and observe the fasts, in short by showing herself to be what in reality she was not: a zealous, believing, Orthodox Christian.

The fact of being a woman played a large part in Catherine's success as a ruler. It was a feminine type of adaptability that enabled Catherine to become in so many respects Russian, a feminine tact that kept her from driving too far the class on which she depended, feminine charm that drew men of the highest talent to work devotedly in her service, without that envy they might well have felt for a male ruler. She was as successful a woman ruler as Elizabeth of England had been in a very different kind of country, and though she differed so much from Elizabeth in her lavish spending and the number of her lovers, she shared with Elizabeth that remarkable intuitive sense of her people's mood, comparable to what a good hostess feels for her guests at a dinner-party.

Did Catherine differ from her male contemporaries in her choice of ends? Yes, but only to a small degree. Catherine advanced Russia's interests wherever she could, much as Gustavus advanced Sweden's and Joseph advanced Austria's. But she did do more than they for education and for the welfare of orphans. A special concern for children is what one might expect from a woman ruler, and is to be found also in Catherine's contemporary, Maria Theresa.

Catherine's remarkable strength of will served her well as a ruler. It showed itself in the tenacity with which she worked for reform and defied both Gustavus and the Sultan in a two-front war, as she had once held out against both Peter and Elizabeth. Its visible expression was unquestioned authority, so strong it persisted even in her absence. Gribovsky tells of the awe felt by visitors to the imperial apartments even when Catherine was not in residence, and a well-founded tradition holds that when he came to the throne her grandson Alexander was to notice a sentry standing guard on a stretch of lawn in the Winter Palace public garden. Day and night a sentry stood alone in the middle of the lawn. Finally Alexander asked the officer in charge why the man was there. The officer replied that, years before, the Empress Catherine had ordered a sentry to that particular spot, to protect the first snowdrop of spring.

Catherine's strength of will was not cold or inhuman. On the contrary, it is one of the central paradoxes of her character that it went with warmth and even protectiveness. One has only to compare her with Frederick of Prussia, so cynical, misanthropic and detached, to realize the extent of Catherine's warmth. She harangued Potemkin to capture Ochakov, but if he was indisposed, trembled for his life. If at times she had something of the schoolmarm, at least she preferred to win pupils round rather than to chivvy them. One recalls Casanova's judgment: 'Catherine, with her undemanding manner, could demand more than Frederick of Prussia and obtain it,' while Dr John Rogerson said, 'Serving her was the most perfect freedom.'

The most striking feature of Catherine's reign is undoubtedly the number and variety of its successes. Without the threats and cruelty employed by Peter the Great, but drawing on his example, Catherine overcame a traditional inertia, and got her people working to good purpose for thirty-four years, until she had transformed the face of Russia. She achieved many if not all the reforms she intended: by the standards of her time she ruled Russia very well indeed and increased its prosperity. She made substantial territorial gains. Her civilizing role, referred to by the *Gentleman's Magazine*, showed itself in literature, building, painting, the theatre, opera and ballet. As regards her relations with her people, according to Prince Adam Czartoryski, a Polish patriot who naturally had some hard things to say of Catherine, 'she succeeded in winning inside her country, especially within her capital, the veneration, even the love of her servants and subjects.' To find a previous similar run of successes over so large an area one would have to go back to the reign of the Emperor Augustus.

On the debit side of Catherine's reign must be placed her handling of Radishchev and Novikov. Her intolerance to these two thinkers clouds her glory, much as the suppression of Port Royal clouds Louis XIV's. Her handling of subversive agents is also regrettable; so too is her treatment of her son Paul, which was later to have grave consequences.

In the light of some such assessment of Catherine the woman and Catherine the ruler we have to decide whether her qualities were such as to deserve singling out by a laudatory epithet. My belief is that they were, and that Catherine deserves to be called 'the Great'. If so, and if she is confirmed in the group of rulers accounted great, she is for the present the only woman among eight men, a position she doubtless enjoys.

In concluding this assessment of Catherine's reign, and as a means to establishing its significance, it is necessary to glance briefly at what followed it.

If God did give him 'the strength and good sense' he had hoped to receive, Paul made poor use of them. He built himself a moated granite stronghold, the Mikhailovsky Castle, each of its façades in a different style, like his own fluctuating moods. From there he ruled as a petty military despot, ending freedom of travel, banning the import of foreign books, determining the cut of his subjects' collars and the shape of their hats, obliging people in the street to kneel in the snow when he passed.

The driving force of his reign was to wipe his mother out of his life. He withdrew from circulation Catherine's *Instruction*, dismissed most of her close associates, called back Valerian Zubov from Persia and Suvorov from central Europe, while pardoning Novikov and, as a mark of his disapproval of Catherine's Polish policy, giving ex-King Stanislaus Gregory Orlov's Marble Palace, where the ageing Pole hung his fine collection of paintings, including Fragonard's *Stolen Kiss*, a reminder of happier days with Catherine.

Paul withdrew from the coalition against France and fell under the spell of the French soldier-statesman who, years before he became known, Catherine had predicted would arise: 'a superior, clever, courageous man, well above his contemporaries, the man of the century perhaps'. Although it cost Russia dear and was disapproved of by the gentry, Paul helped Napoleon by reviving, this time against England, the Armed Neutrality.

In conducting Catherine's funeral as he did, Paul had believed he was avenging a murder. In reality he was indulging a streak of malice that would speedily precipitate a second murder: his own. Paul's reversal of the best features of his mother's reign had already begun to alienate public opinion, his petty cruelties and his attitude to Napoleon, so reminiscent of Peter's to Frederick, completed the alienation. In 1801 history repeated itself; contrary to Marx's dictum, it took the form not of farce but, again, of tragedy. A group of patriots led by Count Peter Pahlen, military governor of St Petersburg, and including Plato Zubov, approached Alexander with a plan for bringing him to the throne. Alexander replied that he would not refuse the crown but he made Pahlen promise that not one hair of his father's head would be harmed.

In the event Paul resisted, cried for help and had to be strangled. Alexander, shocked and guilt-ridden, wished to withdraw but at Pahlen's bidding he appeared before the troops and was hailed by them as Tsar. A statement was issued that Paul I had died of apoplexy – prompting Talleyrand's remark, 'Really, the Russian government will have to invent another disease' – while Alexander made a solemn promise to the troops: 'During my reign everything will be done according to the principles of my beloved grandmother, the Empress Catherine.'

Despite Catherine's Westernizing, Russia had remained in many ways un-European and, after the French Revolution and Napoleon's invasion, even anti-European. It was Alexander's misfortune that he lacked Catherine's commitment by birth to European values, so that Russia's conflict between Western institutions and the patrimonial spirit was fought in his soul without ever being resolved. Just as in private life Alexander showed himself a drawing-room flirt rather than a bedroom lover, so in public life he dabbled in ideas or reform without actually implementing the radical changes prepared by Catherine which his popularity would have allowed him to make.

Alexander opened discussions about a constitution, helped by, among others, Radishchev, who declared that in his provisions for the gentry to elect their own representatives Catherine had laid the foundations for such a constitution. But it did not get beyond the discussion stage, nor did Alexander greatly advance emancipation of the serfs in Russia, though he did emancipate them in Estonia, Courland and Livonia. Catherine's schools were now producing sufficient teachers to staff the universities she had planned; Alexander opened seven universities, and accorded them considerable powers of self-government. That was Alexander's best achievement at home. After defeating Napoleon he became a prey to a characteristic Russian weakness – dreaminess and resignation posing as Christian mysticism – and plans for further reform were allowed to lapse.

The failure of Paul's reign and the comparative failure of Alexander's point up the successes of Catherine's. They show just how difficult it was, in a country like Russia, to enlist public support for major new policies. Moreover Paul and Alexander were native Russians, whereas Catherine of Zerbst had to work in a land highly suspicious of foreigners.

Almost all Catherine's undertakings had repercussions in modern Russian history, even comparatively minor ones like her picture-collecting, her handling of Freemasonry and her use of the fleet in Mediterranean waters. Here it is possible to glance at only one or two.

Catherine's Greek plan inspired her successors, but was realized only in part, and when the Hellenes, with Russia's help, did throw off their Turkish fetters, England's intervention ensured that Greece arose as a free and independent nation.

Catherine's plan for emancipating serfs whenever an estate came up for sale was never applied. She had, however, prepared educated Russians to think in terms of emancipation, and her hope that this would come about within a hundred years was to be realized. But it would be a mistake to single out serfdom as the all-important fact or in Russian life during this period, and to judge Catherine's reign purely on the issue of serfdom. That would be as poor historical thinking as to blame George Washington for not giving the vote to women. Serfdom was merely one item in the larger conflict between European and Asian attitudes, and it could be ended only when it had been proved to be detrimental to Russia's progress as a nation: in 1861, precisely, after Russia's failure in the Crimean War.

By her exceptional energy Catherine had narrowed the gap between Russia and Europe. If only her successors had pursued the same ideals as she had pursued and with the same energy, Russia would have caught up with Europe. In the event they vacillated, and Russia, like her Asian neighbour Turkey, lagged further and further behind. The abolition of serfdom, while removing one injustice, only served to show up others hitherto less evident, such as lack of civic rights, retrograde education and Press censorship. It was after, not before, abolition of serfdom that nihilists and anarchists became prominent, seeking to Europeanize Russia by means of revolution.

One incident from this period shows the falling-off since Catherine's day. Among the colonists Catherine had attracted to the Volga was a group of German Catholics; she gave them land and allowed them complete religious freedom. Catherine's great-grandson, Alexander II, emancipator of the serfs, began to persecute non-Russian minorities; during his reign the little Catholic community were penalized so severely that they left Russia and sailed to the United States, finding a new home in the state of Kansas. Each had brought with him a handful of Turkey Red wheat, and this they sowed on the broad plains, while building a wooden town. The wheat flourished, so did the settlement, which they named after the long-dead Empress who had been their benefactor and allowed them to practise their religion, so that today one of Catherine the Great's memorials is the little town of Catharine, Kansas.

The Tsars, when not actually persecuting, failed to grant Russia the freedoms now being taken for granted in Europe, while the Orthodox Church, which Catherine in old age had described as 'a deep-rooted oak', entered on decline and bigotry. A solution by subversion and force became almost inevitable, and took place in the old context of Russo-German antagonism. When the First World War broke out, the Tsar again had a German consort, but Alexandra, unlike Catherine, failed to show herself a true Russian, and so once more, this time finally, anti-German feeling turned against the throne.

The Russian Revolution took place, and with it men's awe and submissiveness which, had the Church been fulfilling its role, would have gone to God were transferred to the State. By a cruel paradox, just as the French Revolution at the end of Catherine's reign had begun to cut Europe off from Russia, so the Russian Revolution was to cut Russia off from Europe, and a political philosophy from Catherine's Germany was to be refracted into a despotism wholly Asian.

Catherine, who had worked to make Russia European in the best sense of the word, would have disapproved. What she would have thought of the Russia of today, where the descendants of the people she ruled are taught that they are slaves of History and pawns in a Predetermined Future, emerges clearly from a letter she wrote in the middle of her reign:

'Voltaire, my master, forbids predicting the future, because those who predict the future like to make systems, and those who make systems pile into the system what fits and what doesn't, what tallies and what doesn't, and finally self-love becomes love of the system, which produces stubbornness, intolerance and persecution – drugs against which my master has warned me.'

The words of this letter and of her hundreds of other letters are part of Catherine's significance today. There are also her visible achievements: a string of towns on the Black Sea: Kherson, Sevastopol and Odessa; the much enlarged and beautified city on the Neva, of which Edward Clarke wrote in 1799: 'The united magnificence of all the cities of Europe could but equal Petersburg'; there is the bulk of the Hermitage Collection, and in Moscow the Orlov diamond gleaming bluish-white in the imperial sceptre.

But Catherine's significance – and her most effective answer to the system – lies above all in the example of her own life in its best years: her unassumingness, her toleration of all creeds, the beginning she made to thaw the ice of autocracy by giving a measure of power to the 'estates' and by her plan for a national Assembly, her compassion expressed in welfare for the poor, in orphanages and foundling homes and hospitals – in all those acts which won her what as a handicapped girl in Stettin she thought a ruler should try to win: her subjects' respect and affection.

APPENDIX A

The Chief Sources for Catherine's Life

For Catherine's girlhood and years as Grand Duchess the chief source is her **autobiographical writings**. There are nine of them altogether, eight in French, one in Russian, some disjointed, others forming a continuous narrative, written at various dates between 1756 and 1794. All were published in their original languages as Volume 12 of *Sochineniia imperatritsy Ekateriny II* (St Petersburg 1907), with some cuts relating to the unconsummated marriage; curiously, a Russian translation was published without cuts: *Zapiski* (St Petersburg 1907). K. Anthony translated the shorter writings into English as *Memoirs of Catherine the Great* (New York 1927); M. Budberg translated the main continuous narrative (London 1955), occasionally interweaving passages from the shorter writings and adding dates, some of which are incorrect. Not one of the autobiographical writings should be taken in isolation, for differences between earlier and later versions provide important clues to Catherine's development. The most reliable of the writings is the autobiography for Sir Charles Hanbury-Williams, begun in 1756, and included in K. Anthony's translated collection.

Another important source are **Catherine's letters**. By far the most numerous are addressed to Grimm, and they appeared as volume 23 of the Imperial Historical Society's great collection of documents of Russian history. Letters to a variety of correspondents, notably Potemkin, appear in other volumes of the same collection, and are an important source. Revealing of Catherine's private life are her letters to Zachary Chernuishev (*Russkiy Arkhiv* 1881, vol. 3) and her love-notes to Potemkin, edited by Oudard in 1934. Catherine's letters to Voltaire are well known through Reddaway's edition, but in them, evidently overawed by Voltaire's fame, she writes in a stilted, uncharacteristic vein. Her correspondence with Sir Charles Hanbury-Williams shows Catherine's day-to-day reactions to danger.

Catherine's **Instruction** to the Legislative Commission appears in English translation in W. F. Reddaway's *Documents of Catherine the Great* (Cambridge 1931). Catherine's **Edicts** were published in St Petersburg in the nineteenth century as part of *Polnoe Sobranie Zakonov*.

Turning to Catherine's Russian contemporaries, we find a number of major sources. **Derzhavin** was an eye-witness of many important events in Catherine's reign, particularly of the Pugachev rising, which he helped to put down, and the later years, when he held important official positions in St Petersburg. However, his *Memoirs*, written 1811–13, are typical products of their epoch, and were principally written to show their author in the best possible light, to justify his past actions, and to give *his* version of his innumerable wrangles with his contemporaries.

Garnovsky was on Potemkin's staff, and administered his properties in St Petersburg. He was what would now be called an intelligence agent and, although not highly placed socially, was very well informed. He corresponded with V. S. Popov, his opposite number with Potemkin in the field. His memoirs and letters are mainly concerned with the minutiae of everyday politics, and as such of more interest to Russians than to foreigners.

Khrapovitsky, one of Catherine's secretaries, kept a diary from 1782 to 1793. It is written in a very cryptic style; Khrapovitsky hardly ever names the Empress or refers to her directly; the reader sometimes has to deduce that he is referring to the Empress from the context. Some of the entries are very important for an understanding of Catherine's character.

Gribovsky worked for Potemkin from 1787, and later was a member of Zubov's secretariat. His memoirs and diaries are fragmentary. He had a lively pen, and has left a good portrait of Catherine in old age, and a description of her day-to-day life.

P. Sumarokov was a very well-born courtier of Catherine's time, who in 1819 published a collection of anecdotes about the Empress. His chief informant was Catherine's close friend, Maria Perekusikhina. His book is gossipy, and not too much credence should be given to all its contents.

Princess Dashkova was closely associated in Catherine's *coup d'état* and at her death in 1810 left behind *Memoirs*, which she had written between 1804 and 1806. They throw useful light on events leading up to the coup, but overemphasize the importance of her own role. The Princess admired Catherine. Even though she sometimes disagreed with certain actions, she never allowed herself any serious criticism or even analysis of Catherine's character.

Other Russian sources that throw light on minor aspects of Catherine's life are too numerous to discuss here.

Among foreigners who knew Catherine well and wrote about her, two are particularly perceptive: **Sir Charles Hanbury-Williams** for the years 1756 and 1757, and the **Prince de Ligne** for the later reign. **Louis Philippe de Ségur**, who defected to the Revolution – Catherine called him 'a Judas' – is less trustworthy about Catherine the woman than about Catherine's Russia.

Excerpts from the despatches of foreign ambassadors began to be published by the Imperial Historical Society in the nineteenth century, but are no substitute for the full despatches. Of these the **English ambassadors' despatches** in the Public Record Office (State Papers 91) are an unrivalled foreign source for Catherine's reign.

For the conditions of Russians during and immediately after Catherine's reign, our fullest information comes from the accounts of foreign travellers. As a rule those who travelled quickly through Russia formed an unfavourable opinion, those who resided there some time a favourable opinion. Richardson, Macartney, Chappe d'Auteroche, Rulhière and Masson belong in the former group; Guthrie, Tooke, Eton, Atkinson, Levesque (12 years' residence) and Le Clerc (10 years') belong in the latter group. Since their views have received far less attention than the detractors' views, it will help to right the balance to quote three of them on some aspects of serfdom.

Dr Matthew Guthrie, in his unpublished *Noctes Russicae*, in the British Library:

> The Russian like the Roman soldier receives his *Missio Honesta* or honourable discharge at the end of 25 years according to Law, so that if he entered the army at 20, the usual age of recruits furnished by the feudal barons from their *bondsmen* (since the feudal array has been replaced by regular standing armies) he returns to his village a *free man* at 45. Now as every peasant family in Russia has a portion of land alloted to it which they cultivate for their own profit in given days allowed them by laws, and as that portion is very ample in most provinces where they have more acres than inhabitants, a discharged soldier who became a freeman has the right of settling on the land given to his family, and making the most of it by his own industry. We shall take this opportunity of remarking that as the riches of a nobleman entirely depend on the number and affluence of his peasants or bondsmen, who pay him so much per head for every *male*, from five Roubles to 20 according to their abilities; it can not be the interest of a feudal lord to oppress his boors, as by so doing he would fall, for example, in a very few years from a revenue of 40 thousand roubles to 20, an act of too great folly to be generally practised, though in all countries, a few extravagant

madmen and gamesters are to be found, who ruin themselves and all under them.

Moreover every *feudal lord* (for such they still are, though not under the Gothic regulations) must stock every little individual farm given to a peasant, with at least one horse, one cow, some poultry and the instruments of agriculture necessary to cultivate it; so that Galloping Travellers as we have before called them, in merely driving through a country cannot pretend to decide on the state of the inhabitants.

The Polish scholar and traveller **Count Jan Potocki** recorded the following impressions of the countryside near Moscow on 16th May 1797:

I proceed downstream along the Moskva river. The countryside is beautiful and so heavily populated that several villages are in view at any one time. A feast of some sort was being celebrated in one of them just as I passed. What magnificence in the peasants' attire! Women's headdresses and kerchiefs embroidered in gold, and so beautifully made as if they originated from Constantinople itself. Many travellers have spoken about the poverty of Russian peasants; as far as I am concerned, I describe what I have seen myself and not what others have seen. (J. Potocki, *Podróże*. Warsaw, 1959, p. 274. Translated from the Polish by K. A. Papmehl.)

Finally **William Eton**, in *A Survey of the Turkish Empire*:

I appeal to all those who have travelled in Russia whether they ever saw more hilarity in any part of the world. I do not mean to recommend for imitation such a state of things to make men happy; those who have been removed from it cannot go back again; but I affirm that the whole mass of people appear to be more happy (and it is a hard thing to make a man laugh when he is not pleased) than I have seen in three parts of the globe.

When we turn to certain French writers of Catherine's reign or just afterwards, we leave the world of fact for propaganda. First, **Voltaire, Diderot** and others, as part of their battle with the French monarchy, built up a picture of a Catherine who never was and in eighteenth-century Russia never could have been; when Catherine failed to live up to their personal criteria of a philosopher-queen, these writers or their disciples turned against her, expressing emotions ranging from disappointment to an outraged sense of betrayal.

After the Revolution propaganda changed key. **Claude Cardoman de Rulhière** wrote *Histoire, ou anecdotes, sur la révolution de Russie en l'annéee 1762* (Paris 1797; English translations London 1797 and

Boston, Mass. 1798), in which he asserted that the murder of Peter III was carried out with Catherine's connivance. Dr Matthew Guthrie wrote in the introduction to his unpublished translation of Catherine's *The Opera of Oleg* that a French colleague of his, Levesque, who lived twelve years in Catherine's Russia, asked Rulhière in Paris:

> his authority for the most heavy charge against Catherine, re-echoed by all her libellers since, and to his surprise found it to have been an old superannuated Frenchman named Roslain who having been of low birth, commonly said to have come into Russia as a running footman and placed by one of the Court favourites in the Corps of Pages, very possibly to enjoy the airs of the vain old man marching at the head of the boys, which we often saw to our great entertainment. Such was Rulhière's authority for damning the memory of Catherine and which all her Jacobin libellers have copied. In short that horrible accusation depends upon the information of a silly vain old man, who pretended to his countryman that he was a man of much consequence at Court, and deeply versed in its secrets. We well knew the Orloffs, the Marshal Rosomoffsky, and the other conductors of the Revolution which placed Catherine on the throne, we mean in the way of our profession we were frequently with them, and will venture to declare, that instead of confiding their secrets to the old Frenchman, he was an object of their entertainment. It may be asked what interest we take in the memory of Catherine, and we answer that of a man who from sense of justice is shocked to see a number of things which we know to be false appear in print, by needy scribblers, who live on scandal, always a saleable article.

Rulhière also charged Catherine with insobriety. Guthrie replied that 'she was one of the most regular sober women who ever lived.'

Two years after Rulhière's book there appeared a *Histoire de Pierre III* by **Jean Laveaux**. This presented Catherine as not only lascivious, but precociously so. Laveaux stated that Catherine, in Stettin, slept with a certain Count von B-; she would then have been aged thirteen or under. What Laveaux says is contradicted by everything else we know for sure about Catherine's girlhood. Laveaux had never been near Stettin; furthermore he was a Robespierrist writing for Frenchmen at a time when they were bitterly hostile to monarchy and to everything Russian. Almost certainly his story is a libel, like the many similar stories concocted a few years earlier against Queen Antoinette of France, yet still they circulate in one form or another. Too often it is not the evil that queens do that lives after them, but the evil gossip.

C. F. P. Masson was a Frenchman who held a minor post in St Petersburg. He was arrested and expelled from Russia in 1796 by Paul I, who did not like him. In 1800 Masson published anonymously *Mémoires secrets sur la Russie*. It is bitterly anti-Russian and anti-Catherine, and often inaccurate. For example, his allegation that Catherine lived with all the Orlov brothers is certainly not true. The book was a sensational success, was translated into English and German, and an edition appeared in America. As Masson wrote all the things about Russia which foreigners wanted to read and wished to believe, it has been used by non-Russian historians right up to the present day.

Masson is the source of allegations that Catherine indulged in lesbian practices at the end of her life, and of all stories about *l'éprouveuse* – since the French term is always the one used, it seems probable that the source was, indeed, French. On p. 148 of the Amsterdam edition of the *Mémoires* (1800), Masson writes: 'Après quelques entretiens secrets en présence du mentor, Zoubow fut gouté, et adressé *pour plus ample informé* à Mlle Protasow et au médecin du corps.' A note on the same page says: 'On nommoit Mlle Protasow *l'éprouveuse*. Le médecin du corps étoit *M. Rogerson*.'

Masson, a literary man, may have drawn, directly or indirectly, on 'Il Poema Tartaro', written in 1784 by Giambattista Casti, in which Turfana, possibly intended as an amalgam of Countess Bruce and Madame Protasova, says: 'I usually first test the candidate for the favour in order to find out whether he combines with his appearance general merit. And no one gets the position unless he has been beforehand tried and approved by me.' Casti was a Voltairean *abbé gallant* regarded by his contemporaries as an amusing, inventive versifier; as a serious historical source he is worthless.

The only mention of an *éprouveuse* earlier than 1800 is the entry in John Parkinson's diary (first published in 1971) on 10th January 1792: 'Madame Protasov is supposed to be a taster.'

Casanova was in Russia earlier than Parkinson, but he wrote his *Memoirs* in old age, after Catherine's death. He certainly knew Casti's poem and he met Casti after the latter's return from Russia. Yet he does not mention the *éprouveuse*. It seems unlikely that he would have left out such a salacious titbit had he known about it. Casanova's chapters on Catherine's Russia are confirmed by other sources; he is reliable and well informed, and his omission of the story is significant, especially when taken with Masson's known virulence and unreliability.

Going on now to some of the later biographies of Catherine and histories of her reign, we find three outstanding Russian works.

Bilbasov published the first two volumes of a projected complete biography of Catherine; these take events up to the year 1764: *Istoriya Yekateriny Vtoroi*. Vols. I and II, Berlin 1900; vol. XII – a bibliography of non-Russian sources – Berlin, n.d.

Soloviev's *Istoriya Rossii s drevneyshikh vremen* (*History of Russia from the earliest times*), first published in the nineteenth century in 29 volumes, ends abruptly, because of the author's death, in 1773, and thus deals with only the first eleven years of Catherine's reign. However, the coverage of the years 1762–73 is both detailed and reliable, more so than any other history. Soloviev is not interested in Catherine's private life and is only concerned with it in so far as it impinged on Russian state policy, home and foreign.

Klyuchevsky's *Kurs Russkoy istorii* (*A Course of Russian History*) consists of transcripts of 86 lectures delivered at Moscow at the end of the nineteenth century. The reigns of Elizabeth and Catherine are dealt with in vol. 5; there is also a character sketch of Catherine contained in a special appendix. The history is written with dazzling brilliance – and lack of sympathy for Catherine, though he is impressed by the success of her foreign policy, her personal intelligence and her charm, even if bogus, because based on insincerity and guile. It is probably the most readable serious history of Russia in general and Catherine in particular.

Outside Russia nineteenth-century biographers concentrated on Catherine's foreign policy, very topical at a time when the Eastern Question was troubling the chancelleries of Europe. **A. Brückner's** *Katherina die Zweite* (Berlin 1883) is a sound work in this genre.

In *Le Roman d'une Impératrice* (Paris 1893) **K. Waliszewski** wrote an influential psychological biography which brought together much scattered detailed information, especially from French Foreign Office manuscripts. The portrait of Catherine that emerges is, in my opinion, overfull of contradictions, because Waliszewski treats Catherine statically, not as a woman constantly developing, and because he was somewhat undiscriminating in his use of sources, for example of Rulhière and the Chevalier d'Eon.

The twentieth century has seen a proliferation of books about Catherine based, ultimately, on the libels of the French Revolutionary writers. Among serious, reliable recent portraits or biographies of Catherine may be mentioned G. P. Gooch, *Catherine the Great and Other Studies* (London 1954), Ian Grey, *Catherine the Great* (London 1961) and Daria Olivier, *Catherine la Grande* (Paris 1965).

APPENDIX B

Catherine's Children

In an appendix to the first volume of the Russian edition of his biography of Catherine, Bilbasov published a report by M. de Champeaux, *fils*, French Resident in Hamburg, dated 8th September 1758, the original of which is in the French Foreign Office Archives. Champeaux gives an account, which purports to be based on talks with Saltuikov, of how Peter eventually consummated his marriage. According to Champeaux, Peter suffered from a physical malformation, Saltuikov contrived to get him to undergo circumcision, whereupon Peter consummated his marriage, Catherine being still a virgin. This contradicts Catherine's account of the marriage, and the question arises, how much importance should be attached to Champeaux's report?

French diplomats at this period were notoriously ill-informed and tended to spice their despatches, evidently to please Louis XV. Corberon in St Petersburg is one example among many. Then again, the account contains some highly improbable details: Peter sends the Empress the proofs that he had consummated the marriage in a sealed casket, and she rewards Saltuikov with a valuable diamond – though in fact the Empress, in middle age, rarely gave presents. Thirdly, Peter was very self-willed with his men friends, not the sort of person to be gulled by weak Saltuikov. Finally, physical malformation such as Champeaux indicates is extremely rare, whereas some psychological reason for non-consummation of marriage is common among princes and future kings, Louis XVI and Gustavus III being two examples in Peter's own century. Mercy, it may be remembered, picked up comparable gossip about Louis XVI requiring, and undergoing, circumcision, which is without foundation, as I showed in the Appendix to my *Louis and Antoinette* (London 1974).

Champeaux's report is exactly what one would expect from Saltuikov in the circumstances. Frightened by the consequences of admitting that he had been Catherine's lover, and indeed the father of her child, he concocts a story in which he is both hero and the loyal friend of Peter. A physical explanation of the unconsummated marriage was easy for a second-rate minor official like Champeaux to understand and, having no personal knowledge of the Russian Court, he probably expanded it with titillating details for his readers at Versailles. As an explanation of what took place in the winter of 1753–4 Champeaux's report is unconvincing in the extreme, but the possibility that Saltuikov told Champeaux some such story tallies exactly with Catherine's portrayal of him in her Memoirs, and would be one more small additional piece of evidence for their essential truth.

Since Catherine had no motive for lying in making plain, not only in her Memoirs but as early as 1756–7 to Hanbury-Williams, that she was a virgin when she had her affair with Saltuikov, that the affair lasted six months, and that only after a full nine years of non-consummation did she have sexual relations with her husband, I consider that, unless and until any strong contrary evidence emerges, Catherine's account of the marriage has to be accepted, hence that the father of Tsar Paul I was Serge Saltuikov.

It is noteworthy that Parkinson in his entry for 21st December 1792 writes: 'Peter the Third is said to have made a declaration . . . that the Grand Duke was not his son. His father's name was Saltikoff.'

Paul, Bobrinsky and Anna Petrovna (Poniatowski's daughter) are well authenticated and are probably the only children Catherine had.

However, there were always rumours about other children, and Parkinson records in his diary on 15th January 1793 a rumour often found in other foreign sources (e.g. Masson): 'The Empress has other children in the palace. The two mademoiselles Protassoff are supposed to be her daughters.' The fact that, when Anna Stepanovna Protasova (who never married) was made a Countess by Alexander I in 1801, the title, at her request, was also granted to her nieces, whom she had brought up, is sometimes used as evidence to support the theory that the girls were, in reality, Catherine's. But this is not very strong evidence. They could have been Anna Stepanovna's own children, or even real nieces. Foreign, but not Russian, sources suggest these were Orlov's children. Anna Stepanovna was related to the Orlovs in some way, and obtained her position at Court through them.

The Russian Biographical Dictionary lists four illegitimate children of Gregory Orlov; he probably had more. Some sources, for example the Russian Encyclopedia but not the Biographical Dictionary, hint that at least one child (No. 4) may have been Catherine's.

1) Sofia Grigorievna Alekseyeva, who married Buxhoeveden (later Governor-General of St Petersburg).
2) A son, Galaktion, who died young.

3) A son, Ospennyi.
4) A daughter, Elizaveta, who married Friedrich Maximilien von Klinger, 1752–1831, German writer, who spent many years in Russia, author of *Sturm und Drang*.

A. A. Golombievsky, in his *Biografia Knyazya G. C. Orlova*, (Moscow 1904) gives additional, and rather different, information. Golombievsky is a very serious historian, who gives all his sources. He lists the following as, perhaps, Orlov's children. He does not openly attribute any of them to Catherine, with the possible exception of No. 4.

1) Natalya, who married Buxhoeveden in 1777 (not Sofia, as in the Biographical Dictionary).
2) Elizaveta, born 25th April, 1761 (o.s.), who married Klinger in 1788.
3) A third daughter, Ekaterina, who married a Lieut.-Colonel Svinin.

The two boys:

4) Ospinnyi, or Ospennyi, or Ospin.
5) Galaktion.

Ospinnyi: In October 1768 Dr Dimsdale vaccinated the Empress and her son Paul against smallpox. The vaccine was taken from a boy called A. Markov who on 24th November 1768 was admitted to the rank of Nobility and given the name Ospinnyi – a name fabricated from the Russian word for smallpox. Some authorities consider he was Orlov's son, and some even consider that he was Catherine's. The only evidence for this belief is a very ambiguous letter Catherine wrote on 14th December 1768 to Count Ivan Chernuishev, with whom she had a very close friendship. In this letter she mentions the boy as 'Alexander Danilov's son Ospin'; she says he is six years old, a delightful, clever child, and that she spends hours playing with him. She continues:

'If you want to know whose he is, your brother says that with time he will occupy Betskoy's place, and don't ask me any more. Galaktion Ivanovich told me to ask you if he will soon receive the little elephant which you promised to send him from China.'

The reference to Betskoy is obscure. As a girl in Germany Catherine had known Betskoy as a friend of her parents, and on coming to Russia she seems to have associated him in her mind with her parents. She treated Betskoy with unusual respect and rose whenever he entered the room.

Galaktion. Catherine's mention of this boy, in the above letter, is apparently the only contemporary reference. Even his surname is a mystery.

Not very much more is known about Markov-Ospin. He was alive until at least 1796. At first Catherine favoured him, but she later dropped him completely. He lived in great poverty. For some reason, no one would employ him. He made various petitions, in which he spoke of the plight of his aged parents. Catherine may have favoured him at first simply because of the smallpox vaccination which was, after all, an important event.

The Three Girls all had the surname Alekseyev, and were supposed to be the daughters of a Lieut-Colonel Alekseyev. They were brought up at Smolny by order of Catherine.

All Russian sources are extremely reticent on the subject of these children, right up to 1917. One reason may be that two of the Alekseyev girls made quite good marriages and may have had descendants who might have suffered if their illegitimate origins were known. The Bobrinskys, on the other hand, were proud of their origin.

It seems hardly possible that Catherine had a total of ten children: Paul, Anna, Bobrinsky, two Protasov girls, three Alekseyev girls, Ospin and Galaktion, as well as several miscarriages. It will be noted that Elizaveta Alekseyeva, who married Klinger, was born on 25th April 1761, i.e. a year before Bobrinsky and the *coup d'état*, when the Empress Elizabeth was still alive. It seems unlikely that Elizabeth would not have known about it, and, if she did, would not have treated the child as legitimate, as she did with Anna. The Protasov girls are not linked with Catherine in serious Russian sources, only in gossip, mainly foreign.

The fact remains that the only children who can be attributed to Catherine with certainty are Paul, Anna and Bobrinsky. Surmises, but nothing more, can be made about the others.

Sources and Notes

The following abbreviations are used:

Mémoires — *Sochineniia imperatritsy Ekateriny II* Volume 12 (St Petersburg 1907)

Sbornik — *Sbornik imperatorskovo russkovo istoricheskovo obshchestva* (St Petersburg 1867–1916)

CHAPTER 1: A GENERAL'S DAUGHTER

Frederick William I: R. Ergang, *The Potsdam Führer* (New York 1941) and E. Lavisse, *La Jeunesse du Grand Frédéric* (Paris 1891).

Christian August's career: *Allgemeine Deutsche Biographie*, iv, pp. 157–9.

Following a slip in the *Mémoires* (p. 10) and ignoring p. 442, most of Catherine's biographers identify Johanna's godmother, who received Johanna and Sophie at Brunswick, as the Duchess of Brunswick-Lüneburg. In fact she was the Duchess of Brunswick-Wolfenbüttel. Elisabeth Sofie Maria, daughter of Duke Rudolf Friedrich of Holstein-Norburg, was born 2 September 1685, married August Wilhelm, reigning Duke of Brunswick-Wolfenbüttel, as his third wife, on 12 September 1710, and died 3 April 1767. Wilhelm Karl, Prinz von Isenburg, *Stammtafeln zur Geschichte der Europäischen Staaten*, 2 vols bound together (Marburg 1955).

Sophie's reaction to King Frederick William's death: *Mémoires*, pp. 18–19.

CHAPTER 2: INVITATION FOR TWO

Sophie and Fräulein von Kayn: *Mémoires*, pp. 21–2; Sophie and the Countess von Bentinck: *idem*, pp. 25–7.

Sophie's relations with Prince Georg Ludwig: *Mémoires*, pp. 28–30.

The arrival of the invitation: *Mémoires*, pp. 30–2 and 443–4.

CATHERINE

CHAPTER 3: ALL THE RUSSIAS

A typical map of Russia at this period is included in F. C. Weber, *The Present State of Russia* (London 1722). Ill-defined spaces are captioned with shadowy names: 'Here the hordes of Kontash,' 'There the hordes of Otchiurti.'

Peter the Great's visits to Germany: M. Kroll, *Sophie, Electress of Hanover* (London 1973), pp. 191–4, and *Mémoires de Frédérique Sophie Wilhelmine, Margravine de Bareith* (Leipzig 1889), pp. 32–8. A widely read source of information about Peter was John Perry, *The State of Russia* (London 1716). Perry, an English canal builder, revealed that he had received from the Tsar just one year's salary for fourteen years' work.

Empress Elizabeth, her character and accession to power: T. Talbot Rice, *Elizabeth, Empress of Russia* (London 1970).

CHAPTER 4: JOURNEY TO MOSCOW

Mémoires, pp. 33–9; V. Bilbasov, *Geschichte Katharina* (Berlin 1892–7) I, pp. 49 ff; *Sbornik* 7, pp. 1–28. Extracts from documents in H. Jessen, *Katharina II von Russland: Im Spiegel der Zeitgenossen* (Düsseldorf 1970), pp. 27–42.

CHAPTER 5: BECOMING CATHERINE

Sophie's illness: *Mémoires*, pp. 42–3.

Learning Russian: A. M. Gribovski, *Vospominaniya i dnevniki* (Moscow 1899), p. 15: 'When I arrived here, I began to learn Russian with great application. Aunt Elizaveta Petrovna, hearing about this, said to my lady of the bedchamber: "She doesn't need any more teaching, she's clever enough without that." So I could learn Russian only from books, without a teacher, and this is the reason why I don't know Russian spelling well.'

Sophie's betrothal: *Mémoires*, pp. 49–50.

The tour of the Ukraine: *Mémoires*, pp. 51–5. The fireworks at Kiev: *idem*, p. 54; dancing with Sievers at the fancy-dress ball: *idem*, pp. 55–6.

Catherine's resolution: *Mémoires*, p. 57.

Peter's smallpox: according to Katherine Gertrude Harris, who visited her brother, the British ambassador, in St Petersburg in 1778, a man known as Andrenousha, who never spoke and went about almost naked, came to the farm where Peter was ill and made signs that he would deliver him of his disease. When Peter recovered, Andrenousha was taken up by the Empress and lived in her palace 'clothed in fine silk robes like those the Apostles are painted in'. Presently a number of murders were committed without the authors ever being discovered. 'One Strogonoff, a free thinker, had alone the courage to tell the Empress he suspected Andrenousha. This she would not believe and all people, Strogonoff excepted, continued either to believe, or fear Andrenousha too much to accuse him. At length he sent to Strogonoff and offered him much money and women if he would cease to be his enemy. He informed the Empress of this interview and assured her that Andrenousha had spoken to him. However his party was still so strong that this story was only whispered about and he was not discovered and punished till afterwards on account of a Merchant who was murdered and his wife taken from him, when on the murder being very closely looked into it was traced to a band of people who lived underground and in a free Commerce of Men and Women with Andrenousha for their Chief, who had attempted this scheme knowing the weak bigoted ideas of the Empress as the most likely to arrive at supreme power. He was sent as a kind of Galley Slave.' (PRO 30/43, no. 11, pp. 112–112v). The man's name, apparently garbled by Miss Harris, was probably Andriusha.

Catherine's marriage: *Mémoires*, pp. 67–9; Johanna's account of it is in *Sbornik* 7, pp. 52–5. Catherine's wedding dress is in the Metropolitan Museum, New York.

CHAPTER 6: THE MARRIED PRISONERS

Catherine's life at Oranienbaum: *Mémoires*, pp. 260–1.

The Empress's anger with Peter: *Mémoires*, pp. 233–5.

Peter's early life: N. Bain, *Peter III*, *Emperor of Russia* (London 1902). Incident of the oysters: *Mémoires*, p. 287; incident of the King Charles spaniel: *idem*, pp. 269–70.

CHAPTER 7: HUMILIATION

Peter's refusal to go to the steam bath: *Mémoires*, pp. 175–7.

Peter's relations with Catherine Biron: *Mémoires*, pp. 171, 179, 282–5.

Lestocq's dismissal: *Mémoires*, pp. 135–6, 263. The Empress and Catherine's mourning for her father: *idem*, pp. 247–8.

Catherine's illnesses: the many detailed references to them suggest that Catherine may have used the Court Physicians' casebooks to establish the chronological framework for her Memoirs. The extraction of Catherine's tooth: *Mémoires*, pp. 157–8.

CHAPTER 8: MOTHERHOOD BY COMMAND

Alexis Razumovsky's house slips downhill: *Mémoires*, pp. 119–20, 255–7.

Catherine's correspondence with Andrey Chernuishev: *Mémoires*, pp. 197,

263–4. Catherine's reading: *idem*, pp. 245, 269, 348.

Catherine's friendship with Cyril Razumovsky: *Mémoires*, pp. 153–4. Catherine's letters to Zachary Chernuishev, overlooked by most of her biographers: *Russkiy Arkhiv* 1881, vol. 3. (The reference in Bilbasov is incorrect.) In the *Mémoires* (p. 309) Catherine speaks only of a correspondence, not of clandestine meetings.

Catherine's affair with Serge Saltuikov: *Mémoires*, pp. 312–22. The correct date of Madame Choglokova's conversation with Catherine, summer 1752, is given in Catherine's confession to Hanbury-Williams (Anthony's translation p. 248).

Peter and Madame Grooth: *Mémoires*, p. 319. A son of the Court painter in Stuttgart, and brother of George Grooth, the portraitist, L. F. Grooth was an animal painter, specializing in pictures of Elizabeth's horses, dogs, ducks, peacocks and swans.

Paul's birth: *Mémoires*, pp. 341–2. I discuss his paternity in Appendix B.

CHAPTER 9: INDISCRETIONS

Catherine takes charge of Holstein affairs: *Mémoires*, p. 377.

The Shuvalovs: *Mémoires*, pp. 339–43; 365–6.

Sir Charles Hanbury-Williams: D. B. Horn, *Sir Charles Hanbury-Williams and European Diplomacy 1747–58* (London 1930) and *Correspondence of Catherine the Great with Sir Charles Hanbury-Williams*, ed. Ilchester and Longford-Brooke (London 1928).

Peter signs the measures sending an ambassador to France: The Grand Duke 'replied that . . . after he had given the Empress his reasons for his behaviour, he would conclude by saying that he was neither so ignorant nor weak, as not to know that the Empress's will was a law, and that whenever she commanded he would obey, and therefore was ready to sign any paper the moment he received his orders for so doing.' Despatch of Hanbury-Williams, 23 September 1756 (N.S.) Public Record Office, SP 91/64.

Catherine's interview with Sampsoy: *Correspondence of Catherine the Great with Sir Charles Hanbury-Williams*, pp. 158–9.

Lord Holderness's correspondence with Hanbury-Williams: British Library, Egerton MS 3463, August 1756.

Stanislaus Poniatowski: J.-P. Palewski, *Stanislas-Auguste Poniatowski: Dernier Roi de Pologne* (Paris 1946). His description of Catherine: *Mémoires du roi Stanislas Auguste* (St Petersburg 1914).

CHAPTER 10: DISGRACE

The Apraxin affair: *Mémoires*, pp. 362, 387–8, and *Correspondence of Catherine the Great with Sir Charles Hanbury-Williams.*

The birth of Anna: *Mémoires*, p. 401. Bestuzhev's arrest: *idem*, pp. 405–6.
The incident of the cancelled carriages and Catherine's letter to the Empress: *Mémoires*, pp. 414–19.

Catherine's first interview with Elizabeth: *Mémoires*, pp. 422–7. Catherine's second interview: Keith to Holderness, 11/22 September 1758. British Library, Egerton MS 3463.

CHAPTER 11: PREPARING TO RULE

Catherine's relations with Elizabeth Vorontsova: Keith to Holderness, 11/22 September 1758. British Library, Egerton MS 3463. Catherine's handling of Naruishkin: *Mémoires*, p. 395.

Poniatowski saw Catherine in summer 1758, with Peter's connivance, before returning to Poland. Their meetings then, described in Poniatowski's *Memoirs* and inserted by the editor in the English translation of Catherine's *Memoirs* (London 1955), pp. 270–4, belong not before the crucial interviews between Catherine and the Empress, but after.

Catherine and Princess Dashkova: *Memoirs of Princess Dashkov*, trans. K. Fitzlyon (London 1958), pp. 38–44.

Empress Elizabeth's death: *Mémoires*, pp. 499–509.

CHAPTER 12: PETER'S REIGN

Keith's despatches in the Public Record Office, SP 91/69 and 70; the Danish Minister's despatches in the Royal Archives, Copenhagen, TKUA, Russland A III, which stress the ill-feeling aroused by Prince Georg's presence, even among foreign ambassadors, several of whom declined to accede to Peter's wish that Prince Georg receive the honours due to a Prince of the Blood. Also M. Raeff, 'Domestic Policies of Peter III and his Overthrow' in *American Historical Review*, vol. 75, no. 5, June 1970, and N. Bain, *Peter III*, *Emperor of Russia* (London 1902).

The consecration of the chapel: Danish Minister's despatch of 17/28 May. He adds that Melgunov was in Catherine's pay.

The toast to the imperial family: *Memoirs of Princess Dashkov*, pp. 54–5.

Catherine's attempt to borrow English money: Correspondence of Keith and Wroughton with Bute, Feb./Mar. 1762: PRO, SP 61/69, including a letter in Catherine's hand to Bute. 'There were sixty marriages ordered . . .': letter from Wroughton to Grenville from Warsaw, 23 July 1762.

CHAPTER 13: OAK LEAVES AND POISON

The *coup d'état*: Catherine's own account in her letter to Poniatowski 2 August 1762, *Mémoires*, pp. 547–55; also pp. 493–4; Panin's account as given to Asseburg: A. F. von der Asseburg, *Denkwürdigkeiten*, (Berlin 1842) pp. 315–22; *Sochineniia Derzhavina*, vol. vi (St Petersburg 1876), pp. 416–20.

For Peter's murder, Peter's letters to Catherine, in M. Budberg, *The Memoirs of Catherine the Great* (London 1955), pp. 345–6; Alexis Orlov's letters to Catherine, *idem*, pp. 350–1; Earl of Buckinghamshire, *Despatches and Correspondence* (London 1900).

Catherine's coronation: M. I. Puilayev, *Staraya Moskva*, (St Petersburg 1891); N. Leskov, 'Tzarskaya Koronatziya', in *Istoricheski Vestnik*, vol. v (1881), pp. 283–99; V. I. Zhmakin, 'Koronatzii russkikh imperatorov i imperatritz, 1724–1856', in *Russkaya Starina*, XXXVII (1883), pp. 499–538.

CHAPTER 14: REFORMING RUSSIA

The condition of Russia on Catherine's accession: *Mémoires*, pp. 517–25. Economic policy: A. I. Pashkov, *A History of Russian Economic Thought, Ninth through Eighteenth Centuries* (Berkeley, Calif. 1964), Part V.

The development of resources: G. Macartney, *An Account of Russia, 1767* (London 1768). W. Kirchner, 'Samuel Bentham and Siberia', *Slavonic Review*, 36 (1957–8). Trade with China: C. M. Foust, *Muscovite and Mandarin* (Chapel Hill 1969).

Free trade: when she came to hear of Adam Smith's views, Catherine early expounded them in Russia. *Oxford Slavonic Papers*, n.s. vol. 7 (1975).

Provincial Reform: R. E. Jones, 'Catherine II and the Provincial Reform of 1775: A Question of Motivation', *Canadian Slavic Studies*, iv, 3 (1970).

Town-planning: P. E. Jones, 'Urban Planning and the Development of Provincial Towns in Russia, 1762–1796' in J. G. Garrard (ed.), *The Eighteenth Century in Russia* (Oxford 1973).

Education: N. Hans, *History of Russian Educational Policy 1701–1917* (London 1931) and 'Dumaresq, Brown and Some Early Educational Projects of Catherine II', *Slavonic Review*, 40 (1961–2).

Catherine's inoculation: W. J. Bishop, 'Thomas Dimsdale and the Inoculation of Catherine the Great of Russia', in *Annals of Medical History*, n.s. iv, 4 (July 1932).

Catherine's physician: A. Cross, 'John Rogerson: Physician to Catherine the Great', *Canadian Slavic Studies* iv, 3 (1970), and J. B. Wilson, 'Three Scots in the Service of the Czars', *The Practitioner*, 210 (April and May 1973).

Hospitals: I. de Madariaga, *The Travels of General Francesco de Miranda in Russia* (London 1950). H. von Storch, *Historisch-Stätistisches Gemälde des Russischen Reichs am Ende des Achtzehnten Jahrhunderts* (Riga 1797–1803).

CHAPTER 15: THE MOVE TO COMPASSION

Nikita Panin: D. L. Ransel, *The Politics of Catherinian Russia: The Panin Party* (New Haven 1975) and the review by I. de Madariaga in *The Times Literary*

Supplement, 25 June 1976.

The Legislative Commission: P. Dukes, *Catherine the Great and the Russian Nobility* (Cambridge 1967). Catherine's *Instruction* in W. F. Reddaway, *Documents of Catherine the Great* (Cambridge 1931).

Pugachev's rebellion: M. Raeff, 'Pugachev's Rebellion', in *Preconditions of Revolution in Early Modern Europe*, ed. Forster and Greene (Baltimore 1970); J. T. Alexander, *Autocratic Politics in a National Crisis* (Bloomington, Ind. 1969); P. Longworth, *The Cossacks* (London 1969).

Catherine's measures in favour of serfs: I. de Madariaga, 'Catherine II and the Serfs: A Reconsideration of Some Problems', *Slavonic Review*, 52 (1974).

CHAPTER 16: VICTORIES ABROAD

H. Kaplan, *The First Partition of Poland* (New York 1962); P. Longworth, *The Art of Victory. The Life and Achievements of Generalissimo Suvorov 1729–1800* (London 1965).

M. S. Anderson, 'Great Britain and the Russian Fleet 1769–70', *Slavonic Review*, 31 (1952–3), and 'Great Britain and the Growth of the Russian Navy in the 18th Century', *Mariner's Mirror*, 42 (1956). C. de Larivière, *La Princesse Tarakonov* (Paris 1929).

CHAPTER 17: PORTRAIT OF THE EMPRESS

Casanova's experiences in St Petersburg and conversations with the Empress: *Mémoires de Casanova* (Paris 1826–38), vol. 10, chapters v, vi and vii.

Catherine's health: letters to Potemkin 12 October 1786 and 9 October 1787. Sympathizing with Potemkin, who also suffered from 'spasms', Catherine wrote: 'J'ose croire que les spasmes s'en iront avec les vents, je suis d'opinion que tout spasme est causé par les vents.'

The plot by Preobrazhensky NCO's: *Sbornik* 72, pp. 164–5.

The break with Orlov: A. Polovtsov, *The Favourites of Catherine the Great* (London 1940). Orlov's letter to Rousseau, 2 January 1767, in J. J. Rousseau, *Correspondance Générale*, ed. Dufour, vol. 16 (Paris 1931), pp. 325–6.

CHAPTER 18: ENTER POTEMKIN

G. Soloveytchik, *Potemkin* (London 1938); Catherine II: *Lettres d'amour à Potemkin*, ed. Oudard (Paris 1934); Letters to Grimm, *Sbornik* 23.

Catherine's visit to the porcelain factory: Chevalier de Corberon, *Un diplomate français à la cour de Catherine II* (Paris 1901), 9 June 1777.

CHAPTER 19: THE LITERARY SCENE

Catherine and discoveries in the East: according to Rogerson, 'she knew more about the subject than any person whatever'. Letter to W. Robertson 12 September 1773, National Library of Scotland MS 3943. Details of expeditions in H. Chevigny, *Russian America* (New York 1965). On a document concerning the Aleutians addressed to the governor-general at Irkutsk, Catherine added in her own hand the order to 'impress upon the hunters the necessity of treating their new brethren and countrymen, the inhabitants of our newly acquired islands, with greatest kindness'.

The development of history-writing: A. G. Mazour, *Modern Russian Historiography* (Princeton 1958),

K. A. Papmehl, *Freedom of Expression in Eighteenth-Century Russia* (The Hague 1971); W. Gareth Jones, 'The Closure of Novikov's *Truten*', *Slavonic Review*, 50 (1972).

I. F. Martynov, 'English Literature and Eighteenth-Century Russian Reviewers', in *Oxford Slavonic Papers*, n.s. 4 (1971). B. V. Varneke, *History of the Russian Theatre* (New York 1951). Catherine's reactions to *Le Médecin par occasion:* Corberon, *op. cit.* 12 October 1777.

Catherine's writings: A. G. Cross, 'A Royal Bluestocking' in *A Garland of Essays Offered to E. M. Hall* (Cambridge 1970). Catherine's comparative dictionary: *Sbornik* 23, 9 September 1784. A second copy of the vocabulary prepared for Catherine by Butler and sent to Washington is among the George Washington Papers, Series 8D, in the Library of Congress.

G. H. McArthur, 'Catherine II and the Masonic Circle of N. I. Novikov', *Canadian Slavic Studies* iv, 3 (1970). Johanna's alchemy: 'I made the tree of perfection,' says Casanova, 'in the house of the Marquise de Pontcarré d'Urfé, the vegetation of which, calculated by the Princess of Anhalt-Zerbst, gave an augmentation of fifty in the hundred.'

Catherine's search for a cheerful daughter-in-law: letter of 16 January 1772, in Asseburg, *op. cit.*, p. 279.

CHAPTER 20: OF PALACES AND PAINTINGS

A. and V. Kennett, *The Palaces of Leningrad* (London 1973); I. Rae, *Charles Cameron, Architect to the Court of Russia* (London 1971). Catherine's respect for a neighbour's property: V. Esterhazy, *Lettres à sa femme* (Paris 1857), letter of 29 October 1791, pp. 349–50.

The statue of Peter I: *Correspondance de Falconet avec Catherine II 1767–1778* (St Petersburg 1921).

Picture-collecting: P. Descargues, *The Hermitage* (London 1961).

Noteworthy also is Catherine's collection of gems and intaglios. She first bought gems from L. Natter in 1764, and later purchased the collections of

Breteuil, Byres, Slade, Mengs, Lord Beverley, the Duc d'Orléans and J. B. Casanova, Director of the Dresden Academy of Fine Arts, so that by the end she had accumulated 10,000 gems. The brothers William and Charles Brown spent ten years producing 400 cameos and intaglios for her. Catherine wrote to Grimm that 'four men had trouble carrying two log-baskets full of jewel cases containing half the collection.'

The opera *Fedul s Detmi*, usually attributed to Catherine, is in fact not by her, and its music is not by Fomin but by Pashkevich and Martin-y-Soler.

'The Empress has laboured . . .' Buckinghamshire, *op. cit.*, 14 February 1762.

CHAPTER 21: POTEMKIN PREDOMINANT

J. A. Duran, Jr., 'Catherine II, Potemkin, and Colonization Policy in Southern Russia', *Russian Review*, vol. 28 (New York 1969), pp. 23–6.

Catherine's journey to the Crimea: Marquis d'Aragon, *Un Paladin du XVIIIème siècle* [Nassau-Siegen] (Paris 1893). 'Cardboard villages': Helbig, *Russische Günstlinge* (Tübingen 1809).

Catherine's lovers: A. Polovtsov, *op. cit.*; Letters to Grimm, *Sbornik* 23. 'A violent altercation . . .' J. Parkinson, *A Tour of Russia, Siberia and the Crimea 1792–1794* (London 1971). 'Potemkin ordered him . . .' Parkinson, *op. cit.*, p. 54.

The belief that Catherine used an *éprouveuse* originates in C. F. P. Masson, *Mémoires secrets sur la Russie* (Paris 1800), discussed in Appendix A.

CHAPTER 22: THE LATER ACHIEVEMENTS

Alexander's education: F.-C. Laharpe, *Mémoires* (Bern 1864). Plan for a national Assembly: M. Raeff, in *Oxford Slavonic Papers*, n.s. 7 (1975).

Catherine, the old woman and the hen: P. Sumarokov, *Cherty Yekateriny Velikiya* (St Petersburg 1819), pp. 112–13.

Help for the underprivileged: Brevern de La Gardie, *Comte de Stedingk, Choix de Dépêches* (Stockholm 1919), despatch of 3 December 1792, I, p. 339; and J. Parkinson, *op. cit.*, pp. 23–4.

Catherine and the French Revolution: *Sbornik* 23, especially 12 May 1791.

Second and Third Partitions of Poland: *Cambridge History of Poland*, vol. 2 (Cambridge 1950).

CHAPTER 23: LIKE A FLY IN SPRING

Plato Zubov: A Polovtsov, *op. cit.* and *Dnevnik A. V. Khrapovitskavo 1782–1793* (St Petersburg 1874).

Potemkin's last year: G. Soloveytchik, *op. cit.*

'That can't be true . . .' *Sbornik* 23, 14 December 1795. The Persian was Murtasa Kuli, whom Parkinson had met in Astrakhan and described in his entry for 28 June 1793.

CHAPTER 24: CRITICISM AND SEDITION

Punishment of Mamonov and his wife: J. Parkinson, *op. cit.*, p. 61.

'Among other petitions . . .' P. Sumarokov, *Cherty Yekateriny Velikiya* (St Petersburg 1819), pp. 190–2.

A. Radishchev, *A Journey from St Petersburg to Moscow*, trans. L. Wiener (Cambridge, Mass. 1958); D. M. Lang, *The First Russian Radical: Alexander Radishchev 1749–1802* (London 1954); A. McConnell, *A Russian Philosophe: Alexander Radishchev 1749–1802* (The Hague 1964).

Catherine's treatment of followers of revolutionary fashions and propaganda agents: Matthew Guthrie, *Noctes Russicae*, folio 109–109v. British Library, Add. MSS. 14390.

CHAPTER 25: THE DREAM OF A RUSSIAN EUROPE

Catherine at 65: *Vospominaniya i dnevniki Adriana Moisyevicha Grivovskavo* (Moscow 1899), pp. 15 ff. Her dress: V. Esterhazy, *op. cit.*, letters of 1791.

At the end of the reign 158 million roubles in paper were circulating, five times less than the amount of paper money circulating in England, allowance made for the difference in population. Opinion was divided on the issuing of paper money: Ivan Tretiakov, a graduate of Glasgow who held the chair of jurisprudence at Moscow University, approved, while Radishchev disapproved.

Catherine's rejection of flattering titles: to Voltaire, 29 December 1766; to Grimm 22 February 1788.

Gustavus IV's visit: *Sbornik* 9 and 23.

'If I were to live 200 years . . .' Derzhavin, *op. cit.*, p. 606.

Catherine's will: *Mémoires* pp. 702–3.

Catherine's death: the date is given unequivocally by the British ambassador, Charles Whitworth. Writing on Friday 7th November (18th November N.S.), he says: 'last night . . . this incomparable princess finished her brilliant career'. The eyewitness of the funeral was William Eton, PRO, FO 65/35.

CHAPTER 26: CATHERINE THE GREAT

Travelling in Russia in 1793 Parkinson found that 'In speaking of the

Empress it is very much the fashion to say *c'est un grand homme.*' Parkinson, *op. cit.*, p. 132. This 'male chauvinist' phrase had been applied to Catherine by Diderot; earlier, Voltaire had used it of the mathematical Marquise du Châtelet.

The sentry and the snowdrop: Princess Marie Murat, *La Grande Catherine* (Paris 1932).

Paul's reign: P. Morane, *Paul I de Russie* (Paris 1907).

Catherine's prediction of Napoleon: *Sbornik* 23, 11 February 1794.

Catharine, Kansas: M. E. Johannes, *A Study of the Russian-German Settlements in Ellis County, Kansas* (Washington D.C. 1946).

'Voltaire, my master, forbids predicting the future . . .' A. Brückner, *Katherina die Zweite* (Berlin 1883), p. 597.

Index

Index